# Thomas Mann's *Death in Venice*:
## A Novella and Its Critics

This study surveys and analyzes the reception of one of the most famous and most widely read stories in all of modern literature. It treats over seven hundred books, articles, and other reactions to Mann's *Death in Venice* thematically yet within five chronological categories. This comprehensive chronological approach helps put the extensive criticism and scholarship on Mann's story into literary and historical perspective. Issues raised in the interpretations discussed include art and artists, myths, sources, symbols, style, and narrative structure. Those issues also include politics, philosophy, psychoanalysis, homoeroticism, music, and translations. Comparisons of *Death in Venice* to Mann's other writings are considered, as are comparisons to works by authors such as Euripides, Plato, Goethe, Schopenhauer, Platen, Nietzsche, Gide, Conrad, D'Annunzio, and Mishima. Among the critics, scholars, and reviewers cited are Heinrich Mann, Hermann Broch, D. H. Lawrence, Georg Lukács, Lionel Trilling, Wolfgang Koeppen, Susan Sontag, Allan Bloom, Camille Paglia, and Mario Vargas Llosa. Special attention is paid to Luchino Visconti's film *Morte a Venezia,* to Benjamin Britten's opera *Death in Venice,* and to other artistic adaptations of Mann's story.

Ellis Shookman is Associate Professor of German at Dartmouth College. He has previously written a book about the novels of Christoph Martin Wieland, edited a volume of essays on Johann Caspar Lavater, and edited and translated a collection of eighteenth-century German prose. He has also published articles on Brecht, Wieland, Hans Fallada, Arno Schmidt, Hermann von Pückler-Muskau, Lavater, and John le Carré.

*Studies in German Literature, Linguistics, and Culture:*
*Literary Criticism in Perspective*


*Literary Criticism in Perspective*

Edited by James Walker


## About *Literary Criticism in Perspective*

Books in the series *Literary Criticism in Perspective* trace literary scholarship and criticism on major and neglected writers alike, or on a single major work, a group of writers, a literary school or movement. In so doing the authors — authorities on the topic in question who are also well-versed in the principles and history of literary criticism — address a readership consisting of scholars, students of literature at the graduate and undergraduate level, and the general reader. One of the primary purposes of the series is to illuminate the nature of literary criticism itself, to gauge the influence of social and historic currents on aesthetic judgments once thought objective and normative.

# Thomas Mann's *Death in Venice*

## A Novella and Its Critics

Ellis Shookman

CAMDEN HOUSE

First published 2003
by Camden House

Camden House is an imprint of Boydell & Brewer Inc.
668 Mt. Hope Avenue, Rochester, NY 14620 USA
and of Boydell & Brewer Limited
PO Box 9, Woodbridge, Suffolk IP12 3DF, UK

ISBN: 1–57113–056-x

**Library of Congress Cataloging-in-Publication Data**

Shookman, Ellis.
  Thomas Mann's Death in Venice: a novella and its critics / Ellis
Shookman.
    p. cm. — (Studies in German literature, linguistics, and culture.
Literary criticism in perspective)
Includes bibliographical references and index.
ISBN 1–57113–056–x (alk. paper)
  1. Mann, Thomas, 1875-1955. Tod in Venedig.  2. Mann, Thomas,
1875-1955 — Criticism and interpretation.  I. Title.  II. Series: Studies
in German literature, linguistics, and culture (Unnumbered). Literary
criticism in perspective.

PT2625.A44Z4567 2003
833'.912—dc21

                                                2003000501

A catalogue record for this title is available from the British Library.

This publication is printed on acid-free paper.
Printed in the United States of America

"You were going to have Thomas Mann and Leverkühn in scenes together, weren't you? And put that Gustav Aschenbach in with Leverkühn as one of his contemporaries. You call that research?"

"Who's Gustav Aschenbach?" said Hacker.

"A dead man in Venice, Warren."

Joseph Heller, *Closing Time* (1994)

# Contents

# Acknowledgments

THIS BOOK HAS been a labor of love, but I could not have written it without the help of several people to whom I wish to express my gratitude. I would like to thank James Hardin, the general editor of Camden House, and James Walker, editor of the series *Literary Criticism in Perspective,* for their patience and professionalism; my colleagues Bruce Duncan and Steven Scher, both of Dartmouth College, for reading my manuscript; Patsy Carter, Kim Wheeler, and Marianne Hraibi, all of the Interlibrary Loan Office in Dartmouth's Baker/Berry Library, for their readiness to help find even the most obscure sources; Ms. Gabi Hollender of the Thomas-Mann-Archiv in Zurich for her further bibliographical aid; and helpful librarians at Dartmouth, Yale, Harvard, MIT, Northeastern University, and the Boston Public Library as well as the Staatsbibliothek zu Berlin. I also wish both to thank Laurie Wallach and to dedicate this book to her.

E. S.
June 2002

# Introduction

IN ENGLISH, the name of Thomas Mann's novella *Death in Venice* (1912) seems to have become almost a household word. That is what one might think, at least, after finding the phrase "Death in Venice" in the headlines of sixteen relatively recent British and American magazine articles, not to mention the titles of two English mystery novels. The articles appeared in a broad range of magazines, and they treat topics as varied as film, art, architecture, and air pollution in Italy; crime, cocaine, and ailing ducks in Venice, California; and European views on capital punishment. Two of the articles, in *Film Comment* and *The Economist*, are about the Venice Film Festival and are themselves entitled "Death in Venice."[1] In *Sight & Sound*, "Life and Death in Venice" reports on that same event.[2] Two other articles called "Death in Venice," in *Art & Antiques* and *Art Monthly*, are about the Biennale di Venezia, a recurring art exhibition.[3] In *Blueprint*, "Mega Death in Venice" comments on this same exhibition, as does "British Suffer Death in Venice," in *Architects' Journal*.[4] An article on both the Biennale and Titian in *The New Yorker* and one in *Apollo* on a painting by Giovanni Bellini likewise cite Mann's title in their own.[5] "Death in Venice," in *Architectural Design*, moreover, and "Chipperfield takes on Death in Venice," in *Architects' Journal*, describe a plan to extend the historic cemetery on the Venetian island of San Michele.[6] An article in *Discover* about the erosion of marble angels adorning the churches in Venice, Italy, is entitled "A Grimy and Watery Death in Venice."[7] Articles in *Rolling Stone* and *The New Republic* that tell of gangs, crack, and social conditions in Venice, California, again bear Mann's title, as does one in *The Economist* that reports on objections by citizens of that city to their officials' killing of ducks that carry a contagious disease.[8] A further article, "Death in Venice" in *The New Republic*, notes Europeans' support for the death penalty.[9] Finally, two recent mystery novels are named *Another Death in Venice*. Reginald Hill's novel (1976) has far more to do with Luchino Visconti's film *Morte a Venezia* (1971) than with Mann's novella, Visconti's primary source. The surname of Mann's protagonist, Gustav von Aschenbach, though, is fused in Anthony Appiah's (1995) with that of the heiress and art collector Peggy Guggenheim to yield a character called "Peggy Aschenheim." All these allusions to the title of *Death in Venice* might well lead one to conclude that Mann's story is very widely known.

One could draw this same conclusion after learning how many works by other authors have been compared to *Death in Venice,* as well as how often it has inspired further literary and artistic efforts. The list of these authors is long. As studies cited in the following chapters show, it includes ancient as well as modern names that come from many countries and from the fields of psychoanalysis, sociology, philosophy, and history, as well as from belles lettres. Among the names are Alfred Adler, Gabriele D'Annunzio, Maurice Barrès, Charles Baudelaire, Hermann Broch, Anton Chekhov, Cicero, Joseph Conrad, Robert Coover, Euripides, Gustave Flaubert, Sigmund Freud, Jean Genet, Stefan George, André Gide, Johann Wolfgang von Goethe, Gerhart Hauptmann, Martin Heidegger, Ernest Hemingway, Hermann Hesse, Friedrich Hölderlin, E. T. A. Hoffmann, Hugo von Hofmannsthal, Homer, Henrik Ibsen, Henry James, James Joyce, Carl Gustav Jung, Franz Kafka, Yasunari Kawabata, Heinrich von Kleist, Wolfgang Koeppen, Alfred Kubin, D. H. Lawrence, Gotthold Ephraim Lessing, Malcolm Lowry, Samuel Lublinski, Georg Lukács, Heinrich Mann, F. T. Marinetti, Daphne du Maurier, Ian McEwan, Yukio Mishima, Robert Musil, Friedrich Nietzsche, Walter Pater, August von Platen, Plato, Plutarch, Marcel Proust, Georges Rodenbach, Erwin Rohde, Rainer Maria Rilke, Friedrich Schiller, Arthur Schnitzler, Arthur Schopenhauer, Georg Simmel, Oswald Spengler, Leo Tolstoy, Virgil, Max Weber, Walt Whitman, Oscar Wilde, Tennessee Williams, Virginia Woolf, and Xenophon. This imposing list suggests how important Mann's novella has seemed in academic circles. The work has also inspired a poem and two short stories written by Jürgen Theobaldy, Alan Catlin, and Winston Weathers, respectively. It is set to music in Benjamin Britten's *Death in Venice* (1973), an opera with dance sequences choreographed by Frederick Ashton, and it has been interpreted twice in a full-length ballet, first by Norbert Vesak, whose *Death in Venice* was given in Munich in 1986, then by Flemming Flindt in Verona in 1991, with Rudolf Nureyev creating the role of Aschenbach. One staged version of Mann's story premiered in New York in 1980, moreover, another was given in London in 1993, and as I write, the Citizens' Theatre of Glasgow is performing a third at the Manhattan Ensemble Theater. That story is also the ancestor of a film more recent than Visconti's adaptation, namely Richard Kwietniowski's *Love & Death on Long Island* (1997). Finally, many artists have illustrated editions of the novella and portrayed its scenes and characters in paintings, in drawings, and even on medallions. In comparative and creative endeavors alike, then, *Death in Venice* has been highly influential.

Given such popularity and such pervasiveness, one should not be surprised to find that the secondary literature on *Death in Venice* is extensive. The bibliography at the end of this book contains over seven hundred titles, in fact, starting with reviews that appeared in early 1913 and ending with articles published in 2002. To organize so many secondary sources and analyze the major issues they raise, I have divided my account of them into five chapters:

1. *Initial Reactions, 1913–14:* These reactions consist of reviews written either immediately upon or soon after the publication of *Death in Venice*. The novella first appeared in serial form, then as a book, in late 1912 and early 1913. Almost all of the reviews included here are in German.

2. *Increasing Acceptance, 1915–55:* This chapter surveys scholarly remarks on *Death in Venice* made during the First World War, during the Weimar Republic, in the period prior to and including the Second World War, and in the further decade that ended with Mann's death. Among these sources are reviews of the initial translations of the novella into English and French in the 1920s.

3. *Posthumous Praise, 1956–75:* This chapter considers books and articles that appeared over the next twenty years as scholars began to take stock of Mann's entire life and work, in part by exploring his archives and evaluating his correspondence. Visconti's film and Britten's opera sparked wider interest in the novella near the end of this twenty-year period, and scholarly books and articles comparing them to it are included here, as well as in the following two chapters.

4. *Further Developments, 1976–95:* These developments reflect critical and scholarly efforts made during the next two decades, after the centenary of Mann's birth was celebrated in 1975. Such efforts coincided with the publication of his extant diaries and his notebooks, and they ended with the appearance of three major biographies.

5. *Recent Trends, 1996–2001:* Recent scholarship on the novella is surveyed here, to the extent that it has been cited, catalogued, or otherwise made known and available to date. (Four articles from 2002 are mentioned in the conclusion.)

In dividing the vast secondary literature on *Death in Venice* into these five chapters, I have followed the general guidelines that govern Camden House's series *Literary Criticism in Perspective*. Those guidelines stipulate a chronological treatment. Within each chapter, though, I group together studies that discuss similar topics or that take related approaches. The resulting categories are indicated by boldfaced headings. Readers can thus find discussed in one place, for example, all the psychoanalytical studies of *Death in Venice* given between 1956 and 1975, while such readers can also situate these studies in the larger critical climate defined by the other approaches to Mann's story that were taken during this same period. To compare all the interpretations that any single topic or kind of approach has yielded — all the psychoanalytical, all the political, or all the stylistic interpretations, for example — one needs to consult the headings in each chapter and the index. Most of those headings recur in every chapter, but they sometimes vary, a fact that reflects how the evidence supplied and the emphasis lent by the secondary literature have changed over time. The index includes names of persons, titles of works, and keywords that help trace specific issues and themes. It also includes the names of the critics, scholars, and other authors whose works are listed in the bibliography. Finally, each chapter starts with an introduction to the approaches and themes discussed in it. Each of the following sections, in turn, begins with a paragraph that outlines the issues raised by the works treated in that section. A brief summation concludes each chapter except the last. The scope and structure of the chapters in this book thus help divide the reception of *Death in Venice* into manageable, logical, and coherent phases.

Like the five main chapters that precede it, the bibliography is in chronological order. Its entries are listed according to their year of publication, starting with 1913. For any single year, though, the entries are in alphabetical order, according to their authors' last names. The first entry for 1913 is by Wilhelm Alberts, for example, and the last is by Paul Zifferer. Next come the entries for 1914, again listed alphabetically by author, then the entries for 1915, and so on. The text proper seldom mentions titles of secondary works, but it does give their authors' names and their dates of publication. This information will point readers to the appropriate location in the bibliography. The sentence in chapter 3 beginning with "In 1965, Werner Hoffmeister remarked on Mann's skilled use of free indirect discourse . . .," for example, refers to the entry from that year and by that author: Hoffmeister, Werner. *Studien zur erlebten Rede bei Thomas Mann und Robert Musil.* The Hague: Mouton, 1965. In the rare case of an author who published more than one book or article on *Death in Venice* in a single year — for example, Herbert Lehnert in 1964 — both the context of the discussion and references in the text clearly indicate which entry is meant. Page numbers of all quotations are given in parentheses in the body of the text. Thanks to this system of citation, the text is not cluttered with notes or extended parenthetical references. All references to Mann's own works state the volume and page number of his *Gesammelte Werke* (Frankfurt am Main: Fischer, 1974).

My main bibliographical sources are Harry Matter's *Die Literatur über Thomas Mann: Eine Bibliographie 1898–1969* (Berlin and Weimar: Aufbau, 1972) and Klaus W. Jonas's *Die Thomas-Mann-Literatur:* Volume 1, *Bibliographie der Kritik 1896–1955* (Berlin: Schmidt, 1972); Volume 2, *Bibliographie der Kritik 1956–1975* (Berlin: Schmidt, 1979); and Volume 3, *Bibliographie der Kritik 1976–1994* (Frankfurt am Main: Klostermann, 1997). Georg Potempa's *Thomas Mann-Bibliographie:* Volume 1, *Das Werk* (Morsum/Sylt: Cicero, 1992) and Volume 2, *Übersetzungen-Interviews* (Morsum/Sylt: Cicero, 1997) has likewise been helpful. I have also consulted *Germanistik, Bibliographie der deutschen Sprach- und Literaturwissenschaft,* the Modern Language Association Bibliography, and six databases maintained by the H. W. Wilson Co.: Art Index, Essay and General Literature Index, Humanities Index, Readers' Guide to Periodical Literature, Social Science Index, and Wilson Combined Indexes. Such online databases include titles that scholars and students of literature might otherwise miss. The titles cited in the American Psychological Association's PsycINFO, for example, can help one find the many interpretations of *Death in Venice* given by psychologists and psychoanalysts. Other references come from the notes and bibliographies of the books and articles that I cite, as well as from the catalogues of the libraries mentioned in the acknowledgments. Most of those sources are in German or English. A few are in French. Unless otherwise noted, all translations from works in German or French are my own. I have relied on published translations from all other languages.

In addition to using these several bibliographical sources, I have profited from prior remarks on the reception of *Death in Venice*. Most of these remarks are in German, but some are in English, and each of the authors who makes them presents that reception in a particular way. The first extensive remarks in German date from 1968, when Hans Nicklas summarized the major studies written before 1960. Nicklas warned against the tendency to paraphrase Mann's own statements about the novella and to believe Aschenbach's self-justifications. Nicklas included only two reviews from 1913, however, and the total volume of criticism has tripled since his study was published. In 1969, Herbert Lehnert commented on numerous studies of *Death in Venice* in his report about the state of research on all Mann's works. In 1977, Hermann Kurzke's similar report about the research on Mann published between 1969 and 1976 mentioned selected interpretations of *Death in Venice*. In 1979, Gabriele Seitz analyzed over half the reviews published between 1913 and 1915, noting a harshly nationalistic tone in those that were unfavorable. She also observed how Mann tried to influence, manipulate, or "channel" the initial reception of the novella in order to restore both his reputation and his finances. Hans Rudolf Vaget similarly considered roughly half of the initial reviews in 1984, observing how revealing the negative ones can be. He also selectively summarized more recent studies. John Luijs's Dutch thesis of 1987 detailed the reception of the homoerotic element in *Death in Venice*. The early reviewers perceived and judged that element, Luijs argues, but most scholars ignored, avoided, repressed, disguised, or marginalized it until the mid-1970s. Karl Werner Böhm took a similar tack in 1991. Böhm refers to almost fifty early reviews, and he discusses fourteen of them, writing that *Death in Venice* was accepted or rejected according to their authors' views on homosexuality. The more repulsed early critics were by this sexual propensity, he claims, the less favorably they wrote, though respect for Mann's style could make them willing to ignore his homosexual theme or to consider it merely symbolic. Böhm takes this same cogent but narrow approach to subsequent studies. Erhard Bahr, likewise in 1991, excerpted thirty such reviews and studies. In English, T. J. Reed has briefly remarked on the novella's reception, drawing in 1994 on his own copious scholarship. Reed also provided an annotated bibliography. In 1998, again in English, Naomi Ritter explained that reception in greater detail. Ritter's remarks contain many errors of bibliographical fact and are sometimes inaccurate. It is not true, for example, that the most significant criticism of *Death in Venice* before the First World War discusses Mann's implicit foreshadowing of that conflict. In 1999, Susanne Widmaier-Haag surveyed almost three quarters of the psychoanalytical readings of Mann's story, noting how those readings have changed along with psycho-analysis itself. She rightly observed both how loosely some literary scholars apply Freudian concepts and how inadequately some psychoanalysts read fiction. Most of the studies she did not include are in English, but she also drew the mistaken conclusion that none were written in German between 1915 and 1965. Finally, in 2000, Thomas Goll linked the reception of Mann's works to the political culture prevalent in Germany during his ca-reer. Early reactions to the novella were generally positive, Goll wrote, and Mann's story was largely judged literarily rather than politically.

As noted above, my own approach must be chronological. I also make thematic distinctions, however, that resemble the ones drawn by Nicklas and Ritter. Nicklas divides studies prior to his own into six main categories. Those categories comprise differing methods of interpretation and diverse objects: (1) individualistic readings that focus on Aschenbach's psyche, (2) ontological ones that regard him as an artist doomed to death, (3) sociologi-cal ones that find him typical of the German bourgeoisie after Bismarck, (4) formal readings that stress stylistic and structural elements, (5) generic ones that take the history of the German novella into account, (6) all other ap-proaches. Ritter proposes seven such general categories: (1) Greek mythol-ogy and culture, (2) historical/political aspects, (3) literary and other influences, (4) narrative style, (5) major themes, (6) comparison to the work of other authors, (7) psychology and psychoanalysis. Headings such as these can be helpful when trying to comprehend the many topics discussed by scholars and critics of *Death in Venice*. Within the broad categories sug-gested by Nicklas and Ritter and used in the following chapters, those topics include death and Venice, of course, as well as decadence and moral dilem-mas; eros, seduction, and pedophilia; mid-life crises and love in old age; families and foreigners; music and photography; irony and creativity; the image of the tiger and the image of the city; and the histories of the phallus and the literary symbol. Many other such topics have also been raised.

I not only survey and summarize those topics, but also analyze and evaluate them. My analysis and evaluation take several forms. Analytical judgment is implicit in the very arrangement of my chapters, sections, and paragraphs. Such judgment also accounts for the discussion of any given secondary work in one place rather than in another. My remarks on any such work show what I think is most important, most incisive, or most inept about it. They are meant to be as synthetic, comprehensive, and impartial as possible and to reveal the long-term parallels and patterns that connect such works in currents deeper than their authors often knew. I report fewer details about recent research than about earlier work. This is because recent authors often go over the same ground that earlier ones covered and repeat, often unwittingly, what was already known or written. As a whole, moreover, the reception of *Death in Venice* is evaluated in the conclusion at the end of this book.

With the help of such analysis and evaluation, one can see how interpretations of Mann's story have changed along with all the academic fashions and the critical trends that have come into vogue and gone out of style in the ninety years since he wrote it. Readings inspired by Freud, to take one example of such shifting paradigms, also teach their reader other things about its reception. In their sober and sometimes ridiculous diagnoses of Aschenbach and his author, such psychoanalytic interpretations often lack literary refinement. Interpretations given by actual analysts, though, at least seem more professional than remarks by literary scholars who dabble in Freud, and those interpretations attest to the fame that *Death in Venice* enjoys beyond the field of literary studies. Exceptions to the rule of aesthetic incompetence among psychoanalysts who interpret the novella also prove what is true of all ways of reading it: any method of interpretation is only as good as the critic or the scholar who uses it.

This fact becomes especially clear when one considers all the mistakes that critics and scholars have made in their readings of *Death in Venice*. These mistakes are noted in the following chapters, and in the conclusion they are combined in a wildly and intentionally inaccurate retelling of Mann's tale. They are not the stuff of learned disagreement. Instead, they concern names, places, characters, and events that do not exist, do not act, or do not happen in the way that Mann himself describes them. More than a few commentators have thus garbled what Mann wrote, and they often do so for reasons that are highly instructive. Some scholars are so enamored of a pet theory or an interpretive concept, for example, that they ignore or inadvertently twist the fictional facts of his plot. This kind of mistake occurs in many varieties of criticism, but it is especially common in political, deconstructive, and psychoanalytic studies. Further errors result from misunderstandings of Mann's celebrated irony or of passages in his story that are ambiguous. These mistakes, too, are made by critics and scholars of every stripe, but they are particularly common among those who read *Death in Venice* in English translation. H. T. Lowe-Porter's deficient translation of 1928, for example, has been used in North America and Britain for over seven decades, and the reception of the novella reflects her inaccuracies. Fortunately, there are now five more recent, more accurate English renderings — by David Luke (1988), Clayton Koelb (1994), Stanley Appelbaum (1995), Joachim Neugroschel (1998), and Jefferson S. Chase (1999). Readers who do not know German and who want to avoid mistakes of their own should compare these translations. Such readers will thereby get a better idea of the many things that Mann's story can — and cannot — mean than if they rely on only one English translation. With the help of such comparisons, they may also get an inkling of what they are missing by reading *Death in Venice* instead of *Der Tod in Venedig.*

Differences between the reading and reception of Mann's novella in English on the one hand and in German on the other constitute a major theme, then, of the present study. Indeed, I hope not only that this study will raise its readers' awareness of how widely the nature and the quality of comments on Mann's story have varied, and how deeply that story has engaged critics and scholars for many years; I also hope that it will help bridge the growing gap between those who write about *Death in Venice* in German and those who do so English. The distinction between these critics and scholars is not always clear since some of them write in both languages, and it does not always hold even for those who write exclusively in one or the other. Still, the following chapters suggest a difference that is becoming more noticeable every year. Much of the research in German on Mann's story is superb, but some of it is extremely academic and abstract, and it would be enlivened by the creative and comparative approaches taken by some scholars working in English. By contrast, some of these English-speaking scholars seem blissfully ignorant of the German language and thus of both Mann's stylistic complexity and the enormous amount of work in German on his novella. This is the case not only with those who consider the novella alone, but also with those who link it to Visconti's film. The latter scholars' problems are compounded by the many differences between that famous film and Mann's text, and in their comments they sometimes mistake Visconti's images for Mann's words; that is, such scholars sometimes assume that Mann wrote what Visconti shows, and even that he did so in the same way. He did not. I consider secondary literature on both Visconti's film and Britten's opera, by the way, more selectively than the reception of Mann's story itself. I generally do not include accounts of the film or the opera that are published in newspapers or magazines, but treat only those published in scholarly books or articles. I include remarks on technical matters of cine-matic or musical composition, moreover, only when such remarks shed light on the meaning of Mann's prose. Both the film and the opera belong to the reception of his text, however, and critics' and scholars' comments on these two adaptations can illuminate aspects of that text that are neglected in traditional literary studies. May this book, then, help whoever reads or writes about *Death in Venice* — be it Mann's, Britten's, Visconti's, or someone else's — in English, German, or any other language.

Before starting this study and becoming immersed in particular details of *Death in Venice,* such readers or writers may wish to recall the general outline of Mann's plot. His fictional events unfold in the course of five chapters. The initial three constitute the first half of his story. In chapter 1, the author Gustav von Aschenbach, Mann's protagonist, goes for a walk at home in Munich. He is at least fifty years old, and though he is successful in his career, his strength is waning and he is enervated by the writing he tried to do earlier in the day. It is May of the year "19..," a year that poses some unspecified danger to Europe. It is also unseasonably muggy. Waiting for a streetcar at the North Cemetery, Aschenbach sees a Byzantine mortuary chapel and a man standing in its portico. This man's appearance is foreign, and his stare is aggressive. The sight of him prompts Aschenbach to envision a tropical landscape and decide to take a vacation, a trip somewhere south. In chapter 2, Mann tells of Aschenbach's life, works, and career. Those works include a prose epic, a novel, a story, and an aesthetic treatise. Their author was born in Silesia, and he inherited both the sober conscientiousness of his father's side of the family and the more sensual blood of his mother's side. He is famous, disciplined, tense, and tired. His watchword is *Durchhalten* (Persevere), and both his own art and the heroism of his fictional characters are best described by the word *Trotzdem* (Despite). After making artistic mistakes early in his career, Aschenbach has achieved dignity. Denying knowledge, he now cultivates beauty, displaying a moral resolution that raises profound questions about the morality of form. Aschenbach is widowed and has a married daughter. His face shows the strain caused by his art. In chapter 3, he travels to Venice via Trieste, Pola, and an unnamed island off the Adriatic coast. One of the passengers on the boat that carries him from Pola to Venice is an old man made up to look young. As Aschenbach gets off the boat, this old man drunkenly pesters and teases him. The gondolier who ferries Aschenbach to the Lido is likewise unusual. He does not obey Aschenbach's orders, and he disappears at the end of their ride. Among the guests at Aschenbach's hotel is a beautiful Polish boy. Aschenbach admires him, observes him at the beach, and decides that his name is "Tadzio." The hot, thick air soon makes Aschenbach feel ill, and he decides to leave Venice. He delays departing, however, and his luggage is sent to the wrong destination, so he has to stay. He is secretly delighted and returns to his hotel, where he admits that Tadzio's presence made it hard for him to go.

Mann's fourth and fifth chapters constitute the second half of his story. In chapter 4, Aschenbach feels and then understands that he is in love with Tadzio. He thinks of both his surroundings and the boy in terms borrowed from Greek mythology. He watches Tadzio at the beach every day and muses about the link between human beauty and intellectual forms, recalling passages from Plato's *Phaedrus* and other ancient Greek texts. Inspired by Tadzio's beauty, he writes a short treatise on some unnamed topic. He tries but fails to talk to the boy and is ever more intoxicated and transported. After their eyes meet at the end of the chapter, he rushes away and whispers, "I love you." In chapter 5, Aschenbach learns that cholera has come to Venice. Tourists are leaving and the city is being disinfected, but Aschenbach says nothing, hoping that his passion will profit from the attendant disorder. He pursues Tadzio through the streets and canals of Venice. He sometimes stops to consider where his emotions are taking him, but decides that Eros is honorable. Many people lie to him about the epidemic, including the leader of a troupe of street singers who perform one night at his hotel. An English clerk tells him the truth: how cholera came to Europe from India and how the corrupt Venetian authorities have tried to conceal the many deaths it has caused. Aschenbach considers sharing this news with Tadzio's mother, but he is sickened by the idea of going home, and he remains silent. He then has an orgiastic dream about celebrating Dionysus, a dream that terrifies, disgusts, arouses, and destroys him. The barber at his hotel dyes Aschenbach's hair and makes up his face so that he appears younger. Following Tadzio one afternoon, Aschenbach loses his way, then eats soft, overripe strawberries. Again, he recalls bits of Plato's *Phaedrus,* adding that artists, who approach intellect via the senses, cannot attain genuine wisdom and dignity. At the beach a few days later, he sees Tadzio roughly wrestled to the ground by another boy. Tadzio then wades out to a sandbar, where he looks outward, then back at the beach. It seems to Aschenbach as if Tadzio is smiling at him, and he gets up to follow the boy but collapses. He is carried to his room, and the world soon receives the news that he has died. This sketch of Mann's plot is only a crude summary, of course, of a subtle literary text. Many details not mentioned here are cited in the pages that follow this introduction.

# Notes

[1] Harlan Kennedy, "Death in Venice," *Film Comment,* November/December 1986, 34–37; "Death in Venice," *Economist,* 24 September 1988, 120.

[2] David Robinson, "Life and Death in Venice," *Sight & Sound,* November 1998, 6.

[3] Geraldine Norman, "Death in Venice: Older Artists Vanquish Younger Ones at the Biennale," *Art & Antiques,* November 1993, 34–35; Patricia Bickers, "Death in Venice," *Art Monthly,* April 1995, 18.

[4] Simon Grant, "Mega Death in Venice," *Blueprint,* July/August 1999, 72; David Taylor, "British Suffer Death in Venice," *Architects' Journal,* 2 March 2000, 4.

[5] Adam Gopnik, "Death in Venice," *New Yorker,* 2 August 1993, 66–73; Jennifer Fletcher and David Skipsey, "Death in Venice: Giovanni Bellini and the Assassination of St Peter Martyr," *Apollo,* January 1991, 4–9.

[6] Helen Castle, "Death in Venice: The Spectre of the Tragic in David Chipperfield's New Extension to San Michele Cemetery," *Architectural Design,* October 2000,: 44–51; David Taylor, "Chipperfield Takes on *Death in Venice,*" *Architects' Journal,* 6–13 August 1998, 10.

[7] "A Grimy and Watery Death in Venice," *Discover,* February 1986, 8.

[8] Mike Sager, "Death in Venice: The Effect of Crack on Gangs in Venice, California," *Rolling Stone,* 22 September 1988, 64–68; Jennifer Allen, "A Death in Venice," *New Republic,* 5 September 1994, 27; "Californian Ducks: Death in Venice," *Economist,* 12 June 1993, 33.

[9] Joshua Micah Marshall, "Death in Venice: Europe's Death Penalty Elitism," *New Republic,* 31 July 2000, 12–14.

# 1: Initial Reactions, 1913–14

## Introduction

OVER FORTY REVIEWS of *Death in Venice* were written in the two years that followed its initial publication. That publication itself took three separate forms. First, in October and November of 1912, the novella appeared serially in a literary journal, *Die neue Rundschau*. Second, a prior and slightly different version of Mann's text was published in a limited luxury edition by Hans von Weber in Munich. Third, the revised version that, oddly enough, had appeared first, in *Die neue Rundschau,* came out as a book published by Samuel Fischer in Berlin. Von Weber's small edition is dated 1912; Fischer's 1913. Some authors of the earliest reviews read the novella in its serial form. Most referred to the same text in the trade edition published by Fischer. In this chapter, those authors' remarks are divided into five categories. Each reflects a different way in which Mann's story was discussed or understood. First, some critics engaged in literary disputes, disagreeing with each others' interpretations of that story and often attacking or defending its hero or its author. Second, some raised the issue of homoeroticism when writing about Aschenbach's attraction to Tadzio, the adolescent Polish boy whom he admires on the Lido. Third, many focused on the style and structure of Mann's narration. Fourth, some regarded aesthetic and biographical aspects of his portrayal of art and artists. Finally, a few concentrated on other themes or combined those already noted here. Many early reviews mention disagreements, of course, and most address more than one theme. Arranging them according to their main emphases, though, and assigning each of them to one of these five categories best reveals their basic similarities and differences. In the conclusion at the end of this first chapter, those similarities and differences are briefly summarized. Unless cited as being from 1914, all the reviews included here are from 1913.

## Literary Disputes

Three notable literary disputes surrounded *Death in Venice* in 1913–14. These disputes arose when one critic or reviewer attacked or supported the novella, then another replied by taking an opposing and often a polemical stance. The first dispute involved the Austrian novelist Hermann Broch, who defended Mann against the charge of philistinism. The second stemmed from favorable reviews written by two of Mann's relatives: Hedwig Dohm, who was the maternal grandmother of his wife Katia, and his older brother Heinrich. The third dispute occurred after a pamphlet by Bernd Isemann rejected *Death in Venice* in no uncertain terms. Many other reviewers and critics openly disagreed with each other, but their remarks are much more limited and are therefore addressed in subsequent sections of this chapter. The three disputes recounted here are more substantial and more sustained. They also suggest both the aesthetic climate and the personal and partisan motives that affected the early reception of Mann's story.

The first disagreement about *Death in Venice* involved the charge of philistinism leveled at Mann by the critic Carl Dallago. It also involved Hermann Broch's rebuttal of that charge. Dallago criticized the traces of philistinism that he found in Mann's essay on the German romantic author Adelbert von Chamisso (1781–1838). That essay appeared in late 1911, and in it Mann prefers bourgeois solidity to merely interesting bohemianism. Dallago objected, contrasting creative artists with their opposite — the uncultured philistine. Broch objected in turn. His argument is complex. He does not know whether Mann has read Dallago's critique, but *Death in Venice* strikes him as a protest against it, as a rebuttal meant to prove Mann's own artistry. Mann, he argues, not only avoids all traces of philistinism, but does so in a polemic that touches on profound questions of aesthetics. This polemic comes in the second chapter of the novella, Broch writes, the one that recapitulates Aschenbach's career and thereby addresses the phenomenon of creativity, an artist's most profound experience. Mann's novella is an extraordinary exertion of artistic will, moreover, and this is the reason for its high degree of perfection. To show how its story contradicts Dallago's concept of the artist, Broch compares Dallago's definitions of a philistine with Mann's descriptions of Aschenbach. Juxtaposing Dallago's conclusion to his own, Broch sums up this comparison: "'Philister!' — Nein, ein Künstler" ("Philistine!" — No, an artist) (402). In his response to Broch, Dallago agreed that *Death in Venice* is a work of art, one very different from the essay on Chamisso, and concluded that it brings Mann back to the realm of art. Both Broch and Dallago seem to have thought that Mann's remarks on Aschenbach applied to himself.

Broch also gave his own opinion of realism and idealism in art. He cites Schopenhauer's aesthetic principle that artists should see the Platonic idea, the Kantian "thing-in-itself," inherent in actual objects, then manifest that vision in their work. Artistic creativity should therefore result in realism, or even naturalism, that forms around an idealistic core. Mann is accordingly wrong, he adds, to oppose art to philosophy. Broch derives from Plato a principle of equilibrium that he posits in nature as well as in works of art and that he finds realized with rare beauty and clarity in *Death in Venice*. The equilibrium of its plot, excepting the polemic second chapter, he thinks, is connected to that of its mood, its feeling, its style. All of its lines converge, rounding it off in unity yet coming to a point. Aschenbach's destiny follows seamlessly from his character, moreover, intellectual conditions thus translating into apparently coincidental necessities of corporeal life. Broch's argumentation is theoretical, but he notes that music is the purest expression of his principle of equilibrium, and he describes the progress of Mann's narrative in musical terms. Mann starts with a main theme in the form of the wanderer who appears at the cemetery in Munich, for example, and he varies that theme when he describes the old man who poses as a young one on the ship to Venice. After Tadzio appears as a counter-theme, Mann's introduction is complete. The essay that Aschenbach composes at the beach, Broch continues, an essay inspired by Tadzio's pleasing proportions, is a high point but not a hasty allegro. At this point, "das Orchester ist hell ge-stimmt, im Einklang wird das lichte, schlanke Motiv unisono gebracht" (the orchestra is brightly tuned, the light, slender theme is harmoniously played unisono) (413). As Aschenbach admits to himself that he loves Tadzio, a de-monic scherzo begins, and his dramatic pursuit of the boy resembles the plot of an opera. Mann's tempo rushes forward and is allegro furioso in Aschenbach's Dionysian dream, which is followed by a coda and the finale of his death. "Uns aber wäre es nicht seltsam und lächerlich," Broch concludes, "wenn Musik hinter der Szene ertönte und in leisem Rhythmus das Thema übernehmen und langsam verklingen lassen möchte" (We would not find it strange or ridiculous, if music intoned behind the scenes and picked up the theme and, in a quiet rhythm, slowly let it die away) (415). Broch's use of these musical terms conveys the first and most sustained of the many analogies that critics have drawn be-tween Mann's novella and music. Since Mann himself may be casting doubt on Platonic concepts of beauty when he has snippets of Plato's *Phaedrus* occur to the smitten Aschenbach, Broch's Platonic concept of equilibrium might seem unsuitable to interpreting *Death in Venice*. In any case, expressing that concept in musical terms helps him make a strong case for the novella's formal cohesion.

The second literary dispute sparked by *Death in Venice* did not occur on the aesthetic high ground occupied by Broch and Dallago. Instead, it involved a sarcastic charge of nepotism. This charge was made by the critic Alfred Kerr, who objected to two reviews of the novella, reviews that had been written by Mann's relatives. The first was by Hedwig Dohm, his wife Katia's grand-mother. It appeared in a Berlin newspaper on 23 February 1913. Dohm calls *Death in Venice* the confessions of an artist and a psychological study, de-scribing its hero as a "Dichterfürst" (poet-prince). The characteristic trait of the novella, she maintains, is how it contrasts Aschenbach's realistic observa-tion of his surroundings with his inner vision, with the procession of his thoughts into the tabernacle of his soul. In her view, he becomes erotically enflamed in the *morbidezza* of Venice and succumbs to hypnosis and hallucinations. He also allows himself to be barbarically tattooed, as she describes his being made up by the barber, and he does not resist the perversion of his feelings. His terrible dream, with its chorus of horror and satanic orgy, she adds, shows him his soul naked. Finally, he dies in beauty as his eyes kiss the sea and Tadzio's pulchritude. According to Dohm, Mann's novella, however, lives as the work of an author to whom art is a religion. Its language lends every sentence and every expression a classic character. Indeed, Dohm calls that language "eine auf Denkensgrund erblühte Rhetorik von vornehmster Exklusivität" (rhetoric of most noble exclusivity, blooming on the soil of thought). Dohm thus praised Mann's style and his psychological insights. His older brother Heinrich, who wrote the other review, hinted at the social and political import of *Death in Venice*. Poetry can precede reality, Heinrich begins, as it does in Zola's novels about the corruption and collapse of bourgeois culture, novels that preceded and willed the actual downfall of the Second Empire in France. Aschenbach's fate is similarly tied to that of Venice, he says, his psychological adventures calling forth an outbreak of related adventures in the external world. Heinrich's logic, or at least the way he expresses it here, seems vague. He adds that Aschenbach's psyche and the city of Venice combine to produce events of great depth and significance, but he never fully explains the relationship he posits between the individual and the collective. He implies, however, that Aschenbach's Germany, like Zola's France, is ripe for radical change. Although they applied different literary criteria, then, both Dohm and Heinrich welcomed *Death in Venice*. Heinrich's remarks sound tortuous and tepid, though, compared to Dohm's effusive praise.

Responding to these reviews in April 1913, Alfred Kerr faulted Mann for having made the reception of his novella such a family affair. Kerr does not dwell on Heinrich's, which he calls an example of brotherly love, noting its restraint. He also only briefly mocks Dohm for being biased, saving his real ammunition for Mann himself. He recounts an imaginary dream, for example, in which Mann, in a servile letter, thanks Dohm for her review. Two of its sentences suffice to convey the sarcastic tone of that fictional letter. In them, Kerr puts the following words into Mann's mouth:

> Großmama, wir wollen an die Stelle der schon fatal angeschriebenen Freundschaftskritik die schlichtere Verwandtschaftsrezension setzen.
> Großmama ist mein Hirte; mir wird nichts mangeln; Du bereitest mir einen Tisch gegen meine Feinde; Großmamas Stecken und Stab trösten mich.

> [Grandma, let's replace our friends' wholly discredited critiques of our books with simpler reviews by relations.
> Grandma is my shepherd; I shall not want; thou preparest a table before me in the presence of mine enemies; Grandma's rod and staff comfort me.] (637)

The latter of these sentences parodies the Twenty-third Psalm. Kerr also dismisses Mann as an anemic author of kitsch who writes about a poet without being one himself. Mann's German is weak, Kerr thinks, and his pseudo-elevated style is banal compared to the poetry of Friedrich Hölderlin (1770–1843). Kerr concludes by paying Mann a dubious compliment: "Jedenfalls ist hier Päderastie annehmbar für den gebildeten Mittelstand gemacht" (In any case, pederasty is here made acceptable for the educated middle class) (640). In addition to panning the reviews by Mann's relatives and to dismissing Mann as well as his prose, Kerr here takes a final swipe at the homoeroticism that figures so prominently in Mann's story. In this second literary dispute, then, remarks about that story were often highly personal.

The tone taken in the third dispute about *Death in Venice* was even nastier than Kerr's. That dispute began with a pamphlet by Bernd Isemann subtitled *Eine kritische Abwehr* (A Critical Rebuff). Ostensibly, Isemann was loath to write about the novella at all. His only reason for doing so, he explains, is to show that Mann's theory of art is ridiculous, thoughtless, and disrespectful. Aschenbach's burned-out fragility does not make him a hero or a genius, Isemann writes, and artistic creativity is more than sucking the marrow from one's bones. Mann proposes such a theory to justify himself, he adds, and is ignorant of the fact that true artists must possess supreme moral will and great religious sensibility. What Mann praises as Aschenbach's self-discipline is really ignoble fear of losing the few thoughts he entertains. The priestly mustiness of his study is suffocating, moreover, and the accumulation of his many days' work does not add up to greatness. Isemann makes particular fun of this last idea: "Ja, durch Schichtung von zweitausend holländischen Käsen, glaube ich, wird die Größe des Eiffelturms erreicht. Wie neckisch, daß durch Schichtung Größe entsteht" (Sure, I suppose stacking two thousand Dutch cheeses attains the height of the Eiffel Tower. How droll it is to think that stacking results in greatness) (9). Instead of eliciting our sympathy, Isemann also observes, Mann's hero is weak and egocentric. He lacks both all conscience and any sense of humor. His feelings are unclean; his sensuality is crude. The final item on this list especially irked Isemann, who later asks, "Was soll ich denn mit diesem Rezeptbuch, dieser Hausapotheke für geschwächte Geister und Körper anfangen, mit dieser Kosmetik für ein Prischen wertloser Sinnlichkeit?" (So what am I supposed to do with this prescription book, this home pharmacy for weakened minds and bodies, with this cosmetic for a pinch of worthless sensuality?) (12). Isemann also wonders how Aschenbach, in his unclean adventure with Tadzio, can forget the happiness he enjoyed with his wife. Since he can, Isemann argues, he is utterly disgusting, a hollow scarecrow and debauchee of weakness. Mann's fundamental error, Isemann claims, lies in thinking that the imbalance of sensitivity and strength — in other words, hysteria — constitutes the essence of artists and is typical of them. Isemann thus attacked Aschenbach for being an erotically perverse embodiment of Mann's wrong-headed concept of the artist.

Isemann did not stop at finding fault with Aschenbach. He also criticized Mann for writing poorly and producing a useless and an immoral book. Like Kerr, Isemann addresses what he calls the problem of pederasty. Although he is willing to accept this sexual inclination in artists' private lives, he insists that they be real men in their work. Besides, he adds, Mann has written about this problem badly. Homoeroticism can be natural in one's youth, Isemann says, but it becomes unnatural, repulsive, and unfitting in old age. Aschenbach, a "Wrack des Intellektualismus" (wreck of intellectualism) (21), has no inkling of its unseemliness. Mann's whole theory of art is libertine, in fact, since Mann concludes that artists are morally indifferent, even immoral. Isemann presents the corresponding lack of high moral purpose in *Death in Venice* as a matter of national pride: "Wie kommt es, daß eine Nation wie die deutsche sich ohne Widerspruch ein so faules Ei in die Brut ihrer größten Dichter und Denker legen läßt? . . . Ja, all dies ist ein Schlag ins Angesicht des deutschen Geistes" (How can it be that a nation like the German one, without objection, lets such a rotten egg be laid in the brood of its greatest poets and thinkers? . . . Yes, all this is a slap in the face of the German mind) (22). Isemann cannot understand why some critics have not admitted that *Death in Venice* is worthless, much less how others can review it favorably. Kerr, he thinks, is the only one who has taken the proper attitude toward it. Besides applying a moral yardstick to Mann's story as a whole, Isemann objects to particular passages in it. He demonstrates his ignorance when he fails to see what the details of the scene at the cemetery in Munich have to do with the rest of the events in that story. Worse still, he suggests that the book begin differently, even proposing a new opening line: "Gustav Aschenbach bekam Lust zu einer Reise" (Gustav Aschenbach felt like taking a trip) (25). He criticizes the structure of the novella as well as Mann's descriptions of peripheral details that are meant to make its setting seem probable and to disguise the improbability of its psychological plot. Isemann also finds Mann's mode of expression repulsive. Mann's pseudo-classical style is no longer German, he writes, but an unnatural, unappetizing disgrace to literature. The description of the wanderer's naked Adam's apple is especially tasteless, and the passage in which the flirtatious old man on the boat licks the corners of his mouth "auf abscheulich zweideutige Art" (in a disgustingly ambiguous way), as Mann puts it, is both an affront to readers and a blemish on the entire book. This passage is brazen and crude, Isemann concludes, and the book in which it occurs is immoral.

Isemann's vehement tirade did not go unanswered. At least three critics, not to mention Mann himself, quickly replied to it. In August 1913, Friedrich Markus Huebner dismissed Isemann as a provincial poetaster and philistine, calling him a typical dilettante and a wisecracking busybody. Another such response, by Oswald Brüll, appeared in December and in a periodical whose editors had reservations about its strident tone. The motto of that journal, *Der Merker*, proclaims that neither love nor hate should color the judgment it passes. A footnote on the first page of Brüll's article, however, says that those editors were willing to make an exception in this case. An unusual provocation, that note explains, excuses an unusual answer. This suspension of the editors' rules is plain from Brüll's strong words. He lashes out at what he calls Isemann's rabble-rousing attack on Mann, and he decries the anti-Semitism audible when Isemann alludes to Mann as "little Moritz." Brüll also exclaims that critics like Isemann, whose name Brüll makes plural in German, cannot be tolerated: "Nein, kein Mitleid — mit den Isemännern!" (No, no sympathy — with the Isemen!) (946). In his zeal to expose Isemann's ignorance, Brüll sometimes misunderstands *Death in Venice*. He thinks that Aschenbach's earlier rejection of knowledge, for example, and his consequent moral decisiveness are a clear victory of ethics over doubt and intellectualism. He fails to observe that this apparent triumph is only temporary and that it later results in Aschenbach's demise. When he writes that the novella proclaims Mann's own artistry to be a matter of willpower and discipline, moreover, Brüll does not distinguish Mann from Aschenbach. More generally, though he admits that *Death in Venice* lacks the graphic vivacity of Mann's first novel, *Buddenbrooks* (The Buddenbrooks, 1901), he praises its author as one of Germany's most moral writers. Brüll also says that Isemann's innuendo occasioned by the fop's licking his tongue in a "disgustingly ambiguous" way reveals that Isemann, not Mann, has a dirty mind. In defending *Death in Venice,* then, neither Huebner nor Brüll always rose above the low level of Isemann's harangue.

Others, including Mann himself, reacted to Isemann with more restraint, at least in print. Tempers seem to have cooled by August 1914, when Alexander Pache reviewed Isemann's pamphlet. Pache explains that it confirms that authors — Isemann was a minor one — seldom make good critics. Isemann's frightening lack of logic, Pache writes, his transparent bias, his inability to treat a difficult problem objectively, and his almost comical, hair-raising misunderstandings make his failed scribbling unworthy of serious discussion. Referring to what Isemann called the problem of pederasty, Pache praises the courage it took to cast the fundamental idea of the novella in such daring and Hellenistic garb. According to him, Mann has handled this ticklish problem tastefully and chastely. Mann's main subject is not Aschenbach's erotic adventure, he adds, but the mysterious and tender relationship between art and beauty. Indeed, Pache thinks *Death in Venice* is a major development in Mann's career, a turning away from his earlier realism and satire toward a deeper conception of art and life, that is, toward beauty.

These remarks in response to Isemann sound much like Mann's own. In an interview with Ödön Halasi Fischer conducted at Mann's summer home in the Bavarian spa town Bad Tölz in August 1913, the author shrugged off Isemann's attack. In another interview, one given to an anonymous author on 14 September 1913 and published, as Fischer's was, in a Hungarian journal, Mann dismisses Isemann's pamphlet as being so philistine and *ad hominem* as not to deserve an answer. In this second interview, Mann admits that the novella conveys his own skepticism towards art, but he argues that it is not primarily a pathological love story, as his critics contend. Instead, he says, he wanted to describe a fall from aesthetic grace that involves homoeroticism only for greater effect:

> Im "Tod in Venedig" wollte ich einen Mann vorstellen, der auf dem Gipfel des Ruhmes, der Ehrung, der Berühmtheit und des Glücks keine Zuflucht in der Kunst findet, sondern an einer unüberwindlichen Leidenschaft körperlich und seelisch zugrunde geht . . . Nur um den Sturz vom Gipfel in die Tiefe möglichst verhängnisvoll erscheinen zu lassen, wählte ich für meinen Helden die homosexuelle Liebe.

> [In *Death in Venice* I wanted to present a man who at the summit of success, honor, fame, and fortune finds no refuge in art but instead runs aground, physically and psychologically, on an insurmountable passion. . . . Only to make the plunge from the summit into the depths appear as fateful as possible did I choose for my hero homosexual love.] (37)

Mann adds that his source for this story of lapsed greatness was an episode from the life of Goethe. At the age of seventy, he explains, the poet had fallen in love with a sixteen-year-old girl who rejected his proposal of marriage. Once, as the two were playing tag, Goethe stumbled, fell, and was unable to get up — a world-conquering genius reduced to a helpless old man. Mann thus describes Aschenbach as a substitute for Goethe, about whom Mann claims he did not yet want to write. This second interview was translated into German and reprinted three weeks later in a Frankfurt newspaper. Two days after that, on 7 October 1913, a letter to the editor of that same paper, the *Frankfurter Zeitung*, observed that Mann had mistakenly conflated two young women and two separate episodes in Goethe's life. The poet fell while chasing one Fräulein Lade in Wiesbaden, the author of that letter writes, not Ulrike von Levetzow in Marienbad, whom he loved. In any case, Mann gave this explanation of his hero's fall as his answer to Isemann. On 7 December 1913, he gave an anonymous interviewer in Budapest another such account of Aschenbach's similarity to Goethe. Mann added that *Death in Venice* is also a stylistic experiment, an attempt to create a new prose style, and that he had read Goethe's *Wahlverwandtschaften* (Elective Affinities, 1809) three times while writing it.

## Homoeroticism

The issue of homoeroticism in *Death in Venice* has already been noted in Kerr's remark about Mann's making pederasty acceptable to the middle classes and in Isemann's objection to both Aschenbach's passion and Mann's portrayal of it.

This issue also figures in Pache's subordination of Mann's sexual theme to his prose style and in Mann's own explanation that homosexual love simply made Aschenbach's downfall seem steeper. Other reviewers addressed it more extensively. Some regarded Aschenbach's attraction to Tadzio as symbolic or otherwise respectable, but others found this attraction repulsive, offensive, or dangerous. Many thought it less important than the language Mann used to describe it. All of these reviewers' remarks help put Aschenbach's eroticism into the perspective from which it was seen when the novella appeared. Still other reviewers mention his homoeroticism more or less in passing. Their remarks on it are accordingly included in the later sections of this chapter.

To some early reviewers, that homoeroticism was symbolic in the extreme. In July 1913, for example, Franz Herwig gave *Death in Venice* his sentimental approval, showing the high-mindedness connoted by the elevation named in the title of the journal that carried his review, *Hochland*. Herwig praises Mann as a sublime poet, and he senses in *Death in Venice* an indescribable urge toward the divine, an urge alive in all great works of art. Other critics, he says, have missed its simplest and most human point. Greek love is its main theme, but Tadzio is a symbol of something greater by far: "Ein Gleichnis, ja; hinter diesem Gleichnis steht die Gottheit, die absolute Vollkommenheit, die Heimat und die Sehnsucht geht *dahin,* durch das holde Gleichnis *hindurch*" (Yes, a symbol; behind this symbol stands divinity, absolute perfection, home, and *that* is where the yearning goes, *through* the precious symbol) (490–91). This is the core of the novella, Herwig adds, and here we have the yearning that is the best part of humanity, a passionate pressing forward to the eternal. Herwig considers Aschenbach's death, too, symbolic. In beauty reside both the divine and the demonic, he explains, and Aschenbach incurs emotional guilt when he succumbs to the latter. Like Tadzio, his contraction of cholera is a symbol, and he has to die because he has sinned, if only in thought. He also dies, however, of an untamable yearning for perfection and for home. Herwig goes on to note that Aschenbach experiences the insufficiency of even the highest artistic endeavor, and he extols Mann's own "berauschende Steigerung des Ausdrucks" (intoxicating heightening of expression) (491). His focus, however, is on the symbolic nature of Mann's story and its supposed suggestion of all the refuge and rootedness conveyed by *Heimat,* the German word for "home."

Other reviewers similarly described Aschenbach's attraction to Tadzio as highly symbolic. Hermann Joelsohn, for one, interpreted *Death in Venice* according to idealistic concepts of eros, sexuality, and love. Joelsohn contrasts eros and desire in their relationship to artists, and he explains this contrast using the example of *Death in Venice*. The foreign god who appears in Aschenbach's Dionysian dream is the enemy of eros, Joelsohn writes, but also its constant companion at the side of artists, whose mode of knowledge is sensual. Unlike eros, moreover, which begins with the senses and is stimulated by corporeal forms, love lies between the extremes of physical lust and intellectual admiration or respect, and love is what Aschenbach feels for Tadzio. Joelsohn thus subscribes to the Platonic conception of beauty that Mann attributes, but not without irony, to Aschenbach himself. According to Joelsohn, on whom Mann's irony seems lost, Aschenbach's love for Tadzio is not even just erotic, much less merely lustful. E. M. Hamann similarly maintained that *Death in Venice* is a symbolic elegy. The description of Aschenbach's passion for Tadzio is the apex of Mann's art, Hamann maintains, and that description does not seem meant to elicit ugly, impure sensations in his readers. In fact, one follows his plot, after it introduces Tadzio, as if it were the gripping story of some noble, incurable patient. The beauty of Mann's prose is what redeems the novella for Hamann, who thus seems less than keen about its hero's passion. At any rate, he suggests that Mann was writing about a deeply divided type of artist, one who fatally succumbs to the beauty of art that is imperfect because it is immature or unmanly.

Aschenbach's feelings seemed less sublime to two reviewers writing in the Viennese newspaper *Neue Freie Presse*. On 8 June 1913, "p. z." (whom Matter, in his bibliography of 1972, identifies as Paul Zifferer) wrote that the hero of *Death in Venice* is neither Aschenbach nor Tadzio. The boy is more a symbol than a real being, he says, and the hero is Venice, a site of death that recalls Boccaccio's Florence. Dying in Venice is what justifies the dangerous subject of Mann's book, in fact, the somewhat repulsive relationship of Tadzio and the aging Aschenbach. Zifferer is not reassured by the purity of that relationship. It seems to him that Aschenbach lacks not the will to sin, but only the courage and the strength. Aschenbach, he adds, is also terribly serious, melancholy, and almost conscientious about his erotic vice, practicing it as if it were a virtue. His "blond[e] Sinnesart" (blond way of thinking) (31), with its unconvincing guile and this misplaced probity, prompt Zifferer — writing in an Austrian newspaper — to call *Death in Venice* a thoroughly German book. To him, the value of the book lies not in its plot but in its refined art of narration. Zifferer especially likes its style: "Welche Kraft, welchen Reichtum die deutsche Sprache in sich birgt, dies muß man hier staunend wie etwas Neues und Wunderbares erkennen" (One must recognize here with astonishment, as something new and miraculous, what force, what wealth the German language contains) (31–32). Mann's sentences, Zifferer writes, are connected like the arches of a tall bridge. They carry one over abysses, and one never loses a feeling of reassuring safety. Like the sight of a beautiful landscape, moreover, his prose fills one with indescribable joy. His story is seamless and flows so calmly, in fact, that one seems to hear its smooth breathing. Its strength, however, is also its weakness. It derives from art, not life, and thus is a vision, not reality or actual experience. It astonishes us and we admire it, Zifferer concludes, but we are never touched or transported. Just as he rejects Aschenbach's urge for Tadzio and mocks the typically German way in which that urge plays itself out, Zifferer thus expresses mixed feelings about Mann's style.

Writing in the same Viennese paper two weeks later, on 22 June 1913, a reviewer who signed his or her name only as "r." compared *Death in Venice* to Arthur Schnitzler's *Frau Beate und ihr Sohn* (Mrs. Beate and Her Son, 1913). Schnitzler relates the parallel love affairs conducted by a forty-year-old widow and by her son. Both of these stories are novellas written in broadly flowing prose, "r." observes, both recount a curious incident, both are "sündhaft schillernd" (sinfully glittering) (31), and both are often embarrassing and at the limit of what art can do. Mann and Schnitzler, "r." adds, may have been attracted by the unusualness of the events they describe, events that could be conceived easily and playfully enough but that then become "frivol und kichernd und anstößig" (frivolous and giggling and offensive) (31). Many critics after "r." have agreed that *Death in Venice* is offensive, but no one else has ever drawn this conclusion that the events it recounts seem silly and tittering. In any case, "r." thinks both novellas tell of guilt that must be atoned. Like Zifferer, "r." prefers Mann's style to his plot and finds that plot dangerous.

While these two reviews were appearing in Vienna, the first of another pair was published in Budapest. The second corrected this first one in point of fictional fact and took a less literal approach to the theme of homoeroticism and its implications. On 15 June 1913, the Hungarian author and dramatist Sándor Bródy described what had happened when he bought a copy of *Death in Venice* and went home to read it. His reaction was unpleasant. He felt more revulsion than pity for Aschenbach, he says, and was horrified by the novella's success. He cannot understand how what he calls its ugly theme has met with such general interest in Germany. Perhaps this is because Mann lent "einer elenden Schweinerei" (a miserable swinery) (273) a Goethean form. In any case, Bródy thinks that the Germans should share his dislike of it:

> Die Deutschen sollten erschrecken und daraus lernen. Besonders dann, wenn sie es im Zusammenhang mit der neuesten Bevölkerungsstatistik betrachten, die besagt, daß die Bevölkerungszunahme in Deutschland noch ungünstiger ist als in Frankreich, noch trostloser als im ganzen übrigen Europa.

> [The Germans should be horrified and learn from it. Especially when they consider it together with the latest demographical statistics, which show that [the prospect of] a population increase is even more unfavorable in Germany than in France, even bleaker than in all the rest of Europe.] (274)

Bródy thus suggests that Aschenbach's homoerotic emotions are harmful because they diminish the Germans' ability to reproduce. He does not seem to have read *Death in Venice* very carefully, however, for he cites at least two details that are nowhere to be found in it. He claims that Aschenbach dyes his beard and hair while still in Munich, for example, and he explains that as an artist and author, before becoming exhausted and deviant, Aschenbach had both tried to please and been inspired by the feminine sex. He also says that Aschenbach commits suicide. Two of these three details were noted in a letter to the editor of a Hungarian journal other than the one that carried Bródy's article, a letter that appeared two weeks later, on 1 July 1913. Vanda Tóth, its author, writes that Bródy must have perused Mann's novella over dinner, maybe in a bad mood. She observes that it says nothing at all about women being the source or the audience of Aschenbach's art, and she says that Bródy's memory deceived him when he called Aschenbach's death suicide. One could disagree with Tóth about the latter point. Aschenbach has often been said to commit suicide, even if he does not do so explicitly. Tóth might also have objected that Aschenbach's hair is not dyed until he visits the hotel barber in Venice and that Mann expressly describes his face as clean-shaven. In any event, her interpretation is much more incisive than Bródy's. She argues that Mann works consciously and calculatedly, in a way that enables his story to become symbolic and otherworldly. She also considers its sexual theme daring and embarrassing, but expects that most readers will hardly notice it and that the novella expresses something much deeper and more bitter. She thus praises Mann's style and thinks sexuality less important than other issues raised in *Death in Venice*.

Another review published in Budapest, in German, praised both Mann's style and the way he discusses his homoerotic theme. In this review, which appeared in the newspaper *Pester Lloyd*, Ernst Goth welcomes the novella as a masterpiece that no other contemporary German author could write, if only because no one but Mann dares broach its subject matter. In doing so, Goth adds, Mann has shown understanding, tolerance, and tact:

> Denn hier wird ein Thema, das bestenfalls in medizinischen Kreisen mit Ernst und Verständnis behandelt, sonst aber verächtlich unter die widerlichsten menschlichen Aberrationen verwiesen oder gar mit lüsterner Geheimtuerei betastet wird, zum Gegenstand einer rein geistigen, tiefen Tragödie, in der nichts Pathologisches mehr mitschwingt.

> [For here a theme that is treated seriously and sympathetically at best in medical circles, but that is otherwise contemptuously relegated to the most repulsive human aberrations, or even touched upon with lewd secretiveness, becomes the object of a purely intellectual, profound tragedy, in which there is no longer anything pathological.] (28)

Goth goes on to praise Mann's epic mastery, singling out the subtleties of his plot and the power of his language. That power is especially apparent, he adds, when Mann's prose shifts, along with Aschenbach, from being strictly disciplined to indulging in freer rhythms. Goth's main point, though, is that Mann's noble and decent handling of his homosexual subject matter is the most admirable quality of *Death in Venice*. Only Mann's artistry, he explains, could cast things called perverse as forces threatening humanity in general. Goth liked both that Mann treats homoeroticism fairly, then, and that he makes it seem universally relevant.

Other critics shared Bródy's sentiment that homoeroticism was an empty exercise, but they did so in more refined ways. Julius Bab, for one, maintained that the novella addresses the same problem as Mann's unsuccessful drama *Fiorenza* (1905), that is, the opposition of ethical action to aesthetic enjoyment. He also hails *Death in Venice* as a masterpiece of recent German narrative art, praising the epic mastery of its subtle and seemingly effortless telling; the linguistic mastery evident in the contrast between the correct, dry style of its first part and the effusive rhythms that stream forth as Aschenbach's sense of duty dissolves; and, finally, the human mastery thanks to which a so-called perversion is described objectively yet becomes symbolic of a psychological tragedy. Bab, like many other critics cited in this section, thus pays tribute to Mann's prose while considering Aschenbach's attraction to Tadzio important mainly as a symbol. He goes further than most, though, in rejecting the suggestion that the story told in *Death in Venice* is homoerotic:

> Nur die allerhoffnungslosesten Geister werden hier etwas von einem pikanten Stoff verspüren können. Und wenn die sogenannten Führer der sogenannten homosexuellen Bewegung weniger hoffnungslose Geister wären, so könnten sie an diesem Kunstwerk viel über die letzte tragische Bedeutung ihres Themas innerhalb der Geisteswelt erfahren.

> [Only the most hopeless souls will be able to discern any trace of a piquant subject matter here. And if the so-called leaders of the so-called homosexual movement were less hopeless souls, they could learn from this work of art much about the final tragic significance of their theme within the intellectual world.] (170)

The "tragic significance" cited here has to do with the opposition of ethics and aesthetics that Bab finds in both *Fiorenza* and *Death in Venice*. In all heterosexual relations, he explains, there is a will to act as well as the natural will to be fruitful. In delight with one's own sex, by contrast, the soul absolves itself of its ultimate duty, the enjoyment of beauty revolves around itself, and intoxication makes us passive. This purely aesthetic and passive condition, he acknowledges, was valued by the Greeks for inspiring pure intuition, but for Aschenbach, whose life was built on will, work, and deeds, such voluptuous passivity has to mean death. Bab does not imply here that Aschenbach must be punished, but rather that he can live only by his own, active volition.

One brief but telling comment published in July 1914 shows what "the so-called leaders of the so-called homosexual movement," as Bab called them, may have thought about *Death in Venice*. In a yearbook edited by the sexologist Magnus Hirschfeld and devoted to the study of "sexuelle Zwischenstufen" (intermediate sexual stages), Kurt Hiller regretted that the great homoerotic novel had yet to be written. Parenthetically, he added that *Death in Venice* does not deserve that distinction:

> Thomas Mann, seine Technik in Ehren, gibt in diesem Stück ein Beispiel moralischer Enge, wie ich sie . . . niemals erwartet hätte. Die ungewohnte Liebe zu einem Knaben, die in einem Alternden seltsam aufspringt, wird da als Verfallssymptom diagnostiziert und wird geschildert fast wie die Cholera.

> [Thomas Mann, with all due respect for his technique, gives in this work an example of moral narrowness that I . . . would never have expected. The unaccustomed love for a boy, which strangely arises in an aging man, is diagnosed as a symptom of decline and described almost like cholera.] (338)

Hiller here seems to fault Mann for failing to explain the origins of Aschenbach's passion, as well as for making him fall ill and die because of it. This rejection of *Death in Venice* suggests that the novella did not endear itself to all readers who shared its hero's homoeroticism.

## Style and Structure

While some early reviewers focused more or less sharply on the issue of homoeroticism, others' primary interest, one already noted in the disputes cited above, was Mann's style. These other reviewers often stressed topics such as his choice of words, sentence structure, and narrative form. To his most fervent admirers, the plot of *Death in Venice* paled next to its composition, which seemed nothing less than perfect or miraculous. Others found its tone too conscious and too cold. Still others were ambivalent. The most perceptive among them regarded literary form as both a blessing and a curse for Mann. Several compared his stylistic concern and polished prose to those of Flaubert. This comparison was not coincidental — after all, Flaubert's first name was the French form of Aschenbach's: Gustave.

Admiration of the style and structure of Mann's story sometimes came from unexpected quarters. In April 1913, for example, Albert Ehrenstein reviewed the novella in the expressionist journal *Der Sturm*. He judges it to be less a novella than a Platonic monologue, an ethical-epic matter and a transitional work that is not simply an autobiographical account of Mann's own development as an author. Alluding to Mann's prior novella *Tonio Kröger* (1903), and referring to nymphs who are mentioned in Greek mythology, Ehrenstein also observes that this is not the first time that Mann has dealt with its subject, the "Auflösung eines geradezu preußischen Willens im Lande der Lust und der Hesperiden" (dissolution of a downright Prussian will in the land of lust and the Hesperides) (44). Mann's homosexual subject matter is almost peripheral, moreover, for he transforms it into a miracle of composition. Ehrenstein also likes Mann's early scenes for foreshadowing events to come, as well as Aschenbach's tangled emotions and defenselessness against death. Above all, he says, *Death in Venice* is such a miracle thanks to the "Herrlichkeiten der antikisierenden Sprache" (splendors of Mann's pseudo-ancient language) (44). Ehrenstein also notes how important the names of Mann's characters are, explaining that "Aschenbach" suggests a fluid carrying ashes, a fluid that moves only with much effort and is therefore analogous to Aschenbach's will. Given this emphasis on names, it is strange that Ehrenstein gets Aschenbach's first one wrong, dubbing him "Georg." He concludes that some of Mann's other writing is more impressive, regretting that the author is going through a morbid phase.

Like Ehrenstein, Kurt Martens welcomed the way in which Mann narrates his story, expressing minor reservations only after bestowing lavish praise on its style. It is hard to do justice to *Death in Venice,* Martens explains, since it is one of the few works so perfect as to defy analysis. With its psychological language and portraiture, he adds, Mann has surmounted a literary pinnacle. By comparison, its subject matter is indifferent. Even its theme — the mental fall of an aging poet into the abyss of pure form — means little when compared to Aschenbach's prophetic vision and words. Martens also observes that the sensuous world of antiquity and the terrors of modern psychology equally inform Aschenbach's thoughts, though he regrets that Mann's highly conscious artistry leaves little room for the irrational. Like many other reviewers, Martens thus seems to prefer a less naturalistic, more rhapsodic narrative style.

Hans von Hülsen was likewise enthusiastic about Mann's style, not to mention about the confessional nature of *Death in Venice*. Von Hülsen praises the structure, language, and psychology of the novella, and, in its descriptions of Venice, the "dichterische Vision von erstaunlicher Kraft" (poetic vision of astonishing power) (3). He also likes its solemnity and the feeling for nature that Mann displays in his descriptions of the sea. Less incisively, von Hülsen thinks that the novella completely lacks irony and that it makes no use of Mann's usual leitmotifs. In addition to admiring its stylistic virtuosity, von Hülsen welcomes its heroic revelation of Mann's self. "Kein Werk vielleicht im ganzen Umkreise der Literatur," he writes, "gibt so vorbehaltlose Aufschlüsse über Persönlichkeit und Kunstübung seines Schöpfers wie diese Novelle" (Perhaps no work in the entire field of literature is so unreservedly informative about the personality and artistic practice of its creator as this novella) (3).

In Austria, Felix Braun similarly expressed enthusiasm about the structure of *Death in Venice,* which he calls the purest, clearest, and most mature book by Mann, the most refined German writer. Mann's plot is neither rich nor exciting, Braun says, and only after one has finished reading and thinks about his story does one notice the many disguises assumed by death, including Tadzio. The most miraculous thing about the story, he adds, is how subtly and unobtrusively Mann introduces this idea and the characters who embody it. Braun also appreciates how well Mann deals with the second theme that runs through the novella: Hellas. The spirit of the book has everywhere been transformed into limpid form, he continues, so even without its reminiscences of ancient Greece, one can call it a classic. Indeed, Braun thinks its composition as near to perfect as possible: "Die Komposition dieses Buches gehört zu den bedeutendsten Leistungen der modernen deutschen Epik . . . Wenn irgendwo von Vollendung gesprochen werden kann, so ist es hier" (The composition of this book is one of the most significant accomplishments of modern German narration . . . If one can anywhere speak of perfection, it is here) (429–30).

Other reviewers thought almost as highly of Mann's style but were not as impressed by *Death in Venice* as a whole. Oswald Brüll, who took Mann's side against Isemann in December 1913, had already reviewed the novella in May of that year. He had called Mann a "Kasuist der Form" (casuist of form) (375), an author whose many stories about this aesthetic concept recall Flaubert's strong emphasis on literary style. Quoting Aschenbach's musings about the two faces of form, Brüll adds that the subject of the novella is the other side of form, its immorality. *Death in Venice* may treat the same subject as Oscar Wilde's *Picture of Dorian Gray* (1891), he writes, but in it homosexuality has merely accessory meaning, is only a symbol for passion in general. For Aschenbach, form and dignity are closely related, and Mann's focus on artistic form in particular makes Aschenbach's fate that of an artist and a poet. We are not as moved by this sinfully charmed writer, however, as we are by the chaste Tonio Kröger because *Death in Venice* is too concerned with *l'art pour l'art*. Few readers can really enter the world of characters who are artists, Brüll adds, and as Flaubert himself once admitted in a letter to George Sand, more universal and typical people are more interesting. Brüll admires Mann's penetrating composition and masterful style, and he finds the structure of his story faultless. When he adds that the novella contains neither irony nor leitmotifs, however, he seems not to understand Mann's use of such rhetorical and formal devices. In any case, Brüll thanks Mann for providing an aesthetic experience, even though he thinks the content of the novella leaves us cool. This statement in May is warmer than the one Brüll made in December. As he succinctly put it when he summed up his rebuttal of Isemann then, *Death in Venice* is "Marmorglatt und marmorkalt" (as smooth as marble and as cold) (945).

Still other reviewers likewise expressed reservations about Mann's style. In August, a reviewer whose name was indicated only by the initials "F. M." wrote that the novella won fame for its author that, to some readers, has a bitter aftertaste. This is because its style is so coolly objective. Mann describes his hero with the dispassionate calm of an anatomist dissecting a corpse, F. M. thinks, and his style is like that of a delicate etching. *Death in Venice* is a stylistic masterpiece, F. M. adds, but it is not a pleasant one. It is a virtuosic display of its author's art, but nothing more. F. M. also compares it to, and seems to prefer, *Die unterbrochene Rheinfahrt* (The Interrupted Rhine Journey, 1913), a novella by Wilhelm Schäfer (1868–1952). In one of the first monographs written on Mann, Paul Friedrich was similarly ambivalent about his style. Like, Brüll, he praised the language of the novella for being marmoreal. As he explains, "eine ergreifende, blasse Abendröte glimmt feierlich um den vollendeten Sprachmarmor des 'Todes in Venedig'" (A moving, pale twilight solemnly gleams around the perfect language-marble of *Death in Venice*) (13). What is truly gripping and satisfying, Friedrich adds, are Mann's descriptions of the sea and the sky. Mann glorifies the city of Venice, moreover, and he ethereally exalts human beauty. His psychological passages show how eros emerges without being either normal or perverse. We artists, Friedrich writes, know how near to each other beauty and sensuality lie. Despite his praise for Mann's marvelous style, Friedrich finds the novella too long. Its language is beautiful, its subject is remarkable, and its descriptions are chaste and tender, he writes, but its unnecessary length keeps it from being a perfect work of art. Friedrich also thinks that it is too subjective. Its descriptions of Aschenbach's psyche are a bit out of place, he explains, for a hero who does little more than delicately make a fool of himself.

In November 1913, Wolfgang Schumann took a much dimmer view of Mann's style. As "r." had done in June, in Vienna's *Neue Freie Presse*, Schumann compared *Death in Venice* with Schnitzler's *Frau Beate und ihr Sohn*. Mann's book is no match for Schnitzler's, Schumann contends, for the German author Mann is too conscious of his literary task and is unacquainted with the unfettered drives that he anxiously describes. Aschenbach is likewise too dispassionate, and his desire for Tadzio is too reflective to convey either its grotesque and ridiculous sides or its excessive and terrifying ones. As a result, Schumann writes, the novella "macht einen müden, sehr deutlich gesagt: einen langweiligen Eindruck. Wollte sich Mann einmal an einem ihm innerlich gänzlich unzugänglichen Gegenstand probieren, so hätte dies füglich besser unter Ausschluß der Öffentlichkeit geschehen können" (makes a tired, and to speak very plainly, a boring impression. If Mann wanted to try treating a subject to which he has no inner access whatsoever, this could properly have been done better in private) (306). Schumann has especially little patience with Mann's opening sentence. "So," he explains, "begannen alte Kriminalromane, bei deren Lektüre man gefaßt war, auf je einen notwendigen zwanzig überflüssige Sätze zu bekommen" (This is how old detective novels began; when reading them one was prepared to get twenty superfluous sentences for every necessary one) (306). The lack of judgment evident in this remark becomes even more apparent when Schumann adds that Mann's first thirty pages have nothing to do with the rest of his story, a fact Schumann thinks demonstrates its utter absurdity. Schumann also thinks that Mann is like certain older writers who are cool, not capable, and that his overconscious lack of talent results in pedantic dilettantism. His language is highly intellectual but dry and lifeless, Schumann claims, and his supposedly authentic details are wooden and stiff. His hero remains an isolated case of artistic instability, a character whom Mann overestimates, attributing to such an author what only a poet can do. This last distinction had been drawn in Germany ever since Friedrich Schiller (1759–1805) relegated novelists to being only the half-brothers of poets. Like many other reviewers of *Death in Venice*, Schumann thus judged Mann's story according to outdated literary ideals.

Alfred Walter Heymel made similar remarks on 3 August 1913 in the *Frankfurter Zeitung*, the same newspaper that published both the interview in which Mann explained that his story was based on an episode from the life of Goethe and the subsequent letter that noted how he had actually conflated two such episodes. Recounting an ostensible meeting with the editor of that paper, Heymel claims he would have written his review sooner, had he not discovered that *Death in Venice* was incomprehensible, embarrassing, and downright horrifying. At first, he explains, he liked how well Mann casts the net of his diction and how masterfully he hones his syntax, but then he became averse to the entire novella, finding it to be the product of well-harnessed weakness and considering Mann to be identical to Aschenbach. Heymel expresses such mixed feelings in a memorable image: "Ich bewunderte, aus wie wenig Eiern hier ein vorzüglicher Koch einen großen Pudding gemacht hat" (I admired how an excellent cook here made a large pudding from so few eggs) (1). Aschenbach's tragedy is Mann's as well, Heymel adds, for both men lack the liveliness of a poet. Furthermore, one is afraid that Tadzio, that image of a young god, will grow up to be too worldly and have loose morals. Mann's story makes us worried about the fate of this blessed creature, Heymel says, who even at such a young age seems destined to seduce and destroy. Besides, Aschenbach's attraction to him is not so unnatural, and there was no need for Mann, with reminders of ancient Greece, to treat it in such a pedantic and professorial way. On the one hand, then, Heymel admires *Death in Venice;* on the other, it troubles him. His concern about Tadzio's future may be unique. His ambivalence about Mann's style was not. Fritz Hübner, for example, in April 1913, similarly admired the art of Mann's "Satzarchitektur" (sentence architecture) (213) but found the novella marred by gaps, dead stretches, and authorial lapses. He concluded that Mann must be undergoing a developmental crisis.

One of the most astute reviews primarily concerned with Mann's style was written by Bruno Frank. This review appeared in *Die neue Rundschau*, the journal in which *Death in Venice* itself was first published. According to Frank, the novella makes narrative form a matter of discipline, moral economy, indeed moral intransigence. He argues that its author achieves such virtues by resisting the logic that destroys its hero. Like Ehrenstein, Frank is loath to interpret the novella too biographically, confessional though it may be. Instead, he emphasizes how Mann differs from Aschenbach. According to Frank, Aschenbach's problem is that he is threatened by the force of his own intuition, which is sensual. Mann is stronger, resisting this same threat with the irony of having his novella turn against itself. "Niemals war sein Dichter dem Chaos so überlegen," Frank writes, "als da er es bekennerhaft auftat und düster verherrlichte" (Never was its poet so superior to chaos as when he, as if confessing, opened it up and darkly extolled it) (659). Frank does not argue that Mann is a stranger to the fascination with literary form that kills Aschenbach. On the contrary, Frank's point is that Mann needs counterweights to his inspiration and his ideals, needs the ballast that Frank finds in his naturalistic discipline and his "Gehorsam dem Wirklichen gegenüber" (obedience to the real) (664). It is not that Mann rules words, he explains, but that they threaten to overcome him. More like Balzac than Flaubert in this regard, Mann counters his verbal intoxication with his own narrative discipline. According to Frank, it would not be wrong to read *Death in Venice* as an allegory of his struggle between inspiration and narrative will. The art of Mann's novella thus involves its human aspect. That novella is a flawless creation, he thinks, in which Mann practices what he preaches by opposing the ethical will of his creative talent to the lure of self-enjoyment that destroys Aschenbach. Indeed, *Death in Venice* is a perfect miracle, Frank comments, being conceived in dithyrambic intoxication yet drawn out into an epic structure, spinning out its story yet also seeming to stand still and thereby filling its readers with a warm, even glow from its own fiery, hymnic core. More cursory remarks by Frank on Mann's novella, made soon after its publication as a book in 1913, appeared in English in 1947.

In addition to judging form to be Mann's saving grace, Frank had a good deal to say about further ramifications of Mann's style, as well as about both the ideas and details found in *Death in Venice*. Mann's writing has a dual nature, being both ideal and true, he claims, and it is therefore like the ghostly realism of the German romantic E. T. A. Hoffmann (1776–1822). In another such reference to Mann's literary predecessors, Frank writes that the charm of *Death in Venice* often lies in its exactitude, a quality derived from the Mothers in Goethe's *Faust* (1808/1832), the mythological figures who guard ideals beyond time and place. Frank likewise mentions two German philosophers who have left their imprint on the novella. He argues that Mann's moral resoluteness recalls that of Nietzsche. He also contends that Mann — whose heroes, like Nietzsche, are agnostic and therefore all the greater — is the first author who does not merely imitate Nietzsche, but instead bravely goes forth into a godless world. The other philosopher Frank cites is Schopenhauer, in whose *Metaphysik der Geschlechtsliebe* (Metaphysics of Sexual Love, 1844) he finds the first explanation for the emotional changes that overtake middle-aged men such as Aschenbach. Frank thinks

Aschenbach's homosexual love both hopeless and illusory, but he also observes that it is a powerful way of expressing degradation and self-destructive aestheticism. What is more, he links Aschenbach's satisfaction at the thought that Tadzio will not grow old to Aschenbach's rejuvenation at the hands of the hotel barber. Frank also notes structural elements such as Mann's creating an atmosphere of antiquity with subtle allusions to Cicero and Homer, his several variations on the theme of the death's head, and the fact that his hero dreamily sits in a chair at the end of each of the last three chapters, as good as dead after his ride with the spooky gondolier. Although he praises *Death in Venice* as the "Meisterung eines Meisterschicksals" (mastering of a master's fate) (665), Frank differs from many other critics cited so far by regarding Aschenbach's fate as not just that of an artist. Instead, he considers the novella an elegy for individuals in general.

Whereas Frank, writing under the influence of Nietzsche, read *Death in Venice* as the triumph of its author's will, Hanns Sachs argued that its topic and technique paralleled the principles of Freudian psychoanalysis. Sachs's article came out in October 1914 in *Imago,* a journal for the application of psychoanalysis to the humanities that was published under the editorship of Freud himself. According to Sachs, death is the hero of the novella, since it appears from the beginning, not just at the end, and is embodied in a series of fictional characters, not in a skeleton with an hourglass and a scythe. No one can judge this treatment of death as competently as psychoanalysts, he adds, who study the laws of such symbolic representations in dreams. Besides, Mann has tried to lend his story a dreamlike character. Does he do so in the way that psychoanalysis expects? Sachs thinks he does. That the tourist in Munich stands next to the cemetery, for example, illustrates the principle, applied by psychoanalysts in their interpretation of dreams, that proximity indicates connectedness. That the gondolier ferries Aschenbach for free, whereas the Greek Charon was paid for his similar service, illustrates another concept well known to psychoanalysts, Sachs writes, the representation of something by means of its opposite. This concept recurs when the barber rejuvenates Aschenbach and thereby makes plain his surrender to death. In his resemblance to the old man on the boat, an incarnation of death, Sachs continues, Aschenbach now wears death's livery. Likewise, he dies wearing cheerful colors, and only the cloth attached to the abandoned camera is the black of mourning. That only his hatband and tie are red, the color of love and life's blood, demonstrates the displacement of what is important onto seemingly unimportant details. Tadzio, too, wears red, a fact that confirms that he represents not only love but death as well. Sachs also observes that Aschenbach's unconscious foils his attempt to flee Venice and that death and sensual love are closely linked in his violent dream. Sachs interprets *Death in Venice* as if it were itself a dream, then, crediting Mann with having written it in ways consistent with psychoanalytic ideas.

Sachs also had much to say about how Mann's novella treats the subject of homosexuality. Mann's portrayal of homosexual love as repressed but natural, he says, rather than as perverse or degenerate, confirms psychoanalytic ideas about the omnipresence of unconscious homosexuality and the conditions for its spreading beyond the barrier of consciousness. In the novella, Sachs adds, those ideas become transformed into poetry, into truth on a higher level. Sachs does not find the source of Aschenbach's passion damnable, only the fact that it results in the destruction of his sublimations and in his regressing to primitive-sexual wishes. What is more, Sachs says, it is no coincidence that Aschenbach dies of cholera, a disease often associated with loose bladders and bowels. Mann stresses that it is spread by filth, Sachs notes, and these facts suggest the anal eroticism that psychoanalysis has discovered in the history of homosexuality. Aschenbach would not have been defeated by his attack of homosexual love, moreover, had he been able to transform that love into tenderness toward a son, and Tadzio is an ideal son whose father Mann never mentions. While tolerant of homoeroticism in the unconscious, then, and full of admiration for the way in which Mann suggests its presence there, Sachs faults Aschenbach for letting it get out of control and for not avoiding its fatal consequences. He also speaks of such love as a counter-theme to the main theme of death that Mann varies and develops and that combines with love in an intoxicating, resonant final chord. By drawing such parallels to a musical composition, Sachs confirms his interest in Mann's narrative technique.

Important reviews concerned with formal aspects of *Death in Venice* appeared not only in Austria and Germany, but also in England and France. In English, D. H. Lawrence discussed it in July 1913. Germany, he begins, is currently undergoing a "craving for form in fiction" (200). This craving is Mann's subject matter, he adds, and Mann therefore seems "the last sick sufferer from the complaint of Flaubert" (205). Lawrence likes the style of the novella, but he finds this subject matter stale and somewhat banal. In Tadzio, he contends, Aschenbach loves almost a symbol, like Hyacinth, a symbol of life, youth, and beauty. "This, I suppose," Lawrence writes, "is blowing the choking heat to pure flame, and raising it to the kingdom of beauty" (204). He admires such symbolic warmth when it turns up again in the Venetian hot weather: "It is wonderful, the heat, the unwholesomeness, the passion in Venice" (204). In the course of expressing such mixed feelings, Lawrence makes four mistakes. Two of them involve his translations from Mann's German. First, he writes that the old man on the boat mingles among "a crowd of young Poles" (203). In German, though, these passengers are *Polesaner*, residents of the Istrian city of Pola, which now lies in Croatia. Perhaps Lawrence had Tadzio, a Pole, too much in mind here. Second, he observes that the gondolier "will make no concession" (204). It is true, as Lawrence adds, that the gondolier does not follow Aschenbach's instructions to be taken to St. Mark's, but Mann writes that he *has* no concession — that is, no license — a fact indicating that he is not just another Venetian boatman. Lawrence's third mistake is minor: he calls Tadzio "Tadzin" (204). His fourth, though, is significant. He assigns both Mann and Aschenbach the age of fifty-three. Born on 6 June 1875, however, Mann had actually just turned thirty-eight when Lawrence's review appeared. This last mistake may have colored Lawrence's conclusion that "Thomas Mann is old — and we are young. Germany does not feel very young to me" (206). In sum, Lawrence found Mann's novella morbid but well done.

In 1914, a year after Lawrence thus reacted to *Death in Venice* in English, Félix Bertaux reviewed it in French. He, too, stressed its style, and he did so in the same way as Bruno Frank. For Bertaux, the novella is "ciselé comme une coupe où mille arabesques s'enlacent et se dénouent sans jamais aboutir" (engraved like a goblet on which a thousand arabesques enlace and untie themselves without ever abutting) (338). Mann is at once a refined psychologist and a rare stylist, Bertaux says, an author who lingers over details and weighs his choice of adjectives in ways as fastidious as those of Flaubert. Like Aschenbach, according to Bertaux, Mann is also torn between expansive passion and retentive thought. Mann's hero is a writer seized with nameless nostalgia and romantic yearning, and Mann's style is an effort to overcome the romanticism of his own inspiration. By an incomprehensible doubling and an imperceptible deformation of proportions, Bertaux adds, he combines the real and the imaginary to create a fantastic and hallucinatory realism like that of E. T. A. Hoffmann. Bertaux also recalls that Mann is said to have a touch of creole blood, adding that, for whatever reason, something strange lends the work of this German a singularly hot flame, an uncommon passion for sensual and plastic beauty.

## Art and the Artist

A third issue that emerged in many reviews of *Death in Venice* is that of art and the artist. As already noted, this issue was raised in the disputes, in the discussions of homoeroticism, and in the many comments on literary style that the novella also occasioned. Broch and Dallago disagreed about whether Mann and Aschenbach were philistine, and Isemann found Mann's concept of art immoral and Aschenbach's character weak. Joelsohn thought that all artists' mode of knowledge is sensual, and whereas Brüll wrote that artists are not typical enough to be interesting, Frank regarded Aschenbach's story as being that of the individual generally. Other reviewers mentioned these topics and further, related ones, often referring to Mann's second, biographical chapter. Most considered Mann to be more or less like Aschenbach. The ways in which they distinguished between the two, though, between the actual author and the fictional one, reveal striking differences in their opinions. Some of these other reviewers subscribed to the same aestheticism that Aschenbach embraces, while others noted that Mann himself is ambivalent. Some criticized both, and a few even displayed animosity toward Aschenbach. The issue of art and the artist thus has several aspects.

Some critics shared Aschenbach's aestheticism, attributing it to Mann as well. In April 1913, Karl Georg Wendriner observed that Mann's second chapter is supposed to contrast the wildness of an artist's experience with the pure clarity of the resulting artwork. Wendriner thinks this opposition characteristic of Mann himself, whom he deems the purest living German novelist, one whose ways of expressing what he describes make him an admirably exact realist. The following month, Johannes Eckardt explained in far broader terms the idea of the artist implied by that second chapter. Eckardt disliked the naturalism prevalent in literature since the late nineteenth century. Aschenbach's slow and concentrated way of writing, he argues, is "die schärfste Verurteilung der unfruchtbaren Kaninchenfruchtbarkeit des modernen Literatur-Journalismus" (the sharpest condemnation of the unfruitful rabbit-fertility of modern literary-journalism) (265). Aschenbach's development as an artist, Eckardt adds, shows the strengthening of contemporary art, the overcoming of a naturalism described in *Death in Venice* as "unanständigen Psychologismus" (indecent psychologism). This fictional author represents the poetic type, in fact, that has defeated naturalistic inconsolability. According to Eckardt, Aschenbach's own protagonists are typical of the present. They represent the weakening of human character in confrontation with the objective strength of the material world. Furthermore, few present-day artists understand the metaphysical links between art and intellect as well as Mann, who heralds a new age that will overcome materialism and go beyond self-satisfied art, into divine dimensions. Less speculatively, Eckardt also admires how Mann lends external events psychological intensity and thereby elevates the individual to the typical, so that Aschenbach's story is not only the tragedy of an individual but also that of a present-day artist. Eckardt thinks Aschenbach typical of artists of the future, too, even though he calls Aschenbach's tragedy one of age that aspires to greatness but that is increasingly enfeebled. Finally, Eckardt praises Mann's symbolic physiognomies and his monumental style, especially "den Marmor der Sprache, den der Dichter mit feinster Sorgfalt meißelte" (the marble of language that the poet chiseled with the greatest care) (272). Eckardt does not distinguish Mann from Aschenbach, directly attributing the latter's habits of mind to the former, nor does he grasp that Aschenbach's artistic credo hastens his psychological collapse.

Other critics sensed Mann's ambivalence toward his hero as well as toward art itself. Eduard Korrodi, for one, regarded Aschenbach as a composite photograph of Mann's literary contemporaries. Much as Eckardt did, Korrodi considers him "Der Dichter *unserer* Tage!" (The poet of *our* times! (690).

Korrodi thinks that Mann's "type" probably determined Aschenbach's psychology, but he is careful not to identify the two authors too closely. Unlike some other critics, he notes that *Death in Venice* does not declare Mann's own artistic bankruptcy. Instead, it presents the forced talent of a miniature Flaubert, thereby passing general judgment on the narrative literature of Mann's day. Mann exactly describes artistic intoxication, Korrodi argues, and he distances himself from Aschenbach in the end. In contrast to Eckardt, then, Korrodi does not find Aschenbach a tragic hero. He likes Mann's unobtrusive symbolism, moreover, and he comments that one does an injustice to Aschenbach's feelings for Tadzio, the embodiment of beauty, by thinking of the German law against homosexuality. Mann describes these feelings, he writes, "auf einigen Seiten der zartesten und luxuriösesten, aber zugleich geschmackvollsten deutschen Prosa" (on a few pages of the most tender and luxurious, but also most tasteful, German prose) (692). The result is nothing less than a novelistic miracle. Indeed, Korrodi adds that Mann's novella as a whole is a product of the most refined German narrative art.

In one of the first monographs ever written on Mann, Wilhelm Alberts similarly argued that Mann's novella betrays ambivalence toward the artist's profession in general. Alberts had read *Death in Venice* in *Die neue Rundschau,* and his remarks on it are cursory. Like Pache in 1914, he considers the novella proof that Mann is becoming less satirical and is aspiring to beauty in his art. Alberts also calls Aschenbach Mann's new likeness, and he attributes to Mann the same affirmation of life and heightened sense of beauty that Aschenbach has embraced by turning his back on knowledge. Indeed, what is new about this novella, according to Alberts, is the strong and striking influence of Greek concepts of life and art. Its subject matter and its style, he explains, bear witness to Mann's belief in beauty and to his desire for classical perfection, nowhere more so than in the passage that describes Aschenbach's attraction to Tadzio. This attraction is problematic, though, Alberts adds, and its consequences show that Mann is still skeptical of his own profession, that he still thinks something deeply ambivalent, disreputable, and dubious is inherent in the nature of the artist. As Alberts says, "Der Künstler ist ein Abenteurer nicht der Tat, sondern der Gedanken, des Gefühls, hier neigt er unwiderstehlich zu den bedenklichsten Ausschreitungen" (The artist is an adventurer not in deed but in thought, in feeling, [and] here he irresistibly inclines to the most questionable excesses) (175). Although Mann embraces a new belief in practice, then, in theory he remains skeptical of the value of art and artists. Mann himself thus seems torn between the extremes of the "Apollinian" and the "Dionysian," terms Alberts borrows from Nietzsche's *Die Geburt der Tragödie* (The Birth of Tragedy, 1872) and applies to Aschenbach and his intoxication.

A third group of reviews primarily concerned with the issue of art and artists faulted Aschenbach, and sometimes Mann, for being the wrong kind of artist and for writing in the wrong way. On 15 August 1914, for example, Richard Müller-Freienfels had serious reservations about *Death in Venice* when he explained the general relationship between genius and diligence. Mann typifies the latter, he contends, that is, the emphasis placed on form, style, and technique ever since Flaubert. The effort that writing takes is not a measure of its value, though, and writers should not always tell us how careful and conscientious they have been. Because Mann does so in *Death in Venice,* he adds, it is inferior to his *Buddenbrooks.* According to Müller-Freienfels, Mann himself is the hero of his novella, and his description of Aschenbach's writing habits applies to his own. Mann sketches an ideal of the artist, moreover, that will — indeed, that already has — spread erroneous concepts. Mann may not think that Aschenbach's attention to stylistic detail is the criterion of poetic genius, but many youthful readers, Müller-Freienfels writes, have understood *Death in Venice* in this way. Like Korrodi, Müller-Freienfels thus thinks Mann's concept of the artist is typical of his day, inferring criticism of current literary trends. He links Aschenbach and Mann more closely, however, leveling that criticism at Mann himself as well.

Similar remarks on Mann's idea of art and artists were made by the cultural critic Theodor Haecker in 1914. Haecker cites *Death in Venice* as an unfortunate example of the mistaken notion that aesthetic inspiration, the effort of genius, does not differ from work done in the sweat of one's face. In an article on Dostoyevksy, he comments that the novella would have been more glorious without words, implying that it never should have been written. In another article, on Kierkegaard, he was more direct. Calling *Death in Venice* a naïve confession, he says that there is nothing interesting about an author in his forties diligently and accurately setting down what he was too much of a genius to learn in high school. Haecker seems to be referring to Mann's style. He also takes aim at German critics who praised the novella. As psychologists and aestheticians, such critics shared Mann's pain, he rails, the pain that one suffers when one passes wind. They also fell for his misguided descriptions of love. "Und alle ließen es zu," Haecker writes "daß ihnen Gewalt und Geheimnis des Eros erklärt und enträtselt werde von einem, der vom schöpferischen Leben redet, wie ein schweißtriefender Taglöhner vom Backsteintragen" (And all allowed the power and mystery of eros to be explained to them and deciphered by one who talks about the creative life like a sweat-dripping day laborer talks about carrying bricks) (670). What is more, Haecker suggests that the unerotic Aschenbach knows nothing about heterosexual love and was received favorably by critics who are Jewish. Haecker seems to try to discredit the novella by appealing to anti-Semitism. In any case, he dislikes it because he is dissatisfied with what he takes to be Mann's priestly aestheticism.

In June 1913, Carl Busse similarly found Aschenbach's faults to be those of his author. Mann's subject — salvation from an artistic or otherwise shadowy existence — is the only one he seems able to treat, Busse writes, and he does so in a dubious way: "Offenbar waltet doch auch hier ein frommer Selbstbetrug, der eine natürliche Schwäche erhaben auffärbt und zur Stärke macht" (And here, too, there obviously obtains a pious self-deception that applies sublime colors to a natural weakness and turns it into a strength) (310). Busse adds that authors like Mann, Aschenbach, and Flaubert do not sacrifice their lives, as they maintain, on the altar of art. Instead, they pursue art with such exclusive passion because they are too weak, inhibited, and timid to handle real life. In art they find a poor substitute for such life, and by making them into martyrs, Mann has simply made a virtue of his own necessity. Busse has great respect for Mann, but he finds Mann's sense of himself exaggerated. He also doubts that anyone will think Aschenbach, Mann's alter ego and an author of prose, the greatest poet of his age. Even without cholera, Busse says, Aschenbach's death would have been the outward expression of his complete internal collapse. The theme of homosexual love will be embarrassing, he adds, but Mann treats this theme with exemplary tenderness. It involves no incorrect behavior, nothing more than excessively erotic feelings. Besides, in Aschenbach's case, according to Busse, nature simply seems to be taking necessary revenge. Mann's art has also freed this theme as far as is possible "von dem peinlichen Erdenrest, der ihm anhaftet" (from the embarrassing mundane remnant that is attached to it) (311). Busse thinks that too many pages precede the appearance of Tadzio, but that one feels fear and pity for Aschenbach, and that some of Mann's later pages belong to the best German prose of the present day. Having read the novella in Venice, he also finds that it could have no better possible setting.

To Joachim Benn, however, Mann's style did not even partially compensate for his artistic subject. Benn panned *Death in Venice* in a long-winded, pedantic review. He thinks that the ideal reader is skeptical of stories about artists. Such stories are often too personal, he explains, and an artist's fate can easily be too far removed from that of most other human beings. Aschenbach's artistic frailty is not an improper subject, Benn adds, but he is not described objectively enough. He seems not so much a poet — a person who turns the superabundance of life into fictions in the way a tree shoots forth leaves — as he does "ein Kunstmaniakale" (an art-maniac) (308) whose desire for fame and whose destructive exertions bring him to the brink of madness. Benn argues that Balzac could have turned this story into something unforgettable, but that Mann wants to convince his readers of Aschenbach's greatness, and that he thereby puts himself on a plane where they cannot follow him and where he loses touch with them. As the novella progresses, Aschenbach seems more and more like a ghost. He is powerless and pretentious, and his only credible passion is his hunger for fame. As Benn sums up this psychological critique, "Es ist der Versuch gemacht, Größe zu schildern, aber er ist mißlungen" (The attempt has been made to portray greatness, but it has failed) (309). Benn subjects the novella to a formal critique as well. Its events all take place in Aschenbach's mind, he observes, whence it has a strongly monologic character. This is a fault and is apparent in its formless development of the internal action. Mann's many symbolic episodes further obscure the structure of his story and confirm the impression it makes, "den eines einzigen wahnsinnigen Gallimathias über der wüstenhaften Leere der Grundhandlung" (that of one long, crazed jeremiad on the desert-like void of the fundamental plot) (309). Mann's ignorance of the formal laws of art, in fact, results not in a clear plot and a tragic catastrophe but in a maudlin mood-painting. He cannot maintain his striving for classicality either, Benn adds, imitating Goethe but lacking any spontaneous sensuality of diction. His sentences contain too many awkward abstractions and peripheral details; his syntax sounds bombastic, exaggerated, tiring, and even depressing; and like his other unpoetic comparisons of artists and bourgeoises, *Death in Venice* is too narrowly subjective. By opposing ambition to ability, the novella is also a genuine but an unintended tragedy. Benn means that Mann himself has failed as an artist.

A fourth group of reviews concerned with the themes of art and the artist was downright hostile to Aschenbach and at times even to Mann. In May 1913, for example, a reviewer who signed his name as "Götz" (Jonas, in his bibliography of 1972, identifies this reviewer as Bruno Goetz) discussed the novella in a review that largely consists of cryptically aggressive pronouncements. Aschenbach, Götz says, is a self-centered, soulless, and isolated intellect that succumbs to the revenge of its subjugated feelings. Aschenbach, "dieser geschminkte Lüstling" (this lecher in make-up) (560), helps bring on the fevers of Venice with his antisocial amorality. He is also misled by beauty into a void. The fact that nothingness is a form of perfection, a possibility raised by Mann, and that beauty is spiritual, an idea he reveals to be fatal, prompt Götz to observe in oracular fashion: "Das Kunstwerk als Abenteuer: Unsicherheit als Prinzip ist Ausschweifung im Narrendienste leerer Form" (The work of art as adventure: Uncertainty as a principle is excess in the fool's service of empty form) (560). Apparently agreeing here with what he thinks Mann intended, Götz finds Aschenbach deeply maladjusted. He thus differs markedly from all the reviewers who uncritically shared Aschenbach's aestheticism.

One further reviewer criticized Mann's concept of the artist for nationalistic racial reasons. In 1914, Richard Zimmermann described the novella as the self-portrait of an artist and the confessions of an author, dismissing the events of its plot while equating Mann with Aschenbach and denying that irony comes between them. He admires Mann's psychological insights and his crystalline sentences, but he finds his self-concern too solemn and regrets the pale signs of incest always present when a work of art describes an artist's soul. Noting that Aschenbach's mother was foreign, Zimmermann adds that though the German language may be the stuff of Aschenbach's art,

Aschenbach has no roots, as an artist, in the German essence. As Zimmermann puts it: "Gesunde Kraft, Gefühl, Lebensblut, das einem Dichter eben nur aus stammhafter Zugehörigkeit und aus natürlicher Liebe zu seinem Volke zuteil wird, fließt nicht in ihm" (Healthy strength, feeling, [and] life's blood, which is granted a poet only by belonging to a particular race and by natural love for his people, does not flow in him) (357).

Another reviewer disliked Aschenbach so much that he declared war on people like him. In December 1913, that reviewer, Friedrich Stieve, addressed an open letter to Mann's protagonist. Like several other critics cited here, Stieve finds Aschenbach anemic and argues that no real poet needs to pull himself together as strictly as he does. Stieve claims to have no homoerotic tastes and thus to be incapable of feeling offended by Aschenbach's love for Tadzio, but this love strikes him as being purely sensual lust. In this low opinion of it, he thinks he has Mann on his side. Stieve also addresses Aschenbach, saying, "Ihr Dichter stellt Sie ja selbst als höchst verdächtig dar. Und dafür sterben Sie auch noch!" (Your poet himself presents you as highly dubious. And then you die for it, too!) (775). According to Stieve, Aschenbach's primary trait is his ostentatious hollowness, which Mann mercilessly criticizes. No one else, he adds, seems to have noticed that Mann pillories Aschenbach and that Mann does so as a warning to others. Aschenbach's character, Stieve maintains, is both perplexingly contemporary and typical of certain intellectual developments, a symptom of the illness of our generation. Is Germany today not full of this misguided, puffed-up bourgeois type? Stieve thinks so, and he calls upon a new generation of Germans to defeat it: "Krieg, unerbittlicher Krieg gegen den Geist all derer von Aschenbach!" (War, implacable war against the spirit of all those like Aschenbach!) (776).

## Other Approaches

A final group of initial reactions to *Death in Venice* consists of reviews that were written neither as part of a particular dispute, nor with any primary emphasis on the issues of homoeroticism, style and structure, or art and artists. These reviews take either a more comprehensive view of the novella or a narrower one meant to make some special critical point. In May 1913, for example, Josef Hofmiller applied psychological, biographical, erotic, aesthetic, structural, and stylistic criteria in a review that has stood the test of time, having been reprinted in 1955 as well as subsequently. Friedrich Freksa likewise approved of Mann's story on multiple grounds. Other reviewers took less synthetic approaches, interpreting the novella according to their own notions of aging, dying, and the tragically pathological.

Hofmiller incisively traces the origin of *Death in Venice* to an internal experience and an external encounter. These two sources, Hofmiller writes, are successfully related through Mann's art. The experience, he says, which

Aschenbach has, is an abrupt freeing of otherwise strictly harnessed drives and a sudden ambush of reason by the long-crimped sphere of imagination. This experience at least borders on what is commonly called pathological. The encounter, Hofmiller rightly ventures, occurred when Mann, on a trip to Italy, may have noticed a Slavic family, in particular a Polish boy. In any case, the object of Aschenbach's attention could not be a woman, he explains, since any hint of sexual sensuality would have made his hesitation at death's door too sentimental. "Es mußte sein wie eine letzte Liebeserklärung an das schöne Leben selbst," Hofmiller writes, "das in der Gestalt eines schönen, fremdländischen Knaben verkörpert schien" (It had to be like a last declaration of love for beautiful life itself, life that appeared embodied in the form of a beautiful foreign boy) (223). Hofmiller guesses, again correctly, that Mann may also have had the aging Goethe in mind. Aschenbach is no Goethe, however, so his attraction to Tadzio has to have "etwas zart Symbolisches . . . völlig anders, gänzlich unvulgär. In diesem Alter liebt man . . . symbolisch; man liebt das Gefühl, nicht den Gegenstand des Gefühls; man liebt die Liebe" (something tenderly symbolic . . . completely different, wholly unvulgar. At this age one loves . . . symbolically; one loves the emotion, not the object of the emotion; one loves love) (223). Accordingly, what Aschenbach sees at the beach is the vision of an artist who has served beauty all his life and to whom the corporeal is merely a symbol of the cognitive. This artist sees intellectual beauty standing before him, such beauty having now assumed physical form. Hofmiller does not have this symbolic vision himself. In fact, he thinks that Tadzio is something of a *bel idiot* and that *l'art pour l'art* has hardly ever been taken to its absurd conclusion so cogently. He thus suggests that Mann is not identical to Aschenbach. Mann alludes to some of his own writings when he recalls Aschenbach's accomplishments, but Hofmiller finds this similarity embarrassing and unnecessary. Mann, he says, is not Aschenbach; if he were, he never would have invented him. Mann immerses himself in the imaginary world of Greek antiquity that Aschenbach enters, but he does not forget that his hero's experience borders on the diseased, and he does not want us to forget it either.

In addition to interpreting the erotic and aesthetic issues raised in *Death in Venice,* Hofmiller comments on its narrative structure and style. By having Aschenbach die in the place where he desires to go, Hofmiller maintains, Mann lends the scene at the cemetery in Munich the character of a dance of death painted by Hans Holbein the Younger. In the English review discussed above, D. H. Lawrence, too, invoked this image and this artist to characterize the symbolic events that ensue from Mann's opening scene. For Hofmiller, this scene is also the first of many in which the uncanny symbolism of Aschenbach's journey emerges from Mann's everyday details. By putting Mann's descriptions of the wanderer in Munich and the sinister gondolier in Venice into adjacent columns, Hofmiller makes the similarities of these two men apparent. He also juxtaposes Mann's descriptions of the wanderer and the street singer who performs at Aschenbach's hotel, and of Aschenbach and the old man on the boat. Thanks to Mann's artistry, he adds, one notices this series of fictional characters and their symbolic resemblance only upon repeated close reading. Hofmiller also notes in passing that psychoanalysts could make much of Aschenbach's orgiastic dream. His own interest lies in its language. Having noted how charming it is to read *Death in Venice* with an ear to its diction, he explains the rhythm that Mann's prose has when it describes that dream. Prose turns into poetry when Mann writes in hexameters, he says, a Greek meter that seems obvious when Hofmiller divides that dream of Dionysian revelry into individual lines of varying length. He also excuses paying such close attention to formal details, holding *Death in Venice* in high professional regard: "Eine so schön gefügte, so schön geschriebene Prosadichtung kommt dem Kritiker nicht oft unter; das ist fürwahr ein Fest, und bei Festen verweilt man gern etwas länger" (A critic seldom meets with such a beautifully constructed, beautifully written work of prose; that is truly a feast, and at feasts one gladly lingers a little longer) (229). Despite such praise, Hofmiller concludes that Mann's antithesis of the artist and the bourgeois is a vestige of romanticism and that it is resolved less severely in *Tonio Kröger*.

Like Hofmiller, Friedrich Freksa judged *Death in Venice* according to several different criteria. Those criteria are biographical, formal, syntactical, and psychological. Mann's story conveys "die Melodie des eigenen Leides" (the melody of his own sorrow) (773), for example, and with this work Mann has achieved a formal perfection not found in a German novella after 1850. His sentences flow so well, Freksa adds, and his words are so rhythmic that those sentences seem to be constructed from smoothly polished and powerful stones. His psychological and descriptive passages, moreover, end in observations that are universally valid. Freksa also contends that *Death in Venice* lacks Mann's usual recurring motifs and his epic adjectives, but he finds it rich in irony and internal correspondences. It truthfully presents sexual drives and its hero's dissipation, but it does so purely and chastely. Mann's last chapter is not as successful as the others, according to Freksa, but his last scene is magnificent. The novella, then, removes all doubts about Mann's literary talent, doubts that had been raised after the appearance of his less biographical novel *Königliche Hoheit* (Royal Highness, 1909). Here, Mann's work is more closely connected to his personal life, a fact that Freksa conveys in a musical image:

> Müdigkeit und Einsamkeit beherrschen das Buch. Sie erklingen gleich Doppelgriffen auf einer alten Geige, die in der Dämmerstunde von einem Geiger gespielt wird, der sich in Tönen frei machen muß von all dem, was ihm das Herz bedrückt und die Seele beschwert.

[Fatigue and solitude rule the book. They sound like double stops on an old violin that is played in the twilight hour by an old violinist who must free himself in sound from all that oppresses his heart and burdens his soul.] (773)

Freksa concludes that *Death in Venice* is the most beautiful proof to date of Mann's artistry, a book that shows him to be not only a writer but also a poet. Freksa also wrongly thinks that Aschenbach travels to Venice in his fortieth year and that he meets the fop on a boat that takes him there from Trieste.

Other reviewers were less comprehensive. Some put Mann's theme of aging into historical perspective or thought *Death in Venice* more about dying than about death. In a retrospective study of cultural developments during the year 1913, Richard M. Meyer mentioned the issue of aging while praising the rhythm of Mann's sentences and of his story as a whole. The latter rhythm is marked by allusions to Greek myths, he explains, and Aschenbach's unnatural passion is symbolic of his vain attempt to be young again. This passion is also, Meyer contends, a tragic parody of the one sung in Hölderlin's poem "Socrates and Alcibiades." The tragedy of seeking youth is an ancient literary motif, moreover, and Aschenbach's almost pathological fear of aging means that Mann's story has to do with the central literary art: the art of living, of experiencing life. In part, Meyer writes, this art is a matter of how an artist relates to real life, a matter of psychic hygiene and intellectual diet. It also involves the question of how far a poet is allowed to exploit his experience, to make artistic use of real-life models, above all of himself. Mann addresses this question, he thinks, by most artfully combining in Aschenbach truth and poetry, models and imagination. Meyer therefore regards *Death in Venice* as a masterpiece. By contrast, Ernst Heilborn argued that Mann's novella is not about aging or death, but about dying. Heilborn dwells on "das orgiastische Gemütserlebnis des Sterbens" (the orgiastic emotional experience of dying) (1040), claiming that death catches up with Aschenbach only because the sounds of the orgy of dying in Venice have faded away. Aschenbach succumbs to such an orgiastic experience of dying, Heilborn writes, and Mann's failure to delineate him more clearly has the advantage that such dying seems more typical and terrifying, being independent of the person who dies. Heilborn admires how masterfully Mann employs realistic details to suggest Aschenbach's fantastic and painful passing. He thinks so highly of Mann's art, in fact, that he considers *Death in Venice* astounding.

Narrow appreciation was likewise apparent in a review by Willy Hellpach. On 22 October 1913, Hellpach insisted that, in his response to Isemann, Mann misunderstood his own creation. Hellpach had done a study of the pathological and the tragic in modern art, and Mann wrote to him in November 1912, acknowledging that *Death in Venice,* seen from Hellpach's point of view, is indeed a tragic treatment of purely pathological matters. Hellpach quotes from Mann's letter but seems unaware of the irony implied by Mann's emphasis on how the novella must look from Hellpach's own perspective. In any case, Hellpach takes it to be pathological and tragic. Mann describes cholera, he writes, with the talent for writing about illnesses that distinguishes him from all other living writers. Aschenbach's demise is not an elaboration of pederasty, moreover, nor is it caused by his passion. Instead, that passion is a symptom of a deeper crisis. He declines *in* a passionate state, but not *because* of it. Passion does not fell him; instead, the fact that it comes over him is a sign that he is falling. It is not surprising, in Hellpach's view, that Mann thus brings his psychological art to bear on the pathological, abnormal, and perverse. According to Hellpach, Mann succeeds in conveying how rotten and repulsive that passion is in reality, when no longer surrounded by an imaginary aura. Indeed, Mann's novella shows the tragic fate of the poet, the artist, and the beautiful soul, the tragedy of all who live only in the imagination and who cannot survive real life. This interpretation is not the last one given by a critic convinced that Mann's story illustrates his or her own pet theory.

## Conclusion

Initial reactions to *Death in Venice* varied greatly, both in their assessments of Mann's accomplishment and in their levels of literary insight. The critical disputes sparked by the novella and the major issues discussed by its reviewers were often characterized by controversy and extremes. To its admirers, it seemed a literary and linguistic miracle; its hero was a tragic case; and its author was a giant German intellect. To its detractors, it seemed badly written and poorly organized; its hero was anemic, cold, and perverse; and its author preached immorality. Reviewers with mixed feelings liked its style but not its subject, or its subject but not its style, or some, but not all, elements of each. If one keeps score, so to speak, one notices that roughly sixty percent of the early reviews were favorable on the whole, that about twenty percent were mainly negative, and that a further twenty percent were ambivalent. One could also divide the reviews according to their German-speaking country of origin. Only a couple appeared in Switzerland, but no fewer than a quarter were published in Austria, and if one includes those from Budapest, the fraction attributable to Austria-Hungary rises to a third. Is it just a coincidence that Mann's story of decadence and decline elicited this many comments from the Habsburgs' Dual Monarchy only a few years before that empire fell in the First World War? In any event, these early reviews show that the reception of *Death in Venice* was not always smooth. In the beginning, the novella met with much approval, but not all of its first readers liked it. For all its immediate success, it was not an instant classic.

# 2: Increasing Acceptance, 1915–55

## Introduction

*D* EATH IN VENICE took on many new and different meanings in the changing historical and intellectual circumstances of the forty years between 1915 and Mann's death in 1955. Most comments on the novella during these decades, however, developed approaches taken and issues raised in the initial reactions of 1913 and 1914. Heinrich Mann's review had been the only expressly political interpretation among those initial reactions, but such interpretations became more frequent during and after the First and Second World Wars. They included remarks on German society and on Western culture in general. Psychoanalytic readings also became more common. These readings were inspired not only by Freud but also by Alfred Adler, and they routinely address the issue of homosexuality, as do a few other studies. Further readings focused on Mann's attitude toward artists and aestheticism. They often did so in books or articles that, like Alberts's monograph of 1913, discuss this topic in the context of Mann's life and work as a whole. As in 1913–14, however, the issue raised most often was that of literary form — of Mann's narrative structure, symbolism, and style. *Death in Venice* also began to be mentioned in histories of the novella and of German literature, a sign of its acceptance into a national literary canon. Further studies shed light on its theme of death or its setting of Venice. The first English translation of *Death in Venice*, done by Kenneth Burke in 1924, prompted new reviews, as did both Félix Bertaux's rendition of the novella into French in that same year and H. T. Lowe-Porter's English translation in 1928. Burke as well as Bertaux, not to mention other critics and scholars writing in French or about French literature, also compared the novella to the works of André Gide. Other scholars cited Mann's allusions to Xenophon, Plato, and Homer, or the similarities between his novella and texts by Goethe, Schiller, Nietzsche, and Kafka. In addition to these several approaches, issues, and comparisons, there are Mann's own published or otherwise public comments on his story. Those comments mention many of the issues addressed in its reception; they therefore serve as a conclusion to this chapter.

# Politics, Society, and Culture

During and after the First and Second World Wars, many political, social, and cultural aspects of *Death in Venice* largely neglected by its earliest critics became more important. Its story and its setting were regarded as harbingers of those two armed conflicts, and Aschenbach seemed to embody fatefully Prussian virtues and vices. Between 1915 and 1920, some critics found him typical of a society ripe for change or representative of the military spirit needed in time of war, the former because he was so effete, the latter because his ancestors had been Prussian civil servants or because he had once shown disciplined moral resolve. Others saw him as a herald of Germany's political future. Between 1944 and 1955, he seemed to display the rigid Prussian ethic that had typified the German bourgeoisie for decades. The most notable critic to make this argument was Georg Lukács. Other critics and scholars claimed that Mann's novella also describes the intellectual decline and fall of all Western culture.

Readings of *Death in Venice* that reflected the events of the First World War began with an article by Anton Kuh in the German-language *Pester Lloyd,* the same Hungarian newspaper that had carried Goth's favorable review in 1913. Kuh, writing from Vienna in January 1915, argues not only that Mann's book is probably the best recent German novella, but also that it may contain the clearest inkling of war felt in German literature before hostilities started. Kuh is sympathetic to the German and Austro-Hungarian cause, and though he is not impressed by the plot of Mann's story, he explains that cause in relation to Mann's protagonist. For Kuh, Aschenbach is "der Tiptop-Künstler 1913" (the tip-top artist of 1913) (2), an aesthetic bureaucrat who has sacrificed his life to literary art and whose world is too refined and too French. Mann describes Aschenbach's strict style and orderly soul as partaking of Prussian militarism, however, Kuh adds, and if the German call to arms had reached Aschenbach in Venice, he would have stood up, thrown his beach chair far out into the sea, and declared his intention to write a history of Frederick the Great. Kuh here seems to mock Aschenbach — and perhaps Mann himself, whose patriotic essay *Friedrich und die große Koalition* (Frederick and the Grand Coalition, 1915) was published in the same month as Kuh's article. In any case, Mann's long list of Aschenbach's works in the second chapter of *Death in Venice* includes a fictional biography of the famous Prussian monarch. Kuh is wrong when he writes that Aschenbach yearns for the north on his journey to the south and that he stays in Venice after Tadzio has left. Kuh's main point, though, is serious and arguable. In his view, Aschenbach's world lacks the contrast provided by chaos, and if the abyss of existence were revealed by war, Aschenbach would be in his element and in his proper place. Mann's story thus seems a product of its time. Perhaps, Kuh argues, it will one day seem, to a later age, to be the turning point of German art between peace and war. No other work so fully captures the feeling and spirit of 1913, and "kein anderes verliert sich wie dieses gleichzeitig in einen Dämmer der Ueber-reife, als ob es nur gerade auf den ersten Blitz und Donnerschlag wartete" (no other at the same time fades like this one into a twilight of overripeness, as if it were just waiting for the first lightning and thunderclap) (2). Kuh thus analyzes *Death in Venice* as the kind of art mentioned in the title of his article: "Die vorahnende Literatur" (Anticipatory Literature).

Further reflections on Aschenbach written during the First World War can be found near the end of Franz Leppmann's monograph on Mann, a book finished in September 1915. Not long after Mann, in the guise of Aschenbach, had proclaimed "Durchhalten" (Persevere) his own necessity, Leppmann argues, it became the battle cry of the entire German nation. Aschenbach proves worthy of his military forebears, moreover, and the parallel between art and war drawn in Mann's account of his protagonist's work habits is much like the equation of artists and soldiers in his *Gedanken im Kriege* (Thoughts in War, 1914), an essay published in November 1914. Furthermore, Leppmann thinks that the Frederick the Great described by Mann in *Friedrich und die große Koalition* is the brother of Mann's several soldierly heroes, including Aschenbach. Indeed, Leppmann seems preoccupied throughout his book with Mann's concepts of the hero and the heroic. He also has much else to say about *Death in Venice*. Like Frank in 1913, he finds Aschenbach similar to Nietzsche; like Bab, also in 1913, he hails the novella as masterly in every way. He does not distinguish Mann's artistic development from Aschenbach's, seeing clear autobiographical links between them. Since he discerns no narra-tive distance or irony in the novella, he also takes Mann's general statements about life and art at face value, unaware that they may sometimes simply be Aschenbach's means of assuaging a bad conscience. Leppmann is likewise inaccurate when he says that Aschenbach sees Tadzio swimming completely undressed, but he rightly notes that Aschenbach resembles many palaces in Venice in that he, too, presents an empty façade. It is also true, as Leppmann observes, that Mann lends Aschenbach physical features of Gustav Mahler and that India and Brazil both lie in the tropics (at least in part). Leppmann thinks that the latter fact suggests another autobiographical link, since the cholera afflicting Aschenbach's Venice comes from India and since Mann's mother came from Brazil. Leppmann also compares *Death in Venice* to Goethe's *Die Wahlverwandtschaften*. He thinks that Goethe's novel must have struck Mann as a narrative model. It, too, is a tale of psychological destruction, he explains, and Mann and Goethe pass the same moral judgment when each punishes his hero for succumbing to sensuality. Leppmann also sees Goethe's influence in Mann's syntax and diction. This comparison seems far removed from the First World War, but Leppmann concludes it by remarking that Mann has main-tained the moral resolve he allows Aschenbach to lose, a resolve that is the password of the present day.

In 1917, Robert Müller was both more forward-looking than Kuh and less literary than Leppmann. After welcoming the end of liberalism, Müller hails Aschenbach as the modern, conservative petty bourgeois. Sure and resolute, he writes, Aschenbach feels patriotic intoxication at the sight of the productive power of the state. Although a loner, Aschenbach is sensitive to the times and to his fellow Germans, a fact that blurs the boundaries of his person, and he directs his iron will to uphold tradition while he revives the values of his race. He also succumbs to a maelstrom of irrational drives, but Mann makes the heroism of the bourgeois type appealing and dignified in him. According to Müller, *Death in Venice* is the first literary work to present such a new man as a member of society. With its simple and clear account of the sensuality and the consciousness that distinguish modern life, it captures the heroic character of the age. Müller likes such collective virtues, saying, "Jeder Satz ist schwer von den Früchten einer Weisheit, die den Ernten eines ganzen Geschlechts entstammen" (Every sentence is heavy with the fruits of a wisdom that comes from the harvests of an entire race) (33). Müller's main concern, though, is moral leadership. He praises Aschenbach for providing it, for leading the German people and giving youth its ethical criteria again. These criteria are good, healthy, and reasonable, Müller adds, and for thus satisfying the needs of the moment, Mann's hero is a genius, albeit a victim, too. Aschenbach falls so that a new age may triumph, one that no longer regards artists as supreme human beings. While he thus falls in the battle of ethics against aesthetics, Müller continues, his work still stands. Mann has died as the Aschenbach we see at the end of his story, moreover, but lives as the Aschenbach we meet at its outset. For those with ears to hear, Mann's message is clear: human beings are and have to be undisciplined, but they can want nothing other than dignity, discipline, and decency. In sum, Müller thinks Aschenbach a tragic character representative of the coming, conservative revolution. Like Ehrenstein in 1913, he also changes Aschenbach's first name to "Georg."

Things looked different to Felix Braun in Austria after the war. In 1913, Braun had admired the composition of *Death in Venice*. By 1920, he had learned that Aschenbach must be understood as symptomatic, not only because the novella expresses "den sinkenden Charakter eines Zeitalters" (the sinking character of an era) (181), but also because its hero's literary effort is a symbol of all struggles for conservation, preservation, wholeness, and culture. During the war, Braun observes, the only alternative to such conservation was destruction or revolution. The choice of an artist like Aschenbach — and Mann — who preferred form above all, was not in doubt. The question now concerns the fate of the German nation itself. Should one hold fast at all costs? Should one destroy for the sake of a new beginning? Braun answers these questions by turning to Mann's more recent books, referring most often to his *Betrachtungen eines Unpolitischen* (Observations of an Unpolitical Man, 1918). Braun also notes that Germans have often held too fast and therefore have been too limited. He implies that Aschenbach's tragic conservatism no longer has any political future.

Georg Lukács made a related argument in five essays published between 1944 and 1955. In his "Preußentum in der deutschen Literatur" (Prussianism in German Literature, 1944), Lukács associates Aschenbach with Prussia and discusses how Mann reveals their common ethics of composure to be hollow and illusory. Better than Mann's patriotic essays, he argues, the novella shows the complexity of its author's attitude toward Prussia. In "Die deutsche Literatur im Zeitalter des Imperialismus" (German Literature in the Age of Imperialism, 1945), he explains that Mann's brief reverence for Frederick the Great is less important than the social criticism perceptible in *Death in Venice*. Lukács spells out that criticism in "Auf der Suche nach dem Bürger" (In Search of Bourgeois Man, 1945), where he says that *Tonio Kröger* and *Death in Venice* show composure, emotional control, and the profession of art to be the central issues of Mann's literary efforts. The secret of Aschenbach's success, his heroic composure, is Mann's own, Lukács writes, but the later novella is also mercilessly self-critical. A small conflict destroys Aschenbach's composure, he adds, a moral attitude closely connected to the best of bourgeois culture in Wilhelminian Germany. Leading sociologists among Mann's contemporaries tried to "Aschenbachize" — in German, the verb is "aschenbachisieren" (24) — this culture, that is, to lend it moral legitimacy, and Mann's own enthusiasm for Frederick the Great shows that this attitude leads to Prussianism. *Death in Venice,* however, criticizes the worthlessness and irreality of the ethics of composure. In both "Die Tragödie der modernen Kunst" (The Tragedy of Modern Art, 1949) and "Das Spielerische und seine Hintergründe" (The Playful Style, 1955), Lukács draws further parallels between *Death in Venice* and Mann's patriotic essays as well as his other fiction, noting how the novella treats the issue of art and artists in bourgeois society and how it anticipates moral tendencies that became apparent during the First World War. In his own five essays, Lukács thus interprets *Death in Venice* from a Marxist point of view that is tempered with a subtle literary sensibility.

Other critics writing after the Second World War combined criticism of the bourgeoisie with other historical aspects of *Death in Venice*. In 1946, Arnold Bauer called the novella a solitary peak of epic perfection and regarded the prospect that it afforded of the European intellectual landscape. This "Nekrolog auf das abendländische Weltgefühl" (necrology for the occidental sense of the world) (38), he writes, spans the era from Socrates to Nietzsche. Aschenbach abandons his life filled with bourgeois ideals of order, his new life in Venice seems to be a dream, and his romantic consciousness ultimately suspends all bourgeois logic and morality. Bauer also observes that Aschenbach, the learned poet of the early twentieth century, flees to the dreamland of ancient mythology, where Platonic eros overcomes the inner resistance of a proscription that originated in moralizing centuries. In his *Lebensabriß* (Life-Sketch, 1930), Bauer remarks, Mann noted that this story had met with approval, a fact that Bauer relates to historical circumstances. Its unexpectedly deep and surprisingly broad effect on the German reading public, he explains, cannot be separated from the larger intellectual and social situation on the eve of the First World War. Aesthetic neoromanticism and the German youth movement made such a favorable reception of Mann's questionable theme possible, Bauer adds, and *Death in Venice* seemed to ally its author with the intellectual agendas of Nietzsche and the poet Stefan George (1868–1933). It may have been a misunderstanding, though, he concludes, to think that Mann was as subversive as Nietzsche.

While Bauer thought *Death in Venice* saturated with a romantic sense of life, Wolfgang Grothe maintained in 1947 that Mann fought the romantic hegemony of the German spirit. The novella was well received before the First World War, Grothe adds, but readers then could hardly realize that it touches on the general occidental problem, that is, on the hopeless alienation of life and action from observation and thought. It tells us, he explains, that beauty is the sole means by which the isolated intellect can join itself to the flow of existence. Using this means, however, costs the artist his physical and intellectual life. Furthermore, what was a pessimistic prophecy before the First World War is an interpretation of the situation after the Second World War. Mann's novella anticipates the general state of the West, Grothe writes, which, like Aschenbach, was headed straight for the abyss. Its intellect, like his, was isolated and soon reduced to a ruin. And the European continent is now covered with ruins, Grothe laments, with apocalyptic monuments and accusing symbols of wrecked and tragically alienated concepts of culture and society. Grothe concludes on this same note of despair:

> Der Tod in *Venedig* — unversehens ward er zu einem Tod in *Europa,* einem tausendfachen, einem göttlich-natürlichen Ausgleich *nationalistischer* Trunkenheit und Unbrüderlichkeit zu der die *ästhetische* des Herrn von Achenbach [*sic*] sintflutartig anzuschwellen vermochte!

> [Death in *Venice* — it unexpectedly became a death in *Europe,* a thousandfold, divine-natural compensation for *nationalistic* drunkenness and unbrotherliness into which Herr von Achenbach's *aesthetic* kind was able to swell like the Flood!] (758)

As in other cases, such sweeping conclusions come at the expense of accuracy: while some critics get the first name of Mann's hero wrong, Grothe here misspells his last one as "Achenbach."

Aschenbach again stands for all Western civilization in an essay from 1947 by M. L. Rosenthal. Of all Mann's writings, Rosenthal begins, *Death in Venice* best states his general theme, "the inevitable corruption of Western morality and intelligence, leading to a sickness of inaction" (49). This theme is evident, Rosenthal adds, in Mann's opposition of will based on discipline to fatality based on desire. Aschenbach changes as the former yields to the latter, succumbing to corruption of the European soul by the exoticism and decadence of the East and the South. Rosenthal finds this change to be both general and particular, a matter of both Mann's argument and his plot, of form as well as content, so that his pessimism is at once philosophical and aesthetic. He discusses the nature of the artist, for example, on the general level of Plato's *Phaedrus* as well as on the particular, sociological level peculiar to the mind of the European intellectual. The meaning of Mann's resulting near-allegory, Rosenthal argues, is that the sensual and intellectual species of beauty become identical only when the mind degrades itself and descends to the low level of meaningless experience. It is not true that Mann is clearly Platonic, as Rosenthal assumes. Like many other critics, Rosenthal apparently fails to understand that Mann's having quotations from Plato occur to his suffering hero does not necessarily mean that he believed in their import himself. Still, Rosenthal's essay helps show how partisan political readings of *Death in Venice* became broader cultural criticisms.

## Psychoanalysis and Homoeroticism

Political and cultural approaches to *Death in Venice* were not the only ones taken by critics and scholars who discussed it from 1915 to 1955. Like Sachs in 1914, some of those critics and scholars used psychoanalysis to interpret the novella. They often, if not always, addressed the issue of homoeroticism. One of them claimed that the novella attests to both Aschenbach's and Mann's repressed homosexual urges. Another described Aschenbach's artistic career and his attraction to Tadzio as attempts to overcome feelings of weakness. Psychoanalytical comments on other authors and topics noted Aschenbach's wanderlust, his psychic disintegration, and how he unconsciously prepares to commit suicide. Further studies, too, raised the issue of homoeroticism, yet they did not take a psychoanalytic approach to it. One of those studies noted how Mann portrays a homosexual passion in a story that is a work of art, while another argued that homosexual love belongs on the naturalistic level of that story, not on its broader symbolic one.

One psychoanalytic reading was given by Eduard Hitschmann in 1915. According to him, Mann's novella is one of the rare works of fiction that openly treat the issue of same-sex love, and it does so with all the signs of an imagination that comes from the unconscious. Hitschmann argues that Aschenbach is resigned, distinguished, and has a certain morbid decadence about him. His homosexual feelings on the Lido strike him as an impermissible emotional excess, but they hark back to some of his infantile experiences. The fear instilled in him by the series of symbolic male figures, moreover, starting with the wanderer in Munich, marks those figures as objects of his as yet repressed libido. His subsequent love for Tadzio is sadistic insofar as Aschenbach is pleased that the Polish boy is sickly and unlikely to grow old, Hitschmann adds, and Tadzio's defeat when he wrestles with his friend Jaschu clearly appears to come from youthful reminiscences. Hitschmann does not state whether the imagination and the reminiscences he discusses belong to Aschenbach, to Mann, or to both. His conclusion is similarly ambiguous at first, though it later attributes bisexuality directly to Mann. The novella is a genuine product of the unconscious, he writes, as if it were composed of a series of daydreams had by a man who is still only unconsciously homosexual. As in a normal man's dream, this inverted feeling manifests itself as fear before regressing to the infantile and then seeking satisfaction. Mann neither shows nor knows what he wants; a psychoanalyst does:

> Der Autor der Novelle mag weder durch seine Lebensführung, noch sich selbst fragend, seine Bisexualität fürs erste verraten. Dem Psychoanalytiker verrät er unzweifelhaft einen starken gleichgeschlechtlichen Anteil seiner Sexualität.

> [The author of the novella may for now betray his bisexuality neither in the way he leads his life nor in questioning himself. To the psychoanalyst, [though,] he undoubtedly betrays a strong same-sex portion of his sexuality.] (126)

In the end, then, Hitschmann thought that *Death in Venice* enabled its author to unconsciously satisfy repressed desires, at least in his imagination. He also wrongly wrote that Aschenbach and his wife had been childless.

In 1926, D. E. Oppenheim offered a different psychoanalytical interpretation of Mann's novella. Inspired by Alfred Adler rather than Freud, Oppenheim stresses sex less than the attempt to compensate for an inferiority complex. Aschenbach has made such an attempt in his literary career, Oppenheim argues, and his love for Tadzio is a later, related attempt of an aging man to regain his youth. Aschenbach lives in constant fear of death and of its precursor, old age, Oppenheim explains, so he wishes not only for a long life but also for renewed youth. His encounter with the old man on the boat affords a revealing insight into his unconscious because it shows that he wants to be young again and that he regrets having let old age creep up on him. Aschenbach's return to Venice in chapter 3 is likewise significant. Venice is a realm of youth for him, Oppenheim writes, and he seeks some emotional adventure there because he finds new life in love. That he loves Tadzio is less important than his own quest for youth. He may feel attracted to Venice, Oppenheim remarks, and he may feel attracted to Tadzio, but fundamentally he pursues only the one goal of rejuvenating himself. That Aschenbach pursues this goal with the help of the barber's cosmetics, transformed to resemble the old man on the boat, whom he found so repulsive, shows that his fear of old age is irresistible. This fear would not have grown so powerful, Oppenheim thinks, if he had not always suffered from an exaggerated fear of death, a fear that in turn goes back to his feelings of weakness in childhood. With his heroic work habits, he won a victory over his inhibitions and doubts, one that paved the way for his rise to fame, but this triumph was not decisive. The sense of frailty that comes with age now turns his constant struggle against his feelings of weakness into a shameful defeat that devalues his art, the bulwark of his self-esteem.

After addressing Aschenbach's psyche in general, Oppenheim deals specifically with his love for Tadzio. What could be more adventurous and rejuvenate him better, Oppenheim asks, than this abnormal inclination? Besides, he fears succumbing to women, whom he avoids, satisfying his need for love with his own sex instead. In finding males erotic, he also follows the example of the poet August von Platen (1796–1835). When he loses faith in art, Oppenheim adds, his love for Tadzio allows him to keep playing its pedagogical role, for he equates Tadzio with Socrates' Phaedrus. His Platonic love also enables him to flee his profession before he becomes conscious that doing so is the real reason for his trip to Venice. In his dream, moreover, Tadzio turns out to be "der fremde Gott" (the foreign god), as Mann puts it, a deity that is Dionysian because it helps Aschenbach forget himself and foreign because Aschenbach is unable to understand the Polish that Tadzio speaks. Furthermore, according to Oppenheim, Aschenbach alleviates his feelings of guilt by deifying the erotic part of himself in that dream. The more restrained part, being only human, must succumb to this second, divine ego. That this foreign god is Dionysus instead of the less powerful Eros allows Aschenbach to yield to ecstatic intoxication more freely:

> Er, den die Angst, schwach zu werden und weibisch, stets heftiger quält, kann nun, da er trunken ist von erträumter Grausamkeit und Wollust, seiner Männlichkeit ganz sicher sein und darf sich stark fühlen, weil er weh tut.

> [He, whom fear of becoming weak and womanly tortures ever more violently, can now, because he is drunk with imaginary cruelty and lust, be entirely sure of his manliness and feel strong because he causes pain.] (168)

In both his youth and old age, then, Aschenbach flouts established values, seeking proof of his strength. His death keeps him from incurring guilt so great that he loses his fame, and his fate is therefore grand and powerful enough to elevate as well as crush him. Oppenheim thus describes Aschenbach as a hero of weakness, but a tragic one.

Many further revealing comments can be found in the extensive footnotes to Oppenheim's essay. Oppenheim there observes that Mann himself, born four years after his brother Heinrich and encircled by caring women, had good reason to dream of manliness and to fear failure. Oppenheim also defends the practice of regarding Aschenbach as an actual person and Mann's novella as a document providing information about him. Literary historians would study Mann's story differently, Oppenheim writes, but their research can justify treating the psyche of a fictional person according to the same principles that apply to a real one. Oppenheim's own literary remarks are incisive. They include his statement that Mann created Aschenbach in the image of Platen. In addition to having numerous traits and experiences in common, he explains, Aschenbach's and Platen's first names, Gustav and August, are etymologically alike, and "Aschenbach" resembles the name of Platen's hometown, Ansbach. Aschenbach is even more closely related, Oppenheim adds, to the title character of Goethe's *Der Mann von fünfzig Jahren* (The Man of Fifty), a story within the novel *Wilhelm Meisters Wanderjahre* (Wilhelm Meister's Journeyman Years, 1821/1829). Both of these characters have military backgrounds, Oppenheim notes, and seek new life in new love, though Goethe's major is strong enough to renounce his erotic temptation. Besides, Aschenbach's specifically homosexual leanings are more reminiscent of those expressed by Mephistopheles for the male angels who appear at the end of Goethe's *Faust*. Oppenheim also compares *Death in Venice* to Mann's other works, linking Aschenbach to Johnny Bishop, for example, a pretty boy who appears in *Wie Jappe und Do Escobar sich prügelten* (How Jappe and Do Escobar Fought, 1911). In addition to taking a revealing psychoanalytic approach, Oppenheim is thus also no mean literary scholar. Like Ehrenstein and Müller in 1913 and 1914, respectively, though — and despite noting the similarity of the names August and Gustav — he wrongly calls Aschenbach "Georg."

As psychoanalysis gained acceptance, further remarks on *Death in Venice* that were informed by it turned up in unexpected places and in studies that noted its significance for literature in general as well as for Mann in particular. In a study of exoticism in the poems of Ferdinand Freiligrath (1810–76), Meno Spann noted in 1928 how the novella illustrates Freud's point that a strong urge to travel is a disguise for repressed erotic desires. Spann also rechristens Tadzio "Taju." Ten years later, in 1938, Helen V. McLean mentioned the novella in her review of an American collection of Freud's works. She explains that Mann portrays "the disintegration of human personality when repressed unconscious impulses overwhelm the conscious ego" (19). McLean adds that the only solution for a person whose psyche thus disintegrates is unconscious suicide, either psychic or physical. Similarly, and also in 1938, Karl Menninger referred to *Death in Venice* as an example of how novelists show the way in which people who commit suicide begin their self-destruction by bringing about, for unconscious purposes, its apparent justification in external reality. In 1945, Frederick J. Hoffman added that the novella gave a clear picture of the artist as neurotic. Finally, in 1950, Wolfgang F. Michael discussed the date and extent of Mann's acquaintance with the works of Freud. Mann claimed in 1925 that he had written *Death in Venice* under the immediate influence of Freud, Michael notes, and it is not hard to find Freudian motifs and ideas in the novella. Very few of them, he adds, can be traced directly to Freud, though. Mann's story does show the influence of psychoanalysis, Michael thus argues, but that influence was not as direct as Mann later recalled. These several examples indicate that not all psychoanalytical readings of Mann's novella had to do with homosexuality.

By the same token, not all readings that treated the issue of homosexuality were psychoanalytic. In 1919, one Numa Praetorius praised the novella in the same yearbook for "intermediate sexual stages" that in 1914 had carried Kurt Hiller's article denying that it deserves to be called homoerotic. In *Death in Venice,* Praetorius begins, a leading novelist portrays a homosexual passion with highly seductive fervor. From a medical perspective, Aschenbach's love is a case of belated homosexuality that has been latent and repressed but that now dislodges his earlier and always passionless heterosexuality and rouses deeper, stronger, slumbering feelings and drives. One cannot dismiss this interpretation, Praetorius adds, or deny the artistry in Mann's presentation of homosexual passion. Praetorius here takes issue with Hellpach, who in 1913 argued against regarding Aschenbach's fate as an elaboration of pederasty. Praetorius counters that the subject of novella is the fervent and the poetically fascinating depiction of a homosexual passion. Hellpach is wrong, Praetorius thinks, to say that this passion is less important than its physiological causes. On the contrary, Aschenbach's pathological change occurs to illustrate the influence of that passion. Praetorius adds, as Mann had said in September 1913, that a homosexual love makes Aschenbach's fate tragic. Like Oppenheim, Praetorius finds Aschenbach susceptible to such love because he has reached a critical age. It is not correct to claim, as Praetorius does, that Tadzio is fifteen and that Aschenbach dies just when his passion would have made him get to know Tadzio better. Praetorius also notes that Mann depicts homosexual passion not for its own sake but to lend his story a deeper meaning, concluding that *Death in Venice* is a work of art thanks to its masterful literary portrayal of a human passion, though the lover is a man of fifty and his beloved is a boy.

In 1955, Frank Donald Hirschbach likewise discussed the homoerotic attraction that Mann portrays, doing so from an even more purely literary — rather than psychoanalytical — point of view. Mann's story and each incident in it, he explains, have both a naturalistic and a symbolic significance. Aschenbach's homosexual tendencies operate on the naturalistic level. On a symbolic level, *Death in Venice* is about the deterioration and abdication of human will in the face of beauty. Tadzio is but one, albeit the main, agent in this negation of the will. According to Hirschbach, he is also a symbol of a passion that Aschenbach cannot and does not want to fulfill. While Tonio Kröger could contemplate love from a distance, Aschenbach destructively participates in it: "Love seizes him as a storm that blows over an old and hollowed tree, and he is unable to withstand its force" (21). Love and the contemplation of beauty thus have a role in a story about the disintegration of human and artistic will.

## Artists and Aestheticism

Another issue often noted in the reception of Mann's novella from 1915 to 1955 was his attitude toward artists and aestheticism. Aschenbach was frequently considered an artist. In one study, he was said to have an artist's tragic calling. Two other studies of characters like him remarked on the extent to which he and Mann embrace or reject the aestheticism of Stefan George or Hugo von Hofmannsthal. Further studies put the issues of art and aestheticism into the larger perspective of Mann's whole life and work. One such study related *Death in Venice* to Mann's biography and misconstrued the treatise that Aschenbach writes at the beach. A second study showed how reactions to the novella could change, and a third expressed grave reservations about its content and its hero. Other studies remarking on Aschenbach the artist in the context of Mann's career as a whole cited formal, social, psychological, and stylistic implications of his story. Most of these studies are in German, but a few are in English.

Like some of the political interpretations of Mann's novella, one study of Aschenbach portrayed him as an artist who is also a hero. In 1915–16, Paul Hankamer described him as such an artist, as a writer who suffers a tragic modern fate. Like many of Mann's heroes, Hankamer observes, Aschenbach is cut off from bourgeois society and driven to create. The knowledge that life takes a mechanical and a naturalistic course makes him passive, Hankamer adds, when he calms himself with the thought that his artistic existence is a necessity. His author's ethical impulse, a brave "Despite," however, transcends skepticism and passivity. Its image is St. Sebastian, the martyr pierced by arrows. Hankamer thus alludes to how Aschenbach once described greatness and to how a critic described his fictional heroes. Hankamer defines such artists' ethical heroism by similarly quoting the passage in which Mann writes that Aschenbach was called, not born, to the constant tension and to the soldierliness of his career. When he explains the social goal of artists' individualistic calling, Hankamer quotes parts of the passage that tells of Aschenbach's surrender, in his dream, to the foreign god Dionysus. In another allusion to *Death in Venice,* he says that an artist's fate is a life like a clenched fist. Form is also fate, according to Hankamer, who recalls how Aschenbach says that form is moral as well as immoral. *Death in Venice,* Hankamer thinks, is a masterpiece in which iron fate and trembling agony become a formal unity. He uses such lofty rhetoric once again when he sums up how the experience Mann describes is related to the form of the novella:

> In den Worten dieses Werks glutet dumpfste Glut, tiefste Qual und rote Sünde, gebannt von der marmornen Kühle und kosmischen Unabänderlichkeit der Formidee, die wie das Schicksal über allem steht.

[In the words of this work smolders sultriest ardor, deepest agony, and red sin, transfixed by the marmoreal coolness and cosmic unalterability of the idea of form, which, like fate, stands above all.] (186)

In treating the idea of fate and its relationship to the form of Mann's art, then, Hankamer uses the concept of a tragic calling. His remarks on artists' selfless, soldierly heroism seem to reflect that they were written in wartime. Like many other scholars who discuss higher things, Hankamer cites Mann's story selectively and neglects some of its details. Besides praising the ethical firmness that Aschenbach loses by the end of that story, he misspells his last name as "Achenbach."

Other studies that raised the issue of artists or aesthetes came to different conclusions. In 1922, Carl Helbling compared Aschenbach and his author to Stefan George and to Hugo von Hofmannsthal. In *Death in Venice*, Helbling maintains, Mann comes closest to sharing the aestheticism of George and his circle. The novella poses George's problem of beauty and artistic creation, he argues, and like George's poems, Mann's story symbolizes soulful yearning and is not meant for the many. Aschenbach even seems George's spiritual brother, in fact, though much also divides them. Aschenbach cannot overcome his bourgeois scruples, Helbling explains, and when faced with beauty, he is not as strong as George. Socratic doubts about beauty also keep Mann from becoming one of George's disciples. Mann conveys the problematic conscience of such artists and is skeptical of their purity. To Helbling, he therefore seems more like Hofmannsthal, whose works are frequently set in Venice, and whose style, like Mann's, befits the beauty of that city. Mann's story opposes beauty and intellect more radically, however, than Hofmannsthal's *Der Tod des Tizian* (The Death of Titian, 1892). That story also attacks aestheticism, Helbling continues, and the dreams Mann describes are less symbolic than those related by Hofmannsthal. Aschenbach suffers the fate of an artist, though, and Mann shares his heroism of weakness. According to Helbling, *Death in Venice* thus shows both how Mann resembles George and Hofmannsthal and how he differs from them. In 1933, K. J. Obenauer made a similar argument, noting that the novella is Mann's closest approach to neoromantic aestheticism but that it also betrays his skeptical and strictly ethical attitude.

Other remarks on artists and aestheticism were made in studies that treat Mann's career as a whole. In one way or another, all these studies link his life and work. In 1925, for example, Arthur Eloesser interpreted *Death in Venice* in a book as well as an essay. In both, he hails its masterful style and argues that poets such as its hero and its author are not inspired to write in a kind of immaculate conception. Aschenbach's homosexual love heightens his isolation, he observes, and when Mann, a student of Schopenhauer, calls the sea formless, he is under the influence of Indian philosophy. A condensation of Eloesser's argument was published in 1931, in his history of German literature. This condensation appeared twice in English, first in 1933, in a translation of that history, then again in 1947. Eloesser knew Mann well, but he is also the first of many authors to misconstrue the subject of the short treatise that Aschenbach writes in Tadzio's presence. According to him, Mann's protagonist writes two pages about the fatal power of eros. Actually, Aschenbach responds to a request to state his views "über ein gewisses großes und brennendes Problem der Kultur und des Geschmackes" (about a certain large and pressing problem of culture and taste). Mann never mentions the exact nature of this problem, and it is ostensibly "fast gleichgültig" (almost indifferent) to Aschenbach. To be sure, writing his treatise with Tadzio nearby teaches him "daß Eros im Worte sei" (that eros is in the word). The words that Mann uses to describe this creative process, in fact, are often heavily laden with sexual overtones. The connection between Aschenbach's sensual inspiration and finished literary product, though, is indirect. He takes Tadzio as a model of aesthetic perfection, not as his subject, moved by the boy's beauty but not necessarily writing about it. What his act of writing shows, for better or worse, is how artists like him transform experience in an aesthetic crucible. To say that he describes eroticism, much less Tadzio, is therefore a gross simplification, not only of this scene, but also of the complex ties that bind beauty and intellect throughout Mann's story. A strictly biographical critic might also object that the brief essay Mann himself once wrote on vacation in Venice, and in circumstances like Aschenbach's, mused about a new classicism and is called, according to its final title, *Über die Kunst Richard Wagners* (On the Art of Richard Wagner, 1911).

In the same issue of the journal that carried Eloesser's article in 1925, Otto Zarek connected Mann's life and work in a different way. Zarek argues that art creatively transforms an artist's experience. He also reports how he once told Mann that young people had an intimate relationship with *Death in Venice*, not because of its content, but because of their own beliefs about art. Turning away from the novelties of expressionism, Zarek explained, youth had longed for a literary tradition. Mann's story had become a symbol for such readers, he said, since it radiated an atmosphere of classicality. Mann agreed that he had wanted to create a book in the tradition of German prose fiction, according to Zarek, admitting that he had read the same pages of Goethe's *Die Wahlverwandtschaften* daily in order to acclimate himself to the style in which he wanted to write. Later reflecting on this conversation, Zarek thinks that the novella cannot be the beginning of new developments; its style is a stopping, not a starting, point. It can still be the basis of a new tradition, though, he adds, insofar as studying its form helps other authors cultivate theirs. Zarek does not give the exact date of his discussion with Mann, but his article suggests that they had met sometime around 1918. That he changed his mind about *Death in Venice* by the time this article was published in 1925 suggests how reactions to the novella, even reactions of the same reader, could shift.

In 1927, Martin Havenstein was less interested in Mann's actual life than in the inner being and psychic structure revealed by his works. Havenstein had serious reservations about *Death in Venice*. Its noble style conceals questionable content, he writes, and reminds him of the pomp of a funeral procession. Mann's splendid language, he adds, "ist wie eine kostbare Decke, die über etwas gebreitet wird, das an sich geeignet ist, Widerwillen zu erwecken" (is like a costly cover that is spread over something that in itself is suited to awaken revulsion) (239). Havenstein misunderstands Mann's story when Aschenbach strikes him as the victim of a fate that others conspire to realize and that is purely coincidental. He also is satisfied with the explanation of the novella given in Mann's *Betrachtungen eines Unpolitischen*. That work notes that *Death in Venice* shows the ethical risks posed by an artist's life. Havenstein finds the novella admirably self-critical, though he thinks that Mann was wrong to make Aschenbach so similar to himself. What is more, Aschenbach is the object of Havenstein's scorn: "Er ist eine Treibhauspflanze, die in der frischen Luft zugrunde gehen muß und der wir den Untergang wünschen" (He is an indoor plant that must perish in fresh air and that we wish destroyed) (245). Aschenbach is also an unsympathetic snob, he says, a far cry from the title character of Goethe's *Torquato Tasso* (1790):

> Er bleibt bis zum Ende der eiskalte, gegen jedermann bis oben zugeknöpfte Großmogul der Literatur, der seinen Ruhm "verwaltet" und es wohlgefällig bemerkt, wenn die Kellner vor ihm katzbuckeln.
>
> [To the end, he remains the ice-cold Grand Mogul of literature, completely aloof from everyone, who "manages" his fame and notes with pleasure when waiters bow and scrape before him.] (247)

Most readers would have more sympathy with Aschenbach, Havenstein says, if his erotic passion did not take an unnatural turn. His suppressed vitality becomes perverse, and his whole life and work are unhealthy and abnormal. Havenstein thus sometimes seems to lump an artist's life and work together after all.

Other studies that raised the issues of artists and aestheticism with regard to Mann's career reached different conclusions about *Death in Venice*. In 1935, Ferdinand Lion noted that the novella combines aestheticism and naturalism, classical form and morbid content, in an ambiguous *conjunctio oppositorum*. Lion likes the result: "Welche Klassik mit Karbolgeruch!" (What classicism with the smell of phenol!) (84). Like Zarek in 1925, Lion calls the novella a *non plus ultra*, finding that Mann could go no further in his critical portraits of artists. What is more, he thinks Aschenbach horrified by the first signs of the homosexuality found liberating in Gide's *L'immoraliste* (1902). Lion also remarks that eros can be like music as well as sculpture in Mann's fiction, especially in *Death in Venice*. In 1947, Lion made a related point, telling how the novella takes the form of musical variations. The Venetian lagoon, Venetian politics, and Venice itself, he argues, correspond to Aschenbach's art, life, and essence. For Hans Mayer in 1950, Aschenbach runs aground because his intellect is not in tune with his social environment, because his psychological experiences are no longer realizable within his society. In 1953, Hans Eichner claimed that Aschenbach succumbs to a fate that is his own doing. In Eichner's view, he is an artist uniquely unaware that there is more to life than work. Mann has never ennobled the raw material of his fiction more than in this novella, Eichner writes, never transformed its unseemly subject with such artful narration. The novella is not only classical, though, he adds, but also parodistic.

All of the studies mentioned so far in this section were written, at least at first, in German. A few others originally appeared in English. James Cleugh's book on Mann from 1933 contains quotable prose as well as glaring errors. One cannot say, as Cleugh does, that *Death in Venice* silenced hostile critics for a long time. The first chapter of the present study proves that this was not the case. It is also incorrect to claim that the novella contains none of Mann's usual irony and that it almost totally lacks leitmotifs. Several critics cited so far make this surprising assertion. Cleugh is closer to the mark when he explains Aschenbach's state of mind. In his opinion, "Nietzsche would have approved this modern, dispassionate pilgrim of the decadence and used him as a stick with which to beat the unregenerate Wagner" (137). This sentiment, though overstated, is not far from the one expressed in Mann's essay *Über die Kunst Richard Wagners*. Cleugh is wrong again, though, when he writes that Aschenbach's tragedy amounts to asking whether any man can ever really be called fortunate and beyond evil destiny. Finally, Cleugh may be right to say that Mann's novella is an imperishable monument of German literature, but it sounds ludicrous to announce that "critics were silenced by this inexpugnable affirmation of mortality in a prose worthy of the great Aschenbach himself" (145). In 1942, Joseph Gerard Brennan thought *Death in Venice* an allegory of the artist that tells how creative asceticism causes spiritual dissolution. It shows Mann's "inextricable union of disease and the artist nature" (48), "disease" here meaning psychological disturbances resulting from a tension between knowledge and form. Brennan views Aschenbach as an artistic genius, one whose moral example Mann does not recommend: "Anyone who would find in his statement of artist morality an incitement to general moral anarchy would thereby betray a total misunderstanding of the man and his work" (129). This warning may be a result of Brennan's interest in Nietzsche. Aschenbach's longing for the sea as nirvana, he claims, recalls an aphorism in Nietzsche's *Morgenröte* (Dawn of Day, 1881). In 1951, Henry Hatfield wrote that the novella, Mann's most heroic portrait of the artist, shows Aschenbach's death wish rebelling against his categorical imperative. Hatfield's use of these concepts suggests that Mann stages a conflict between the principles of Freud and Immanuel Kant. Hatfield also concludes that *Death in Venice* is the least bourgeois of Mann's works, calling it "at once consummately civilized and deeply barbaric" (63).

## Structure, Symbols, Style, and Literary History

Another approach to *Death in Venice* taken from 1915 to 1955 was concerned with formal features such as its structure, symbols, and style. This approach proved fruitful in several different studies. One of those studies stressed the narrative form of Mann's story, the symmetry of its chapters, and the differences between its literal and figurative levels as well as between experience and art. A second argued that Mann's symbolism is ambiguous, synthetic, and subtly effective, while a third demonstrated how Mann's choice of words and the way in which he arranges them sum up Aschenbach's psyche in a single sentence. A fourth study contrasted Aschenbach's fate with the freedom of Mann's narrator, showing how the narrative medium of the novella, like its psychological symbolism, is an existential message. A fifth study maintained that Mann's story is not about amoral ambiguity, and a sixth contended that it is too subversive, both aesthetically and ethically. Other studies discussed its leitmotifs and its symbols in further ways or revealed how efficiently Mann wrote it. Finally, *Death in Venice* began to be mentioned in histories of the novella as a literary genre and in histories of German literature.

In 1927, Marianne Thalmann made a forceful case for regarding the structure of *Death in Venice*. Thalmann takes issue with Isemann's pamphlet of 1913, which she criticizes for being too concerned with Mann's subject and with moral demands. Instead, she explains the novella's narrative form. For her, the fact that it consists of five chapters is at least as important as the fact that it discusses an erotic experience. The third and longest of those chapters, she writes, is its formal and thematic center. That chapter treats the motif of travel most revealingly, establishing the novella's main, north-south axis between Munich and Venice. The other chapters surround it symmetrically: chapters 2 and 4 are monological, for example, while 1 and 5 are dialogical. Chapters 2 and 4 are also complementary: 2 is a cold chronicle of Aschenbach's family background; 4 is more psychological, egotistical, and stylized; 2 shows youth, a northern work-ethic, and the puberty of Apollinian man; 4, rejuvenation, southernly idle hands, and the puberty of Dionysian man. Two vocal parts accompany the resulting amoral polyphony of the artist, Thalmann notes, one vernal, the other autumnal. The first is audible in chapter 1, the second in chapter 5. Thalmann's argument becomes awkwardly abstract when she adds that these chapters lie in concentric circles on a spatial plane, a horizontal extension expanded by the figurative, vertical tendency of the symbols of death. The result, she claims, is that Mann's subject transcends experience as that subject is drawn upward into eternity. It is also a simplification to say, as she does, that the erotic incident is peripheral because it takes place solely in chapter 5. Thalmann is more perceptive when she explains that Tadzio is not the focus of the novella, but rather the last in the line of foreign, erotic, and similarly dressed males repre-senting death. She also justifiably questions Oppenheim's psychoanalytic approach. Is it proper to treat Aschenbach as if he were a real person, she asks, and Mann's novella as if it were Platen's biography? Thalmann poses such questions for the same reason she refutes Isemann: like him, Oppen-heim does not distinguish art from life.

A second study of formal elements in *Death in Venice* was written by Vernon Venable in 1938. Venable examines the novella's "symbol structure" (72). Like Thalmann, he describes two narrative levels. On one of these levels, Aschenbach's trip to Venice and fatal love for Tadzio occur; on the other, Mann repeats the theme of life and death. This argument recalls those of Broch in 1913 and Sachs in 1914 when Venable explains these two levels in terms borrowed from music, comparing them to the treble voice and ground bass of a passacaglia. He also notes that though Mann links his symbols with almost mathematical precision, they are not so obvious as to seem artificial. At the cemetery and in the gondola, though, such symbols connote the antithesis of life and death in the realms of physical things, ideas, and emotions alike, resulting in "rather dull arithmetic" (73). Those same symbols become ambiguous, however, resulting in synthesis. Since each suggests both life and death, they are no longer discursive, Venable adds, but synoptic. By repeating them, Mann intensifies their effect. He exercises strict narrative control, but does so below the level of readers' conscious attention, achieving a poetic simplicity of mood. Venable also argues that the wanderer, gondolier, and flirtatious old man are really images of Aschenbach and Tadzio, and he calls that old man a "loathsome travesty of the Sebastian-like hero type" (67). Furthermore, he thinks that Tadzio is Aschenbach's creation, even Aschenbach himself. Venable notes how Tad-zio's smile is that of Narcissus, too, and he concludes that Aschenbach is thus confronted with the image of his own beauty. Some of these claims and conclusions suggest that Venable was too eager to synthesize all of Mann's symbols in one uniform meaning. In any case, it is not true, as he maintains, that Tadzio is twelve years old. He points out the phallic imagery in Aschen-bach's vision of the jungle, however, and tells just how this middle-aged artist "goes to seed in a most shocking way" (64).

Oskar Seidlin wrote the next notable formal study of *Death in Venice* in 1947. In microscopic detail, he analyzed the syntax and diction of the opening sentence of Mann's second chapter. That sentence comprises six-teen lines, he explains, and is divided into five sections by semicolons and a colon. The first thirteen lines discuss Aschenbach's career, while only the remaining two or three are about his private life. This disproportion shows how work oppresses the man, who is only an appendage to his résumé. The symbolism of Mann's syntax, Seidlin adds, is also apparent in the length of the four sections that describe Aschenbach's writings. As the volume of those writings increases, so does the length of the section, the last being almost four times as long as the first. By listing a biography, a novel, a moral story, and an aesthetic treatise in turn, these same sections also show the progressive spiritualization of Aschenbach's subject matter. Aschenbach himself is called an "Autor" (author), then a "Künstler" (artist), then a "Schöpfer" (creator), then a "Verfasser" (composer, writer), a series of appellations, according to Seidlin, that tells how his creativity becomes more elevated and esoteric. This spiritualization is balanced, though, by the increasing intimacy that results from the ever more detailed descriptions of his readers' reactions. Seidlin notes that adjectives and other expressions used to characterize Aschenbach's work similarly hint at its significance. Mann's describing Schiller's essay on naïve and sentimental poetry as a "Raisonnement," for example, shows Aschenbach's antithetical, Latinate cast of mind, while using the title "Friedrich von Preußen" (Frederick of Prussia) instead of "Friedrich der Große" (Frederick the Great) suggests his Prussian sense of discipline and duty. To Seidlin, the word "Epopöe" (epopee), used in place of "Epos," even sounds like a fittingly martial fanfare. He finds similar connotations in the rhythm and tempo of Mann's sentences and in the increasingly high pitch of his vowels, admiring not only the architecture but also the music of *Death in Venice*. According to him, this piece of German prose is "in seiner stilistischen Vollendung ein Stück Architektur auch, ein Stück musikalischer Komposition" (in its stylistic perfection, also a piece of architecture, a piece of musical composition) (448).

In 1950, Fritz Martini likewise subjected the style, structure, and narration of the novella to a close reading. Just as Seidlin focused on the first sentence of Mann's second chapter, Martini concentrates on the last five paragraphs of his fourth. Martini's interpretation recalls the one given by Bruno Frank in 1913. Like Frank, Martini contrasts Aschenbach's story and Mann's narration, linking the latter to the influence of Nietzsche. Although Aschenbach is doomed and defenseless, Martini argues, a passive victim of forces and of a fate beyond his control, Mann's narrator is free. This narrator is sympathetic to Aschenbach but also distinct from him, and his sovereignty preserves an equilibrium that prevents Mann's story from being hopelessly pessimistic. This equilibrium is a means of self-preservation, however precarious, against death and despair. By achieving it, Martini writes, intellect defends itself as a will to form, and form creates at least the illusion of distance from the destructive forces that constitute life. In other words, Mann's subjectively narrated prose is proof of human beings' intellectual freedom. Martini's stylistic considerations thus seem motivated by existential concerns. For him, Mann's highly cultivated prose is a paradigm of linguistic perfection, but it is also a form of seeing and of experience, a means of distancing oneself from reality. He accordingly mentions not only its complex syntax, attributive style, and repetition of words, but also its irony, allegorical images, skeptical distance, consciousness, ambiguity, and almost overwrought intellectualism. Martini, then, relates details of style and composition in what he describes as a unified work of art that bespeaks its author's general intellectual attitude.

A different version of Martini's essay appeared in 1954. While this version presents much the same interpretation, often in a rearranged order, it differs from the original one mainly in the emphasis it places on Mann's symbolism. Contrasting *Death in Venice* with *Bahnwärter Thiel* (Flagman Thiel, 1888), an earlier novella by Gerhart Hauptmann (1862–1946), Martini shows how Mann went beyond naturalism and told his story by using synthetic symbolic constructions that convey Aschenbach's state of mind. He notes the repetition of symbolic figures and situations as well as the functional character of Mann's symbols, which change in the course of the story and are limited, in their reference, to that story itself. The sea is symbolic in this way, as is the erotic, both in the old dandy and in Tadzio's narcissistic smile. Like Venable, Martini concludes that Tadzio is Aschenbach himself. He means that Tadzio embodies Aschenbach's yearning for perfect beauty. In such symbolic constructions, he adds, Mann's narration operates on two levels. One is realistic and psychological; the other, symbolic and mythical. By means of psychological analysis and distanced irony, moreover, Mann wins the battle that Aschenbach loses. Stating this case more forcefully than he had in the earlier version of his essay, Martini writes that Mann's intellectualism is a way of defending himself against life. The style of Martini's essay is often rambling, and its structure is far from clear, but Martini expresses this same thought concisely when he explains, "Die Form ist die Moral dieses Schriftstellers" (Form is this author's morality) (201).

In the expanded version of a book originally published in 1952, Hermann Pongs, in 1956, objected to the emphasis that Martini's second essay places on ambivalence and ambiguity. Behind Mann's ironic combination of myth and psychology, Pongs argues, lie parody and satire. From its very first page, he observes, the fundamental word of *Death in Venice* is "falsch" (false). This word occurs several times in the novella. A "falscher Hochsommer" (false high summer) makes May in Munich sultry, for example, and the old man on the boat turns out to be "false" — that is, not young — and to have false teeth. From such evidence Pongs draws the dramatic conclusion that "der schwarze Engel des 'Falschen' schattet über diesem ganzen Werk, seiner Fabel, seinem Helden" (the black angel of the "false" overshadows this whole work, its story, its hero) (334). Pongs seems even more emphatic when he exclaims that Aschenbach is all "Falsch, falsch, falsch!" (334), as if some teacher, he adds, had written the word "false" into a notebook that belonged to this confused student of life. Pongs faults Martini for not taking this falseness into account and for not concluding that Mann cites it to condemn Aschenbach's ambiguous world. Pongs may have a point when he contends that there is an innermost realm, by which he means some firm core, in Mann's ambiguous attitude. He seems mistaken, however, to infer the existence of such a realm from Mann's supposed awareness of the fact that the simplicity of the German *Volk* is a virtue.

In 1955, Robert Ulshöfer likewise interpreted *Death in Venice* according to Mann's "Begriff der 'falschen' Natur" (concept of "false" nature) (19). Like Martini, Ulshöfer concentrates on a few particular passages. Like Pongs, he draws unwarranted moralistic conclusions. The warm weather in Munich is not the only thing that is false, he contends; so are several aspects of Aschenbach's itinerary. Indeed, the concept of false nature is clearly a leitmotif of Mann's novella, and readers are meant to become aware of the falseness around and within them. On learning of Aschenbach's death, Ulshöfer writes, such readers notice how terrible and destructive is the world, and how miserable, worthless, and dishonest is all human effort and all talk of the superiority of intellect to nature. Mann thus contradicts the classicistic aesthetics apparent in the works of Goethe, and the gap between form and content is the second leitmotif of his story. Whereas Goethe's characters show a healthy harmony of body and mind, Ulshöfer thinks, Mann shows illness, aging, and abnormal sexuality. Mann's description of the wanderer at the cemetery in Munich, he adds, reveals that innate physical traits such as one's physiognomy determine one's soul and intellect. Captivated by that bizarre wanderer, Ulshöfer also observes, Aschenbach did not even notice the many healthy people whom he certainly encountered on the same day. This obsession with the false paralyzes and destroys him, and with images of a reality that is sick and lacks metaphysical being, Mann consciously negates Goethe's images of a genuine, meaningful reality created by God. Ulshöfer admits that Mann's story has some empirical and psychological truth to it, but he insists that there is more to life than Mann's psychophysical reality and that Goethe is greater. Writing for teachers of German, Ulshöfer also adds that he thus explains *Death in Venice* so that young students are not indecisively and relativistically allowed to regard the sick as normal and the bizarre as beautiful. Like Martini's existential assumptions and Pongs's apparent need for certainty, this pedagogical concern may reflect ethical unease in postwar Germany.

Other studies of the formal features of Mann's novella offered further insights into its leitmotifs, its symbols, and its composition. For Leander Hotes in 1931, it was "ein Meisterstück leitmotivischer Komposition" (a masterpiece of leitmotivic composition) (120). By contrast, Ronald Peacock, in 1934, found that it contained no leitmotifs at all. In 1955, Robert Faesi called cholera a symbol of the epidemic inside Aschenbach. In that same year, William York Tindall, like Venable in 1938 and Martini in 1950 and 1954, cited the ambivalence of Mann's symbols, among them Tadzio, "the object of senile passion" (224). The camera left standing on the beach at the end of the novella is enigmatic, for example, yet it "corresponds to dying

Aschenbach and concentrates the feeling of abandonment — not only his but that of society" (118). Benno von Wiese, again in 1955, noted what he took to be Mann's purely artistic symbolism. He argues that Mann's series of phantom-like characters is ambivalent, comprising actual men who, on an allegorical level, are messengers of death. Like Venable, von Wiese finds such symbols limited to their function within Mann's story. The special thing about them, he writes, is that they occur in an unrelated series and become symbolic only through their function in the narrative. Mann's symbolism is conscious, subtle, and suggestive, he adds, and almost forced insofar as his symbols no longer represent a world beyond their narrative function. Finally, in 1950 James F. White examined a sheet of notes Mann used while writing *Death in Venice*. Everything on the sheet went into its final version, White explains, and only a few of its items were rearranged. The sheet thus shows "the economy and efficiency of Mann's planning, of his ability to project the skeleton of a story, and then to fill out its live contours, utilizing every planned *motif* and every verbal formulation" (75). In addition to the narrative virtues cited by others, then, it seems that Mann did not waste words.

Such studies of the form of *Death in Venice* are related to others that treated the history of its genre. These histories of the novella as a literary genre are seldom original, and they often simply repeat the results of other research. They nevertheless help show how Mann's story was received by readers other than specialists. In 1928, Arnold Hirsch explained how Mann intensifies Aschenbach's aversion to work in a plot interrupted only by the biographical second chapter. While the plot rises in a formal sense, Hirsch claims, it declines in an ethical one. Mann's story is not about Aschenbach's particular attraction to Tadzio, moreover, but about the general opposition of intellect to sensuality. Mann's dual frame of reference, realistic as well as symbolic, Hirsch adds, approximates ineffable and amorphous psychological motives, making them seem rational on the surface of his story. In 1934, E. K. Bennett found *Death in Venice* too symbolic. Aschenbach's demise seems unjustified and unmotivated, Bennett argues, a fate presented so intellectually as to preclude any emotional reaction from Mann's readers. *Death in Venice* is the last novella that Bennett treats in his history of the genre, and Mann's style and symbolism appear to him to reach a point beyond which no other author can go. Indeed, he calls Mann's novella "a work which exhausts the last possibilities of which the genre is capable" (248). Johannes Klein added in 1954 that *Death in Venice* recalls but also differs from Mann's earlier novellas about decadence. If its subject were not so tender, Klein writes, it would be a monumental German novel. It is still one of the most important, a music drama in words, he thinks, in which love and death finally unite in a way reminiscent of Wagner's *Tristan und Isolde*. Klein's comments are marred by several errors of fact. Contrary to his assertions, Aschenbach is not disappointed by the cloudy sky upon arriving at his hotel, he does not surrender to the music performed in front of its terrace because passion makes people relax, and he does not want death more than love so as to uphold his former reputation.

*Death in Venice* also received increasing attention in general histories of German literature. One of those histories betrays a way in which its reception changed over time. In an early edition of his study of recent German writing, an edition published in 1928, Albert Soergel notes both how Aschenbach succumbs to a love scorned by society and how Walt Whitman's line that only love and death are ultimately beautiful could be the motto of Mann's story. As Soergel knows, Mann quotes this line in his essay *Von Deutscher Republik* (On the German Republic, 1922), where he hails Whitman as an advocate of democracy that involves social eroticism and homosexual love. Soergel concludes, moreover, that the novella would be among Mann's most enduring works if its concept of the artist were generally valid, not highly questionable. Instead, it is simply his most confessional and most polished. In a revised edition of Soergel's study, an edition that appeared in 1961, *Death in Venice* is introduced as a tragic parody of the writerly existence. Relying on Hofmiller's review of 1913, this later edition cites Mann's use of Platonic categories in Aschenbach's dream of a Socratic address to Phaedrus on the subject of beauty. Mann's style in this passage resembles that of a mediocre translation of Plato, it adds, and is an attempt to lend his and his hero's dubious substance credibility. The entire novella is too polished, moreover, and lacks inner freedom. Its image of artists is egocentric and narcissistic, and "ein Tropfen ironischen Öls hätte das Bild zerstört" (a drop of ironic oil would have destroyed the image) (864). The revised edition thus puts no ironic distance between Aschenbach and his author. Finally, that edition calls Aschenbach's homosexuality a symbol of the fact that he loves only himself. Both editions of Soergel's literary history thus criticize Mann's concept of the artist. Compared to the one from 1928, however, that of 1961 takes a dimmer view of the novella and seems less sympathetic toward homosexuality. *Death in Venice,* then, did not automatically gain respect with the passage of time.

## Death and Venice

A few studies of *Death in Venice* that appeared between 1915 and 1955 specifically addressed the issues mentioned in its title: death and Venice. Those studies present these two issues in different ways, often drawing contradictory conclusions about them.

In the 1930s, four studies addressed the issue of death in Mann's works. In 1932, Lydia Baer observed that his novella is "saturated with Death" (34). She explains that death is the end result of Aschenbach's inner dissolution; that he is ripe for it; that it appears as fate, love, and beauty; and that it is both mystical and a metaphysical state, as well as a merging with the absolute. Baer also thinks that the novella shows Mann's "negative concept of Death which opposes Death to Life and which destroys Life" (38). Hans Kasdorff described *Death in Venice* similarly, also in 1932, arriving at the conclusion that death is not Aschenbach's destruction, but his release, satisfaction, and fulfillment; not his demise, but a revelation of his essence, desire and innate tendency. It is death, Kasdorff thinks, in Schopenhauer's sense. It is also less a death in Venice than a death at the sea that is the background for Aschenbach's contemplation of Tadzio, and the sea, according to Kasdorff, always meant nothingness and eternity for Mann. In 1934, Fritz Nolte had doubts about how Mann handles the contrast of life and intellect, calling *Death in Venice* an ethical low point in Mann's career. Equating intellect with death, Nolte argues, since intellect seems superior to life, here results in an extreme case of tragic error. In 1935, Hellmut Rosenfeld wrote that Mann's story objectifies and generalizes the eroticism of death, an eroticism that is suggested by the Eros from Centocelle. This statue is assumed to be a copy of an original sometimes attributed to Praxiteles. It is a kind of statue often used in funerary monuments showing a beautiful youth with a torch, a figure that represents death. Rosenfeld thinks that Mann's story is patterned after it.

Other studies treated the theme of Venice. In 1937, Thea von Seuffert said that Venice, which she calls the epitome of beauty and the dreamland of the German soul, is the theme of the novella. In no other place could Aschenbach's encounter with Tadzio be so moving, she writes, since Venice symbolizes beauty. Other authors describe the beauty of the city itself, but Mann has Venice suggest an aesthetic atmosphere. Like Goethe in *Die Leiden des jungen Werthers* (The Sufferings of Young Werther, 1774), he explains how exaggerated aestheticism proves fatal. Beautiful but deadly, according to von Seuffert, Venice is not just the setting of his novella, but also one of its characters. In 1955, Walter Pabst examined how Venice had become a literary constant since Shakespeare. Mann turns its landscape into that of ancient Greece, Pabst notes, and Tadzio is an incarnation of Hermes. The boy's name is a variation of "Thaddeus," Pabst adds, the surname of one of Christ's disciples. As a divine messenger, then, Tadzio is both heathen and Christian. With their red hair and vertical furrows in their brows, furrows that suggest the devil's horns, Pabst also observes, the wanderer, the gondolier, and the street singer represent Satan. Tadzio is in league with these demonic figures, and Aschenbach's Dionysian dream is accordingly the work of the devil. The novella as a whole, Pabst writes, exemplifies St. Paul's saying that sin brought death into the world. There is a religious component, then, to Aschenbach's psyche. By going to hell via Italy and succumbing to heathen beauty, Pabst notes, Aschenbach also varies a grand romantic theme. Finally, Tadzio's name may allude to other Slavs, actual and fictional, who have visited Venice. Many of these same points were made by Hellmuth

Petriconi in 1955 (though his article appeared in the 1953–54 issue of a German journal). Petriconi also links the smell of phenol to the devil's supposed foul odor, and he distinguishes Mann from his strict Protestant narrator. Mann divides his setting, Petriconi adds, placing the devil in Venice and the Greek gods on the Lido. Those gods seem to exist independently, he thinks, and Aschenbach's guilt makes Mann's theme moral, not Christian. Pabst and Petriconi thus debated the importance of Greece and Christianity in *Death in Venice*.

## Translations

In addition to taking the approaches and to treating the issues already discussed in this chapter, scholars and critics writing about *Death in Venice* from 1915 to 1955 considered its translations into English and French. In both of these foreign languages, the novella appeared serially in 1924 and as a book in 1925. In the United States, the first translation was done by Kenneth Burke. This translation was initially published in *The Dial,* then by Alfred A. Knopf, and American reviews of it were almost always favorable. The first British translation appeared in 1928. It was done by H. T. Lowe-Porter and published by M. Secker. Starting in 1930, Knopf published it, too, and reviewers and scholars have often noted its many and serious flaws. The first French translation was done by Félix Bertaux, who had reviewed the novella in 1914, admiring both its style and its passion. This translation initially appeared in the *Revue de Genève*. When it was published as a book by Simon Kra, its title page listed Charles Sigwalt as Bertaux's co-translator. The novella has also been translated into over thirty languages other than English and French, languages spanning the alphabet from Afrikaans to Yiddish. The first of these translations were in Danish and Swedish; the most recent one noted in Potempa's bibliography of Mann's works is in Gaelic.

In 1925, reviews of Burke's translation often praised Mann's style and the treatment of his sexual theme. On 1 February, William A. Drake said *Death in Venice* is "an extraordinary study of emotional dualism." He thinks that Burke's translation is not very successful. One week later, on 8 February, Ernest Boyd wrote that the novella shows the extreme degeneration of the bourgeoisie. The bourgeois in Aschenbach is frightened and crushed, Boyd argues, by his quest for beauty in "the most perfect of Mann's achievements." On 22 February, the *New York Times Book Review* called Aschenbach's longing for a sensual life "the old Faustus motif whose roots are set deep in Germanic subconsciousness." The actual cause of his death is an overcharged heart, according to the anonymous author of this statement, but his story is written with "exquisite tact and delicacy and . . . its implications will only be misunderstood by the coarse and literal mind." The reluctance to accept limitations, a reluctance like Aschenbach's, may also explain the collapse of the "swollen schemes of modern Germany." On 28 February, Edwin Bjorkman noted how Aschenbach has made fetishes of discipline and success, and then is seized by a form of love "generally condemned as perverted." His story is daring, Bjorkman writes, but its telling instills "a sense of immaculate purity," and its "more or less abnormal twistings of natural instincts" are aesthetically, not erotically, suggestive. One of the rare negative reviews of Burke's translation appeared on 21 March in the *Independent* and called the novella a tedious and strained description of the Teutonic artist, whose temperament is too alien. On 25 March, Joseph Wood Krutch noted the "gravely sensuous mood" of *Death in Venice*. Its hero succumbs to merely sensuous beauty, Krutch maintains, and declines "into the refined voluptuary." Mann's self-conscious art is so perfect, he adds, as to seem artificial. In May, Boyd again called the novella Mann's most daring exposition of bourgeois degeneracy, while Cuthbert Wright admired it, describing its story as somewhat simplistic but finding it beautifully wrought. According to Wright, Aschenbach is "shaken by an abnormal emotion so intense that he commits what is essentially a crime" (424), but Mann transforms the primary emotion into an intellectual problem, a latent story into a secondary value. Wright himself transforms the one-and-one-half pages that Aschenbach fills in Tadzio's presence, mistakenly calling this short treatise a book. On 27 June, Louis Kronenberger praised the novella as a flawless, tragic, and perfectly ordered story, observing how Mann "molds with strong fingers this record of weakening and capitulation." Two other brief comments from 1925 differed markedly. *The Open Shelf* found *Death in Venice* — along with *Tristan* (1903) and *Tonio Kröger* — satisfying and finely wrought, but *The Booklist* called the narrative appeal of these stories very limited. According to Helen Rex Keller's *Reader's Digest of Books* in 1929, Aschenbach remains in Venice for the sake of Tadzio, his obsession, but then does not feel well and dies suddenly.

While most reviewers in America admired Mann's story, most said little about Burke's translation. Lowe-Porter's subsequent version, however, was sometimes criticized. In February 1929, Cecil Roberts found it to be poor. Roberts described the novella itself as sensitive and powerful. He mistakenly thinks Aschenbach an "old professor" (294). In 1930, in a preface to Lowe-Porter's translation, Ludwig Lewisohn called Mann's theme the artist's dizziness at the edge of the abyss of art. He also argued that Mann, in Aschenbach, projected a personal vision of his own later years. Like many other commentators, Lewisohn concludes that "The miracle of art . . . is here achieved" (128). He is speaking of *Death in Venice* in Mann's German, not in Lowe-Porter's English. In 1945, Marianne Zerner pointed out many mistranslations in that English. Among other things, she explains how Lowe-Porter ignores thematic keywords and fails to convey Aschenbach's strict bourgeois ethos. Lowe-Porter often falls lamentably short, Zerner remarks, in her characterization of Aschenbach. Her inadequacies include overstating and shifting the emphasis of his exacting slowness and misinterpreting basic characteristics such as his magisterial style. She also detracts from the Greek symbolism of Mann's descriptions of Tadzio, whom she calls "Prince Charming" rather than "Dorn-auszieher" (Thorn Puller) and a "lure" instead of "Psychagog" (psychagogue). Zerner reveals that most of Lowe-Porter's inaccuracies, however, are either syntactical errors, lost nuances, omissions, overstatements, understatements, changes of focus, interpretations of what Mann only suggests, or neglected technical devices. These inaccuracies include the sentence "Aschenbach was the one poet among the many workers on the verge of exhaustion." Mann wrote, "Aschenbach war der Dichter all derer, die am Rande der Erschöpfung arbeiten" (Aschenbach was the poet of all those who labor on the brink of exhaustion). Zerner rejects this "ludicrous misunderstanding of the hero and his art" (186). What is more, Lowe-Porter renders the phrase "[dem] unter der Schminke Fiebernden" ([the man] fevering beneath his make-up) as "under the fever of his cosmetics" and so, Zerner writes, "bungles the first indication that Aschenbach was stricken with the plague" (187n4). According to Zerner, Lowe-Porter's omissions also lead to oversimplifications. When she leaves out a paragraph of the episode in the gondola, for example, the English text is ambiguous. She also obscures Mann's several allusions to his other works in the passages about Aschenbach's career, losing a subtle link between the two authors. Zerner is right, then, to fault Lowe-Porter's "amazing jour-nalistic nonchalance" (186).

# Sources and Comparisons

Further comments made on *Death in Venice* from 1915 to 1955 compared it to the works of other authors. Some of the authors are from ancient Greece; others are from modern France and Germany. Two scholars noted how Mann alludes to Xenophon, quotes Homer, and emulates Plato. Those scholars found parallels of form, content, and theme between the novella and works by these ancient authors. Bertaux and other reviewers and schol-ars writing in French or about French literature routinely compared Mann to André Gide. To these reviewers and scholars — and Burke, too, is among them — *Death in Venice* often seemed typically German. The fact that Bertaux as well as Burke drew such comparisons shortly after each had translated the novella suggests how closely translation and comparison were related before comparative literature became an academic discipline. *Death in Venice* was likewise compared to aesthetic, philosophical, and literary works by Schiller, Kafka, Nietzsche, and — above all — Goethe. These comparisons illuminate its themes, style, setting, and characters, as well as its social criticism and ironic parody.

Two scholars discussed Mann's ancient sources. In 1946, Lorraine Gustafson noted that Mann alludes to Xenophon when Aschenbach thinks that Jaschu should travel for a year to recover from kissing Tadzio. The scene in which Aschenbach has this thought parallels a Socratic dialogue contained in Xenophon's *Memorabilia,* Gustafson explains, and is an example of his erudition. The dialogue, together with Plato's *Phaedrus,* she adds, can be considered the text of *Death in Venice.* Xenophon's themes, characters, plots, and incidents are strikingly similar to those of Mann's novella: both works tell how sensual beauty causes a kind of madness; Xenophon's Critobulos is like Jaschu, his son of Alcibiades is like Tadzio, Xenophon himself is like Aschenbach, and his Socrates is like Mann; the degeneration of Aschenbach's character parallels Socrates' description of the effects of beauty on its beholder; and Xenophon almost seems to suggest Aschenbach and Tadzio's silent exchange of glances. According to Gustafson, Mann's story therefore recalls an ancient philosophical problem and demonstrates timeless moral dangers. In 1952, Franz H. Mautner found similar Greek references. Mann's hellenizing style, he explains, indicates his psychological plot as well as his Platonic problem. Aschenbach speculates that the gondolier could send him to "Aides," Mautner writes, a spelling of "Hades" that is especially reminiscent of Greece. The Greek cast of Mann's prose begins in the third chapter, moreover, and it dominates the fourth as Aschenbach embraces a Greek view of life. Mautner also observes that the lines at the end of the third paragraph of chapter 4 — "Dann schien es ihm wohl, als sei er entrückt ins elysische Land . . ." (It seemed then to him as if he were carried away to Elysium . . .) — are taken from the *Odyssey* (IV, 563–68). In Homer, he adds, these lines foretell the death of Menelaus. In Mann, they describe Aschenbach's contentment in Venice, and their echo of Homer reveals how that contentment will lead to death. Like Hofmiller in 1913, Mautner discusses how Mann incorporates such hexameters into his prose. He also says that Mann emulates the style of Plato's dialogues, and he contends that Tadzio is an abstraction distinct from its embodiment, like a Platonic Idea. Allusions to Platen, Mautner also observes, reinforce Mann's link between the classicistic concept of beauty and homoeroticism, and the novella as a whole shows his recourse to myth.

In France, critics found Aschenbach very German and disagreed about his infatuation. In 1925, Bertaux introduced his translation as an intellectual biography of Mann himself, as a book that describes Mann's vacillation between artistic and bourgeois values. In *Death in Venice,* he says, a "roman psychologique d'incontestable valeur documentaire" (psychological novel of incontestable documentary value) (11), Aschenbach is both man in general and a product of a particular time. He is caught between universally opposing forces, that is, but he is also a German of 1913 and an intellectual of the Wilhelminian age. He may even represent German thought itself, adds Bertaux, which has known extremes like his and which now, after the First World War, is trying to expand its former horizons. Bertaux also argues that

Aschenbach's love for Tadzio is only part of Mann's story, a story that should not be compared to Gide's *Corydon* (1911). Aschenbach's passion is symbolic, Bertaux explains, and the significance of the novella would not change if he succumbed to an entirely different impulse, for example, to a taste for gambling or a craze for cocaine. Jean Fougère doubted this logic in 1947, and Edmond Jaloux had already read the novella differently in 1925. Jaloux notes how traces of German romanticism recur in Aschenbach just before the First World War. Among those traces are the old German attraction to death. Jaloux also argues that Aschenbach is often like the hero of Gide's *L'immoraliste,* and he faults Mann for not telling enough about his hero's previous love life: "Cette passion anormale est-elle la première de ce genre qu'Aschenbach ait connue? Ces abîmes auxquels M. Thomas Mann a fait allusion ont-ils quelque rapport avec l'homosexualité?" (Is this abnormal passion the first of its kind that Aschenbach has known? Do those abysses to which Mr. Thomas Mann has alluded have some connection to homosexuality?) (3). Incorrectly, Jaloux claims that Aschenbach has been ennobled by an emperor who considered him one of the most representative minds of his country. Jaloux also misspells Tadzio's name as "Tandzio." In other French responses, Geneviève Bianquis cited Mann's romantic inspiration in 1929, and Marcel Brion contrasted his aestheticism with the political partisanship of his brother Heinrich in 1930.

Other critics and scholars offered further remarks on Mann's similarity to Gide and to other French authors. In 1931, Burke contrasted *Death in Venice* with *L'immoraliste.* Although the two books share the themes of sickness and "sexual vagary" (120), he maintains, their emphases differ. Mann conveys resistance, resignation, and self-discipline, whereas Gide provides unclean details. Burke also observes how Aschenbach's mind tricks him, mentioning his "delirious remembrance of lines from the *Phaedrus*" and "his own diseased reworking of the Platonic dialogue" (120). Tadzio's freshness, liquidity, and immaturity, Burke adds, are "the sinister counterpart to the desiccation of Aschenbach's declining years" (119). In 1950, Martin Schlappner opposed Mann's gruesome content to his ethically inspired form, finding this form a counterweight that demonstrates the classicality Mann recommends in the essay *Über die Kunst Richard Wagners.* His vision of Venice as beautiful yet deadly is that of every romantic, Schlappner writes, but he also overcomes the romanticism and decadence that the city symbolizes. He thus resembles certain French authors, most notably André Saurès and Maurice Barrès. Gide, too, advocated a new classicism, moreover, and *Death in Venice* is like his *Corydon* since both link classicism and homosexuality. Schlappner discerns this same link in Goethe's remark that men are more aesthetically pleasing than women, and he finds this notion fundamental to Mann's story. He also calls that story similar to Wagner's *Tristan,* and he relates Tadzio's name to an adagio that Nietzsche heard in Venice.

In 1951, Albert J. Guérard wrote that *Death in Venice* and *L'immoraliste* both tell "essentially the same story of latent and unrecognized homosexuality leading to self-destruction" (113). Although Aschenbach has fewer homosexual reactions than Gide's Michel, he explains, both men rationalize their inward drives, neither of them wants his boy to grow up, and both externalize their psychological conflicts. Aschenbach is an obtuse observer, he adds, whereas Michel is an obtuse narrator. Gide's story is more purely Freudian because Mann's hero is more conscious, but both authors unnecessarily cite outside pressures such as the loss of Aschenbach's luggage. In realistic descriptions like that of Tadzio's sisters, Guérard continues, Mann also offers "a great deal of irrelevant detail" (116).

Still other scholars compared *Death in Venice* to works by three German-speaking authors: Schiller, Kafka, and Nietzsche. In 1949, Bernhard Blume explained that the novella shows the tragic conflict of intellect and beauty. It portrays the former striving for the latter, he argues, as does Schiller's essay *Über naive und sentimentalische Dichtung* (On Naive and Sentimental Poetry, 1795–96). In 1951, F. D. Luke likened *Death in Venice* to Kafka's *Die Verwandlung* (The Metamorphosis, 1915). Both books are about outward and inward degradation, Luke explains, both their protagonists are tragically isolated and die voluntarily, both betray sinister ambiguity, and both are artistic *tours de force*. Luke also observes that Mann's story is more firmly related to the external world of conventions, objects, society, and reality. Whereas Mann's "dream-logic" — a term used in that story to introduce Aschenbach's last monologue — is an artificial literary construct, moreover, Kafka's is genuine. Lacking Mann's analytical reflections, Luke concludes, Kafka's prose is more furtive, economical, and radical in its view of the human condition. Two years later, in 1953, Paul Böckmann argued that Mann's novella recounted an artist's fate in the spirit of Nietzsche's *Die Geburt der Tragödie*. In his story about the proximity of beauty and death, Böckmann notes, Mann, too, shows art confronted by Dionysian and demonic forces. Aschenbach's analytic consciousness attests only to human frailty in the end, he writes, whence Nietzsche's linking art to life by means of minds such as his is questioned. In 1955, R. A. Nicholls added both that Aschenbach's courage derives from Nietzsche's concept of German heroism and that his lack of inspiration corresponds to Nietzsche's analysis of modern decadence. Like Aschenbach, Nicholls also comments, Nietzsche had to leave Venice because of its oppressive climate. He also claimed that cholera had broken out there and that the city had been quarantined. For Mann and Nietzsche alike, Nicholls observes, Venice had a twofold character: beautiful but decaying and corrupt.

The author most often mentioned together with *Death in Venice* was Goethe. In 1948, Marianne Thalmann compared the novella to Goethe's *Der Mann von fünfzig Jahren,* the story in his *Wilhelm Meisters Wanderjahre* linked to it by Oppenheim in 1926. In 1927, after describing the epic form of the novella, Thalmann criticized Oppenheim's psychoanalytic approach. Now she cites Aschenbach's psychological troubles while lamenting how the world has changed since Goethe. All that is left of Goethe's story, she says, are Aschenbach's psychologically interesting symptoms of old age. His heart has been damaged by dividing life from intellect, the list of his publications reads like a medical history, and he is a hero of modern sublimations, what psychoanalysis calls a neurotic character. He is a modern intellectual, Thalmann also notes, a man who seems more than he is, and he succumbs to the repressions and psychoses of an individualistic century. The dissatisfaction implicit in these remarks is clearer when Thalmann adds that Aschenbach's death is the end of individualism and when she comments that he is a nineteenth-century man who knows how to play the stock market, a person no longer rooted in Goethe's simpler society:

> Er ist herausgetreten aus dem Kreis, in dem noch Axt und Säge gilt, und gehört in den Schlafwagen, in die Hotelhalle, den Wartesaal, die Gondel, auf das Pflaster.

> [He has stepped out of the sphere in which ax and saw still count, and he belongs in the sleeping car, the hotel lobby, the waiting room, the gondola, on the pavement.] (72)

Thalmann's argument sounds simplistic when she bemoans the modern rift between head and heart, but she adds an existentialist twist when she says that Aschenbach both fears and dies of time itself, a fear that shows a lack of a humane center. She welcomes Mann's novella as a critique of bourgeois Germany, moreover, but she thinks this critique more reminiscent of Schiller than Goethe, more reflective and antithetical than immediate and balanced. Mann, she comments, speaks only to a particular group of educated urbanites. She thus regrets a loss of social wholeness and appears beset by a conservative postwar malaise.

In 1955, R. Hinton Thomas drew another comparison between Mann and Goethe. Like Leppmann in 1915, Thomas read *Death in Venice* in light of *Die Wahlverwandtschaften*. Mann liked Goethe's contrast of classical form and daring content, Thomas writes, and *Death in Venice* is similarly dualistic. In Zarek's interview of 1925, Mann also noted that he meant to parody Goethe's style. Thomas shows how such ironic parody works. Goethe's Eduard and Mann's Aschenbach are alike in that demonic passion shatters their strict lives, he explains, and Aschenbach's relationship to Tadzio seems one of elective affinities, the concept mentioned in Goethe's title. According to Thomas, thematic parallels are misleading, however, for life is less benign in Mann, as is clear from the fact that Goethe's story involves heterosexual normality, not homosexual perversion. Mann's Tadzio is also not nearly as sweet a child as Goethe's Ottilie. As Thomas says, "Decadence lies at the very root of his being, and it is not childlike innocence that his smile expresses" (106). Thomas also maintains that Goethe's novel bears none of the thematic or stylistic characteristics that make Mann's novella classical. Mann admired the rhythmic charm of Goethe's prose, though, he says, and what their works have in common is syntactical poise and balance. Goethe portrays inner states through external events, moreover, but Mann evokes inward movements of his hero. What seems external in Mann expresses Aschenbach's state of mind, as in the detailed description of Tadzio coming to breakfast, a description that reflects Aschenbach's subjective mood and private fantasies. Mann's style is not as moderate as Goethe's, Thomas adds, because his hero is less restrained. His syntax is also more extravagant and sophisticated. Thomas notes that descriptions of Aschenbach as seated and relaxed replace Goethe's motif of the walk and that the abandoned camera at the end of the novella belongs to the theme of blackness suggested by the gondola. Such elements show how the structure of Mann's story is musical, he writes, while that of Goethe's is architectonic. Like Schlappner in 1950, Thomas points out that Aschenbach first hears Tadzio's name as "Adgio," a word that may suggest an adagio that Nietzsche recalled hearing in Venice. In sum, Thomas argues that Mann makes Goethe's theme and style nearly unrecognizable in a parody that preserves as well as subverts. A revision of these remarks appeared as a chapter in Thomas's book on Mann, a book published in 1956.

## Mann's Own Interpretations

Mann's own remarks on *Death in Venice* help sum up many of the issues that critics and scholars raised from 1915 to 1955 and that have been discussed in this chapter. He often referred to the novella in his other writings, and his comments clarify its political, stylistic, cultural, moral, aesthetic, biographical, and psychoanalytical aspects. Those writings, like the interview recalled in Zarek's article of 1925, also help assess its reception, which they frequently influenced. The most extensive of Mann's comments occur in three such works, but these three are complemented by many others that shed further and sometimes surprising light on what he had in mind when he wrote his story, what he thought it meant, and how his interpretations of it changed. To cite all these remarks is not to suggest that one must take them at face value, of course, or that Mann has to have the last word. For that matter, not all of his comments are included here, since he often repeated himself, giving the same information and opinions again and again. Knowing his own, most important interpretations, though, does help decide how much he is — and is not — like Aschenbach; help understand his characters, setting, ideas, and images; and help comprehend the conception, composition, and publication of *Death in Venice*.

Mann made his most extensive remarks on his novella in three longer works. In *Betrachtungen eines Unpolitischen,* the treatise of 1918 cited by Braun in 1920 and Havenstein in 1927, he explains how much he shares an "Entschlossenheit" (resoluteness) opposed to the "unanständigen Psychologismus" (indecent psychologism) (XII, 28) of the prewar era — terms used with reference to Aschenbach in the novella. Nonetheless, he argues that critics misunderstood his style. The hieratic atmosphere and masterly style of the novella are not his own ideals, he writes, but rather adaptation and parody, qualities that he only ironically attributed to Aschenbach. Mann also notes that the exhausted Aschenbach, with his strict and heroic work ethic, is a modern-day bourgeois. Furthermore, he calls his novella a problematic but an honest work of art. Compared to Barrès's *La mort de Venise* (1902), he adds, the tentative overcoming of decadence in *Death in Venice* is distinctly Protestant, Kantian, and Prussian. The novella is also a product of its time, its tensed will and its morbidity coming just before the First World War. As Mann observes, "sie ist auf ihre Art etwas Letztes, das Spätwerk einer Epoche, auf welches ungewisse Lichter des Neuen fallen" (in its way, it is something final, the late work of an epoch, [a work] onto which fall uncertain lights of the new) (XII, 212). He also says that he experimented with the rejection of psychologism and relativism, letting Aschenbach's will, morality, intolerance, and determination result in a skeptical and pessimistic catastrophe, and doubting that an artist could ever achieve dignity. Aschenbach's failure strikes Mann as moral, since doubt and despair seem more moral to Mann than either "Führer-Optimismus" (Führer-optimism) (XII, 517) or politically gullible democracy. Artists cannot achieve dignity, moreover, he writes, because they are caught between intellect and sensuality, the two souls at war in the breast of Goethe's Faust. Beauty partakes of both these extremes, as Plato says, and beauty is not the road to dignity. Accordingly, Aschenbach learns

> daß seinesgleichen notwendig liederlich und Abenteurer des Gefühles bleibe; daß die Meisterhaltung seines Stiles Lüge und Narrentum, sein Ehrenstand eine Posse, das Vertrauen der Menge zu ihm höchst lächerlich gewesen und Volks- und Jugenderziehung durch die Kunst ein gewagtes, zu verbietendes Unternehmen sei

> [that his sort necessarily remains dissolute and adventurers of feeling; that the masterly attitude of his style is a lie and foolishness, his honorable status a farce, the masses' trust in him supremely ridiculous, and the education of the people and youth through art a risky enterprise that ought to be forbidden.] (XII, 573)

In a second longer work, his *Lebensabriß* of 1930, Mann recalls his own trip to Venice in May 1911 and the series of curious circumstances and impressions that helped give rise to the idea realized in *Death in Venice.* He writes that he had intended the novella to be a quick improvisation and an interlude in his work on the yet unfinished novel *Bekenntnisse des Hochstaplers Felix Krull* (Confessions of the Confidence Man Felix Krull, 1954). Aschenbach's story acquired a will of its own, though, he adds, and went well beyond the meaning he had intended to give it. Its elements coalesced as if in a crystal, he remarks, and everything fit together. Actual details of his own trip were inherently symbolic and structurally appropriate. Nothing was invented. The wanderer at the cemetery in Munich, the dingy ship from Pola, the old dandy on it, the suspicious gondolier, Tadzio and his family, the departure thwarted by lost luggage, the outbreak of cholera, the honest travel agent, and the malevolent street singer — all he had to do was combine them. This fact, Mann goes on to say, helps explain why he felt transformed and borne along during the difficult process of writing the novella. The moved reaction of the friends to whom he read it at his summer house, he adds, prepared him for its stormy public reception. For German readers, it effected a moral rehabilitation of the author of the lighter *Königliche Hoheit,* he thinks, despite its dubious subject matter. Mann also notes with approval the sympathetic reception of *Death in Venice* in France, and he traces the interest taken in him by the Nobel Prize Committee to 1913, when this novella proved that he could go beyond his *Buddenbrooks.* In *Der Zauberberg* (The Magic Mountain, 1924), he also observes, he planned a comic reduction of his tragic treatment of the fascination with death, of the victory of supreme chaos over a life founded on and devoted to order. He took the easy tone of the later novel, he explains, as if to recover from the severity of the novella. Mann is also pleased that *Death in Venice* corresponds to *Der Zauberberg* just as *Tonio Kröger* corresponds to *Buddenbrooks;* it is the counterpart to that earlier, northern novella.

Mann made further remarks on his story in two lectures that he gave at Princeton University in May 1940. These lectures are known as *On Myself* and were published in 1966. In them, Mann notes that the fundamental motif that first occurs in his early *Der kleine Herr Friedemann* (Little Mr. Friedemann, 1897) recurs in *Death in Venice* and in the part of *Joseph und seine Brüder* (Joseph and His Brothers, 1933–43) about Potiphar's wife: the collapse of a carefully cultivated composure, the defeat of civilization and the howling triumph of suppressed drives. Mann also describes the subject of the novella as a devastating eruption of passion, the destruction of an ordered and a seemingly controlled life devalued and made to appear absurd by the "foreign god" Eros-Dionysus. Originally, he claims, he meant to write about the elderly Goethe's love for Ulrike von Levetzow, that is, about the degradation of intellect through a passion for life. He did not dare conjure the figure of Goethe, though, and instead created a modern "*Helden der Schwäche*" (hero of weakness) (XIII, 148–49), a hero with the external features of Gustav Mahler. Mann also notes that Aschenbach is not a naturalistic portrait of any actual model, however, but a heightened and stylized figure in which the features of such a model mix with material derived from other sources. He did portray Goethe in *Lotte in Weimar* (1939), and that novel, too, he explains, tells of a dignified artist who hides his true self from the world under a rigid mask. Finally, Mann comments that *Death in Venice* marked a turning point in European history as well as in his own career. The novella corresponded to the problem of individualism in the bourgeois epoch that was headed toward the catastrophe of the First World War, he maintains, and although his story contains elements of a post-bourgeois way of life, it takes them *ad absurdum*. His skepticism toward artists, whose sensuality keeps them from achieving true dignity, Mann adds, is more extreme in *Death in Venice* than in his earlier works. It is also a curious moral self-chastisement. His prose style, with intentional irony, displays the same dignified and masterful attitude that his story shows to be foolish and deceptive. He also observes that the story castigates his own pedagogical aspirations with almost flagellatory pessimism. It is his sharpest and most concentrated treatment of the problem of decadence and the artist. There was no going forward on the personal path that had led him to it, he says, and his friends wondered what he would do next.

Besides these three longer works, with their extensive remarks on *Death in Venice,* many of Mann's other writings briefly refer to the novella. Some of those writings reflect his patriotism during the First World War as well as his later political change of heart. In the essay *Gute Feldpost* (Good News from the Field, 1914), for example, Mann takes great pride in the fact that German soldiers encamped at Verdun have written to tell him that *Death in Venice* has never felt closer to them. To him, this news seemed to refute early critics of the novella:

> Ein Gebild, welches heute und dort *besteht,* vor den Augen derer, die dort draußen ein Leben der höchsten, wirklichsten Ehrenhaftigkeit führen, und welches ihnen "nie näher war", — kann es so falsch, so schmählich sein, wie viele von euch ausschrien, als ich es hingab? Welche Feuerprobe verlangt ihr, worin es sich als Affekt, als Geist, als Wahrheit bewähre?

> [A creation, which *holds its own* today and there, in the eyes of those who lead a life of the highest, most real honorableness out there, and which "was never nearer" to them — can it be as false, as disgraceful as many of you cried out when I presented it? What ordeal by fire do you demand in which it might prove itself as affect, as intellect, as truth?] (XIII, 527)

Besides putting these questions to his critics, Mann takes this good news about his novella as proof that intellect is justified in real life. Later, in a foreword to a volume of essays called *The Order of the Day* (1942), a foreword first published in *The Nation* in 1942, Mann claimed that *Death in Venice* was neither ignorant of the problems of its time nor unconcerned with them. He also observed that it was rooted in the German intellectual tradition that he had defended in *Betrachtungen eines Unpolitischen*. His subsequent distance from that tradition and its political manifestations was plain in an article that first appeared in the *Atlantic Monthly* in October 1944. Mann there expressed satisfaction with Georg Lukács's remark that one could not accurately judge the extreme patriotism Mann had displayed during the First World War without considering it together with *Death in Venice,* a novella about an ironically tragic demise of the Prussian ethic.

In addition to these statements about *Death in Venice* and the first of the two world wars, Mann made other remarks on it that anticipate the second. Those remarks link Aschenbach to National Socialism. Aschenbach and Hitler's agenda are related, Mann thought, since both are willfully irrational. In the essay *Bruder Hitler* (Brother Hitler, 1939), for example, he wrote that *Death in Venice* knows a thing or two about renouncing psychologism and about a new resoluteness and simplification of the psyche. He took these matters to a tragic conclusion in his novella, he maintains, and he distances himself from the extreme form they have since assumed:

> Ich war nicht ohne Kontakt mit den Hängen und Ambitionen der Zeit, mit dem, was kommen wollte und sollte, mit Strebungen, die zwanzig Jahre später zum Geschrei der Gasse wurden. Wer wundert sich, daß ich nichts mehr von ihnen wissen wollte, als sie auf den politischen Hund gekommen waren und sich auf einem Niveau austobten, vor dem nur primitivitätsverliebte Professoren und literarische Lakaien der Geistfeindlichkeit nicht zurückschrecken?

> [I was not without contact with the inclinations and ambitions of the time, with that which would and was to come, with strivings that, twenty years later, became a rallying cry on the streets. Who is surprised that I wanted nothing more to do with them when they had gone to the political dogs and played themselves out on a level from which only professors in love with primitivity and literary lackeys of the enemies of intellect do not recoil?] (XII, 850)

Mann had also considered this implication of *Death in Venice* in a diary entry from May 1933, an entry first published in his *Leiden an Deutschland* (Suffering from Germany, 1946). He there rails at those who had attacked his essay *Leiden und Größe Richard Wagners* (The Sufferings and Greatness of Richard Wagner, 1933). They are idiots, he writes, who pride themselves on having broken the shackles of rational analysis. These critics forget that he had had such thoughts twenty years ago, in *Death in Venice,* and that he therefore cannot entertain those thoughts with much enthusiasm, now that they have become so common. The manifesto denouncing Mann's essay — a *Protest der Wagner-Stadt München* (Protest of the Wagner-City of Munich) — likewise prompted a reply by Mann, a reply addressed to the composer Hans Pfitzner (1869–1949). Pfitzner had signed that manifesto and then remarked on it in an article that appeared in the *Frankfurter Zeitung* on 2 July 1933. Mann wrote his reply in France later that same month, though it was not published until 1974. He remarks that his thinking and writing are not without connections to the modern heroism that is now so proudly and so consciously opposed to a psychologism that degrades and enervates life. *Death in Venice*, he explains, tells of an artist who has set an example of a morality determined to deny, to reject, and to go beyond knowledge, insofar as such knowledge weakens and paralyzes the will, the deed, and the creative impulse. That the story ends badly, he says, does not disprove its author's interest in such heroism. He cannot praise such heroism as enthusiastically, though, he continues, as someone who has only recently discovered it. Finally, in a diary entry from March 1934 that was first published in 1946, again in his *Leiden an Deutschland*, he reported that a Nazi commissar visiting Switzerland, where Mann was living in exile, said that German pupils no longer read literary works such as *Death in Venice*. This commissar seemed ashamed, Mann notes, that the German niveau was so ruined.

Mann's remarks about his novella and its reception also mention how and why Austrian, German, and French responses to it differed. In a speech to the PEN-Club of Vienna on 11 June 1925, he observed that the best readers of *Death in Venice* lived in the Austrian capital. He made this same remark in his *Verhältnis zu Wien* (Relationship to Vienna, 1926). Perhaps such readers' skill had to do with the fact that Vienna was the home of Freud and psychoanalysis. In *Mein Verhältnis zur Psychoanalyse* (My Relationship to Psychoanalysis, 1925), Mann noted that psychoanalytic critics had been sympathetic to the novella. Those critics understood Aschenbach's determined denial of knowledge as an example of repression, he adds, but what gives such neurotic artists courage is better, albeit less scientifically, described as "ein Aufsichberuhen lassen" (a letting the matter rest) (XI, 749). In the essay *Freud und die Zukunft* (Freud and the Future, 1936), he similarly expressed his appreciation for the friendly interest that individual disciples and representatives of psychoanalysis had taken in his works, including *Death in Venice*. Both of these last two essays first appeared in Vienna. Mann thought that many responses to the novella in Germany, by contrast, had been colored by the literary and social status of novelists there. In his *German Letter [VI]*, which first appeared in *The Dial* in October 1925, Mann wrote that thanks to the social, moral, and intellectual upheavals that Germany has suffered since the war, novelists can now enjoy the public esteem previously reserved for playwrights. When he anticipated such national stature in *Death in Venice*, he recalls, people told him that doing so was not credible. In Germany, they said, no novelist could ever receive the honors accorded his Gustav von Aschenbach. In a letter to his fellow author Jakob Wassermann (1873–1934), a letter written in April 1921 and first published in a book about Wassermann in 1935, Mann said that novelists can never be as prominent in Germany as they are in France. In *Death in Venice*, he adds, he acted as if a German novelist could. In *Les Tendances Sprituelles de l'Allemagne d'Aujourd'hui* (The Spiritual Tendencies of Germany Today, 1927), a lecture given in Paris in January 1926, Mann praised Edmond Jaloux's remark that the novella demonstrates the traditional German attraction to death. As noted above, Jaloux's review appeared in 1925. In *Lebensabriß*, he similarly notes how well the novella fared among critics in France.

Mann's own estimation of the novella changed over time, and he often compared it to his other fiction. In an interview with Alfred Neumann in June 1920, he contrasted Aschenbach with Hans Castorp, the younger and healthier hero of *Der Zauberberg*, a work he calls more broadly epic than *Death in Venice*. In *Erfolg beim Publikum* (Success with the Public, 1928), he explained that *Death in Venice* corresponds to *Der Zauberberg* and is the literary counterpart to *Tonio Kröger*, as he would explain again in *Lebensabriß*. In a *curriculum vitae* first published in Sweden in 1930, the year after he received the Nobel Prize there, Mann called *Death in Venice*, along with *Tonio Kröger*, his most valid accomplishment in the field of the novella. In an interview with Karl Schriftgiesser in the *Washington Post* on 1 July 1935, Mann said that he liked *Death in Venice* best of all his own books. When he tried to explain why, a minor comedy ensued as he and his wife Katia took turns translating the word *geschlossen*. He said, "It is the most closed." She said, "The most accomplished." He said, "The most all right." She said, "What he means is, O.K." (6). Schriftgiesser adds that Mann, who had once told how death came to Venice in a heat-sent plague, did not like the sweltering summer in the District of Columbia. In an interview published in a Swedish newspaper on 1 September 1939 and signed "Colomba," Mann said that his new novel, *Lotte in Weimar*, was about Goethe, as he had originally wanted *Death in Venice* to be. As noted above, he made this same comment in *On Myself*. Further remarks on the novella occur in *Die Entstehung des Doktor Faustus* (The Genesis of Doctor Faustus, 1949). Commenting on how he incorporated Theodor W. Adorno's statements about the style of Beethoven's music into his novel *Doktor Faustus* (1947), Mann claimed that Adorno's ideas about death and form, about the ego and objectivity, were reminiscent of his own Venetian novella. He also approvingly quotes Lukács's remark of 1945 that *Death in Venice*, along with Heinrich Mann's *Der Untertan* (The Loyal Subject, 1918), signaled the danger of barbarism that lies within and that necessarily attends modern German civilization. Mann observes that this remark indicates the connections between that Venetian novella and *Doktor Faustus*. Finally, in an interview with Helmut Lamprecht that appeared in April 1953, Mann said he liked *Death in Venice* less than *Tonio Kröger*.

In addition to all the various foregoing comments on *Death in Venice*, Mann made statements about its hero's face, its setting, its length, and its publication. Those statements shed further light on what the novella meant to him. In a letter to Wolfgang Born that became, in 1921, the foreword to a book of Born's nine lithographs illustrating scenes from the novella, Mann told how he had given Aschenbach the facial features of Gustav Mahler. He had met the composer in Munich, he writes, and was impressed by his strong personality. While vacationing on Brioni, the Adriatic island that became the model for Aschenbach's stop on the way to Venice, he followed Austrian newspaper reports of Mahler's illness and death in May 1911. Still shaken by this event when he got the idea for his novella, he gave Aschenbach not only Mahler's first name but also his "Maske" (mask) (XI, 584). Writing to Born again in 1942, Mann expressed delight with two "intellectualized and surrealistic" (15) drawings of Aschenbach done by one of Born's students in America, Joan Waddell. Mann's statements about the location of the novella were sometimes light-hearted. In *Lübeck als geistige Lebensform* (Lübeck as an Intellectual Form of Life, 1926), he playfully dubbed the marzipan produced in his hometown "panis Marci," bread of St. Mark, the patron saint of Venice. He thus felt at home in the setting of *Death in Venice*, he explains, a tale which is, so to speak, marzipan. In a *curriculum vitae* originally published in English in 1936, he drew similar parallels. His statements about the length of his story mention how his works often turned out longer than he intended. In 1939, for example, introducing his *Zauberberg* to students at Princeton, he said that he had meant *Death in Venice* to be a short story for *Simplicissimus,* a satirical German magazine. Mann's statements about the publication of *Death in Venice* are no less revealing. In *Brief an Wolfgang von Weber* (Letter to Wolfgang von Weber, 1924), a letter written on the death of Hans von Weber, he recalled an irritating incident. Von Weber had published the limited luxury edition of the novella, apparently in late 1912. When Mann proofread the typescript, he missed two or three misprints, and this oversight upset von Weber's subscribers. That was bad, Mann says, and he still cannot pick up the handsome volume without feeling pangs of conscience. In a newspaper article published in December 1954, moreover, Mann told Georg Gerster that after he finished the novella in 1912, he seriously wondered if he should actually send it to the *Neue Rundschau*. Given the high status it had attained in the meantime, a status confirmed by almost all the authors cited in this chapter, Mann's reason for hesitating sounds incredible: "Ich fand sie einfach nicht gut genug" (I found it simply not good enough) (391).

# 3: Posthumous Praise, 1956–75

## Introduction

THE REPUTATION OF *Death in Venice* was further reinforced in the twenty years between Mann's death in 1955 and the centenary of his birth. During these two decades, scholars gained access to his archives and read his correspondence. Research based on these sources helped illuminate his ideas, his intentions, and the genesis of his text. Other research was more speculative and put the novella into broader perspectives. One group of studies treated it with regard to issues of aesthetics, artists, and Mann's other writings. These studies debated the ethics of Tadzio's beauty and its beholder; assessed Aschenbach's art, criticized his flaws, and examined his ego; and compared the characters, narration, and origin of the novella to those of fiction that Mann had planned, published, or would later write, or to his essays, treatises, and his own interpretations of it. A second group of studies focused on myths, sources, and comparisons. Their authors remarked on Hermes, Apollo, and Dionysus, especially as these gods figure in the works of Euripides, Nietzsche, and Erwin Rohde; tracked down sources in texts from ancient Greece and Rome or from eighteenth-century Germany; and linked *Death in Venice* to nineteenth and twentieth-century European and American literature. A third group of studies was concerned with style, symbols, and literary history. These studies stressed narrative nuances, subtle allusions, and wider ramifications of Mann's story, especially the gap between its author and its narrator. A fourth group interpreted that story in light of philosophy, politics, and psychoanalysis. Such studies related it to the intellectual history of German idealism; described it in the ideological terms of Marxist class consciousness; and treated it as a case study of oedipal conflict, repressed desire, suicidal impulses, fears and fantasies, sibling rivalry, Jungian archetypes, and neuroses and narcissism. A fifth group of studies raised other issues: fictional names, homosexuality and gender, decadence and death, the suspension of time, looks and language, and Italy and Venice. A sixth group concerned music, film, opera, art, and texts. These studies cited the life and works of Richard Wagner; or Gustav Mahler, whose music figures in Luchino Visconti's cinematic adaptation of Mann's story; or Benjamin Britten's operatic one; or works of art done to illustrate scenes from the story; or differences between Mann's life and literature, as well as the ambiguous artistry of his text. The biography of Mann by Peter de Mendelssohn, with its full account of how he wrote *Death in Venice,* thus brought to a conclusion, in 1975, two very fruitful decades of scholarship.

## Aesthetics, Artists, and Mann's Other Writings

As in 1913–14, many studies of *Death in Venice* published from 1956 to 1975 treated the related topics of aesthetics and artists, often with regard to Mann's other writings. Those about aesthetics considered art to be at war with the good in a great moral dilemma, read Aschenbach's story as an example of irreligious isolation, found fault with him and his author, or described differences between beauty in art and beauty in life. Those about artists found Aschenbach Faustian, tragic, decadent, or ambiguously motivated; criticized his lack of creativity, his criminal tendencies, and his pathologic moral decline; and probed his divided, problematic, and generally ambiguous self. Studies that regarded Mann's other writings examined the several works that he attributes to Aschenbach, expressed doubt about his interpretations of the novella, and linked it to his *Buddenbrooks, Tonio Kröger, Der Zauberberg,* or *Die Betrogene* (The Deceived Woman, 1953; translated as *The Black Swan*). In one way or another, all of these studies also compared and contrasted Aschenbach with his author.

Some critics concerned with aestheticism raised moral or religious issues. In 1956, George N. Shuster described Aschenbach's problem as serving high art with ascetic fidelity, as reverently as a monk at prayer. His sudden, sordid affair — "the flame in which he, unbelievably turned moth, must die" (25) — derives from his awareness of beauty. Mann's novella has universal cultural significance, Shuster adds, being an almost clinical dissection of an obsession, not in a Freudian sense, but rather of the European dedication to high art. A similar defeat of the will can be found in Paul Bourget's novel *Le Démon de midi* (1914), Shuster writes, but Mann describes the dichotomy between the beautiful and the good in the terms of a German romantic, revealing how beauty invades and destroys Aschenbach's egocentric cosmos. Shuster's moral approach is subtle, leading only occasionally to mild overstatement. Passages from Aschenbach's writings are included in German schoolbooks, but not because he enunciates noble ethical principles, and he does not garble Plato's *Phaedrus* so badly as to make its Socrates identify the good with lechery. He does not leave his initial vacation spot on the Adriatic, moreover, because he is "bored to the point of extinction" (28). In 1960, Anna Hellersberg-Wendriner argued that *Death in Venice* shows the ethical danger of living in aesthetic isolation. By equating form and death, she explains, it exaggerates Mann's main problem, the idea of detachment, treating it more radically than his other works. Such detachment is clear from Aschenbach's selfish art, from the fact that he never talks to Tadzio, and from his "Genealogie von Einsamkeiten" (genealogy of solitudes) (69), that is, his Silesian ancestors' unnatural careers in the service of foreign Prussia. The wanderer's contradictory appearance is a similar sign of unrelatedness, Hellersberg-Wendriner writes, and Aschenbach's sexual degeneracy likewise is a symbol of his self-absorption, since in Tadzio he loves merely himself. Such aesthetic symbols are also ontological, she notes, for they show a lack of transcendental connections and a death of form far from God.

Another reading of *Death in Venice* that mentioned aestheticism from a moral point of view was given by Ronald Gray in 1965. Gray argues that the novella only appears to be about yielding to a desire for perfect beauty, and he is harshly critical of both Aschenbach and Mann. According to him, Aschenbach is less concerned with artistic integrity than with public recognition. Considering all forms of human conduct acceptable, he deliberately deceives most of his readers. Sharing his amoral insights with them, Gray contends, would damage his prestige and be disastrous for his country. In Gray's opinion, Aschenbach wants fame even at the expense of truth, and Mann's story is itself untruthful. The description of a sunrise in its fourth chapter is a mere imitation of classicism, for example, an imitation meant to deceive, and a parody of rococo classicism rather than a faithfully imagined reality. Aschenbach's dream of Socrates near the end of the novella contains a "mass of illogicalities" (148), moreover, and his Socrates' remarks on beauty are irrelevant, since Aschenbach's pursuit of beauty reflects his own corruption and complacency. Gray also thinks Mann's meaning is ambiguous, since the end of the novella can be read as showing not only Aschenbach's ignominious collapse but also his assimilation into a greater perfection, into the nothingness symbolized by the sea. Aschenbach himself, Gray writes, is both a saint and a devil. Mann never deals with the issues of art, truth, and beauty, Gray goes on to say, and thus tricks and deceives his readers, whose ability to discern is mocked by his style. His contempt for those readers is pernicious, and he himself is an "insidious force for evil" (155). In drawing this drastic conclusion, Gray overlooks the fact that Aschenbach himself has foresworn moral relativism. More broadly, Gray also maintains that *Death in Venice* records a traditional German fatalism.

Other studies concluded that aestheticism in *Death in Venice* was more ambiguous. In 1963, Elisabeth Seidler-von Hippel wrote that Mann's theme is not errant sensuality or formlessness as such but rather the encounter of an artist with corporeal beauty that is perfect, that threatens an artist's critical distance, and that can lead to death. In 1965, Fritz Martini similarly argued that *Death in Venice* is not about a pathological tryst but rather about the conflict between aesthetic creativity and sensual, beautiful life. It is classical not only in that it alludes to Plato's concepts of beauty and to Greek myths, Martini writes, but also in its own concentrated narrative form. Its classical form is ironic and parodistic, moreover, insofar as it tells how Aschenbach descends into chaos and succumbs to the demonic. Beauty never loses its divine luster, though, since Tadzio summons him to a merciful, liberating death. In 1970, Frank Baron interpreted *Death in Venice* with the help of Mann's essay on Goethe's *Die Wahlverwandtschaften,* noting that Mann valued how that novel balances sensuality and morality. Mann's own second chapter expresses reservations about Aschenbach's greatness, Baron says, especially in matters of aesthetics. Aschenbach's preoccupation with form offsets his moral resolve, he adds, a fact that pertains to the phenomenon of all artistic creativity. Cynicism about art and artists seems justified, Baron claims, yet Aschenbach's defeat makes it possible to affirm their morality. Creative as well as destructive, the forces of morality and sensuality maintain a precarious tension in Mann's novella, an equilibrium depicted with its author's characteristic irony. In 1972, Erdmann Neumeister wrote that the novella poses the problem of beauty and truth in ways related to turn-of-the-century *Jugendstil,* which conceived of beauty as a synthesis of extremes like Mann's antitheses of love and lust or of knowledge and morality. In 1975, Claude Gandelman maintained that Aschenbach dies of an aesthetic narcissism that results from an excess of empathy with beauty. Mann notes this same empathy in his essay *Die Erotik Michelangelo's* (Michelangelo's Eroticism, 1950), Gandelman observes, and Michelangelo may have been one of his models for Aschenbach.

Further scholars saw Aschenbach as a Faustian, a tragic, a decadent, or an ambiguous artist. In 1958, Constance Urdang connected him to Faust. The true theme of *Death in Venice,* she writes, is that the artist cannot avoid his destiny, just as Faust could not avoid his. By renouncing the romantic abyss, Aschenbach tries to escape the punishment of Faust, to ignore the artist's Faustian role, a role he plays because his art is the result of evil and demonic forces. Whereas other critics liken Aschenbach to Faust because both are rejuvenated, Urdang thus suggests that Aschenbach sells his soul to the devil. She also discerns an overt reference to the Faust legend in his "dream Walpurgisnacht" (266). It may be stretching the evidence to find, in details of his early career, a "parallel to Faust's researches in all branches of knowledge" (266). Doing so, though, allows her to see in the novella "an initial statement of the Faust theme" (267). W. H. Rey regarded Aschenbach as a tragic figure, also in 1958. One reason for his tragedy is his one-sided disposition as he dies to life in order to create, Rey writes, adhering to an overstrained morality of discipline and form instead of achieving a harmony of human qualities. His position between intellectual relativism and emotional excess seems hopeless, but Mann shows a way out: the prospect of the infinite to which Tadzio points in the end. Aschenbach's death and transfiguration, moreover, come after he writes his short treatise at the beach, a work that accomplishes the artistic ideal for which he destroys — or rather, sacrifices — himself. In 1960, Georges Fourrier considered Aschenbach as one of Mann's variations on the theme of the artist. Fourrier describes the sources, narration, and subject of *Death in Venice,* arguing that it reveals an artist's education to be illusory and vain. In showing that decadence is inherent in artists' nature, he adds, Mann passes judgment not only on aesthetes like Stefan George, but also on partisan authors like his own brother Heinrich. In 1966, Anthony Woodward read the novella as the downfall of an aesthetic superman, a story in which "shaggy monsters of instinct" (162) recalling German romanticism add to a "sinister threnody" (165). Aschenbach's pursuit of beauty toward lower rather than higher things, though, makes his story a "*Symposium* in reverse" (165) as well, one that is unforgettably poignant and evoked with tragic compassion. Woodward also suggests that Mann resembled Tonio Kröger more than Aschenbach since his bourgeois values saved him from the latter's fate of ambiguous aestheticism.

Some scholars were highly critical of Aschenbach. To Margaret Church in 1962, he was a second-rate artist unable to synthesize beauty and truth. While Church may be right to note the similarity of the names of Aschenbach's stopover and Tadzio's homeland — "Pola" and "Poland" — she reads too much into their relationship when she adds that on one level Mann's story is about the "seduction and overcoming of other countries by a Germany which . . . has become a slave to its disciplined rigidity and thus subject to decay and death" (649). It is not true, moreover, that Aschenbach "throws himself on the darkened beach in an absurd and abject frenzy" (650). Finally, to call Aschenbach's vision at the cemetery a "rank African scene" (649) is to miss the point that he imagines the Indian origins of Dionysus. It is plausible, though, as Church says, that the camera left on the beach symbolizes the death of the artist. In 1970, C. A. M. Noble went even further, writing that Aschenbach is ill and criminal, a symbol of the pathology of artistic creativity. Psychologically abnormal and criminally irresponsible in Noble's view, he does dubious things such as entering his hotel by the back door. Noble lends emphasis to such claims by often putting them in italics. Aschenbach's reason for staying in Venice is of a "*purely personal, diseased-criminal kind*" (123), and by secretly pursuing Tadzio through its canals, "*He approaches his work in the same way that a criminal commits a crime*" (127). Thanks to his immoral love for Tadzio, "*The novella is the sublimation of a fundamentally criminal experience*" (121). Indeed, Aschenbach demonstrates "*the creative person's wavering on the threshold of the chaotic, diabolic, and criminal*" (119). Mann's bourgeois consciousness kept him from a similar life of crime, Noble thinks, and in Aschenbach he overcame his own criminal urges. In the end, even Noble recognizes that "criminal" may be too strong a word. More judiciously, Louis Leibrich added in 1974 that the novella poses the problem of a writer's moral responsibility. This problem involves spirituality as well as sensuality, Leibrich writes, and

Mann judges his solitary hero's comportment severely in his artistic but objective study of a pathological process of self-destruction.

Still other scholars discerned larger human issues in Mann's portrait of an artist. In 1962, Eugene McNamara argued that Mann makes an observation on living in harmony with diverse human nature, writes about being both spirit and matter, that is, both an angel and an animal. Aschenbach suffers from his "submerged animal nature," and his admiration of Botticelli's *St. Sebastian* suggests "sublimated masochism" (233). Mann's ambiguous imagery, McNamara adds, points to the destruction and disintegration of such a tragically divided self. In 1966, Horst Daemmrich similarly noted that the novella showed the dangers of the reflective-analytic artist's one-sided preoccupations with intellect and instinct. In 1967, Burton Pike considered *Death in Venice* Mann's finest illustration of a "problematic self" projected into the external world. According to Pike, Aschenbach is not a symbol for the artist in general. Instead, his public success is shabby and hints at his fatal misconception about an artist's function. He is a flawed artist who is acclaimed by a flawed society, a man whose will falters even before he sees Tadzio. The treatise that he writes on the beach is not art, and he is pathetic, not truly tragic. The narrator presents him in a negative light, then, providing a "whole sad catalogue of Aschenbach's deficiencies" (136). Pike also argues that the novella is built on the separation between the narrator and the protagonist, and that this distance increases as Aschenbach descends and the narrator rises. Aschenbach is deceived by appearances such as Tadzio, Pike contends, while the narrator sees their general, latent pattern and lends them mythical significance. The narrator is thus the real artist in the novella, and "Aschenbach is diminished so that the narrator may triumph" (137). In Mann's stylistic mimicry and in the autobiographical links to his protagonist, moreover, such a genuine artist is shown to create form out of existing chaos. Mann's resulting detachment enables him to project part of his problematic self onto Aschenbach and to exorcise it by destroying him in a ritual sacrifice. As Pike puts it: "Mann could call down the sentence of death vicariously on his totem, while remaining alive himself" (140).

Other scholars, too, regarded Aschenbach as an example of the artist's self, personality, or consciousness. In 1957, Hans M. Wolff explained how the author and the hero of the novella are related. The death of Aschenbach's wife, for example, corresponds to the long absence of Mann's, who went away to a sanatorium in Davos, Switzerland, in the spring of 1912. While Aschenbach has realized Tonio Kröger's aesthetic agenda of coldly conscious art, though, Mann shows how it leads to sterility and artistic decline. Mann's own later writings, Wolff adds, are accordingly less constrained. In 1963, Heinz Peter Pütz argued that Aschenbach, a writer, is less threatened by life than Mann's heroes who are musicians. Pütz also observes that Mann's artists and their audiences are bound by sympathy like the kind that obtains between

Aschenbach and his fictional public. In 1966, Peter Heller remarked on Mann's ambivalence and ambiguity. Like his other heroes, Heller explains, Aschenbach helps show how the phantasmagoria of temporal life is transparent, how sex is the agent of despiritualization, how artists can disparage art, and how a life led in public causes personal problems. As Heller writes, Aschenbach is "the victim of his own attempt to force his personality into the representative role" (201). Also in 1966, Ignace Feuerlicht linked the hero of *Death in Venice* to the nameless stranger who likewise wants a life free of egoistic constraint in Mann's other Venetian story, *Enttäuschung* (Disappointment, 1898). Aschenbach's need to spend his vacation at the sea, Feuerlicht thinks, reveals his nihilistic taste for chaos. Mann may have meant the novella to show that art has nothing to do with dignity and is incompatible with intellect, moreover, but if it is a *Candide* directed against art, it is one belied both by Mann's own narrative accomplishment and by the new kind of dignity Aschenbach wins in his pursuit of beauty and love, not to mention by the untarnished fame of his books. Feuerlicht may be right when he calls *Death in Venice* a critique of a particular kind of art, one that was not Mann's own, but he seems to put too much distance between Mann and Aschenbach when he adds that Mann never experimented with Aschenbach's classicistic style. Mann did so in *Death in Venice* itself. Feuerlicht, like Wolff and Heller, nonetheless shows how the novella ambivalently tells of a literary artist's loosening up and letting go. In 1971, finally, Gabriel Josipovici noted that the hero of *Death in Venice* is a man uncertain about the propriety of being an artist. Aschenbach is a normal, traditional novelist, he adds, who turns into a neurotic, romantic poet. He is not his author, however, who is able to describe his decline into silence. For Mann himself, *"the end is not silence but the articulation of silence"* (288).

Many of the foregoing studies of aestheticism and the artist in *Death in Venice* mention Mann's other works. Other studies draw more extensive comparisons between them. Some examine those that Mann himself had planned to write but then attributed to Aschenbach. Three such studies appeared in 1965. In that year, Hans Wysling interpreted the same long sentence about Aschenbach's works that Seidlin had subjected to stylistic close reading in 1947. Drawing on Mann's notebooks and on recently rediscovered letters, Wysling proves that between 1900 and 1911 Mann had conceived all of the works cited in that sentence — not only a novel about Frederick the Great, but also the novel *Maja*, the story *Ein Elender* (An Outcast) and the treatise *Geist und Kunst* (Intellect and Art). These last three titles left traces in Mann's subsequent notes and writings as well, Wysling claims, though he never finished any of them. Mann alludes to works that he did complete — to *Buddenbrooks, Fiorenza, Königliche Hoheit*, and *Felix Krull* — a few pages later in his second chapter, adding them, too, to Aschenbach's list of publications. Hans-Joachim Sandberg, also in 1965,

similarly noted that Mann describes Aschenbach's Schillerian aesthetic treatise in a way that reveals how ambitious his plans for *Geist und Kunst* had
been. Herbert Lehnert, again in 1965, compares Aschenbach's last work, the
short treatise he writes on the beach, to Mann's essay *Über die Kunst Richard Wagners*. Mann wrote this essay on stationery from the same hotel
where he has Aschenbach stay, Lehnert explains, and though Aschenbach
writes something very different, it is an autobiographical link to his author.
Mann is ambivalent about Wagner in the essay, Lehnert notes, but the
composer also suggested liberating possibilities for the use of myth, possibilities pursued in Mann's novella. Another study of *Geist und Kunst,* one
by T. J. Reed, appeared in 1966. According to Reed, this treatise figures as
one of Aschenbach's works "as a form of wish-fulfillment" (53), another of
Mann's unrealized plans that Aschenbach vicariously executes. In *Death in
Venice,* Mann experiments with a new literary approach, with a mature
classicality that he entertained while trying to write that treatise. The experiment ends tragically, though, for Aschenbach "had abandoned some of
the values Thomas Mann attached to *Literatur* — and had paid the price"
(95). In 1975, Peter Richner added that Mann symbolically completed a
novel about Frederick the Great by attributing it to his hero.

Mann's writings *on,* not just those *in,* his novella also received attention.
Those writings are mentioned at the end of the previous chapter. In 1964,
Herbert Lehnert cast a critical eye on the reliability of Mann's own, often
conflicting, interpretations of *Death in Venice.* Mann intended it to be more
serious, Lehnert thinks, than the light improvisation he recalled in *Lebensabriß,* perhaps planning a portrait of Goethe comparable to the earnest one of
Schiller given in his story *Schwere Stunde* (A Difficult Hour, 1905). His
interest in Goethe's late love affair with Ulrike von Levetzow and in the style
of *Die Wahlverwandtschaften* was serious and seems credible, and a similar
interest in Goethe figured in *Felix Krull.* Lehnert notes that Mann also told
how elements of *Death in Venice* had fused as if in a crystal, a simile Goethe
used in his autobiography to describe the composition of his *Die Leiden des
jungen Werthers.* In 1911, moreover, when he saw a Polish boy who served
as the model for Tadzio, Mann forwent love as Goethe once had. According
to Lehnert, the origin of *Death in Venice* lay in this combination of literary
plans and personal circumstances. Its transformation of satiric autobiography
into myth, however, goes beyond Goethe, he explains, and reveals the influence of Erwin Rohde's *Psyche* (1894), a book about Greek beliefs in the
immortality of the soul. Lehnert also explains how Mann's comments on the
novella during the First World War were defenses against its critics. Mann's
emphasis on its parodic style and on its hero's simplified morality, for example, were reactions to expressionistic critics. Lehnert does not agree with
Mann's statement that the novella denies all dignity to the artist, noting that
the ambiguity of Mann's art is lost in most of his self-interpretations. Indeed,

despite Mann's parody of classicism and his comments on current events, the novella is famous predominantly as fiction. Lehnert adds that Mann's later remarks on the novella link Aschenbach's Nietzschean disregard for knowledge to tenets of fascism. Mann himself thus started the ideological readings given by Lukács. Mann's own interpretations simplify his story, Lehnert concludes, offering insights but also leaving it tarnished. Readers take those interpretations seriously, Lehnert thinks, and criticizing them helps set his fiction free so that we can see it afresh.

Other studies likened *Death in Venice* to Mann's other fiction. In 1957, Joseph Mileck compared the novella to *Die Betrogene*. Mann started both after putting aside his *Felix Krull*, Mileck explains, and the heroine of the latter, Rosalie von Tümmler, undergoes essentially the same ordeal as Aschenbach, succumbing at the age of fifty to a passion accompanied by moral and physical dissolution. Mileck notes many striking similarities in these characters' mixed feelings, as well as the theme of life and death, which is highlighted by Mann's use of the colors red and yellow. Mann seems more sympathetic to Rosalie, apparently no longer feeling that "the consequences of a moral aberration need be as severe or as inevitable" (127–28), but her story expands and verifies the Schillerian moral philosophy of *Death in Venice*. Marianne Welter compared the same two works in 1965. *Die Betrogene* seems to be a pendant to *Death in Venice,* Welter writes, and Mann could be called the poet of late love. In both works, such love is that of an older person for a young man, and in both it takes the form of an illness dear to its sufferer. Rosalie von Tümmler's fate is not as severe as Aschenbach's because she is simple, Welter adds, whereas he knows what he is doing when he lets his neglected sex-drive take its final revenge. Welter seems to overrate the effect of this late love on his art. The essay he writes at the beach is his last work, as she observes, but Mann gives no hint that it is also his greatest. In 1969, Herbert Lehnert similarly drew a structural comparison between the novella and Mann's *Tristan* and *Tonio Kröger*. Like the last, he writes, it interests its readers in its hero but does not invite them to identify with him fully. Instead, the narrator remains at a distance and encourages readers to do so as well. Such readers are attracted by Aschenbach's attempt to transcend his bourgeois routine, Lehnert thinks, but are filled with anxiety by the loss of accustomed order. The narrator reinforces such ambivalence with his mix of internal and external perspectives on Aschenbach's life, providing readers both the liberating bliss of imaginary myths and the skeptical insight of the workaday world. According to Lehnert, Mann's sympathy thus belongs to bourgeois readers.

Other scholars compared *Death in Venice* to two of its author's great novels. In 1974, T. J. Reed analyzed the novella to explain the origins of *Der Zauberberg*. Mann, Reed writes, meant both works to show a fascination with death and the triumph of disorder. Many motifs in their heroes' trips and trysts are similar, he observes, and both convey an impression of fatefulness with the same stylistic means. The healthy Hans Castorp could thus have fallen even further than Aschenbach. In this way, Reed explains how Mann originally intended his famous *Bildungsroman* to be a satyr play and humoristic counterpart to the novella. In 1975, Helmut Koopmann twice compared *Death in Venice* to *Tonio Kröger* and to *Buddenbrooks*. In a book, Koopmann argued that Aschenbach, like the title character of the earlier novella, is a heightened version of Mann himself and embodies many of Mann's ideas and concerns. He is even a substitute for Mann, Koopmann claims, having finished several works that Mann had not. He is not the same as Mann, however, who had already overcome Aschenbach's problems. According to Koopmann, his story is nonetheless even more personal than *Buddenbrooks*. Like that novel, it treats the theme of fathers and sons, of successive generations. Aschenbach has no son, but he embodies youthful revolt as well as paternal tradition in a fruitful yet destructive way. This same conflict occurred within Mann himself, Koopmann adds, who now sees it from both the father's and the son's point of view. As in his novel, both the old and the new generations are destroyed. In many respects, Tadzio is like Hanno Buddenbrook, though, and in him the deceased Hanno lives. Koopmann made this last point in an article as well. He there writes that *Death in Venice* repeats and heightens the epiphany of the handsome boy that also occurs in *Buddenbrooks* and *Tonio Kröger*. Noting their similar ages and delicate physiques, he proclaims that "Tadzio ist Hanno redivivus" (Tadzio is Hanno redivivus) (61). In fact, he adds, Tadzio is unthinkable without Hanno; he is Hanno elevated to a god. He is not only a mythologized Hanno, moreover, but a personification of Mann's own youth and art as well.

## Myths, Sources, and Comparisons

Besides treating the themes of aesthetics and artists, and besides comparing *Death in Venice* to Mann's other works, studies of the novella that were published from 1956 to 1975 also examined its use of myth, cited its written sources, and compared it to texts by other authors. Scholars interested in myth noted Mann's penchant for Hermes; his parody of a "monomythic pattern" and of Nietzsche's *Die Geburt der Tragödie;* societal consequences of worshipping his "stranger god"; and the influence of Euripides, Schopenhauer, Wagner, and Nietzsche. Related research identified Mann's sources in writings by Erwin Rohde, Homer, Plato, Plutarch, Cicero, and Schiller. Comparative readings drew parallels between the novella and texts by Ernest Hemingway, August von Platen, Hermann Broch, Heinrich Mann, Joseph Conrad, Walter Pater, James Joyce, Leo Tolstoy and Anton Chekhov, Virgil, and André Gide. These studies of myths, sources, and comparable texts sometimes overlap, and boundaries between them are not always clear.

International in scope, though, and including both ancient and modern authors, they all help their reader put Mann's novella into literary-historical perspective.

One aspect of myth in *Death in Venice* is its introduction of Hermes. In 1956, Walter Jens maintained that the wanderer at the cemetery in Munich is not only Thanatos, a figure representing death, but also Hermes, who escorted dead souls to the underworld. The wanderer's hat recalls that god's similar *petasos*, Jens adds, and another, erotic incarnation of this god is Tadzio, who guides Aschenbach to a realm of both beauty and death. In an essay that expanded on a newspaper article she had written in 1955, Heidi Heimann noted in 1958 that Hermes is disguised in *Death in Venice* and leads Aschenbach on, instead of just leading him, more a seducer, that is, than a guide. Heimann also notes that Hermes is embodied not only in the wanderer and Tadzio, but also in the gondolier and the street singer. Like the wanderer, she explains, the gondolier wears a hat. Hermes invented the lyre, moreover, and the street singer plays a guitar. Atsushi Yamamoto reached similar conclusions about Hermes in 1960.

Mann's use of myth also appeared pioneering, but ironic and parodistic. In 1965, Isadore Traschen argued that Mann used myth earlier than T. S. Eliot or James Joyce. Indeed, *Death in Venice* was the first work to use "the mythic method as a way of giving shape and significance to contemporary history by manipulating a continuous parallel between contemporaneity and antiquity" (166). Traschen also applies Joseph Campbell's concept of "monomyth," the pattern that divides a hero's adventure into a departure, an initiation, and a return. Mann uses this mythic pattern ironically and parodistically, Traschen writes, and his story includes several "parodies of the transformation and rebirth of the monomythic hero" (171), including Aschenbach's surrender to maenads and his lack of transcendentalism. According to Traschen, Mann also treats Nietzsche's *Die Geburt der Tragödie* ironically, parodying its ideas: Aschenbach's dream is not a metaphor for Apollinian art, his demise does not suggest that Dionysus saves, and homosexuality is not the kind of "fraternal union" (177) that Nietzsche thought Apollinian and Dionysian forces should have. Traschen's insights are often astute: cliffs in Istria do not allow easy access to the sea, the object of Aschenbach's death-wish; Socrates had a snub-nose like that of the wanderer and of Mann's related characters; Saint Sebastian unwittingly charmed the homosexual emperor Diocletian and was also a patron saint in times of the plague; the gondolier's muttering foreshadows Tadzio's foreign language; Tadzio's curly hair is like the curling waves; Aschenbach is like Theseus when he loses his way in the streets of Venice; and the abandoned camera, a tripod reminiscent of Apollo's shrine at Delphi, suggests the death of Apollinian art. Traschen also astutely divides the events of Mann's novella into three phases: Christian, pagan-Apollinian, and pagan-Dionysian. Other remarks

94 ♦ POSTHUMOUS PRAISE, 1956–75

are too speculative or are inaccurate because Traschen quotes Lowe-Porter's deficient translation. At times, Traschen also discerns parody where none necessarily exists. Mann's suggestions of homosexuality, for example, do not mock Nietzsche's idea of a Dionysian "union between man and man" (176). In Nietzsche's German, the word occurring in this phrase is *Mensch,* which denotes human beings of either sex. It nonetheless seems right to conclude, as Traschen does, that Mann was ambiguous about using myth as a modern form of knowledge.

Mann's "stranger god" also occasioned a mild diatribe against assorted ills of modern life. In 1971, A. E. Dyson noted how Aschenbach falls victim to this "stranger god." A Bacchic interpretation of this fateful process seems justified by Mann's allusions to Euripides' *Bacchae,* Dyson writes, which tells a tale of similar repression and degradation. Bacchic forces determine Aschenbach's fate, too, and that fate is prophetic. Such forces, Dyson notes, have also led to the excesses of the Hitler Youth and Charles Manson. Dyson is especially troubled by the Bacchic fulfillments sought in the pop and drug culture of the 1960s. Aschenbach is a typical modern hero, Dyson says, and his story helps explain how modern life has become brutal and impoverished. It is post-Christian in that he cannot think of love without sex and egocentric possessiveness. Dyson thus opposes post-Freudian acceptance of the "nag of lust" (19). Aschenbach's antithesis of the bourgeois and the bohemian is similarly irreligious, Dyson remarks, and this antithesis attests to a coarseness of Mann's intellectual structure. In its artful telling, however, his story transcends this framework. By beautifully and memorably depicting the dark side of the dark gods, it is "one of those works of art which enriches our education, humanises our culture, haunts our imaginations, safeguards our religion itself" (14). According to Dyson, then, Aschenbach is a symptom of forces that shape modern squalor, and there is a God far stranger than Bacchus.

The function and meaning of myth in *Death in Venice* were analyzed especially well by Manfred Dierks in 1972. Dierks posits that Mann got the idea for *Death in Venice* — the fatality of Apollinian one-sidedness — from *Die Geburt der Tragödie.* Mann also found in Nietzsche a paradigm for his story: *The Bacchae.* Both Aschenbach's fate and Mann's narrative structure, Dierks explains, are modeled on this tragedy: Aschenbach is similar to Euripides' Pentheus, his and others' hats allude to the wreath worn by Dionysus, the wanderer and his successors are messengers of Dionysus, Venice resembles ancient Thebes, and the cholera epidemic recalls Dionysian ecstasy. Mann's interest in Nietzsche, Euripides, and Rohde's *Psyche* thus preceded and is more important than the influence of Lukács, Plato, and Plutarch, or than his scattered references to Greek mythology, Homer, and Xenophon. His relationship to myth was still dilettantish, Dierks adds, as is obvious from his references to Hermes. According to Dierks, Mann also made individual persons such as Aschenbach seem mythically typical in the manner of Wagner's operas, though he modified his symbolism in accordance with Nietzsche's sharp critique of Wagner in *Nietzsche contra Wagner* (1895). Mann's knowledge of metahistorical types also derives from Schopenhauer, he explains, as do Aschenbach's dream, the title of his novel *Maja*, and the idea that the sea suggests nirvana. Mann writes that Aschenbach was born in the Silesian city of "L.," moreover, which Dierks identifies as Liegnitz. Dierks notes that this city not only figured in the campaigns of Frederick the Great, but was also the site of a battle against the Golden Horde in 1241. Heinrich II of Silesia was killed then, and Aschenbach is likewise defeated by eastern or oriental forces. Among other things, *Death in Venice* is about this kind of cultural typology. Finally, Dierks shows that this same opposition of Asia to Europe, of the Dionysian to the Apollinian, underlies the relationship between the Egyptian priestess Mut-em-enet and the title character of Mann's *Joseph und seine Brüder*. In an appendix, Dierks adds selected notes that Mann made while composing *Death in Venice*. In 1969, Hans Wysling similarly maintained that the novella is an attempt to translate *Die Geburt der Tragödie* into the epic genre and that its scattered mythological motifs do not attest to an interest in myth as such.

In addition to describing how Mann employed myth, studies of *Death in Venice* also revealed and debated his specific sources. Two of those studies focused on Nietzsche's friend and correspondent Erwin Rohde and his *Psyche*. In 1959, Wolfgang Michael noted that Mann modeled Aschenbach's Dionysian dream on a passage from this book. Even his diction recalls Rohde's, Michael explains, though he transformed Rohde's scholarly prose into subtly structured and artful language. The main idea of the novella is tied to this dream, moreover, for the eruption of the Dionysian is Aschenbach's attempt to join a human community and thus to overcome every artist's feeling of loneliness. In 1964, Herbert Lehnert added that *Psyche* sparked Mann's general interest in myth. Myth complements naturalism in *Death in Venice*, Lehnert explains, and the world into which its narrator leads Aschenbach and its readers suggests a mythical interpretation. Rohde's book is a major source of that world. Mann marked passages in his copy, Lehnert adds, and his notes for the novella contain excerpts from it. Lehnert gives two examples cited by Mautner in 1952: the expression "House of Aides," and lines 560–69 from book IV of the *Odyssey*. Mann altered Rohde's translation of these lines, Lehnert argues, since he did not want to display learned material, but to transform Aschenbach by means of classical myth. Aschenbach's experience of the sunrise, details of the cult of Dionysus, and other passages more or less closely connected to the novella, he observes, are further examples of such borrowings from Rohde. Lehnert also argues that Aschenbach's decline, illness, passion, and death are superseded by his transformation as he opens his soul to a mythical world in a religious experience. Mann's feeling, Lehnert claims, was that "what Rohde writes is close to Aschenbach's fate" (301). A transformation into a life with Dionysus also occurs in Hugo von Hofmannsthal's *Ariadne auf Naxos* (Ariadne on Naxos), Lehnert thinks, and it is no accident that this libretto appeared in 1912, as did *Death in Venice.*

Two other studies related the novella to Homer's *Odyssey.* In 1963, John S. Martin told how Mann develops the theme of "Circean seduction" found in books X and XI of the *Odyssey.* Aschenbach is seduced both by Venice and by Tadzio, Martin says, and the latter stands in a dual relationship to him, as Circe does to Odysseus, enriching his life with unaccustomed abandonment. The theme of salvation through seduction illustrates Mann's mythical consciousness, then, and since it also occurs in *Der Zauberberg,* it supports his claim that he originally intended that novel as a humorous counterpart to the novella. In 1965, Herbert Lehnert acknowledged that another tidbit of *Death in Venice* comes from the *Odyssey.* The phrase "oft veränderten Schmuck und warme Bäder und Ruhe" (often changed jewels, and warm baths, and rest), he explains, comes from book VIII, line 249. Lehnert also notes that Mann used a version of Johann Heinrich Voss's famous German translation of Homer's epic, a translation first published in 1781. Mann likewise made incidental use of other lines from book VIII to describe Aschenbach, Tadzio, and Venice. As Lehnert sums up the significance of such lexical borrowings, "Classical beauty, restrained in dignified verses, is never allowed to be completely independent of the forces of dissolution" (307).

Three studies mentioned Mann's debt to Plato and other ancient authors. In 1966, Vittorio Santoli introduced an Italian collection of Mann's stories, observing how Mann treats some of his typical early themes with the help of Plato's *Phaedrus.* Nothing could be further removed from Plato, Santoli writes, than Aschenbach's romantic attraction to diseased beauty, however, and Plato did not condemn art, only artists. *Death in Venice* is thus a notable example of decadent neoclassicism, a modern work whose style and symbolism betray its author's Alexandrian imitativeness. In 1971, Willy R. Berger regarded Mann's allusions to Greek mythology, noting that Tadzio's similarity to Hyacinth and Narcissus derives from Ovid's *Metamorphoses;* that his pose on the balcony of the hotel during the street singers' performance recalls a passage in Philostratus; that Mann knew of Rohde as early as 1902, confirming that the elements of Greek antiquity in *Death in Venice* can be traced to Mann's interest in Nietzsche; and finally, that Mann's allusions to Plato range from loose paraphrases to literal quotations and help Aschenbach to sublimate his homoerotic passion. Berger thinks that Aschenbach's entire philosophy of art is Platonic as well, but he explains that Mann's knowledge of Plato came from reading Schopenhauer. Taking his cue from Berger, Ernst A. Schmidt, in 1974, studied the antinomy and antagonism of intellect and sensuality inherent in Mann's story. In a complex argument, Schmidt explains how intellect wanes, sensuality waxes, and the treatise Aschenbach writes at the beach synthesizes them. Aschenbach perverts and paganizes Plato's concept of intellectual eros, Schmidt thinks, as is clear from modifications that Mann makes when he paraphrases part of a dialogue on love from Plutarch's *Erotikos*. Aschenbach also alters the meaning of Plato's *Phaedrus* and *Symposium* by mistakenly equating his feelings for Tadzio with contemplation of beauty itself. Platonism thus turns into an alibi for pagan sensuality. According to Schmidt, Aschenbach's brief treatise can nonetheless synthesize Platonism and paganism, intellect and sensuality. Like a line from Euripides' *Stheneboia*, it demonstrates the effect of eros as a muse. By positing that Aschenbach otherwise misunderstands the Platonic concept of eros conveyed in Lukács's essay "Sehnsucht und Form" (Longing and Form, 1911), and that Mann knew Plutarch's *Erotikos* via Schopenhauer, Schmidt, like Santoli and Berger, regards the Platonism apparent in *Death in Venice* as derivative.

Another ancient author cited as a possible source of Mann's novella was Cicero. In 1967, John Conley related two of its passages to the Roman orator. The opening paragraph of the novella attributes the expression *motus animi continuus* to Cicero, Conley begins, so one might want to regard the image of a clenched fist, which Mann uses to indicate Aschenbach's strain, as another borrowing from Cicero. After all, he explains, Cicero uses it twice, in his *Orator* and his *Academica*. Mann himself, however, had written to Conley in 1946 that the Austrian poet Richard Beer-Hoffmann (1866–1945) once used this image to describe Hugo von Hofmannsthal. Besides, as Conley adds, Mann was known to have found the phrase *motus animi continuus* in one of Flaubert's letters in 1910. Answering Conley, Herbert Lehnert added in 1967 that Mann read Flaubert's letters in 1906 and that the image of a clenched fist also occurs in a letter by Goethe from 1823. Goethe there uses it to describe the effect of music, Lehnert writes, which he says makes him unwind in the way one lets a clenched fist relax. He does so just after referring to Ulrike von Levetzow, moreover, the young woman who inspired the passion in Goethe that Mann originally intended his novella to treat. Lehnert agrees, however, that Beer-Hoffmann is a better source insofar as the novella attributes the image to a man in Vienna. He also notes the rhythmic similarity of the names "Gustav von Aschenbach" and "Hugo von Hofmannsthal." Hofmannsthal thus seems to be another actual person partially embodied in Mann's protagonist.

Not all of Mann's possible sources were thought to date from antiquity. In 1966, Lida Kirchberger linked *Death in Venice* to the eighteenth century, in particular to Schiller. Citing Mann's published letters, Kirchberger argues that he planned the novella as early as March 1909. His speculations on the nature of beauty show the inspiration of eighteenth-century German writers, she adds, and the Homeric atmosphere of his fourth chapter suggests the meditatory influence of Goethe's *Die Leiden des jungen Werthers*. Prussian attributes innate to Frederick the Great, moreover, are only adopted by Aschenbach, who is from Silesia, a province whose conquest by Frederick is symbolic of Aschenbach's defeat. Kirchberger's main point is that Mann found a paradigm for his story of collapsed dignity and personal disintegration in Schiller's *Der Geisterseher* (The Ghost Seer, 1787). While there are many differences between these two works, she argues, there are also many similarities between their plots and narrative structures: both are set in Venice, both their heroes are emotionally deprived and fall victim to their sensuality, both involve envoys of death, and both relate the pursuit of a beloved who personifies an aesthetic ideal and discloses the mortal dangers of excessive preoccupation with beauty, a beloved made more alluring by his or her exotic, incomprehensible speech. Kirchberger cites such similarities to suggest that *Death in Venice* is an indictment of apolitical aestheticism and to connect it to Mann's novel *Königliche Hoheit.* "Mann," she explains, "must have been aware of the *Geisterseher* as a model for his Venetian Novelle" (331). *Death in Venice* therefore acknowledges Schiller more than Goethe.

Beyond citing Mann's sources, studies of his novella also compared it to other texts. Two such literary comparisons were drawn by Joachim Seyppel. In 1957, he explained how Mann's story and Hemingway's *Across the River and Into the Trees* (1950) both treat the theme of beauty and death in Venice. They do so differently, Seyppel says. Mann's novella is more psychological, Freudian, and philosophical, and Hemingway's hero is attracted to a woman, not to a boy. Both Aschenbach and Richard Cantwell are badly worn down, though; both begin womanless, homeless, and lonely; both go to their hotels in ominous boats; both observe bad weather that foreshadows their end; both encounter pleasure and death in the streets of Venice; both are rejuvenated by a hotel's barber; both fall in love with young people who embody classical perfection; both seem pure compared to the sexual creatures around them; both of their lovers are linked to the sun; cemeteries figure in both of their stories; and both die in Venice after decaying from within. It is not true, however, as Seyppel maintains, that Tadzio's mother is "mildly tolerating and even reluctantly encouraging in the ways of the woman eternally divided against herself" (11). In 1959, Seyppel drew similar parallels between Mann's hero and Platen. Like Aschenbach, Seyppel argues, Platen was devoted to beauty and drawn to Venice while in Munich. He also visited Venice in May, found himself oddly changed there, and bared his soul in love for a young man. In one of his Venetian sonnets, his beloved, too, looks like a work of art and is unattainable. Another sonnet describes the sights Aschenbach sees while approaching St. Mark's. Platen did not think he needed make-up like Aschenbach's, Seyppel adds, but he did fall ill after eating mushrooms that may have been poisonous and thereby resemble the strawberries Aschenbach ingests. Platen also fled Venice but hated to leave and did not do so before listening to musicians like those who perform for Mann's hero. Besides, Platen thought he might die of cholera and met a tragicomic end. His bureaucratic forebears and his interest in Poland are other parallels. Finally, according to Seyppel, the irony with which Mann describes Aschenbach is like the irony showered on Platen by Heinrich Heine.

Two scholars likened *Death in Venice* to Hermann Broch's *Der Tod des Vergil* (The Death of Virgil, 1945). As Doris Stephan showed in 1960, Broch's novel bears traces of the review of Mann's novella that he had written in 1913. Stephan cites similarities as well as differences: each novel treats a historical subject of current interest to its author, and Broch learned from Mann how to write about the problem of artistic creativity; in each, the main character is a poet or writer near death, guided by a boy in which he encounters both himself and his art; both Tadzio and Broch's Lysanias dominate a final scene set at the sea, moreover, and both represent Hermes Psychopompos, about whom Mann and Broch alike learned from the Hungarian mythologue Karl Kerényi. Stephan also observes that Broch's Virgil is conveyed in a trireme, sedan chair, and boat that correspond to Mann's gondola, and that his novel has a musical structure like the one he had discerned in *Death in Venice;* that Broch's prose, like Mann's, sometimes flows in hexameters, and that he quotes Virgil just as Mann quotes Homer, Xenophon, and Plato; and that both authors relate myth and music in the style of Richard Wagner. Broch, however, Stephan says, transforms such corresponding concepts according to his title character's attitude toward art, which differs from Aschenbach's. Stephan also argues that the sea symbolizes an end in Mann but a beginning in Broch, and that Broch is far more critical of beauty. In 1968, Manfred Durzak similarly revisited Broch's review, observing how its analysis of Aschenbach corresponds to Broch's own epistemological concerns. Durzak draws many of the same parallels of form and content as Stephan. He also faults her for describing Mann's concept of the sea too negatively. Like her, though, he thinks that Mann questions art less fundamentally than Broch. *Death in Venice* does so in the framework of a subjective antinomy of the artist and the bourgeois, he argues, whereas Broch's deeper reflections on the ethical relevance of beauty result in a new idea of poetry.

Other scholars compared Mann's story to works by his brother Heinrich. In 1962, Ulrich Weisstein noted that Aschenbach undergoes a development similar to that of the hero of Heinrich's *Professor Unrat* (1905), albeit in an artistic realm, with no social consequences. In 1967, Rolf N. Linn wrote that Unrat, like Aschenbach, is uneasy about the standards he upholds and that he surrenders to degradation and chaos. Unrat is less communicative than Aschenbach, however, Linn notes, whose dissolution is not such a public phenomenon. In 1972, Renate Werner read *Death in Venice* as a reply to Heinrich's *Die Göttinnen* (The Goddesses, 1903). Both books present the experience of beauty as orgiastic intoxication with life,

Werner argues, and show the demise of a protagonist in ecstasy. They are also similar in that some of their characters seem mythological and even have the same physiognomic features. Like Tadzio, she explains, Heinrich's Nino represents love and death, Eros and Hermes. Both boys also show symptoms of decadence. Such correspondences leave no doubt that Thomas consciously alludes to Heinrich's trilogy, Werner says, and he does so to criticize *l'art pour l'art*. The idea that beauty, as supreme perfection, transports its beholder is a Nietzschean one found in Heinrich's novel, she adds, and Aschenbach's reborn naïveté corresponds to the superficial aestheticism of Heinrich's heroine. Thomas concedes that aesthetic intoxication is essential to art, moreover, and Aschenbach's fate thereby repeats the fate of Heinrich's heroine Violante von Assy. According to Werner, Heinrich's essay on Platen in Italy likewise anticipates Aschenbach's fate. Werner also traces some of Aschenbach's traits to Heinrich's essay on Flaubert, claiming that Thomas associated its subject with the extremes shown in *Die Göttinnen* to describe how the cult of form could turn into unintellectual, sensual intoxication. Furthermore, Aschenbach's vision of a sultry tropical jungle alludes to a letter in which Flaubert regrets that he may never see the bright eyes of a tiger crouched in bamboo forests. In contrast to Wysling and Lehnert, Werner sees in Thomas's use of myth not a new beginning or a new classicality, but a result of his references to Heinrich's story. Thomas's irony reveals their fundamental difference, she says, and he criticized *Die Göttinnen* vehemently because he felt threatened by its aestheticism.

Another text compared to *Death in Venice* was Joseph Conrad's *Heart of Darkness* (1899). In 1961 and 1965, Lionel Trilling connected the two works, claiming that Mann describes the birth of tragedy in Aschenbach's orgiastic dream, a birth that he identifies with the ritual killing and eating of a goat whence tragedy is traditionally derived. Trilling also argues that Aschenbach's end is not tragic, since he becomes conscious of a new reality. Aschenbach does not die at the height of his powers, as Trilling claims, however, and though goats are mentioned and the bacchanals fall upon animals in Aschenbach's dream, Mann does not seem to recount any particular ritual sacrifice. In 1962, Harvey Gross added that Aschenbach and Conrad's Kurtz are both discontent with their civilization. They are culture heroes, Gross writes, and their stories are allegories of culture. Both feel destructive forces that their culture can no longer contain, and each breaks under the strain of "living beyond his psychic income" (136). Aschenbach's collapse is not as scandalous or public as Kurtz's, but his story, too, shows that "European civilization was built over a sinister fault" (139). Gross is justified in arguing that Aschenbach "descends into the chaos of the id" (138), but it is not so clear that he dies with the tragic knowledge that he has been punished for denying his own nature or that Mann shows how artistic creation results from preconscious terror, aggression, and disease.

Mann is indeed ambivalent and ironic, as Gross thinks, and one can certainly say that he thereby tames anarchic impulses and brings order to libidinal force, but it is not obvious, as Gross believes it is, that his novella is a parable that teaches us, too, how to handle such destructive powers. In 1975, Allan J. McIntyre drew a further comparison between *Heart of Darkness* and "its spiritual German cousin" (218). McIntyre remarks on the striking similarities of their themes, structure, and style: both are romantic critiques of civilized life, both express *fin de siècle* pessimism about the moral sickness of civilization, and both criticize entrepreneurial society; both books also recount a journey that is a descent and that involves encounters with death, and both link a psychic or moral landscape with the physical world in a symbolic style; Aschenbach and Conrad's Kurtz are both hollow, moreover, like the civilized enterprise they represent; and Aschenbach, like Kurtz, is also an exceptional man because he has abandoned his illusions and is honest with himself. McIntyre also observes that Aschenbach's name is epigonic, echoing that of Wolfram von Eschenbach (circa 1170–1220), the author of the medieval epic *Parzival* (circa 1210). While the name of this truly aristocratic medieval poet suggests the strength of the ash tree (*Esche*), he explains, that of Mann's belatedly ennobled protagonist implies that he is strained, tired, and ashen. Mann's "introverted athlete of the will" (222), in fact, soon becomes, in spirit, "a besotted pederast" (223).

Walter Pater and James Joyce were other authors writing in English whose works have been compared to Mann's novella. In 1968, Catherine Cox wrote that *Death in Venice* helps explain Pater's similar but less fully articulated *Apollo in Picardy* (1893). Their plots resemble each other, Cox explains, and each is furthered by "the motif of the 'return of the gods'" (144). Like Apollo, she adds, Tadzio and Pater's Apollyon are associated with music, the sun, and beauty — attributes that are mixed blessings for the men attracted to them. In search of perfect beauty, for example, Pater and Mann show how creative artists subject themselves to a cruel and degrading master. Such beauty enables each hero to see, but his resulting achievement of formal perfection fills each with disgust. Beauty is inspired by sensuousness that entails moral hazards, Cox notes, and to beauty the artist is sacrificed. Mann, Cox concludes, makes these points more artfully than Pater. In 1968 as well, Peter Egri studied the function of dreams and visions in *Death in Venice* and in Joyce's *Portrait of the Artist as a Young Man* (1914–15). Both stories explore the psychology of the artist, Egri writes, and dreams and visions in both suggest a new kind of literary representation. Similarities in the subject matter and in the treatment of the dreams and visions had by Aschenbach and Stephen Dedalus, he explains, reveal an expression and annihilation of the aesthetic attitude as well as the increasing importance of such subjective phenomena. Mann differs from Joyce in that the dreams he relates do not spill over into the objective world. Mann's distance from his hero, in fact, and Aschenbach's similarity to the autobiographical Dedalus mean that "Aschenbach stands nearer to Joyce than to Mann" (101). Egri's point is that Mann, unlike Joyce, modernized but did not disintegrate traditional realism. Egri also interprets Aschenbach's final dream differently than Trilling did in 1961 and 1965. Egri stresses the "horribly repulsive, suffocatingly stinking goats appearing in Aschenbach's dream and personifying his sins" (98).

Besides being compared to works by American, German, Austrian, Polish, English, and Irish authors, *Death in Venice* also seemed much like the life as well as the work of two Russians: Tolstoy and Chekhov. Alois Hofman, in 1967, related the novella to these authors' personal crises. Tolstoy was torn between the same extremes of lust and moral purity as Aschenbach, Hofman notes, and was seized by the same unrest when he considered his career as old age approached. Before the First World War, negative aspects of Tolstoy's character influenced Mann. According to Hofman, similar concerns with the meaning of life and the dubiousness of art relate Mann to Chekhov. The hero of the latter's *A Boring Story* (1889) is another Aschenbach, he explains, a successful and learned man who declines at the end of life. In addition to these parallels, Hofman draws forced connections between the novella and contemporary politics. It may be true that Aschenbach's fears and confusion, as he observes, were characteristic of the European intelligentsia. It is less persuasive to say that Mann criticizes literary colleagues who lack a simple, healthy relationship to their fellow men. According to Hofman, moreover, "Aschenbachs Weg zur Schönheit ist mit spitzen Steinen seiner unnatürlichen Leidenschaft gepflastert" (Aschenbach's path to beauty is paved with sharp stones of his unnatural passion) (252).

That passion was presented more understandingly by Ernst A. Schmidt in 1974. Whereas Stephan and Durzak compared Aschenbach to Broch's fictional Virgil in 1960 and 1968, respectively, Schmidt connected *Death in Venice* to the actual Virgil's second eclogue. The novella and this famous poem are revealingly related, he explains, not only because a poet or writer loves a boy in both, but also because both show a crucial link between pederasty and art. Parallels apparent from studying their genesis, Schmidt thinks, confirm the importance of this link for interpreting them. Virgil and Mann both first planned to write about heterosexual love, Schmidt says, then wrote about homosexual love instead. Rather than a grotesque novella about the aging and amorous Goethe, a story about dignity lost because of passion, Mann told the tale of the degradation of an artist as such. Goethe longed for renewed youth, but Aschenbach yearns for beauty. Like Virgil, Mann thus saw in pederasty a desire for beauty. He did so in his essay on Platen as well, Schmidt adds, an author whose influence on him corresponds to that of the Hellenistic poet Kallimachos on Virgil. Virgil's biographers do not distinguish him from his Corydon, Schmidt notes, as carefully as many scholars avoid automatically identifying Mann with Aschenbach.

Finally, in 1975, Frederick Wyatt compared *Death in Venice* to Gide's *L'immoraliste*. Mann's writings often suggest a "homo-erotic matrix of phantasies" (215), Wyatt argues, and his choice of the topic of his novella has "psychodynamic significance" (217n2). His motives for writing it may have included an infatuation with a man, Wyatt explains, but this possible unconscious attitude did not disrupt it, for it orders and controls its tale of dissolution and chaos. In this respect, *Death in Venice* differs from *L'immoraliste*. Both works involve travel to romantic, foreign places and a narcissistic fascination with beauty. Both are also records of inhibition and tell of characteristic male fantasies. Aschenbach's love includes strikingly little sexuality, though, and the eros at work in his attraction to Tadzio is not the explicitly homosexual kind that moves Gide's Michel. Instead, Wyatt continues, it may be hermaphroditic. In any case, the women in Mann's story are either distant memories, mindless girls, or cold and arrogant. Like sexuality in general, these women seem perilous and potentially destructive, and Aschenbach's so-called discipline may really be a deep fear of love. In sum, Mann and Gide may have chosen their related topics for similar reasons, but Mann's composition is more controlled, his conflict more contained. Wyatt seems unaware of the comparisons between Mann and Gide already drawn by Jaloux in 1925, Burke in 1931, and Lion in 1935. While he mentions Guérard's book of 1951, moreover, he cites 1969 as its date of publication and 1965 as that of Mann's review of it. These dates seem odd when one recalls that Mann died in 1955. Actually, his review had appeared, in English as well as German, in 1951. Furthermore, although Aschenbach does stand helplessly outside Tadzio's hotel room, Mann's readers do not find him, as Wyatt thinks, "mumbling a fervent declaration of love at the latter's door" (231).

## Style, Symbols, and Literary History

A third category of research on *Death in Venice* done from 1956 to 1975 consisted of remarks on its style, its symbols, and its place in literary history. Studies of its style looked into Mann's combination of what he called "myth plus psychology"; his famed irony; his classical rhetoric and linguistic consciousness; the motifs and narrative structure of his story; his integration of linguistic and thematic elements; his charlatanic artistry; and his parody, syntax, free indirect discourse, and suggestions of ancient Greece, as well as his phantasmagoria, diction, and grotesques. Research on its symbolism noted connotations of the sea and of various animals, as well as allusions to Greek mythology. Scholars mindful of literary history argued about its import as a German or a modern novella, or remarked on its similarity to the critic Samuel Lublinski's idea of neoclassicism and its parallels with the life and works of Goethe. This entire category of research thus concerned literary language, form, and tradition.

One important aspect of Mann's style is his combination of "myth plus psychology." In 1956, André von Gronicka defined these terms and the way Mann applies them, most notably in his novella, where he develops "a bifocal view of life that encompasses both the transcendent and the real" (191). His locale, plot, and characters spring from that view, which is rooted both in this world and in the realm of myth and legend. Mann "informs reality with myth's timeless grandeur," von Gronicka writes, "while rescuing myth from abstract remoteness and endowing it with a vibrant immediacy" (193). He synthesizes the present and the past, the contemporary world of bourgeois civilization and the wide vistas of our cultural heritage. His descriptions of Venice, for example, are at once naturalistic and stylized, providing realistic detail but also symbolical meaning. The wanderer is similarly both a Bavarian tourist and Satan, at once psychologically explicable and suggestive of a numinous atmosphere and surrealistic qualities. According to von Gronicka, Tadzio, too, is similarly a realistic character raised to the level of myth, a boy whose resemblance to Hyacinth, Hermes, and Narcissus can be explained as a figment of Aschenbach's imagination but who also seems symbolically divine to us. Aschenbach himself is both a case study and an eternal type, and Mann's ambivalent attitude toward him is the source of this "dialectical polarity of style" (201). Aschenbach's pet ravens at home, moreover, recall the mythological bird kept by the Nordic god Odin or Wodan. Finally, the passage from the *Odyssey* that Mautner regarded in 1952 identifies Aschenbach with Menelaus to suggest that Aschenbach's death, too, is an apotheosis. Mautner responded to this last point in 1958, noting that he and von Gronicka were both wrong about this passage, since Mann admitted he had never intended this parallel. Mautner seems to assume that texts should be interpreted according to their authors' intentions. In any case, von Gronicka amplified the foregoing remarks in 1970. He then said that the novella shows artists' ambivalent drives as well as its author's pessimistic awareness of such artists' "tragically problematical nature" (11). Echoing his remarks of 1956, he also calls the novella Mann's "psycho-mythical masterpiece" (110).

Another aspect of Mann's style that drew scholars' attention is his irony. In 1958, Erich Heller wrote that Mann's experiments with the incongruity of meaning and manner, the ironical juxtaposition of substance and form, were most successful in his novella, where "a composition of classical order and serenity is used to tell a most unclassical tale of disorder and decomposition" (23). Mann's parodistic idiom also distinguishes him from Aschenbach, even though his "parodistic semblance of mythic innocence" (100) indicates their similarity. His poetic account of Aschenbach's obsession parodies the classical manner with Wagnerian methods, moreover, and *Death in Venice* is not only a parody, but also a paradox, a work of art that rejects art itself. Does such a paradox, Heller asks, deserve to be taken seriously?

Heller thinks so, concluding that it is an ironic assertion of Mann's radical moralism. In any case, Heller justifiably laments that Mann's irony often gets lost in translation: "In English, alas, the ironically draped velvet and silk often look like solemnly donned corduroy and tweed" (103). In 1960, John G. Root applied Friedrich Schlegel's romantic concept of irony to analyze the effect of Mann's syntactical patterns. *Death in Venice* is a unique source of syntactical irony, Root explains, a variant of stylistic irony that is more subtle than semantic or situational irony. Mann achieves such syntactical irony, he adds, by using the devices of recurrence, digression, oscillation, and apposition, not to mention the parody of externals, that is, parody implying that outward behavior does not reveal inner nature. All these devices detach Mann from Aschenbach, Root says, opening a gap between them meant to be sensed by Mann's readers. In 1964, Reinhard Baumgart read Aschenbach's story as one of ironic disillusionment. Aschenbach, Baumgart thinks, has forgone ironic impartiality in his rejection of relativistic knowledge. Mann's irony is negative insofar as it exposes Aschenbach's pathetic ideal without offering an alternative, he adds, and it is liberating insofar as it replaces his illusion with reality. It is also transparent in Mann's final line, which broadly hints that Aschenbach was not what he seemed. Usually more subtle, according to Baumgart, ironic consciousness in Mann's novella overcomes the pathos of the ascetic ideal.

Other studies presented *Death in Venice* as a demonstration of Mann's classical rhetoric or linguistic consciousness. In 1964, Frederic Amory argued that the novella should be read as a fictional life written in the classical style of Alexandrian biographies. Like ancient authors of such lives, Amory claims, Mann had to deal with the fact that his hero's outward deeds were unremarkable and not worth recording. He did so rhetorically, Amory adds, maintaining an interaction of words and deeds that does not exist, a discrepancy that characterizes and condemns Aschenbach. Amassing content and manipulating detail, he compensated for his hero's lack of an external life. Mann had to impose artistic unity, though, without unduly verbalizing phenomena. Accordingly, he employed learned as well as artistic prose, stylistically shifting between metonymy and metaphor, between realism and symbolism. His stylisms include parallelisms, periphrasis, and epithets, and his configuration of biographical form, euphemistic style, and erotic content also occurs in Christoph Martin Wieland's novel *Agathon* (1767). Amory also notes that Mann recorded the last instance of pandemic disease in Europe, the Asiatic cholera of the summer of 1911. In 1969, Ulrich Dittmann took a related approach to Mann's narration. *Death in Venice,* Dittmann argues, addresses a skepticism toward language that Mann shared with Nietzsche and Hugo von Hofmannsthal. Indirectly, Dittmann adds, Mann overcomes this skepticism. He suggests correspondences between internal and external realms of reality, and he implicitly criticizes Aschenbach's aestheticism. His narrator — whom Dittmann takes to be Mann himself — is more conscious than Aschenbach, and the language of the novella negatively indicates a universal human wholeness. Mann's knowledge that artistic language is self-satisfied (Dittmann seems to mean that Mann thought such language merely self-referential) prevents him from presenting such wholeness directly. Amory's argument is sometimes obscured by its dense stylistic details, and Dittmann's often sounds vague, thanks to its theoretical abstractness. Both, however, reveal how Mann's words help constitute what he describes and how they thus confer meaning on his story.

In 1964, Walter Weiss examined Mann's art of linguistic and thematic integration. He noted several elements of Mann's style. He explains, for example, how Mann transforms adjectives into nouns that identify his fictional characters. The first sentence of *Death in Venice* states that Aschenbach went for a walk alone, and he then grows increasingly isolated, described as "der Einsame" (the solitary). When he first sees Tadzio, he finds him perfectly beautiful, and Mann later refers to the boy as "der Schöne" (the beautiful [one]). Weiss also analyzes how gestures are used to suggest the opposition of closed form to letting go. Aschenbach's life had been like a clenched fist, for example, but he relaxes his hands and arms when he accepts his fate and declares his love for Tadzio. His laughter on his way back to the Lido after he misses his train is another gesture that indicates dissolution, Weiss argues, as is his urge to skip school, that is, to flee from order and duty. The distortion of the facial features of Mann's messengers of death thus should not be seen in isolation. What is more, according to Weiss, the word "Tadzio" is music to Aschenbach, which shows Mann's suggestive use of names, and the sea, swamp, and jungle that Mann describes are landscapes that occur in his other fiction, too. The image of the sea in *Death in Venice* is also connected to its themes of expansion, alienation, and relaxation, not least since it is a horizontal plane, and Venice is a swamp like the one Aschenbach envisions in Munich. Weiss also notes leitmotifs that recur in almost all Mann's works. The hourglass Aschenbach recalls is such a motif. The characters who prefigure his death come from far away, moreover, and suggest the importance to Mann's heroes of the far-reaching and far-off. *Death in Venice,* Weiss adds, exemplifies the repetition and connection of these and other leitmotifs. Not only does it contain the linear repetition of motifs such as the Byzantine architecture Aschenbach sees in Munich as well as Venice; almost all of the various leitmotifs are also related by being described as alien, alienating, or alienated. They thus contrast with what is usual for him, and they contribute to Mann's antithesis of tension and relaxation, order and chaos. Weiss also observes that antithesis makes Mann's irony more pointed in some of his works, including *Death in Venice,* than in others; that the novella belongs to those works whose dialectic is unresolved; that he quotes himself when he describes Cipolla, in *Mario und der Zauberer*

(Mario and the Magician, 1930), in terms he had already applied to the ticket-seller on the boat to Venice; and that Cipolla shares the homoeroticism of Mann's solitary artists such as Aschenbach.

The motifs and narrative structure of *Death in Venice* were similarly analyzed by Hans W. Nicklas in 1968. Nicklas's study was the first monograph on Mann's novella, and it treats those motifs and that structure at considerable length. It often adds little to what had already been known, but besides surveying the extant secondary literature, Nicklas makes several trenchant points. He explains that the tropical vegetation in Aschenbach's initial vision includes lotus flowers, which symbolize beauty rooted in chaos and which lure Aschenbach, like Odysseus, into lethargy. Between this initial vision and Aschenbach's bacchantic dream, a series of trance-like states shows him drawn to the realm of death or Tadzio. A narrator's presence, Nicklas adds, is palpable in comments, judgments, interruptions, and intrusions. This narrator both evaluates and explains Aschenbach's behavior, though often otherwise presenting Aschenbach's point of view. According to Nicklas, moreover, Aschenbach's conversations with the gondolier, English clerk, and hotel barber reveal his passivity and increasing loss of control, while his discussions with himself, inner monologues, reported thoughts, and free indirect discourse show how Mann focuses on internal events. Irony in the novella is direct less often than it is compository, Nicklas notes, apparent only after Mann's plot proves initial appearances deceptive. Aschenbach can be ironic about his fatal attraction, but his irony is itself ironic, a transparent attempt to maintain his intellectual superiority to events and emotions that destroy his dignity. He leaves Munich two weeks after deciding to do so, moreover, travels for twelve days before arriving in Venice, and stays there for five or six weeks. The events in the novella thus occur over the course of nine weeks. The weather, Nicklas says, plays a part in the story by paralleling his moods, helping lull him into complacency, and spreading cholera. Furthermore, the title of the novella anticipates its ending, making what happens seem less urgent than how it comes to pass and thereby helping integrate its motifs. Nicklas's main point, in fact, is that the form and content of the novella are inseparable and that Mann integrates all his motifs into one seamless whole.

Another, related interpretation of Mann's style in *Death in Venice* was given by Eva Brann in 1972. Brann claims that Aschenbach and his author are charlatans, then tells why the novella is nonetheless worth studying. Mann's descriptive use of words and his compositional care, she explains, along with the timeliness of his story, make it interesting. It also tries to comes to terms with the decadence of modernity. To these main aspects of Mann's artistry, Brann adds seven spheres of reference. In the autobiographical sphere, Aschenbach's professional crisis parallels Mann's; in the cosmopolitan sphere represented by the hotel manager, modern means of transportation suggest that Aschenbach's "secret and catastrophic adventure of the soul" (2) occurs against a background of progress or civilization that is French; in the topography of Mann's spiritual sphere, the North, South, East, and West stand, respectively, for melancholy, decadence, lust, and rationality; the Protestant sphere reveals Aschenbach's silent innerliness and his ascetic "Kantianism of decadence" (3); in a further sphere, Mann imitates the style of Goethe's prose; in the sphere of romanticism or counter-revolution, the passion his hero feels is musical and fatal; in that of Greek antiquity, Mann refers to myths, statues, Homer, and Xenophon, usually when he describes Tadzio. In Mann's diction, composition, and modernity, that is, his battle with decadence, Brann also observes parody. That he lends his story meaning by referring to Greek myths — that such reference itself *is* meaning — strikes her as unsafe but better than ignorant and brutal varieties of decadence. Mann's parodistic style derives from his romantic irony, she adds, and the polarities he describes come from Schiller, Schopenhauer, and Nietzsche. His novella is about the "decadent artist's confrontation with a living work of art" (8), moreover, and in Aschenbach's apostrophes to his Venetian Phaedrus, his two soliloquies addressed to Tadzio, Mann parodies and reverses Plato. The problem Mann poses is that of "romantic reaction" and of a "false relation to the passions and to the past" (9). This conclusion comes at the end of Brann's odd apology for reading *Death in Venice*, an apology that praises but also distrusts Mann's language, parody, and irony. Odd, too, is Brann's declaration that the novella is set in 1909.

Other research mentioned further characteristics of Mann's style. In 1963, Hermann Stresau called the novella a parody of a purely formal existence, citing its parodistic use of Homeric hexameters along with the tension created by Mann's long sentences. In 1965, Werner Hoffmeister remarked on Mann's skilled use of free indirect discourse, by which he conveys his hero's strict intellectual consciousness of the external world. According to Walter A. Berendsohn, also in 1965, the most important element of Mann's style is his suggestion of ancient Greece. In 1971, R. J. Hollingdale explained that the novella achieves the "total transformation of reality into phantasmagoria" (90). Details of Mann's story deprive it of all realism, Hollingdale maintains, leaving nothing naturalistic. Aschenbach is less a character than a concept, moreover, and the most striking thing about *Death in Venice* is the utter lack of sympathy shown for its wretched hero. His world becomes so unreal, in fact, because we must not be emotionally affected by his death, not be able to pity him. These claims about Mann's style and its motivation seem one-sided. Hollingdale likewise oversimplifies the case by calling Aschenbach's end "as meaningless a death as any man could well die" (94). In 1975, Hans Ternes argued that both the demonic characters whom Aschenbach encounters and his own tragicomic loss of dignity are grotesque. Mann, Ternes posits, may have known Jacques Callot's sketch of a guitarist who looks like the dubious street singer at Aschenbach's hotel. In any event, Mann's pseudo-classical style softens the effect of the grotesque, he explains, which is not as nastily distorted in *Death in Venice* as it had been in his earlier stories. Erich Fried, also in 1975, argued that one could no longer describe death as Mann did when he described the wanderer. The way people die in modern life had made such an exaggerated description anachronistic even before Mann wrote it, Fried maintains, and even if he meant to parody the polite convention of such descriptions, less would have been more. Fried, himself a poet and a creative writer, seems eager to escape Mann's shadow. Again in 1975, and perhaps for similar reasons, Wolfgang Koeppen, whose novel *Der Tod in Rom* (Death in Rome, 1954) alludes to Mann's story, similarly praised its author and its hero only ironically.

Related to studies of Mann's style were those that interpreted his symbols. In 1965, Bengt Algot Sørensen claimed that *Death in Venice* transforms the real world into dreams and suspends time, and that it does so in connection with the experience of the sea as an intellectual glimpse of eternity. This circumstance, Sørensen argues, determines its symbolism. In 1967, Hertha Krotkoff identified the two apocalyptic animals flanking the stairs above which Mann's wanderer appears as those symbolic of the Antichrist in Revelation 13. Since Krotkoff did not find these animals when she visited the burial chapel in Munich that Mann describes, she concludes that he invented them to suggest that Aschenbach's actions are evil. The furrows on the wanderer's forehead recall marks cited later in Revelation 13, she says, and thus show that he worships such animals. The scene at the cemetery thereby hints that Aschenbach will be judged from a Christian point of view. Quoting Carl Gustav Jung, Krotkoff adds that the tiger in Aschenbach's vision is the dynamic force hidden in his unconscious. In his orgiastic dream, this force is sexual, she writes, as is implied by the fact that Dionysus rode a tiger on the way to India. While the apocalyptic animals stand for Christianity, moreover, the tiger represents ancient Greece. In these symbols, readers encounter equivalent myths from different cultures. Krotkoff also notes how both the burial chapel in Munich and the cathedral in Venice convey Aschenbach's state of mind; how Tadzio's sailor-suit links him not only to the sea, but also to the similarly dressed gondolier; how that gondolier and the characters like him resemble the goatish Pan and thereby underscore the sensuality of Aschenbach's "panic life"; and how Aschenbach drinks pomegranate juice that ties him both to Persephone and to Dionysus. Like Krotkoff, but in 1971, Christoph Geiser mentioned animals. The exotic birds in Aschenbach's jungle, Geiser writes, foreshadow the beauty, dissolution, and immobility that kill him. By recalling similar birds in poems by Charles Baudelaire, and by analyzing Aschenbach according to Stéphane Mallarmé's idea of *stérilité*, Geiser relates Mann's symbols in *Death in Venice* to French symbolism.

Mann's symbolism also figured in studies that read his story with regard to the genre of the German novella. In 1956, Benno von Wiese expanded the argument that he had made the previous year. Taking issue with Martini's essay of 1954, von Wiese contends that events in *Death in Venice* are symbolic. Mann's treatment of them, he explains, makes his story a modern dance of death. Without his symbolism, that story would be nothing more than a psychological study, a pathological case of perverted love. Beyond their psychological motivation, for example, the wanderer and Aschenbach's vision both have mythological import. Contradicting the claims made by Venable in 1938, however, von Wiese adds that Mann's several messengers of death — the wanderer, cashier on the boat, gondolier, street singer, and Tadzio — are all ambiguous, seeming real as well as symbolic. They are not merely figments of Aschenbach's imagination, and their symbolic connection is suggested by Mann's mention of their teeth. Such symbolism is both deliberate and disguised, von Wiese writes, and Mann makes symbolic interpretation possible without making it obvious or absolutely necessary. He thus treats his symbols consciously, playfully, and ironically. In sum, Mann's symbols make cholera and Aschenbach's passion seem two manifestations of the same demonic disruption. According to von Wiese, that symbolism is consciously artistic, though, not cosmic, and it is valid only for *Death in Venice*. In its symbolic density, von Wiese says, Mann's novella meets requirements of its genre, but the deliberate and limited functionalism of his symbols also runs the risk of losing epic gravity. In 1957, Fritz Lockemann noted the artificiality of Mann's symbols. He also observed that *Death in Venice* is a novella about chaos and as such is at odds with the conventions of the genre established by Boccaccio. In 1975, Mary Doyle Springer read Mann's story as an example of "degenerative 'tragedy'" in the genre. We would feel affectionate concern for the hero of a genuine tragedy, Springer remarks. "For Aschenbach," however, "we cannot weep" (104). Perhaps Springer thinks this because she misconstrues his vain attempt to leave Venice as the result of merely physical enervation.

Another approach to such issues was taken by Hans Rudolf Vaget in 1973. Although he liked to portray himself as an intellectual loner, Vaget argues, Mann was firmly rooted in contemporary literary life. The theme and artistic character of *Death in Venice* betray the influence of neoclassicism, Vaget explains, and without this literary movement in early twentieth-century Germany, he would not have written his story the way he did. According to Vaget, Aschenbach takes tenets of that movement *ad absurdum,* and Mann thus exposes its pedagogical claims. He thereby also analyzes anti-social and anti-psychological currents as well as the Prussian work ethic of his time. This criticism of neoclassicism, however, Vaget adds, came only after he had entertained it himself. As shown by his letters of 1904–10, Samuel Lublinski was his most important connection to it. He also alludes to Lublinski in the second chapter of *Death in Venice,* which mentions an incisive and intelligent critic. This critic's remark that Aschenbach's kind of hero is a modern St. Sebastian, Vaget observes, is a literal quotation from Lublinski's favorable remarks on

Mann's *Buddenbrooks*. Having become skeptical of Wagner, Vaget says, Mann turned to neoclassicism and, because of Lublinski, looked instead to Goethe and Nietzsche. Mann's revival of Greek myth can likewise be traced to his exchange of ideas with Lublinski, Vaget adds, who opposed it. Vaget recalls that such a modern revival also occurs in the second part of Goethe's *Faust*. Aschenbach's journey to Venice has a model in Goethe's Classical Walpurgis Night and in his episodes about Helen of Troy. A further element of *Faust* that recurs in Mann's novella is Hermes, who guides souls in both works. According to Vaget, then, Samuel Lublinski stimulated a re-orientation in Mann first manifested in *Death in Venice*. In 1975, Vaget adduced further proof of how the novella shows Mann's growing interest in Goethe. It addresses the problem of being a public figure, he explains, a problem faced by both authors. It also contains a wealth of Goethean elements, though it is not the grotesque account of Goethe's senile passion that Mann initially planned, starting in 1905. Its narrative art, economy, and musicality, Vaget maintains, all derive from Goethe's *Die Wahlverwandtschaften*. From that novel, Mann learned how to use motifs such as symbolic gestures. When Aschenbach leans his head on Tadzio's door, moreover, and gives the begging street singer a very large coin, he follows examples set by Goethe's Eduard. What is more, in *Faust* (ll. 9220–31), Goethe describes Hermes in language like that used to characterize Tadzio at the end of Mann's story. That story is not as parodistic as Mann sometimes claimed, Vaget notes, but its genesis, themes, structure, and style leave no doubt that it is a product of his initial reception of Goethe. It is therefore a turning point in the development of Mann's oeuvre. In 1978, Vaget added that Mann's interest in neoclassicism reflected his reading of Lukács's *Die Seele und die Formen* (The Soul and the Forms, 1911).

## Philosophy, Politics, and Psychoanalysis

The application of philosophical, political, and psychoanalytic concepts to *Death in Venice* resulted in a fourth kind of research conducted from 1956 to 1975. Scholars interested in philosophy interpreted the novella according to Schopenhauer's concept of the will, Hegelian logic and irony, the tradition of German idealism and romanticism represented by Schiller and Heinrich von Kleist, and Nietzsche's ideas of Apollo and Dionysus. Scholars concerned with politics often castigated Aschenbach and the Prussian bourgeoisie in Marxist readings less subtle than the ones Lukács had given between 1944 and 1955. Such scholars routinely found the bourgeoisie barbaric and a precursor of fascism. Marxist politics were also linked to liberating eros from bourgeois constraints. Practicing psychoanalysts considered the novella both in remarks on Mann and his protagonist, and during their treatment of real-life patients, demonstrating more or less literary sophistication. Several literary scholars, too, read it in light of Freud. While most studies cited so far in this chapter regarded *Death in Venice* as a work of literary art, the approaches examined in this section often treated it as proof of some preconceived, nonliterary theory. These approaches differ from each other in many ways, but they are alike insofar as they almost always use Mann's story as grist for an abstract, ideological, or otherwise speculative mill.

Philosophical readings displayed this tendency in varying degrees. In 1957, Fritz Kaufmann observed that a passage in the fourth chapter — "Der strenge und reine Wille jedoch . . ." (The strict and pure will, however . . .) — best demonstrates Mann's idea that artists' representations manifest the universal will. This idea, Kaufmann writes, shows how highly Mann regarded Schopenhauer. Since Mann was skeptical about regaining a "classical" naïveté, moreover, Aschenbach is "an abortive attempt to overcome the predicament of the modern artist" (95). Mann himself was more dialectical. Kaufmann also traces Mann's Sebastian motif to the young Goethe. In 1964, Rainulf A. Stelzmann read the novella as "an exercise in, and a masterpiece of, Hegelian logic and irony" (161). It fuses opposite elements such as reality and unreality, Stelzmann explains, and thus is reminiscent of Hegel. In its perplexing ambiguity, he adds, it is both a caricature and a mystical statement about pure being — or nothingness. The inscriptions that Aschenbach reads at the cemetery in Munich are both Protestant and Catholic, Mann's symbols are both Christian and Greek, the novella expresses ideas of Nietzsche as well as Schopenhauer, and Aschenbach's name signifies life and death alike. His own death is final, though, and such opposed concepts negate reality and cancel each other out. As Stelzmann sums up this logic, $-X + X = 0$. In 1970, Stelzmann added that Mann's irony in *Death in Venice* distances him from Nietzsche's opposition of the Dionysian and Apollinian. Aschenbach's animalistic dream, Stelzmann notes, exaggerates and devalues the Dionysian, presenting it as obscene. Mann describes the Apollinian negatively as well, he writes, by filling that dream, which should be Apollinian, with Dionysian content. In 1972, A. F. Bance explained the novella according to the "triadic structure" posited in Schiller's treatise *Über naive und sentimentalische Dichtung* and in Kleist's essay *Über das Marionettentheater* (On Marionette Theater, 1810). This structure, Bance argues, involves stages of simplicity, self-consciousness, and a second naïveté, a progression that explains Aschenbach's status as a tragic hero. He is a representative figure, Bance writes, an idealist striving for a romantic synthesis, and the lingering credibility of this synthesis makes his story tragic. In it, the three phases of the triadic structure are inverted: from a false synthesis of knowledge and nature, he regresses to dividedness and confusion. The story is therefore a version of the "tragedy of German dualism" (156). Indeed, "Aschenbach has tragically destroyed for himself a whole cultural tradition — the striving for synthesis, for the ideal of harmony" (159). Bance seems to overrate Aschenbach's consciousness when he adds that it orders such self-destruction and leads to tragic self-recognition.

Other studies of *Death in Venice* treated such philosophers and ideas in connection with Nietzsche. In an article about Schopenhauer and Nietzsche in Mann's early work, André Banuls remarked in 1975 that Schopenhauer's thoughts are easy to recognize in the novella. Aschenbach lives in the world of representation, Banuls claims, until the will overwhelms him. Also in 1975, D. J. Farrelly considered Nietzsche's concepts of Apollo and Dionysus. These two gods, and the concepts they represent in Nietzsche, are intrinsically interrelated in Mann, Farrelly writes, so one would be wrong to think that his story is about a conflict between art and life. Despite the polarity of those gods, Mann suggests that art is not confronted by its opposite, but composed of such opposites. "The artist," Farrelly notes, "must consequently acknowledge and sustain the tension between the two gods, the two *acknowledged opposites*" (14). Farrelly finds evidence of both gods in Aschenbach's inherited traits and in his facial features, adding that Tadzio embodies their synthesis. In Tadzio, moreover, both Apollo and Dionysus destroy Aschenbach. Farrelly observes that Tadzio's mother is Apollinian and that Aschenbach's attitude does not change insofar as he adheres to his daily régime. He still gets up early, for example, albeit to see Tadzio, rather than to work. Tadzio's scorn for the Russian family on the beach, however, has more to do with the fact that his native Poland had not yet regained its independence when Mann wrote *Death in Venice* than with his "destructive Dionysian attitude" (11).

Most political readings of the novella took a strict Marxist line. In East Germany in 1959, Inge Diersen made many valid observations about its motifs, its symbols, and its narrator, but her conclusions betray her ideological biases. Like Lukács, she explains that Aschenbach is a typical bourgeois of the imperialistic epoch and that his tragic fate is that of his social class. His bourgeois attitude contains the seeds of fascism, moreover, and his story ends in inhuman intoxication because he anticipates fascistic tendencies of people like himself. His national fame serves and depends on the ruling class, Diersen adds, he speaks for the bourgeoisie and represents its interests, and his collapse foreshadows its own demise. His wanderlust is an attempt to escape bourgeois-imperialist Germany, moreover, imperialism makes him unable to feel love that is not barbaric, and in his orgiastic dream he takes part in a barbaric cult that shows how imperialism will lead to fascism. Diersen is too preoccupied with this regression into barbarism when she wrongly claims that the excesses of that dream include cannibalism. Politics similarly informs the distinctions she draws between Mann and his protagonist. Aschenbach is too attached to his class, she explains, to distance himself from the spread of imperialism. Mann, however, maintains such a critical distance. Aschenbach has renounced literary realism, she adds, conservatively upholding the political status quo. Mann's symbols are rational and realistic, though, in that Aschenbach's psyche is a function of his social circumstances. Diersen also notes the tension between Mann's motifs of composure and seduction, and she thinks that his narrator embodies Aschenbach's earlier attitude, a bourgeois humanism that both ends in fascism and is powerless to oppose it. The contrast between this narrator and Aschenbach, she maintains, lends the novella historical tension and a political perspective. Diersen admits that the novella is not directly political, but she insists that its handling of personal and intellectual matters invites political interpretation. *Death in Venice,* she writes, reflects the great upheaval of the bourgeois-capitalist world-system that became apparent in the political crises that preceded the First World War. In her later analysis of the novella, in 1975, Diersen takes a milder tone. She notes Aschenbach's secret ambition to be like Goethe, and she explains how Mann examines and experiments with his own intellectual, moral, and ideological possibilities. She also repeats some of her earlier argument, though, and she believes that the knowledge Aschenbach has renounced is of the hollow and brittle condition of the existing social order.

Other political interpretations sounded similar, often echoing Lukács and Diersen. Two such interpretations were given in the 1960s. In 1962, R. Schmidt argued that the novella addresses the problem of the bourgeois artist in imperialistic society and shows how the formalism favored by the ruling class leads to barbarism. Mann distances himself from the forces that influence Aschenbach, Schmidt notes, but he cannot overcome them because he has not recognized the historical role of the working class. Mann's lack of historical consciousness also makes his symbols, motifs, recourse to antiquity, and Aschenbach's decadent dream abstract, subjective, and unrealistic. Schmidt misreads Mann's prose when he claims that the German Emperor rewards Aschenbach for supporting the reactionary ideas of the Hohenzollerns. Eberhard Hilscher interpreted the novella less stridently in 1965, though he, too, concluded that it foreshadows the rise of fascism.

Similar political readings were given in the 1970s. In 1973, Wolfgang Frühwald added two new twists to conclusions like Schmidt's and Hilscher's. Aschenbach, he writes, is the representative of a declining bourgeois age and the Wilhelminian epoch. In criticizing Aschenbach's literary attitude, Frühwald adds, Mann objects to the barbarism about to erupt in the external world as well. The motif of cholera similarly conveys his criticism of an ideology soon expressed in Oswald Spengler's *Der Untergang des Abendlandes* (The Decline of the West, 1918). Mann's own personal limitations, however, kept *Death in Venice* from being a more direct fiction of fascism. To this standard Marxist line, Frühwald adds that Aschenbach's individual fate is that of an epigone and that his crisis is ironic and unoriginal. Aschenbach's search for beauty in Greek antiquity reproduces eighteenth-century neoclassicism, he explains, and Mann's criticism of this long aesthetic tradition links Mann to anarchist and socialist authors. Frühwald also infers concrete historical dates from Mann's descriptions. Aschenbach was born in 1838 and ennobled in 1888, he claims, and is thus seventy-three years old when the fictional events of the novella occur, namely in April 1911. Frühwald is in error here, for those events start in the month of May. These speculations may account for Frühwald's mistaken notion that Aschenbach's hair has turned white when he visits the hotel barber. The barber and Aschenbach both say only that it has gone gray. Duncan Smith's comments on the novella in 1975 combined radical politics with eroticism, Karl Marx with Herbert Marcuse. Smith criticizes the intellectual establishment's "cultural use" (74) of *Death in Venice*. According to him, the story is an "aesthetic glorification of the death wish within middle class culture" (74). Aschenbach's homosexual love is narcissistic intercourse with the self, he observes, intercourse made necessary because bourgeois culture casts males and females as antagonistic opposites. With regard to such love, the novella is also "a dream turned nightmare but not yet protest" (75). Aschenbach dies, moreover, because he repudiates the bourgeois "performance principle" (78). Mann is wrong to associate the death wish, homosexuality, and eros because they all betray this principle, Smith thinks, and his condemnation of eros seems both contrived and mistaken.

Like such political readings, psychoanalytic commentaries on *Death in Venice* were variations on a standard theme. In an essay presented in 1948 and published in 1957, Heinz Kohut interpreted the novella as Mann's attempt to communicate and to sublimate threatening personal conflicts. In Kohut's view, the four mysterious men Aschenbach meets are a threatening father figure returning from the grave. Swollen veins on the street singer's forehead, Kohut explains, allude to this feared father's sexual excitement or rage. Goethe is a father figure for any German writer, moreover, a fact that supports the idea that Mann's central theme is the father conflict. A compulsive personality, according to Kohut, Mann split this ambivalent figure: the four men embody the bad, threatening, and sexually active father, while Aschenbach identifies himself with the good father who loves only his son. Indeed, Aschenbach's love for Tadzio is what he wishes his own father had given him. His Dionysian dream reveals both his unsuccessful struggle with such a bad, barbaric father and the breakdown of his sublimation of homosexual desire. It also describes a primal scene that is the origin of Aschenbach's homosexual fears and desires and of his detached, defensive artistic attitude. Mann's reasons for writing such a story may have included feelings of guilt occasioned by the suicide of his sister Carla, Kohut adds, as well as both paternal affection and heterosexual abstinence caused by a temporary absence of his wife Katia. In any case, Aschenbach's disintegration is a return of unsublimated libido, and Mann displaced a personal conflict, safeguarding his own creativity. This general argument sometimes distorts Mann's details. Aschenbach goes to the other side of the boat that takes him to Venice not because he tries to avoid the flirtatious old man, for example, but because his deck chair has been placed there. That man's remarks to him do not concern love for a woman, moreover, as Kohut thinks when he quotes Lowe-Porter's translation, which wrongly uses the feminine "her" in those remarks, where Mann used only the neuter "Liebchen." Finally, if Mann implies a deeper similarity between his hero and Gustav Mahler by giving Aschenbach Mahler's facial features, it is not because he had intimate knowledge of Mahler's personality. Despite these mistakes, Kohut's essay has been reprinted in anthologies and translated into German, Spanish, and French.

Whereas Kohut discerned in *Death in Venice* psychological conflicts of its author, Riva Novey recounted, in 1964, its effect on one of its readers. That reader was a young man named Robert, and he suffered an identity crisis after reading Mann's story. He had written a paper on *Death in Venice* while in college, Novey relates, and had been struck by his similarity to Aschenbach. He was similarly intellectual, loveless, and attracted to a blond boy, and he became worried that his suppressed emotion might disintegrate his personality. Robert then went to Novey for treatment. Mann's story thus encouraged him to seek treatment, she writes, and enabled him to convey his sense of danger. Novey explains how Robert's improvement was interwoven, in his associations, with Mann's themes. He linked Mann's poisoned strawberries, for example, with strawberry shortcake his father gave him, to poisoned meat his father sold in Robert's dreams, and to his poisoned dog. Novey, who is more interested than Kohut in pre-Oedipal reunion with the mother, also explains that those strawberries may symbolize nipples. Robert, she notes, also linked his preoccupation with homosexuality to Mann's story. He imagined himself in love with a television actor whom he called "Tadzio," and as his heterosexual interests later increased, certain handsome boys reminded him of the death figures that Aschenbach meets. Identifying with Aschenbach not only made Robert feel threatened, though, but also released his feelings and relieved his guilt. "A chance acquaintance with the novel, Death in Venice," Novey concludes, "led him to see himself more clearly . . . It appears that reading the story and undergoing analysis worked together to advance the patient's hitherto arrested ego development" (51). Both Robert and Novey sometimes misunderstood that story. Robert wrongly thought that Aschenbach meets the wanderer in a mausoleum and that the latter's eyes are strawberry colored. The wanderer's eyelashes are red, but his eyes are colorless. Novey incorrectly adds that Mann's hero has just won a distinguished literary award. Like Kohut's essay, which she faults because she believes that Mann was merely expressing conflicts rather than resolving them, Novey's appeared in *The Psychoanalytic Quarterly*.

Two other psychoanalytic readings of *Death in Venice* were published in *American Imago*. They appeared in the same issue in the summer of 1969. Harry Slochower regarded both the development of long-repressed forces in Aschenbach and Mann's function as the interpreter of Aschenbach's dream. This dual approach implies that *Death in Venice* is not just a clinical case history. Indeed, Slochower calls it "perhaps the greatest short novel in world literature" (104). Mann's dialectic technique, he explains, casts a magic spell broken by realistic details that divert our attention and limit the emotions he explores. Slochower notes Mann's main motifs and imagery. The crouching tiger introduces the theme of sexual assault, for example, and the redness characteristic of all the ominous male figures suggests sexual temptation. In the red sunrise, Aschenbach experiences an aesthetically transfigured primal scene between his mother and father, Slochower writes, and in meeting Tadzio, he relives the meeting of his parents before this union. Slochower stresses such tension between paternal and maternal elements in Aschenbach. His slow death, which culminates in oceanic feelings, consists of stages of reunion with the mother, and Mann's ironic art, Slochower remarks, both celebrates this surrender and warns against thus submitting to Eros and Narcissus. Similarly, Slochower thinks Aschenbach androgynous. He begets the entire series of strange men, including Jaschu, and Tadzio is his "esthetic issue" (118). His voyeurism, his watching and looking at Tadzio, is even "esthetic onanism" (106). In fact, essentially, *"the boy is Aschenbach's 'double'"* (106). When Jaschu and Tadzio wrestle, however, the first event that is not a narcissistic projection, Slochower adds, Aschenbach is released from his fantasy, for he can no longer mold Tadzio as he wishes. According to Slochower, this is an affirmative element, and like Goethe's *Faust*, *Death in Venice* warns against both "the bed of sloth and the ravages of vagabondage" (122). Slochower also observes that Kohut's analysis of Mann's sublimated attitudes and expiated guilt does not do justice to his irony, ambivalence, and dialectic style. Kohut's mistakes seem most obvious in a letter that Slochower quotes. Kohut there writes that pronouncing Tadzio's name produces "the melancholy sound of a foghorn" (121 n 21), a sound linked to Mann's childhood, when he must have heard it in his Hanseatic hometown of Lübeck and on the nearby shores of the Baltic. While some of Slochower's own conclusions seem far-fetched, he reads accurately for the most part, as when he explains that "The leading affect in *Death in Venice* is the sensual, not the sexual" (112). Mann's text, though, nowhere states that Aschenbach moved from Silesia to Bavaria after being knighted.

The other essay on *Death in Venice* published in *American Imago* in 1969 was written by Raymond Tarbox. Thanks to its vivid and complete description of Aschenbach's brief manic phase, he considers the novella as a notable example of "literature of the depressive response" (123). This phase is one of four that Aschenbach experiences in an ecstatic suicidal process. Like the literary hero of Ernest Hemingway's *The Snows of Kili-*

*manjaro* (1936), Aschenbach is a masochistic "institutional author" who adopts a "pleasure-seeking manic-ideal" (125) and then sinks into depression before dying in a final fantasy. During the first of these four phases, Aschenbach has derived only limited joy from his "erotically tinged submission to authority" (128). During the second phase, he identifies with the good but controlling mother of the second and third year of life, a mother like Tadzio's. Aschenbach also falls in love with Tadzio, who represents, among other things, Tarbox writes, the maternal breast. Indeed, what the narcissistic Aschenbach seems to find most satisfying is "the fact that the boy is an ecstasy-provoking embodiment of the maternal breast . . . Also like the breast, Tadzio is described as being white, smooth, pure, soft and creamy" (135). In the third phase, the city of Venice turns sickening and thus likewise seems a maternal object that offers the breast, then suddenly withdraws it. In the fourth phase, Aschenbach can finally "enjoy the fantasy of rejoining the mother and sleeping at her breast" (144). Drawing this conclusion, Tarbox relies on a phrase that occurs earlier in the novella, a phrase that he quotes in Lowe-Porter's translation, in which Tadzio guides Aschenbach's glance out into the "bosom of the simple and the vast." Tarbox links this suicidal process to an "oral triad" that posits in the nursling three wishes: to eat, to be eaten, and to sleep blissfully at the mother's breast. These wishes manifest themselves in various ways, he explains, as Aschenbach interacts with the ominous strangers and Tadzio. He projects his own unconscious sadism and his wish to incorporate through the eye onto the wanderer, for example, but he orders and controls his visions of Tadzio in an aesthetic "code." Tarbox also notes that Aschenbach seems to transfer his hostility toward Prussian authorities to the authorities in Venice.

Further psychoanalytic readings of *Death in Venice* were less ambitious but nonetheless suggestive. In 1969, E. Pumpian-Mindlin argued that the lack of physical contact between Mann's characters symbolizes Aschenbach's isolation and detachment. Mann himself feared what might happen if his wife died of the tuberculosis for which she was away being treated while he was writing the novella, and the novella is thus "a fantasy of the author as to what the future held for him: empty, lonely, sterile success" (238). In other words, according to Pumpian-Mindlin, it was an attempt to master the fear and fantasy of losing his wife, to symbolically disintegrate and die in order to continue to live. Pumpian-Mindlin rings a new change on the narcissism mentioned by other psychoanalytic critics, contending that Tadzio is Mann returned to his youth, to a time when he had not yet chosen the way of life that now looked so bleak: "Tadzio, then, is not merely Tadzio, but von Aschenbach himself, fresh, beautiful, enjoying life uncommitted" (239). Pumpian-Mindlin's point is that Mann expressed his anxieties in literary form to protect himself from the threat of disintegration. In 1974, Hunter G. Hannum read *Death in Venice* according to an idea of Carl Gustav Jung, calling it a "dramatization of the archetypal pattern of enantiodromia" (48). This pattern involves one-sidedness, an inhibition of conscious performance, and the emergence of an unconscious opposite as the epiphany of an archaic god. It also occurs, Hannum notes, in Goethe's *Faust* and Hermann Hesse's *Der Steppenwolf* (1927). Mann's story, he reasons, places a traditionally German emphasis on the irrational, the anarchic, and the instinctual. In Venice, moreover, Aschenbach seems to be an island of consciousness surrounded by water representing the flood of the unconscious. While some critics praise the ending of the novella as an apotheosis, Hannum wonders if it is simply a sentimental appendage, "a kind of dated *Jugendstil* decoration tacked on to a realistic psychological work" (57).

All the psychoanalytic studies cited so far in this chapter are in English. In 1965, however, Peter Dettmering interpreted the novella in German in his study of the problem of suicide in Mann's work. Quoting Melanie Klein, Dettmering explains that Aschenbach has been abandoned by a woman, his dead wife. He holds fast to her image and has turned away from a female love-object in real life. Indeed, he has become the mother, loving Tadzio as he himself was once loved, or wished he had been. He identifies with the female object, moreover, and needs to be completed by a male. His love for Tadzio is feminine, Dettmering adds, and his orgiastic dream reveals to him that he wants to be conquered, overwhelmed, and subjugated. His desire to be passive and to be wooed himself explains why he woos Tadzio only with admiring glances and cannot establish actual contact with him. What is more, his underlying motive is fear of the destructive aspect of the feminine, and he flees the reality of the feminine for a homoerotic myth. Dettmering also notes Aschenbach's latent rivalry with Tadzio's mother. In 1969, he similarly presented *Death in Venice* as a story of suicidal impulses stemming from an Oedipal conflict. In addition to identifying with the mother, he explains, Aschenbach is a father attempting to regain his son. Mann distances himself from this father-figure, he adds, and he informs his readers about the state of mind in which such failed figures commit suicide. The foreign god is a subjugating and rapacious father, Dettmering maintains, and the sea symbolizes the original unity with the mother that is regained in death. In 1973, Lajos Székely combined Freud and Marx, interpreting Aschenbach's dilemma of composure and dissolution in light of Mann's conflict with his brother Heinrich, who, Székely writes, was both his literary rival and his political opposite. In the literary dialogue born of this fraternal conflict, *Death in Venice* is Thomas's ambivalent attempt to outdo Heinrich's similar *Professor Unrat*. Székely thus understands Thomas's story as a case of sibling rivalry. In Aschenbach, he adds, Thomas condemns his artistic ego, his own narcissism and homosexual libido. Like Novey in 1964, Székely also recounts the effect of *Death in Venice* on a patient, a woman who had seen Visconti's film. He explains that this woman unconsciously identified with

Aschenbach and that she also identified Tadzio with her dead sister, the repressed object of her lesbian love.

In addition to all these readings by actual psychoanalysts, similar remarks on *Death in Venice* occur in the work of several literary scholars. Some of those remarks were made in the 1950s and 1960s. In 1956, Erich Heller argued that the novella supplies an example of a moral problem, the problem of responsibility for one's decisions and actions. Its hero's failed attempt to leave Venice, he writes, is a Freudian accident that reveals his true will to stay. Aschenbach might seem innocent by traditional moral standards, Heller adds, but he is responsible according to those of psychoanalysis. An English version of these remarks, which are in German, appeared in 1984. In 1962, Frederick J. Beharriell, taking issue with Michael's study of 1950, regarded elements in the novella that are reminiscent of Freud as evidence of psycho-analytic influence in Mann's work prior to the 1920s. Beharriell believes Mann's own statement of 1925 that he wrote *Death in Venice* under Freud's immediate influence. In 1967, J. R. McWilliams considered the novella as a psychological document and its story as the failure of a repression. Mann's "series of Stygian figures" results in an "apocalyptic culmination," and the effect is that of a "powerful dirge" (233). Such signs and symbols, McWil-liams writes, convey Aschenbach's notion that the wages of his sin and degradation are death. They show his need for chastisement. Seeing the wanderer, for example, makes him "fully conscious of the fact that death is the reward for the liberation of his tyrannized senses" (237). Stressing this "penitential factor" (237), McWilliams seems to overrate Aschenbach's awareness. In any case, he sounds moralistic when adding that Mann shows "the ghastly and shocking results of unrestricted indulgence" (240). More subtly, he explains that Aschenbach makes symbolic contact with Tadzio through the boy's wrestling match with Jaschu.

Further remarks on *Death in Venice* inspired by psychoanalysis were made in the 1970s. Robert Rogers, citing Kohut in 1970, noted the no-vella's "doubling by multiplication of similar bad fathers" (115). Adolf Schweckendiek, again in 1970, portrayed the homosexual Aschenbach as suffering from arrested development and a hunger neurosis. In 1972, in the expanded version of a book originally published, it seems, in that same year, Herbert Anton claimed that no psychoanalytic theory of narcissism can explain Tadzio's self-absorbed smile. C. A. M. Noble, also in 1972, added that Aschenbach is not aware of the real reason for his neurotic-like relation to life because Mann did not yet know of Freud's insights into ambivalence when he wrote *Death in Venice*. Finally, Jean Finck argued in 1973 that Mann's relationship to psychoanalysis was extremely ambivalent. With his reference to Aschenbach's rejection of "indecent psychologism," Finck claims, he undeniably alludes to Freudianism, and the novella attests to the dilemma that he faced thanks to the psychoanalytic concept of repression.

While Mann acknowledges psychic causality, however, he also tries to transcend it, Finck adds, tries to assert the morality of artists against the iconoclastic view of art taken by psychoanalysis. Aschenbach is a neurotic, his sexuality may be abnormal, and his repression pathological, according to Finck, but even in defeat, he has his artistic dignity.

## Other Approaches and Themes

A further kind of research conducted on *Death in Venice* from 1956 to 1975 consists of studies that took other approaches and treated other themes, and that do not fall into any of the four broad categories cited so far. Four of those studies speculated about the etymology and connotations of Tadzio's name, while another included that of Aschenbach. Two located Aschenbach in literary and cultural traditions of homosexuality, one contrasted his sexual love with caritas, and a further one saw in him Mann's dialectic of the male and the female. Six remarked on human, existential, or literary aspects of Mann's treatment of decadence and death. Two observed how and why his narrative suspends time. Two others traced his related motifs of mute glances and of the death of language. A final three analyzed the actual and imaginary sites of his story: Italy in general and Venice in particular. These several miscellaneous studies are often striking, for their authors tend to present *Death in Venice* from fresh perspectives and in innovative ways.

The name "Tadzio" occasioned surprisingly free associations. As noted in chapter 2, Schlappner in 1950 and Thomas in 1955 thought that this name may suggest an adagio that Nietzsche heard in Venice, while Pabst in 1955 linked it both to Thaddeus, the disciple of Christ, and to other real and fictional Slavs who had visited Venice. As noted above, moreover, Slochower in 1969 quoted Kohut's strange statement that the sound of the name "Tadzio" resembles that of a foghorn like the kind Mann must have heard as a boy. The conclusions reached in 1962 by Lee Stavenhagen were stranger still. Convinced that Tadzio's name cannot be arbitrary, Stavenhagen, like Pabst, compares it to that of the apostle Thaddeus, who was also called Lebbeus. These two names, Stavenhagen notes, come from Syriac and Hebrew nouns for "breast" and "heart." They thus connote love and compassion. To this "remarkably fortunate etymology" (21), Stavenhagen adds an allegorical dimension, remarking that Thaddeus is St. Jude of the Latin hagiologies, who is depicted as a young man and who preached in the East and died a martyr. He is also confused with another Thaddeus who taught in the sensuous Orient. Furthermore, men enthused to Aschenbach's manic degree embody the holy madness known as *hagios*, a word that an Italian or Pole might pronounce as "Adgio." Stavenhagen hails Mann's erudition and imagination in selecting such a symbolic name. In fact, Mann simply thought he heard it called to the boy he spied on the Lido in May 1911. In 1963, James B. Hepworth wrote that Erwin Rohde's *Psyche* describes ancient Greek rites like the events of Aschenbach's final dream and mentions "Sabazios," another name for Dionysus. Hearing "Tadzio" must thus have reminded Mann's hero of Dionysus, Hepworth reasons, and the youth is a reincarnation of this foreign god. In 1968, Ignace Feuerlicht observed that three of the six letters in Tadzio's name spell *Tod*, the German word for "death."

Such tenuous connections between Tadzio's name and its import continued to be drawn in the 1970s. In 1971, Christian Schmidt noted that Mann mentions this name in connection with music and that it hints at Nietzsche's sympathy for Poland and Chopin. While Schmidt agrees with Schlappner, he is critical of Stavenhagen and Hepworth, and his remarks are accordingly more cautious. In 1975, Siegmar Tyroff tied the meaning of the names of Mann's characters to their sounds. Only three of those characters, Tyroff remarks, have names at all: Aschenbach, Tadzio, and Jaschu. As in Mann's other fiction, he adds, these names are sometimes misheard and misunderstood, and they convey concepts like the opposition of East and West. The *o* in "Tadzio," for example, signifies that the Polish boy plays the same aesthetic and attractive role for Aschenbach that Ingeborg Holm, whose last name likewise contains a long *o*, does for Tonio Kröger. Tyroff also writes that the vowels in "Gustav" correspond to the dark atmosphere of Mann's story and anticipate those of "Tadziu." Many of the words Mann uses to describe Aschenbach's dream, he adds, similarly contain *u* and *a*. "Gustav" recalls "Detlev," moreover, the first name of the aesthete Spinell in Mann's *Tristan*. According to Tyroff's acoustic laws, Mann's hero in *Death in Venice* could also have been named "Wenzel"! Furthermore, according to Tyroff, "von Aschenbach" was the name of a Prussian noble family, and the "ash" (*Asche*) in it establishes some connection with the Asiatic and with the river Ganges. Tyroff does not define this connection. In any case, he thinks that this surname also encourages associations with ideas such as glowing or smoldering embers about to be extinguished. Finally, Tyroff wrongly claims that Aschenbach is still married. Mann's story explicitly states that Aschenbach's wife has died.

Other scholars cited traditions sympathetic to homosexuality, contrasted Aschenbach's sexual love with caritas, or described his progress as a change from the male principle to the female one. In 1962, Marion Luckow argued that Mann's idea and plot are both fundamentally Christian. *Death in Venice* also concerns Greek antiquity, Luckow writes, which had been more tolerant of Aschenbach's kind of love. Mann did not want to condemn his hero's homosexual leanings, Luckow adds, and their fulfillment and punishment are intellectual and visionary, rather than realistic. With help from Plato, then, Mann meant to humanize the Christian mythos. Luckow compares Mann to Balzac, Gautier, Gide, Proust, and Genet — and mistakenly calls Tadzio "Adgio." In 1969, Thorkil Vanggaard entitled the last chapter of his history of the phallus "The Breakdown of Gustav von Aschenbach." Vanggaard maintains that all men share Aschenbach's sexual disposition. Mann does not tell of an odd perversion, then, but relates a myth of universal validity, one reminiscent of Euripides' *Bacchae*. Thanks to his psychological insight, he lucidly exposes "a fundamental conflict of the mind in the Europe of recent times" (189). According to Vanggaard, that conflict stems from the fact that most men, like Aschenbach, are ignorant of their repressed homosexuality. David Myers, again in 1969, argued that Aschenbach's passion for Tadzio is sexual love that leads to disorder and destruction. Aschenbach denies both this love and caritas, according to Myers, and suffers an unhappy fate when he meets the symbolic apparition of the beauty he tried to create. That Mann links such sexual lust to disease and death shows "sexual pessimism" (596). Inta Miske Ezergailis approached the subject of sexuality differently in 1975. Aschenbach's formerly clenched fist is an emblem of the male principle, she explains. It signifies tension and self-discipline. By contrast, the fertile swamp that Aschenbach envisions suggests the female principle, which Ezergailis associates with relaxation, widening, openness, and passivity. Venice, too, stands for the female principle — indeed, the city is "a symbolic Woman" (53) — whereas Aschenbach's house in the mountains is clearly connected with the male. "As Aschenbach becomes engulfed by the female principle," moreover, "time ceases to exist for him" (55). According to Ezergailis, Tadzio is another incarnation of the female principle. His attributes often seem those of a girl, she explains, and Mann associates him with the mother, the communal meal, art, the sea, music, and transparency — all of which Ezergailis finds female. In the end, Aschenbach's dream enacts "the final triumph of the female principle — the yielding of the self" (65). Such judgments seem based on sexual stereotypes.

Scholars who treated the subjects of decadence and death updated results of the studies of the latter done by Baer and Kasdorff in 1932 and by Nolte in 1934. Two of those scholars published their remarks in the 1960s. In 1964, P. J. Van der Schaar maintained that Mann's having cholera come to Venice by way of that city's valuable spice trade shows how he projected himself into its "infrastructure of decay" (72). In 1966, Jeannette Lander (whom Matter, in his bibliography of 1972, identifies as Joachim Seyppel) explained that the aging Aschenbach, who fears death, assigns subjective significance to Mann's series of ominous characters, whence his meeting with them is an objective-phenomenal encounter with death. Mann presents death as the essence of Aschenbach's life, Lander writes, death as the end of *Dasein* and as the means to authentic existence. In his active, voluntary being-unto-death, Lander adds, death becomes part of life for Aschenbach, as it was for Rilke. In his novella, then, Mann anticipated the existentialism articulated by Martin Heidegger. In 1967, Wolfdietrich Rasch added that life and death are equated in much literature written around 1900. Like Lander, Rasch cites both Rilke's poems and Mann's novella as examples of such literature.

Further remarks on decadence and death were made in the 1970s. Albert Braverman and Larry David Nachman, in 1970, read *Death in Venice* as Mann's most consummate statement of "the dialectic of decadence and culture in bourgeois society" (289), and as his attempt to address the issue of "the status of the free human spirit in the context of the life of the body, whose end is death" (291). Aschenbach's sudden desire for life results from the imminence of death, they argue, and his love is selective to an unhealthy and a depraved degree. The novella thus shows the danger of personal development estranged from the world and the body. According to them, Mann not only explains how a superior personality and decadence are related, though. By invoking Socrates near the end of his "supreme and final tragedy of pure romantic individualism" (298), he also hints at a synthesis of eros, reason, and society. Braverman and Nachman base this conclusion on a notion of Socrates that they find in Nietzsche's *Die Geburt der Tragödie*. René Girard considered Mann's story in 1974 as an example of how the plague is presented in literature and myth. While the plague, as Girard argues, heightens the sense of Aschenbach's decay, and while he even may be said to ally himself with it when he does not tell Tadzio's family to flee, Girard associates them too closely by claiming that, "The writer has become the very embodiment of the plague" (848). In 1975, Ludwig Uhlig wrote that Tadzio embodies both eros and death, and thus differs from Mann's series of skeletal characters. This contrast, Uhlig remarks, between a friendly ancient and a fearsome medieval incarnation of death goes back to Gotthold Ephraim Lessing (1729–81). Aschenbach yields to the former, not the latter, Uhlig observes, though his dying in ecstatic self-surrender is decidedly modern.

A further theme examined in studies of *Death in Venice* was time. In 1966, Hans-Bernhard Moeller wrote that Mann develops insights of the philosopher and sociologist Georg Simmel, who in 1907 published an article that told how time seemed to stand still in Venice. Moeller thinks Mann's novella is an epic experiment with the category of time. The odd men his hero meets all recall Hermes, for example, and by thus having Hermes appear repeatedly, Mann devalues and transcends the passage of time. Two such "hermetic" characters — the wanderer and Tadzio — perform the task of pointing to another world at both the beginning and the end of Mann's story, Moeller adds, a fact that shows how the same events recur and how Mann negates narrative time. Aschenbach also remembers Platonic dialogues twice, a repetition that likewise blurs the elapsing of time. He finds himself in the same erotic situation as Socrates and Platen, moreover, a circumstance that shows how human fate has stayed the same since the days of the Greeks and how time thus proves to be powerless. With variations of the same imaginary events, then, Mann circumvents progress and disables temporal orientation. Both in his novella and in history, according to Moeller, the present, the past, and the future are identical. This narrative timelessness suggests mythical simultaneity and a taste for ahistorical types, Moeller adds, and Mann's use of it in *Death in Venice* precedes the use of it found in Joyce, Proust, Wolff, and his own *Der Zauberberg*. It recalls techniques suggested in Karl Gutzkow's novel *Die Ritter vom Geiste* (The Knights of the Spirit, 1850–51), though, and seems inspired by Schopenhauer's *Die Welt als Wille und Vorstellung* (The World as Will and Representation, 1819). It is no coincidence, then, that days on the Lido do not differ from each other and that Aschenbach leads a mythical life of timeless simultaneity there. In contrast to Moeller, Winfried Hellmann argued in 1972 that *Death in Venice* describes tension between the present and the timeless. The novella shows this tension more clearly than Mann's essays, Hellmann notes, and only later did he incorporate it into his thoughts about history.

Two especially trenchant studies raised the issues of looks and language. In 1968, John R. Frey explained the function of the gaze and the power of seeing in Mann's story. Martini, in 1954, had mentioned in passing the mute encounter between Aschenbach and Tadzio. Frey finds that such visual links sustain Mann's psychological plot. They consist of physical looking, he argues, as well as intellectual visions. After the headstones at the cemetery in Munich occupy Aschenbach's "geistiges Auge" (intellectual eye), as Mann says, for example, the wanderer's hostile glaring makes him avert his actual glance. In his vision of a jungle, moreover, "Seine Begierde ward sehend" (His desire became seeing). The word "sah" (saw) occurs several times in that vision, Frey adds, in which Mann mentions staring birds and a tiger's ocular "Lichter" (lights, eyes). While the wanderer gives Aschenbach the evil eye, moreover, Tadzio exchanges glances with him. Tadzio, too, looks threateningly at the Russian family. Aschenbach is "der Schauende" (the seer) in his presence, however, a fact that proves how physical looking at actual objects can become an intellectual vision of mythical realms. Furthermore, while listening to the street musicians, Frey writes, Tadzio observes Aschenbach, and their eyes meet. Their relationship is ambiguous and tense precisely because it is visual. According to Frey, the function of gazes both holds Mann's plot together, then, and demonstrates his narrative virtuosity. In 1972, Graham Good likewise stressed nonverbal elements of *Death in Venice*. He reads the novella in terms of the crisis of language that Hugo von Hofmannsthal, Karl Kraus, and Ludwig Wittgenstein noted in the early years of the twentieth century. Good describes a conflict between Aschenbach's pure writing and the vulgar speech of Venice. Abandoning his art, he explains, Aschenbach is seduced by language as music and meaningless sound. He is surrounded by a mixture of languages, his own dialogues are few and ineffectual, and the words he hears are often incomprehensible. As language around him degenerates, Good adds, so does moral order. Spoken and written German both vanish from his hotel, and his unspoken feelings for Tadzio become unspeakable. According to Good, "veracity and persuasiveness, the sense and the music of language, have parted company, leaving a choice between lifeless truth, flattering lies, and silence" (51). The short treatise that Aschenbach writes is an exception to this rule, as is *Death in Venice,* Good thinks. Aschenbach neither imitates "corrupted Venetian speech patterns" (47), however, nor desires to be soothed by "the Venetians' musical lies" (48).

A final miscellaneous theme was the setting of *Death in Venice.* Studies that mention this setting recall that of von Seuffert in 1937. In 1969, Ilse-dore B. Jonas similarly noted that Venice has an important part in Mann's action, that it increases the fascination that Tadzio holds for Aschenbach, and that its deceptiveness increases Aschenbach's susceptibility. She also notes that Italy signifies antiquity. Jonas made this same argument again in 1972. In 1974, Wolfgang Leppmann looked through old Italian magazines and found that the campanile outside St. Mark's was covered by scaffolding in 1911, a fact, he notes, that Mann never mentions. Leppmann also found that Italian tourists were not scared away from Venice by reports of cholera that year. Mann thus describes the epidemic as being far more drastic than it actually was. What is more, Leppmann learned that men in Italy routinely had their hair dyed, just as Aschenbach does. In his fiction, then, Mann worked narrative magic by transforming unremarkable elements of reality. In the expanded, English version of his remarks, a version that appeared in 1975, Leppmann added that Mann's omission of historical details such as the heat wave that hit northern Italy in the summer of 1911 raises his story above traditional coordinates of time and place. His omissions, Leppmann thinks, thus lend it a patina of classicality, a classical dimension.

## Music, Film, Opera, Art, Texts

A final kind of research conducted on *Death in Venice* in the twenty years after Mann's death reflected interests in various media, especially in music. Five scholars linked the novella and Richard Wagner, relating Mann's hero, central episodes, structure, and narrative tone to Wagner's residence and death in Venice, to the erotic and romantic high points of his operas *Tannhäuser* (1845) and *Tristan und Isolde,* to his use of leitmotifs, and to his artistic decadence. The work of two other scholars avoided and corrected some of the misunderstandings that arose when Luchino Visconti transformed Aschenbach into a composer much like Gustav Mahler in the film *Morte a Venezia.* Some critics thought this film hopelessly flawed because it distorted Mann's story, but others appreciated its director's bold attempt to adapt and interpret the story in an independent cinematic creation. Other remarks on the relationship of fundamentally different arts can be found in the early reviews of Benjamin Britten's *Death in Venice.* Music critics found this opera more congenial and less controversial than many film critics found Visconti's film. Besides being given new life as a film and an opera, Mann's novella inspired several works of art. It was also published in new, improved editions. A revised version of Kenneth Burke's translation from 1924 appeared in 1970, and it included an afterword by Erich Heller. An edition of the German text, with an introduction in English by T. J. Reed, came out in 1971. Heller and Reed both discussed autobiographical aspects and the genesis of *Death in Venice,* citing similarities as well as important differences between Mann's life and his fiction. Their remarks are an antidote to Visconti's film, which revived interest in Mann's novella and helped boost its sales, but which also conveyed visual images that have since skewed many interpretations of Mann's verbal artwork.

Five scholars linked *Death in Venice* to the life and works of Richard Wagner. Three did so in the late 1950s or in the 1960s. In 1958, Werner Vortriede noted that Wagner's autobiography was published in 1911, the year that Mann began his novella. In the middle of an artistic crisis, Vortriede explains, Wagner had fled to Venice in August 1858. Seeking beauty on the edge of the abyss, and arriving in Venice beset by visions of death, he resembles Aschenbach. Indeed, as an artist, Vortriede argues, Aschenbach is partly a biographic copy, partly an artistic interpretation of Richard Wagner. The novella is accordingly the first of Mann's studies of Wagner, whom it regards in light of Nietzsche's critique of the decadent composer. This fact is hidden and unacknowledged, Vortriede adds, but all three men are the same figure, Aschenbach and Mann being musical variations on the theme of Wagner. Aschenbach's dream, moreover, recalls Tannhäuser's bacchanalian vision of the *Venusberg.* In 1964, William H. McClain cited the parallels between Mann's novella and Wagner's tales of suffering and dying for love, especially his *Tristan* and Brünhilde's death in *Götterdämmerung* (The Twilight of the Gods, 1876). Such parallels of form and content are more important, he argues, than Aschenbach's resemblance to Wagner. McClain notes Wagnerian overtones and thematic structures in the novella, especially leitmotifs of falseness, encounter, yearning, death, fleeting time, love, and nirvana. These elements make Mann's last scene very Wagnerian, he adds, though the scene also alludes to a poem by Theodor Storm (1817–88) that represents death as a beckoning boy. Like Isolde and Brünhilde, McClain also writes, Aschenbach dies in hopes of infinite, eternal love. Horst Petri, likewise in 1964, similarly cited Mann's use of leitmotifs.

Further remarks on Mann's novella and Wagner were made in the 1970s. In 1973, Erwin Koppen argued that both Maurice Barrès's *La mort de Venise* and *Death in Venice* derive from Wagner. Like Vortriede, Koppen also speculates about associations between Mann's story and Wagner's arrival in Venice in 1858, as well as his death there in 1883. Such associations suggest a "Wagnerization" (232) of that story under the auspices of literary decadence. Finally, in 1975, James Northcote-Bade described the novella as an expression of the "Wagner-crisis" that Mann underwent between 1909 and 1911. It is an attempt, according to Northcote-Bade, to sever his ties to Wagner. In it, he rejected Wagner's Germanic myths in favor of Greek ones, the essay that Aschenbach writes at the beach is Mann's own skeptical *Über die Kunst Richard Wagners,* and autobiographical links between Aschenbach and Wagner relate the latter to the former's decline. When Northcote-Bade argues that Mann also rejected Wagner's psychologistic style, citing as proof Aschenbach's elegant prose and artistic discipline, he seems to overlook the fact that Mann shows how anti-psychologism hastens Aschenbach's fall.

The other composer tied to Aschenbach was Gustav Mahler, whose music constitutes the soundtrack for much of Visconti's film. In 1960, Hans Tramer remarked on the close similarity of Aschenbach's and Mahler's physical features, a parallel first noted by Franz Leppmann in 1915. In 1973, Ernest M. Wolf noted this same similarity, then went on to clear up the misconception that Mahler had been the prototype for Mann's story. In an interview with Hollis Alpert of the *Saturday Review,* he writes, Dirk Bogarde, the English actor who played Aschenbach, repeated a story that Visconti once heard. The story was that Mann had met Mahler on a train in 1911 and that the distraught composer confessed that he was coming from Venice and had fallen in love with a thirteen-year-old boy. Wolf quotes Alpert's expressions of doubt about this lurid story, and Wolf himself rejects it as pure fabrication. Wolf also quotes letters to the editor of the *Saturday Review* that were written in response to the interview, letters by Mann's wife, by Mahler's daughter, by the author of an unpublished dissertation on Mahler, by Visconti, and by Alpert. The first four rejected the story as false. Wolf seems wrong to blame Alpert for being "the instigator of the Mann-Aschenbach controversy" (49). In any case, the mistaken idea that Mann based the character of Aschenbach on Mahler had also been spread in 1970 by Margaret Hinxman. This was the first but not the last time that Visconti's film and its viewers skewed the reception of Mann's novella.

Four early critics of Visconti's film objected to it on stylistic grounds. In 1971, David I. Grossvogel wrote that Mann's prose style allows his readers to know more about Aschenbach than Aschenbach himself acknowledges as he "descends the Platonic ladder to his perdition" (53). Mann thereby lends his protagonist's degeneracy a speculative dimension. Visconti, Grossvogel also notes, omits much of Mann's symbolism. His Aschenbach goes to Venice to recover from a prior illness, for example, and he ingests only one strawberry, doing so "with the prissy punctiliousness of a headmaster taking a laxative" (54). Furthermore, Visconti's camera sees more than Mann's hero does, most notably the hero himself, and it presents his mien, not his mind. Tadzio, moreover, is merely one particular actor, rather than Aschenbach's subjective image of perfection or Mann's individual readers' ideal of beauty. "It is this unfortunate density of the flesh," Grossvogel notes, "which, combined with the equally physical definition of Aschenbach, gives Visconti's motion-picture too much of a mundane and sexual quality" (55). Grossvogel also notes Visconti's insertion of flashbacks, of scenes from Mann's *Doktor Faustus* (1947), and of excerpts from Mahler's third and fifth symphonies all fail to make Aschenbach a convincing character. Geoffrey Nowell-Smith dismissed *Morte a Venezia* in 1973 as an empty, pretentious, and parasitic film and as a pathetic pastiche of Mann's novella. Instead of producing a visual discourse comparable to Mann's subtle interweaving of Aschenbach's mind and Mann's commentary, he explains, the film is a "vulgar-materialist reduction of discourse to a level of landscape with figures" (203). In 1974, Epi Wiese claimed that Visconti had not captured Mann's ambiguity: "His Aschenbach is not sublime and, simultaneously, contemptible. He is not tragic. He is silly" (204). Mann's hero is a moral sentimentalist like Schiller, Wiese adds, but Visconti's seems "'a very familiar and not at all mysterious expression of inanity'" (210). Wiese quotes these strong words from a remark on human faces, a remark made by the Swiss novelist and illustrator Rodolphe Töpffer (1799–1846). In 1975, Wolfram Schütte added that Visconti's many alterations, additions, and omissions made his film less Platonic, ironic, and dialectic than Mann's text. The film also fails, he explains, to connect the beauty and the decadence of Venice.

Four other critics similarly faulted Visconti for misrepresenting Mann's characters, plot, and setting and for thereby changing the essence of his story. In 1971, Joan Mellen wrote that Visconti's decisions to make Aschenbach a composer and to overwhelm his cinematic scenes with Mahler's music were disastrous. He also made the mistakes, she notes, of beginning with Aschenbach already on the boat to Venice, of making him a dirty old man, not a tragic character, and of substituting melodrama for Mann's subtle psychological analysis of repressed sexuality. Visconti also grossly simplifies Mann's insights into the amorality of art, Mellen says, and he fails to grasp Aschenbach's social and historical import. He also turns Tadzio into "an outrageous flirt" (43). As a result of these mistakes, his film is "painfully callow" (47). Mellen herself sometimes fails to grasp Mann's story. Compared to Mann's Aschenbach, for example, Visconti's does indeed seem a "repressed, priggish gentleman" and a "whining, whimpering man in need of smelling salts," but it seems unlikely that Mann was speaking for "those who would avert their eyes from men too weak or too sensitive to survive in a puritanical, callous, and self-centered age" (41). It is likewise true that Mann seems more consistent for never letting Aschenbach's bourgeois admirers see him as a sham, but his hero does not succumb, as Mellen thinks, to filthy and corrupt impulses that Aschenbach himself taught the bourgeoisie to disdain. Bernd Schmeier, also in 1971, called Visconti's film a sacrilege, a sin, a crime, and a *malheur*. Its Tadzio is a boy prostitute, Schmeier writes, and its Aschenbach is vulgar. He wrongly adds that the latter, in Mann's novella, is a historian. Mann's brother-in-law Klaus Pringsheim, again in 1971, objected to Visconti's film for more personal reasons. Pringsheim had studied with Mahler, whom he thinks the film dishonors. He also thinks the film misrepresents Mann's story, and he promises to take action against this double defamation:

> Es muß und wird etwas geschehen, um ein unverzeihliches Unrecht wiedergut-zumachen und um die Namen zweier Giganten der europäischen Literatur und Musik vor weiteren Beleidigungen zu schützen.

> [Something must and will be done to redress an unpardonable injustice and to protect the names of two giants of European literature and music against further insults.] (10)

In 1972, B. M. Kane similarly described Mann's Aschenbach as a composite figure whose ambiguities Visconti destroyed by modeling him closely on Mahler. In general, Visconti's film offers "a heady feast for eye and ear but does scant justice to the depths and subtleties of the original" (74). Its attention to detail, its exquisite images, and its "impeccable surface accuracy" (75) add up to an impressive visual tour de force, but they do not convey the psychological or the mythological dimensions of Mann's story. Visconti's principal fault is the way in which he portrays Venice, Kane adds, since he fails to capture the sinister atmosphere that it has in Mann. Nostalgic for its bygone and bourgeois world, he instead suggests a "mood of extended sentimental whimsy which is a travesty of the sultry and demonic aestheticism which surrounds Mann's Venice" (81).

Other critics saw pros as well as cons in both Mann's book and Visconti's film. In 1971, Joachim Günther told how the film made him reread the book. Günther compares them and reflects on the latter. Mahler's music does not correspond to Mann's prose, he claims, and the film clumsily ruins Mann's subtle psychology of the artist. Mann's own exact descriptions may not leave much room for readers' imagination, he adds, but films leave none at all, a fact that precludes all fantasies about Visconti's Tadzio. Although the boy looks much the way Mann describes him, he also seems alarmingly like a male prostitute. Furthermore, readers who do not share Mann's stylistic morality will lay the story aside, bored by its thin and ambiguous plot. At the same time, Mann's high art of the word makes reading it in one sitting barbaric. Its protagonist's eroticism is improbably naïve, moreover, and its true theme is the autumn of life. The story no longer seems shocking, as it did when it first appeared, Günther writes, but it is also remote from the present, which is less intellectual about art. When we think of the book now, he argues, we shall also think of the film, in spite of all its flaws. Also in 1971, Jean Améry similarly argued that from now on there would be two versions of *Death in Venice*. The novella and the film are both valid, Améry claims, being congruous in some respects and contradictory in others. The images and the music from the film shame our imagination, he contends, yet it is the de-materializing process of language that changed the good looks of a boy whom Mann once saw into fatally intellectual beauty. The Aschenbach of the film also proves the impossibility of conveying consciousness by means of physical gestures. Here, too, Améry adds, the facticity of images collides with the suggestive vagueness of words. Visconti has nonetheless, according to Améry, interpreted Mann and created a new *Death in Venice*. In 1975, Geoffrey Wagner regretted that Visconti had interfered with Mann's stylization by inserting common reality. Dirk Bogarde, moreover, looks too much like "an absent-minded professor who is in reality a lecherous fag" (343). The film is an assault on Mann's story, in fact, which it nevertheless successfully complements "in the manner of some richly visual footnote" (345). Visconti interprets Mann's sense of pessimism with integrity, Wagner adds, and his film is an analogy that has to be respected. Wagner also observes that Aschenbach's degrading collapse recalls that of Oscar Wilde. He is rightly cautious about allowing that the youthful coarseness Mann attributes to Aschenbach may involve visiting a prostitute like the one Visconti adds. The treatise that Mann's Aschenbach composes on the Lido, however, is not a "frankly pornographic eulogy of Tadzio" (341).

Further critics expressed more positive views of the film. In July 1971, Urs Jenny noted that Visconti is faithful to much of Mann's story, although his Aschenbach is very different. His film, Jenny explains, is phenomenal in its high-handed appropriation, which transforms Mann's world into Visconti's. Its music triumphantly conveys, he adds, what language could only crudely express. In the same month, July 1971, Wolfgang Limmer wrote that one might now see Aschenbach's fall as the decline of the bourgeois class and epoch more clearly than in Mann's day. In November 1971, Michael Mann, Thomas's youngest son, wrote a laudatory open letter to Visconti. More than a mere transposition of the novella from one medium into another, he exclaims, the film is its legitimate complement. By linking Aschenbach to music, in fact, Visconti improves on Mann's story. Michael dislikes Visconti's having turned Aschenbach into a neurotic oddball who lacks tragic pathos and seems incapable of the works attributed to him. In conclusion, however, he praises Visconti for bringing Aschenbach up to date. In 1972, Robert Plank observed that, "Ironically, more people may in the end know *Death in Venice* the film than *Death in Venice* the book" (95). He also asks what light the former sheds on the latter, and he finds fault with the "beckoning quality" (98) of Visconti's Tadzio. Plank also notes that internal processes in the book become external events in the film, a shift that changes their psychological significance. In the novella, for example, Mann's hero only thinks he sees Tadzio gesture to him. At the end of the film, Tadzio actually does. With a flashback to a heart attack his Aschenbach has suffered, Plank adds, Visconti also implies that people die only of natural causes. He thereby alters Mann's moral tragedy, perhaps making it more modern. In 1974, Alexander Hutchison argued that the novella and film both address the ethical paradox of form. Visconti borrows and develops Mann's leitmotifs, Hutchison writes, but he sometimes changes their import. His Aschenbach, unlike Mann's, knows that he wants to leave Venice because he loves Tadzio, who becomes an erotic conspirator. Hutchison occasionally misconstrues the novella. Visconti's Aschenbach may believe that beauty results from labor, for example, but this is not, as Hutchison claims, the aesthetic point made in Mann's dialogues between Plato's Socrates and Phaedrus.

In contrast to these critical and ambivalent assessments of Visconti's film, initial reactions to Britten's opera hailed it as skillful and even brilliant. In an introduction to it broadcast by the BBC in 1973, and in notes for a recording of it issued in 1974, Donald Mitchell made a strong case for setting the novella to music. Ironically, Mitchell observes, Mann's otherwise articulate hero cannot express his powerful feelings for Tadzio. Britten seized the opportunity that this speechlessness presents: "That there is no verbal communication in *Death in Venice* certainly creates a situation that is ripe for music" (240). Music is able to convey what cannot be spoken, as is ballet, Mitchell adds, and Britten employs both these nonverbal media. The latter is especially prominent, Mitchell says, in the choral dances that he adds in a scene called "The Games of Apollo." In all of its alien complexity, moreover, the percussion music that he uses to characterize Tadzio is "quite the equal of Mann's elaborate literary construct" (244). Peter Evans, likewise in 1973, argued that the opera was remarkably true to Mann. Its musical details, he explains, afford insights comparable to those of Mann's verbal subtleties. According to Evans, Britten both underscores Aschenbach's detachment and, since he substitutes soliloquy for Mann's third-person narration, makes his self-scrutiny more pronounced. A few words in Myfanwy Piper's libretto impoverish or even vulgarize Mann's text, Evans notes, but that libretto, on the whole, accurately conveys the inner conflict of Mann's hero. Indeed, Evans thinks the opera "a sustained study of festering obsession" (490). Commenting on the New York première of Britten's opera in 1974, Andrew Porter contended that Mann's novella lends itself to music, thanks to its leitmotivic composition. By revealing the hymnic celebration of beauty that Mann intended before he cast a colder narrative eye on his hero, Porter claims, Britten's music succeeds where Mann thought words failed. By expressing his thoughts aloud in Britten's recitatives, Porter adds, Aschenbach becomes even more self-conscious than he is in the novella. The opera, however, reflects the fact that Mann never has him speak to Tadzio, his family, or his friends: it casts them as dancers who do not sing.

Besides the cinematic and the operatic versions of *Death in Venice* done by Visconti and Britten, there was a drawing published with Jürgen Theobaldy's poem "Die Erdbeeren von Venedig" (The Strawberries of Venice), and there were three medallions and a medal inspired by the novella and issued to commemorate the hundredth anniversary of Mann's birth. The poem, an irreverent take on Aschenbach's pursuit of Tadzio and consumption of tainted fruit, appeared in 1974. Berndt Höppner's drawing depicts Gustav Mahler regarding a giant strawberry perched on an ottoman. The medallions and the medal were all done by female artists: Louise Metz, Lenore Gerber-Sporleder, and Elisabeth Baumeister-Bühler. As Otto Marzinek described these works in 1975, they almost always show Tadzio naked and Aschenbach drowning in the Venetian lagoon.

Finally, *Death in Venice* appeared in two important new editions in the early 1970s. Both these editions included scholarly commentaries. In an essay appended in 1970 to a revision of Kenneth Burke's 1924 translation, Erich Heller considered the tenuous links between autobiography and literature. Heller thinks that Mann may have been trying to hide his own experience of feelings of "forbidden love" when he claimed that he originally planned a story about Goethe. At any rate, Heller contends, Mann transformed his life into an aesthetic composition. Mann clearly alludes to his own career when he describes Aschenbach's, for example, but he is not identical with his fictional hero. Giving that hero Mahler's facial features, moreover, may have been an attempt to lend his tale universal meaning by distracting from its autobiographical nature. As Heller writes when summing up such possibilities, "It is fascinating and instructive to observe the autobiographical hide-and-seek that Thomas Mann is so fond of playing in the unreliable border-region between the empirical and the imaginative truth" (107). The gap between these two kinds of truth is clear from how the views on neoclassicism that Mann expressed in his essay *Über die Kunst Richard Wagners* differ from those embodied in his novella. As Heller explains, he wrote the essay on stationery from the hotel in which he has Aschenbach lodge, and his criticisms of Wagner foreshadow Aschenbach's aesthetic ideal. The content of the novella, however, is at loggerheads with its classical form, for its author parodies a beloved but bygone classical literary tradition. Heller also notes that Mann's strawberries recall Eve's apple in the Garden of Eden. A German version of this essay appeared in 1972. In English, Heller made similar remarks on autobiographical aspects of the novella in 1976.

The other new edition of Mann's novella, this one in its original German, included an introduction and notes, both in English, by T. J. Reed in 1971. Like Heller, Reed discusses the issue of autobiography. While *Death in Venice* lends itself to formal analysis, he writes, it also reflects several literary issues Mann faced. Those issues, Reed explains, inform its psychological theme of decline and its general theme of the dangers of beauty. It is a "hypothetical autobiography" (27), in fact, that criticizes the possible course of Mann's own career. In it, he experiments with Platonic idealism but ultimately remains true to his usual methods of psychological analysis, ironic distance, and moral judgment. His initial impulse in writing it was hymnic, Reed argues, but he later tempered this impulse with a skepticism toward Plato that he found in Georg Lukács's essay "Sehnsucht und Form." According to Reed, the result was a moral fable that he had not intended, and traces of his original, hymnic conception make it ambiguous and ambivalent. The meaning of its final scene, for example, is uncertain. Aschenbach's death could be either an apotheosis or a moral criticism. In any event, Reed thinks that Aschenbach's moral decline has less to do with his homosexual attraction as such than with his failure to make it a matter of purely spiritual beauty. A condensed version of these remarks was published in 1973. In the fuller version that appeared in 1974, Reed added details about how Mann's story develops the issues raised in its second chapter, which almost seems an obituary of Aschenbach; how Mann's career had come to a standstill; how his originally affirmative conception underwent a diametrical change to become more critical; how Mann was thus a reluctant moralist; how he combined the insights of Plato and Lukács; and how his elevated style indicates his original, hymnic intentions. Reed thus studies ambiguities resulting from the genesis of the novella. As he explains, "Precisely this negative reworking of what was at first a positive conception would account perfectly for the strange mixture *Der Tod in Venedig* actually is, of enthusiasm and criticism, classical beauty and penetration, elevation and sordidness" (167).

# Conclusion

In his unfinished biography of Mann from 1975, Peter de Mendelssohn lamented that two generations of literary scholars had already plumbed *Death in Venice*, that a third was currently at work, and that a person could no longer take in all of their research. Those scholars have turned the novella over and over, de Mendelssohn notes, have taken it apart and put it back together, submitted all of its details to close scrutiny, and observed and analyzed it, in whole and in part, from top to bottom as well as side to side. Besides much worth knowing, he adds, these scholars have teased things out of Aschenbach's story that Mann never dreamed, much less intentionally thought, of putting there. The large number and variety of studies cited in this chapter help explain de Mendelssohn's exasperation.

His own approach is strictly biographical, and it produces tangible, limited results. From Mann's notes for the novella he confirms, as Dierks suggested in 1972, that Aschenbach was born in the city of Liegnitz. Mann calculated Aschenbach's age to be fifty-three in 1911, moreover, and the date of his birth to be 1858. De Mendelssohn adds that Mann thereby adheres closely to the dates of Mahler, who was born in 1860 and died on 18 May 1911. As Mann noted, he also remarks, Aschenbach leaves Munich four days later, on 22 May, then spends ten days on the island of Brioni, and quits it for Venice on 2 June. The outbreak of cholera begins in the fourth week of his stay there, around 27 June. De Mendelssohn observes that these dates follow those of Mann's own trip to Venice in the spring of 1911 by about a month. He seems to mean by a week. He also clarifies some of the parallels between these imaginary and actual trips that Mann himself drew in *On Myself.* According to Mann's wife Katia, for example, the actual luggage misdirected in Venice belonged to Heinrich, not Thomas. As reported in 1965 by Andrzej Doegowski, moreover, (de Mendelssohn spells his name "Dolegowski") Mann modeled Tadzio on Baron Władysław Moes, who was fourteen when he and his family vacationed in Venice in 1911, and who learned of his role in the novella when it was translated into Polish in 1923, but who did not publicly acknowledge that role until 1964. His friend Janek Fudakowski, the model for Jaschu, later recalled joking with Moes about the "old" man — the thirty-five-year-old Thomas Mann — who kept looking at them on the Lido. De Mendelssohn goes on to say that it took Mann a year to write *Death in Venice,* that he sent the manuscript to *Die Neue Rundschau* on 21 July 1912, that the limited luxury edition published by Hans von Weber presumably appeared by Christmas, and that the edition published by Samuel Fischer came out in February 1913. De Mendelssohn mentions several of the early reviews, adding that Mann liked it when people told him *Death in Venice* was a moral, a puritanical, even a soldierly book.

De Mendelssohn not only cites such biographical facts and the wealth of details from Mann's life that recur in the novella, but also tries to make sense of them. He wants to determine what the novella meant in Mann's life and what it says about that life. Among the many questions he asks, the main one is: Did Mann portray himself in Aschenbach? Or, put another way: Just who is this Aschenbach? De Mendelssohn admits that these questions prove vexing. The novella has many qualities suggesting that Mann intended it as an example of the new classicality mentioned in his essay *Über die Kunst Richard Wagners.* As de Mendelssohn writes, "Ihre Architektur ist die eines antiken Tempels mit fünf Säulen; sie hat auch die Struktur einer Symphonie in fünf Sätzen" (Its architecture is that of an ancient temple with five columns; it also has the structure of a symphony in five movements) (910). There is also more of Mann's self in Aschenbach, he explains, than Mann's own professions of stylistic mimicry and parody imply. Aschenbach thus strikes him as more legitimate and more credible than Mann intended. In the end, though, de Mendelssohn admits that *Death in Venice* cannot be clearly deciphered on an autobiographical level alone. The plethora of studies that he decries may thus not be entirely unnecessary after all. At any rate, he explains that Fischer published the novella in an initial printing of 8,000 copies, which immediately sold out; that by the end of 1913, this figure had risen to 18,000; that during the First World War, it reached 33,000; and that by 1930, it was 80,000. As Wolfgang Mertz reported in 1975, moreover, sales of the paperback German edition alone increased more than

# 4: Further Developments, 1976–95

## Introduction

SCHOLARLY RESEARCH ON Mann's novella, not to mention other forms of its reception, did not diminish in the two decades that followed the centenary of his birth. The scope and depth of such research increased, in fact, as did its volume. In part, this increase was due to the publication of his previously sealed diaries and his notebooks. Most studies of *Death in Venice* that appeared in those twenty years, moreover, fall into the broad categories established in the previous chapter. First, there is the issue of aesthetics and artists, including comparisons drawn between *Death in Venice* and Mann's other writings. Second, there are the myths and the other sources that figure in his story, along with all the similarities that scholars have found between that story and works of other writers. Third, there are matters of style, like irony and narrative voice, and of symbols, considered together with the place of the novella in literary history. Fourth, there are philosophical, political, and psychoanalytic readings. Fifth, there are studies that focus on homosexuality, often in light of Mann's diaries and their revelations about its significance in his own emotional life. Those studies treat this topic more extensively and often more provocatively than previous scholars had, a fact that distinguishes this period of the reception of *Death in Venice* from earlier ones. Sixth, there are other issues such as the reception or rereading of the novella, attributes of Tadzio and his historical model, miscellaneous aspects of Mann's style, and the setting of Venice. Finally, there are remarks on music and on illustrations of scenes from the novella as well as on adaptations of it. The last include not only Visconti's film and Britten's opera, but also two ballets and two plays. While these seven categories are almost identical to the ones found in the previous chapter, the reception of *Death in Venice* from 1976 to 1995 became far more complex. Nicklas's study of 1968 had been the only book-length treatment of the novella, but five such works appeared in these two decades, and this higher total includes neither Luijs's thesis of 1987 on the reception of its homoerotic element nor the introductory and didactic commentaries of Frizen in 1993 and T. J. Reed in 1994, not to mention commentaries whose authors have not otherwise contributed to research on the novella. Similarly, while the scholarship of the prior twenty years included one major biography — de Mendelssohn's of

1975 — that of the next two decades included four. All the categories in this chapter contain correspondingly larger numbers of sources. The increased quantity of those sources was not always attended by an increase in quality.

## Aesthetics, Artists, and Mann's Other Writings

Studies stressing issues of aesthetics and artists in Mann's story continued a critical tradition established in the initial reviews of 1913–14 and revived in the many books and articles devoted to those issues from 1956 to 1975. The studies of aesthetic matters saw in that story dichotomies such as intellect and sensuality, form and formlessness, and inspiration and consciousness, or reflected on the Platonic concept of beauty or on Aschenbach's artistic ethics. Those concerned with artists described the aesthetic mind, the artistic psyche, the ideas of artists' dignity and nature, and the demise of Aschenbach, whom other studies portrayed as a representative of trends in literary history such as aestheticism, decadence, and modernism. Studies that tied *Death in Venice* to Mann's other writings told how it is and is not like *Tonio Kröger* and his other stories, his novels, and his essays, or how it quotes and is quoted in those other works. In keeping with the biographical tone often taken in appraisals of Mann's novella between 1976 and 1995, many of these studies link their topics to his personal life and his career. Some also betray the influence of increasingly abstruse literary theory. Several are remarkably inaccurate about the fictional facts of Mann's plot.

In the first book since Nicklas's study of 1968 devoted solely to *Death in Venice*, Hermann Luft, in 1976, analyzed the conflict between intellect and sensuality. As an artist, Luft argues, Aschenbach goes from one extreme to the other. The short treatise he writes in Tadzio's presence at the beach briefly balances these extremes, showing that he has achieved an ideal artistic state. Tadzio himself is symbolic, embodying intellect that has become visible and thus sensual. Luft addresses the problem of the artist, then, which he calls the main theme of Mann's oeuvre. In life as well as art, Luft explains, Aschenbach has cultivated external form at the expense of his inner emotion. His feelings are reawakened at the beginning of Mann's story, Luft adds, and in his relationship to Tadzio. That relationship changes, starting as aesthetic admiration and paternal affection before becoming more sensual. Tadzio has a dual function in this process because his beauty is real as well as symbolic, both human and mythological, and both sensual and intellectual. Aschenbach achieves a golden mean in his treatise, but its equilibrium and harmony are precarious. As Luft writes:

> Es ist, als stünde er auf dem Grat eines hohen Berges, dort, wo sich zwei Steilhänge treffen, von welchen einer in die eisig-leblosen Tiefen der Geistigkeit und der andere in die glutvoll-lebendigen Schluchten der Sinnlichkeit abfällt.

[It is as if he were standing on the ridge of a high mountain, there where two steep slopes meet; one of them drops off into the icy-lifeless depths of intellect, and the other into the fiery-vivid gorges of sensuality.] (77)

Aschenbach loses his balance, Luft observes, but what he then wants is sensuality and emotion for their own sake, so Tadzio is just a means to an end. Aschenbach's intoxication becomes sexual and narcissistic, moreover, and he dies like a tragic hero, an artist at war with himself. While Mann is sympathetic to him, Luft notes, Aschenbach is an example not to be followed. So cautiously assessing the conflict between the intellect and the senses, Luft often relates it to the proverbial two souls in the breast of Goethe's Faust.

Other scholars similarly thought that *Death in Venice* turned on one or another fundamental dichotomy. For R. D. Miller in 1976, that dichotomy was one of form and formlessness. According to Miller, Mann's story only appears to show form defeated by formlessness. Actually, he argues, Mann commends the former and condemns the latter. Aschenbach worships form and then is overwhelmed by formlessness in his passion for Tadzio. Mann portrays this process as tragic, and he approves of the formal, spiritual aspects of Aschenbach's love. As the embodiment of form, Tadzio is the "perfect objective correlative of Aschenbach's aestheticism" (183), and in the end he beckons him toward a Platonic realm: "Aschenbach, having paid the price of formlessness in this world, gazes beyond to the next, where form, uncompromised by the world's materialism, shines in absolute perfection" (193). Interpreting Aschenbach's vision of a tropical jungle, Miller remarks that an association of formlessness with foreign countries and the embodiment of this association in a tiger also occur in the diary kept by Ottilie, the girl fatefully courted in Goethe's *Die Wahlverwandtschaften*. For Karen Drabek Vogt in 1987, Mann's novella portrayed the polar mental states of consciousness and inspiration. Like Miller, Vogt argues that Mann not only shows a creative process gone awry but also hints at one that works as it should. Aschenbach has lost his inspiration, she explains, and has become too rational and too critical to be creative. He renews that inspiration, but passion and emotion then avenge themselves on him. Mann thus suggests that artists need to balance such extremes. Vogt is right to observe that Mann linked creativity to a fondness for autobiography. Her remarks, however, contain many mistakes. Aschenbach has not "taught his readers (and himself) not to dwell in the abyss of superficial psychological understanding" (32), there is no "image of Tadzio in the essay written on the Lido" (39), and it is not the case that Aschenbach "will not confront the truth that Tadzio is internally unsound" (39). Vogt is right to relate Aschenbach's psyche to that of the German nation, moreover, but she exaggerates Mann's power to alter the course of history. "If Europe," she says, "had seen 'Death in Venice' as a warning against instead of support for decadent and aesthetic tendencies, it might have avoided the destruction of World War One" (54).

Many studies about artists and aestheticism note Plato's concept of beauty. In 1978, Walter K. Stewart did so in order to describe Aschenbach's "path to insight." This insight comes at the climax of the novella, he maintains, and that climax is reached in Mann's second dialogue based on Plato's *Phaedrus*. First, Stewart tells how Mann triggers such insight by modeling Aschenbach's degradation on that of the elderly Goethe, then having his hero gain "insight into the abyss" (52), an experience tied, both here and in Mann's other fiction, to bodies of water. Second, Stewart locates the origin of that insight in Plato's ambiguous notion of beauty. While beauty can stimulate creativity, he explains, excessive devotion to it can upset the artist's balance between the spirit and the senses. Stewart's argument here resembles the one made by Luft and draws heavily on the work of T. J. Reed. Aschenbach's belief in beauty is absurd, he adds, and "there can therefore be no doubt that Mann always conceived of *Der Tod in Venedig* in negative terms" (54). Other scholars, including Reed, express just such doubt. It is also not true, as Stewart claims, that the treatise Aschenbach writes at the beach is about art and taste. Richard White made a similar case in 1990. According to him, Mann's story calls into question not only Plato's conception of beauty but also the arguments of every other philosopher who attributes redemptive powers to art. *Death in Venice,* then, has to do with the problem of art and the history of aesthetics. Implicitly, it is a profoundly anti-Platonic critique of Plato. Indeed, White deems it "a challenge to every idealizing impulse, including that of Plato, which seeks to justify the erotic impulse or the pursuit of beauty for the sake of something higher" (61). Its hero's Platonic concern for beauty leads to his dissolution and death, White thinks, a fact that disproves Schopenhauer and Nietzsche. White is mistaken when he claims that Aschenbach's mother was the daughter of a composer.

Some scholars regarded the relationship between aesthetics and ethics in Mann's story. In 1980, Hermann Kurzke quoted *Death in Venice* to open an essay about how the two prove irreconcilable in its author's early work. Only later, Kurzke argues, did Mann imply a narrative ethics. Franz Maria Sonner's strange book about the novella used a similar term in 1984. Sonner reflects on Aschenbach's aesthetic ethics, which he explains both by examining Mann's story and by relating the themes he finds there, as his cryptic subtitle proclaims, "mit dem zeitgenössischen intellektuellen Kräftefeld" (with the contemporary intellectual force field). In other words, he connects Mann's story to discourses drawn from sociology, psychoanalysis, and politics. In the end, he even compares Aschenbach to medieval Christian mystics. Sonner discovers in all those discourses a battle for control of the body — the body of individuals as well as the body politic. Both kinds of body contain great disjunctive energies. The themes that he treats include Aschenbach's economical work habits, which recall the Protestant ethic and the spirit of capitalism linked by Max Weber, and his irrational "heroism of weakness," which parallels traits proposed by Oswald Spengler to account for the decline of the West. Sonner also argues that Aschenbach suppresses his feelings to heighten his aesthetic pleasure and that he desires both form and formlessness. Tadzio's perfection embodies both these extremes, he adds, and Aschenbach's ambivalent attraction to it, his acceptance of its immediacy and ethical polarity, results in a state of mind like the ecstasy described by mystics such as Meister Eckhart (circa 1260–1327). There is a sacred potential to Aschenbach's aesthetic ethics, then, and he ultimately experiences the body as a celibate machine. Sonner illustrates this complex argument in many schematic tables. Unfortunately, he also obscures his intriguing insights with much unnecessary theory, derived largely from Michel Foucault. One gets a sense of the resulting abstractness by noting that he does not even mention Mann or *Death in Venice* until the last lines of his thirty-five-page introduction.

Two other studies linking aesthetics and ethics in *Death in Venice* were written by Harvey Goldman in 1988 and 1992. Like Sonner in 1984, Goldman explains Aschenbach's decline in terms coined by the German sociologist Max Weber. In 1988, Goldman interpreted the novella as showing the death, in life, of the artistic personality. Aschenbach is imprisoned in such a personality, Goldman argues, and can no longer perceive the world as it is or feel a passion for a real human being. Neither Mann nor his narrator understands, he adds, that their story is "ultimately about a man entrapped within his own personality in the prisonhouse of the calling" (188). This calling is soldierly service, a burden on the self, and it exhausts Aschenbach, who thinks that the struggle it takes and the suffering it causes lend his life meaning. Through such devotion to work, Goldman notes, he hopes to regain naïveté and artistic conviction. Mann and his narrator tell us about Aschenbach's dilemma and doom, moreover, and they present his true identity as feminine. Aschenbach's struggle in his calling thus seems gendered, Goldman writes. In fact, though, Mann tells "the story of a burden and tragedy great enough to call into question both the whole meaning of art pursued as a calling and the personality constructed and enrolled in its service" (199). Aschenbach's self-conquest, then, the nature of the calling as a way of life, is suspect. In Goldman's view, his tragedy is that he lives completely in symbols. His love for Tadzio is actually an artist's passion for beauty, for example, a fantasy of himself mastering and possessing the beautiful. Living only for art, he has died to life. The rest of his story follows from this premise. According to Goldman, the story thus shows the consequences not only of a calling gone wrong, but also of a calling gone right. The idea and ideology of the calling itself is the problem. Goldman added in 1992 that *Death in Venice* shows how "ascetic practices that shape the self have potentially unforeseen, and potentially disastrous, consequences for the self" (19). In *Betrachtungen eines Unpolitischen*, Goldman notes, Mann took up positions he had criticized in his novella, re-identifying himself with Aschenbach and with the German nation founded by Frederick the Great.

Another reading of *Death in Venice* in terms borrowed from Max Weber was given in 1994 by Edith Weiller. According to her, Mann's ideas are similar to Weber's but also go beyond them. She explains that Mann considered Aschenbach, with his strict work ethic, to be representative of his age. Mann's story of this ascetic artist, she adds, shows how even the realm of the aesthetic is rationalized in the way that Weber posits when he describes the secular transformations of religious self-discipline. Aschenbach's heroic perseverance, Weiller says, takes Weber's notion of the modern personality to an extreme where repressed needs threaten a conscious subject weakened by its own asceticism. Moreover, Aschenbach's refusal to know himself as he succumbs to sensual desire, his refusal to acknowledge the erotic motive for his visions of beauty, recalls the intellectual sacrifice that Weber thinks made in ascetic Protestantism. Aschenbach's mastery of aesthetic forms results from an ethical imperative to control his natural inclinations, Weiller also observes, but his self-discipline actually releases the sensuality that it was supposed to contain and destroys the innocence that he tries to achieve. Mann thus shows the personal consequences implied by Weber's idea of the calling.

Five further studies examined the artist's mind, psychology, dignity, and nature. In 1978, Daniel Albright argued that *Death in Venice* is the culmination of Mann's stories exploring the aesthetic mind. It is psychomachia, Albright explains, and an allegory of the workings of that mind. It calls art itself into question as the external world of the novella becomes congruous with Aschenbach's soul and conforms to the power of his imagination. Tadzio, for example, becomes consubstantial with him. In this tale about "the progress of the artist's image through the temporal world," though, Tadzio is also increasingly involved in "the turgidity of the corporeal" (231). This loss of ideality shows a descent of artistic power into material life. Albright thinks that Mann later would have liked Aschenbach to avoid "contaminating himself in the humid apparatus of personal expression" (233). In any case, Albright finds fault with aesthetic solipsism. His remarks sometimes sound trenchant but are often overblown and occasionally inaccurate. The fop on the boat does not tease Aschenbach about his mistress, for example, and though Tadzio may be Aschenbach's fiction, as Albright argues, Aschenbach does not try to "liberate Tadzio into words" or translate him into an "enraptured essay on aesthetic theory" (230). In 1992, Martin Travers similarly found "a new vision of artistic psychology" (48) in *Death in Venice*. The novella examines Aschenbach's heroic pose, Travers argues, ending on a note of banality, for he must "drain the dregs of his inauthentic life and philosophy" (57). In 1989, Esther H. Lesér similarly wrote that Mann recounts a loss of artistic dignity. While Lesér may be right to remark that he shows Plato's Socrates clashing with Nietzsche's, she also makes several mistakes. Platen, not Dante, occurs to Aschenbach on his approach to Venice, for example, and Tadzio does not respond with a sigh to Aschenbach's glance after the street musicians entertain the hotel guests. In a note, Lesér remarks that Goethe, like Aschenbach, was ennobled at the age of fifty. In 1994, Irvin Stock added that *Death in Venice* was, until *Doktor Faustus*, Mann's "blackest exposé of the artist-nature" (32). The details of his own Venetian trip that he used in it, Stock writes, enabled him to "go thrillingly far in self-realization" (33). In 1982, Susanne Otto likewise stressed the biographical function, for Mann, of Aschenbach's art. That art is socially acceptable, Otto explains, and by describing Aschenbach's fate, Mann asks if art and bourgeois respectability meet all his own needs, or if he is still vulnerable. The novella confirms his position as an author and a husband, she adds, and compensates him for unrealized pleasures. With the motifs and themes that make his personal experience seem general, it also demonstrates his professionalization. According to Otto, Mann thus shows the limits and the dangers of his own kind of artistic life.

From a related angle, J. Brooks Bouson misinterpreted *Death in Venice* in 1989. Bouson stresses, as the title of his chapter about the novella announces, its "defensive aestheticism." Mann, he says, deflects readers' attention from Aschenbach's horrible demise by encouraging them to ponder stylistic and structural features. Readers thus avoid full awareness of his disintegration and translate narcissistic anxieties into literary discourse. Mann's narrator likewise retreats from the tale he relates, according to Bouson, and even critics of the novella shield themselves from the anxieties that it enacts. Whatever merit this argument has, it is incorrect to characterize prior research as, by and large, shying away from the awful truth about Aschenbach. Mann's narrator is hardly "writing himself into the text" (110), moreover, in speaking of a "shrewd critic" of Aschenbach's weak heroes. As noted earlier, this term alludes to Samuel Lublinski. Furthermore, Bouson often misreads Mann's story because he knows it only in Lowe-Porter's deficient translation. He claims that Aschenbach's essay is an attempt to grasp Tadzio's beauty and to seize and possess him, quoting the verb "snatch up." In German, though, Mann uses *tragen*, which means that Aschenbach wishes to "bear" or "carry" Tadzio's beauty into the realm of intellect. Bouson also thinks that Mann's narrator creates the illusion of a reading community by calling Aschenbach "our traveller," "our solitary," and "our adventurer." In German, though, Mann uses no such possessive pronouns, referring to Aschenbach only with definite articles: *the* traveling, solitary, adventuring one. Similarly, Bouson notes Aschenbach's "hypercathexis of the visual mode" (112) after quoting Mann's supposed phrase "the language of pictures." This phrase is Lowe-Porter's invention. In German, Mann compares Amor to mathematicians who show children comprehensible images of pure forms. Finally, Bouson argues that the presence of "phallic women" (113) in Aschenbach's lurid dream marks the return of the repressed. The waists of maenads in that dream, he thinks, are surrounded by coiling snakes. As Marianne Zerner pointed out in 1945, though, this is another of Lowe-Porter's many careless mistakes. In Mann's German, things are the other way around: the snakes are held in the middle of *their* bodies by the women. Bouson's many flawed conclusions, then, show how hasty it can be to judge *Death in Venice* without reading it in German.

A final type of study concerned with aesthetics and artists cast Aschenbach as representative of literary aestheticism, decadence, and modernism. In 1982, Hinrich C. Seeba called *Death in Venice* the classic expression of the *fin de siècle* interest in how art can displace life. Aschenbach's thoughts on Tadzio's statuesque form, Seeba adds, make him seem like the eighteenth-century art historian Johann Joachim Winckelmann. The last sentence of Mann's story, he thinks, could apply to Winckelmann's death in Trieste in 1768. In 1985, Walter Schmitz wrote that the existential dilemma of the Protestant aesthete Aschenbach, in the social and sensual setting of Catholic Venice, conveys the irresponsibility of aestheticism. Mann, Schmitz notes, also alludes to Munich. Aschenbach's story, he explains, exposes as false the claim made by Munich's literati to represent German culture. It thus is a *roman-à-clef* like Mann's *Beim Propheten* (At the Prophet's, 1904), which debunks Stefan George's bohemian disciples. In 1986, Wolfdietrich Rasch wrote that the novella demonstrates Mann's inner attachment to decadence and its themes. Relativizing Aschenbach's attempt to renounce decadence, he argues, is a tentative experiment typical of Mann. In 1988, Franz Norbert Mennemeier claimed that Mann attributed his own artistic coldness to Aschenbach and succumbed in the latter's final dream to his own decadent weakness. Like his distanced narrator, Mennemeier writes, Mann also practiced a poetics of indifference, a poetics characteristic of aestheticism. In 1991, René-Pierre Colin likewise traced Aschenbach's fall to an aestheticism from which Mann distanced himself. In an extended essay on *Death in Venice* and the decadent spirit, Colin concludes that Aschenbach is tragically unable to bear his Dionysian revelation of the power of passion and instinct. Finally, in 1995, Hubert Ohl called Aschenbach a textbook decadent, an artist who leads an exclusively aesthetic existence. Mann himself uses aesthetic categories to describe Aschenbach's works, moreover, a fact that troubles Ohl, who faults the formal morality Mann attributes to Aschenbach as well as to Aschenbach's own protagonists. The treatise Aschenbach writes at the beach, Ohl adds, should have had an explicit modern theme. Mann's allusions to Greek mythology make the fictional events of his story seem justified and timeless, but they also stylize them at the expense of their relevance to the present. With its ahistorical classicism, then, the Venetian novella documents its author's apolitical detachment. Ohl thus seems to find Mann himself too aesthetic.

The foregoing studies of the related themes of art, artists, and aesthetics often mention Mann's other fiction. Further studies more directly connect *Death in Venice* to his other writings. The work cited most frequently in those further studies is *Tonio Kröger*, and the most revealing comparison of these two novellas was drawn by Richard Sheppard in 1989. Sheppard goes against the grain of much previous scholarship, arguing that they are more different than alike. *Death in Venice,* he explains, is informed by a different problematic and sense of reality. While writing it, Mann's imagination eluded his conscious control, "seized and saturated by a powerful sense of what Nietzsche called the Dionysiac with which he was able to suffuse, mythologise and transcend his earlier Naturalism" (94). Both novellas address the problem of the artist, Sheppard adds, both show the influence of Nietzsche, and both have an auto-biographical dimension. Tonio resembles the young Aschenbach, moreover, and their stories share formal and linguistic features. All these common elements, however, have different functions. *Tonio Kröger* is about a human being, an adolescent crush, middle-class normality, and a positive ideal. By contrast, *Death in Venice* is about a mythological power, a demonic obsession, pathological hubris, and apocalyptic destruction. *Tonio Kröger* is a work of bourgeois realism, then; *Death in Venice,* of visionary modernism. To support this argument, Sheppard contrasts many telling details. In *Tonio Kröger,* for example, there is a tiger confined to a cage. This Dionysian animal is on the loose in *Death in Venice.* Similar differences distinguish Mann's respective versions of storms, dances, and the leitmotif of blondness. Concepts such as life and art thus mean one thing in one novella, but something different in the other. Sheppard also notes that the easygoing Russian family wisely balances Nietzsche's Apollinian and Dionysian poles, while Aschenbach has lost the saving grace of irony. Along with his luggage, Sheppard writes, he also loses his cultural riches. The problem of the artist, Sheppard concludes, is more complex in *Death in Venice,* and this later novella therefore implies a deeper love of humanity.

Other comparisons of *Death in Venice* and *Tonio Kröger* drew less nuanced conclusions. In 1992, Heinrich Detering wrote that the later novella comments on the homoerotic characteristics of the earlier one. According to him, there is an exact correspondence between the scene in which Tadzio first smiles at Aschenbach and the one in which the mature Tonio thinks he sees Hans Hansen again. Both scenes occur very near descriptions of a sunrise and of the surf, for example, that have erotic connotations. The one in *Death in Venice* repeats and intensifies the one in *Tonio Kröger,* Detering argues, and in retrospect Hans prefigures Tadzio. Both boys wear sailor suits, and both are objects of homosexual desire. They are therefore functionally equivalent. The grown Tonio, then, sees Hans in the same way that Aschenbach sees Tadzio. Both novellas thus derive from Oscar Wilde's *Picture of Dorian Gray.* In 1994, Detering incorporated this comparison into a larger study of the history of homoerotic camouflage and its literarily productive possibilities in German and in Danish literature since the mid-eighteenth century. *Death in Venice* stands at the end of that history, he argues, marking the point where such camouflage stops. By writing an unambiguously homoerotic story, he thinks, Mann, himself a homosexual author, breaks an old taboo. Indeed, "*Der Tod in Venedig* ist das *coming out* der deutschen *mainstream*-Literatur" (*Death in Venice* is the coming out of German mainstream literature) (34). The novella not only contains a decidedly homoerotic interpretation of *Tonio Kröger,* Detering adds, but also turns the earlier story on its head in a self-travesty by making repression and sublimation of homosexuality an issue for Aschenbach, not for the text. Finally, Detering suggests that such repression and sublimation in *Death in Venice* do not implicitly belong to Winckelmann but to the educated bourgeois class that pacified his ideas and that Aschenbach represents. The novella, then, shows the original unity of homoeroticism and aesthetics. In 1993, G. A. Wells called *Tonio Kröger* a "wholesome corrective" (89) to the ambiguous morality attributed to artists in *Death in Venice.* Since the latter novella was written a decade after the former, this statement seems anachronistic. In any case, Aschenbach is certainly not "something of a 'Heimatkunst' author, castigating immorality by writing stories that can be taken into school syllabuses to make children into decent citizens" (87). Excerpts of his prose are taught because its style is formal and polished, not because its content is homespun or uplifting.

Further scholars compared *Death in Venice* to other writings by Mann. Four of them did so in 1978. Louis Leibrich wrote that Aschenbach, like the Schiller of Mann's story *Schwere Stunde,* is an artist who risks exploring the extremes of the human condition. James Northcote-Bade noted the effect of the interruption in the composition of Mann's *Felix Krull* caused by *Death in Venice.* According to Northcote-Bade, the break Mann took in 1911 and 1912 to write *Death in Venice* had just as great an effect on that novel as the later one he took from 1913 to 1951. He had difficulty writing in a humorous style again, for example, but also became aware of ways to treat the theme of homosexual attraction less earnestly. In this regard, *Felix Krull* is "a sort of antidote" (277) to *Death in Venice.* Also in 1978, Susan Sontag contrasted the novella with *Der Zauberberg.* Whereas disease simplifies and further reduces Aschenbach, she argues, it individualizes and promotes Hans Castorp: "In one fiction, disease (cholera) is the penalty for secret love; in the other, disease (TB) is its expression" (37). That same year, Peter Heller related the novella to almost all of Mann's short fiction, from *Vision* (1893) to *Die Betrogene.* Mann's basic theme, Heller writes, is present in all these stories. Mann, he notes, defined that theme as the overwhelming of a cultured, civilized person by the destructive drives of eros and thanatos. This affliction is social as well as psychological, Heller adds, and *Death in*

*Venice* presents it as refreshment through regression. The novella also real-izes the principal of the leitmotif, he explains, which is related to the psycho-analytic concept of repetition compulsion. To the extent that the end of Mann's story fulfills its beginning, he thinks, it can be read in a quasi-theological way, as being about original sin. Aschenbach would thus die because he eats forbidden fruit. In any case, Heller remarks that Aschen-bach's walk in Munich is heightened by his trip to Venice and final journey to the beyond; that embodiments of the force that destroys him come closer to him as his ego disintegrates; that the camera left standing at the beach could mean that sublimated voyeurism no longer satisfies him; and that he remains Apollinian, able to conceive of and recognize the ideal. In the end, Heller writes, his story tells not only of destruction, but also of liberation.

In other years, other scholars compared *Death in Venice* to further fiction by its author. In 1976, Reinhard Baumgart linked it to his later *Die Betrogene*. Mann wrote both these novellas, which both tell stories of love and death, during interludes in his work on *Felix Krull*, Baumgart notes, and the end of the latter recalls the former. Rosalie von Tümmler, its heroine, suggests trav-eling on the Rhine by gondola, he explains, and its last sentence, which de-scribes her death, echoes the one that tells of Aschenbach's. These allusions seem relatively harmless and mild, however, and Baumgart thinks Rosalie less culpable and less severely punished than Aschenbach. He also finds her less representative of social and historical circumstances. Baumgart concludes that the more relaxed *Die Betrogene* reads as if the con man Felix Krull had experi-enced and written *Death in Venice*. In 1993, Eckhard Heftrich tied *Death in Venice* to *Joseph und seine Brüder*. The story of the Egyptian priestess Mut-em-enet, he argues, relates eros, beauty, and art in much the same Nietzschean and Wagnerian way as Mann's Venetian novella.

The most extensive comparison between *Death in Venice* and Mann's other writings was drawn in two books by Rolf Günter Renner published in 1985 and 1987. In both, Renner's style is as dense as his argument is intri-cate. In the first, he notes the nonverbal communication and familial fanta-sies common to all of Mann's early novellas, adding that *Death in Venice* relates self-reflection and communicative behavior in a way characteristic of them. In thematizing the opposition of order to disorder, of rest to restless-ness, Renner argues, its opening passage contrasts Aschenbach's social effec-tiveness as a writer to his autistic-emotional thinking. His initial vision of a jungle, moreover, expresses intrapsychic tensions presented as a conflict between characters, tensions that can be explained by using a psychoanalytic theory of primary socialization. Those characters also offer a model of com-municative relationships, that is, of relationships grounded in language. Aschenbach tries to fantasize that he is Tadzio's father, Renner adds, playing a role in an imagined familial constellation that includes the sea as the boy's mother. By construing Tadzio as Hermes or Phaedrus, Aschenbach also cites mythology and philosophy as culturally mediated systems of discourse, systems in which the self is forced to express itself. To put it another way, Aschenbach's sexual desire relies on discourses of knowledge and culture to communicate itself. Renner's approach thus combines psychology, intellectual history, and the analysis of cultural discourses. It also presents Mann as an author who eventually came to live in his work by appropriating the lives of others, as an author who constituted his self by substituting fictional for actual biography. *Death in Venice,* Renner observes, does not yet implement this strategy. It develops psychological issues raised in Mann's earlier writings, but it still ends fatally. Only his later fiction successfully displaces his basic psychological conflict in borrowed discourses. Besides thus relating *Death in Venice* to the rest of Mann's oeuvre, Renner notes that Aschenbach's initial vision recalls a state of yogic mediation mentioned by Carl Gustav Jung; that his death shows the power of self-censorship; and that he appears to die of apoplexy, not cholera.

Renner made a similar but lengthier argument in his second book, the one published in 1987. It is devoted entirely to the relationship between *Death in Venice* and Mann's other writings, and its five chapters elucidate its title, *Das Ich als ästhetische Konstruktion* (The Ego as Aesthetic Construction). First, Renner discusses the novella as a double text. Aschenbach's state of mind hints at the multiple levels of Mann's text, he explains, levels defined in terms of waking and dreaming, dream and text, eros and word, and myth and psychology. Dreams compete with or substitute for conscious communication, for example, while myth relates psychological conflicts and literary models. Second, Renner highlights cultural systems of inscription, an expression that refers to the influence of Plato, Schopenhauer, Nietzsche, and Wagner. Mann appropriates these authors, he argues, to address his own problems of socialization, sexual love, and artistic creativity. Third, Renner reveals the original script of Mann's own inner biography. He describes *Death in Venice* as a vexation that both hides and reveals that secret text. Mann's fiction transforms his sexual wishes, Renner argues, as well as his psychological insights into his homoeroticism. Like his essays, the novella thereby displaces conflicts that Mann analyzes with ever greater consciousness. It thus is part of his self-analysis. Fourth, Renner writes that Mann's later works further develop this process of self-analysis and creative projection. Those works include his essays on Freud and his autobiographic sketches. It is *Felix Krull,* however, where the antagonism of life and works shown in *Death in Venice* is finally resolved in creative narcissism and successful socialization. Fifth, Renner considers other approaches. He likes Visconti's filmic interpretation of the novella since it, too, links Mann's story to his other works. Renner's didactic suggestions and his remarks on other scholarly methods seem to take his own approach as the measure of all things. In any event, his main point is that Mann not only literarizes psychological conflicts, but also tries to overcome them. The strength of his case lies less in his interpretation of details of *Death in Venice* than in his synoptic view of Mann's career as a whole. Renner's generalities can be extremely abstract, though, and his academic German is often vague and oracular.

A further approach linking *Death in Venice* to Mann's other writings was taken by Gert Bruhn in 1992. Bruhn shows how and why Mann both quotes such writings in the novella and quotes it in them. He often does so, Bruhn argues, when discussing his belief in artists' heroic creativity and suffering. His self-quotations thus show how closely his life and his work are related. When Mann writes that Aschenbach once said somewhere that almost everything great exists as a "Trotzdem" (Despite), for example, he quotes from his own essay *Über den Alkohol* (On Alcohol, 1906). He thus indicates Aschenbach's similarity to Schiller and hints at how he identifies with both of these authors. That one of Mann's own favorite words — "Durchhalten" (Persevere) — is also one of Aschenbach's, Bruhn adds, shows his solidarity with his protagonist in another way. This word is ironic when applied to Aschenbach's decadent mania, though, and Mann thus seems to regard him, Bruhn notes, as a parody of Schiller. In his essay *Gedanken im Kriege,* moreover, Mann quotes his statement from the novella that art is a war, an exhausting struggle. This statement sounds ironic in the novella, Bruhn thinks, but not in the essay. When Mann writes that Aschenbach used the expression "Wunder der wiedergeborenen Unbefangenheit" (miracle of reborn naïveté), he is similarly quoting his own failed drama *Fiorenza.* The expression is ironic in both works, Bruhn adds, and the novella alludes to its earlier use, which it also parodies. This same expression recurs in his *Versuch über Schiller* (Essay on Schiller, 1955). Its un-ironic use in that essay, Bruhn argues, attests to Mann's belief that Schiller achieved the "miracle" that eluded Aschenbach. Bruhn also observes that Mann quotes several passages from *Death in Venice* in his *Betrachtungen eines Unpolitischen.* Mann uses the words "Durchhalten," "Entschlossenheit" (resoluteness), and "unanständigen Psychologismus" (indecent psychologism), for example, all in quotation marks and all with regard to his own writing. Similarly, he mentions a passage about the style and the audience of Aschenbach's works, applying it, too, to his own. All of these self-quotations, Bruhn explains, show Mann's intellectual sympathy and identification with Aschenbach. This is also true in his *Deutschland und die Deutschen* (Germany and the Germans, 1945), an essay in which he quotes a line from the novella about artists being fruitful at all stages of life. Bruhn concludes that such quotations are a means of epic montage, a narrative method Mann used at least since *Death in Venice,* and that this method helped him overcome the artistic crisis he later described suffering after he finished the novella.

## Myths, Sources, and Comparisons

In addition to raising the issues of aesthetics and artists, and to comparing *Death in Venice* with Mann's other writings, readings of the novella that were given between 1976 and 1995 considered its use of myths and sources and compared it to books by other authors. In this respect, too, these readings resemble those published in the previous twenty years. Myths such as those of Narcissus, Theseus, and Dionysus were cited to explain Aschenbach's psyche as well as Mann's sources and style. Scholars also found or remarked on further sources in writings by Plato, Euripides, Lukács, and Goethe, among others. Finally, comparisons were drawn between the novella and numerous other works. Most of those works are in German or English, but some of them are in further languages: French, Italian, Spanish, Norwegian, and Japanese. Like earlier such studies of myths, sources, and comparisons — the ones published from 1956 to 1975 — those cited here cannot always be clearly distinguished from each other. Here, too, their subjects often overlap. As in the earlier studies, however, such related subjects all show the wide range of literary-historical interest taken in *Death in Venice*.

The role of narcissism in Mann's story and his life was cited by Luft in 1976, Renner in 1987, and Bouson in 1989. Other authors writing between 1976 and 1995 related *Death in Venice* to the myth that gave rise to this concept. In 1977, Herbert Anton claimed that the novella alludes to Ovid's description of Narcissus in *The Metamorphoses*. Aschenbach falls in love with his own narcissistic ego, Anton explains, a fact that has less to do with homoerotic passion than with the psychoanalytic idea of object love. In 1984, Lawrence Thornton stressed Aschenbach's romanticism in a study of narcissism and the modern novel. That romanticism, Thornton claims, is linked to Aschenbach's confusion of art and life. With his "analogical habit of mind" (176), he imaginatively transforms Tadzio. Associating the youth with the homoerotic Narcissus, Thornton adds, Aschenbach betrays a new awareness of and obsession with the self. Furthermore, his "solipsistic obsession, and the 'dark satisfaction' it breeds resonate with the destructive implications of Romantic literature, the sea, and the death music of the *Liebestod*" (181). Isolde's final aria again serves as an example of music connoting dissolution and death when Thornton invokes Wagner to interpret the cloth shrouding the camera left at the beach: "That black cloth snapped by the wind is also the black sail signaling disaster in *Tristan*" (185). Thornton has a point when he explains that the mist obscuring Aschenbach's first sight of Venice is a barrier between his conscious and unconscious, but he misidentifies the poet who wrote the verses occurring to Mann's protagonist then. That poet is Platen, not Byron. Edward Engelberg, in 1989, similarly thought of Mann's tale as "Narcissus by the Seaside" (96). It tells of an unlived life, Engelberg writes, of the terrible waste that results from having too long withheld love from the son that

Aschenbach finds in Tadzio. The abandoned camera shows such useless isolation. Finally, in 1991, Junichi Suzuki argued that Tadzio paralyzes the self-reflexive system of Aschenbach's narrative world. Narcissus himself, Suzuki writes, thus proves stronger than narcissism.

Other scholars stressed the myth of Theseus and the minotaur, the way in which Mann used his limited knowledge of such myths, and the function of mythical parallels in *Death in Venice*. In 1986, Bernhard Frank argued that Mann refers to the myth of Theseus on a romantic, a realistic, and a symbolic level. Tadzio is much like "the Phaeacian sailor who piloted Theseus' ship" (31), Frank claims, Venice is a labyrinth, and Aschenbach pursues the minotaur of passion. Frank thinks previous studies all but ignore Aschenbach's addressing Tadzio as "little Phaeax." In his article of 1965, however, Herbert Lehnert noted that Aschenbach quotes a line from the *Odyssey* that describes the easy life the Phaecians liked. In the context of Aschenbach's thoughts on how Tadzio can sleep as late as he wants, this source makes better sense. In 1990, Manfred Dierks explained Mann's use of mythology more generally, adding to his earlier remarks of 1972. *Death in Venice* is the first of Mann's works to make mythological allusions, Dierks notes, and though Mann did not yet know much about their sources, he used them to lend his fiction timeless, typical meaning. Two paths led him to mythology. First, he read Wilhelm Jensen's novella *Gradiva* (1903) and Freud's famous interpretation of it. He thus learned about the return of the repressed, the psychoanalytic concept that structures his story. He added the ideas of the Apollinian and Dionysian, Dierks says, and the result was *Death in Venice*. In 1995, Zoltán Szendi explained how Aschenbach's mythological visions and dreams convey his psychological conflict. Referring to Dionysus, Socrates and Phaedrus, and Hyacinth and Hermes, those visions and dreams are both barbaric and humane, Szendi argues, and they establish a tense balance of sexual liberation and cultured dignity. Szendi thus explains the logic of the structure, rhetoric, and composition of Mann's story. He notes, for example, that questions about the artist posed in its second chapter are taken up in the dreams and visions of its fourth and fifth. Szendi also remarks on its counterpoint, polyphony, and rhythm, joining the many other critics and scholars who have cast *Death in Venice* in terms of music.

Two other researchers discussed the multiple sources and the significance of Mann's Dionysus. In 1991, Hans-Joachim Sandberg identified twelve such sources: Mann's mother's guide to Greek and Roman mythology by Friedrich Nösselt; Goethe's *Faust;* Nietzsche's *Götzen-Dämmerung* (Twilight of the Idols, 1889) and *Die Geburt der Tragödie;* Jacob Burckhardt's *Griechische Kulturgeschichte* (Greek Cultural History, 1898–1902); Ricarda Huch's *Blüthezeit der Romantik* (The Blossoming of Romanticism, 1899); an eighteenth-century translation of a French treatise about how the ancients beat the women they loved; Gabriele D'Annunzio's *Il Fuoco* (The Flame,

1900); Samuel Lublinski's *Die Bilanz der Moderne* (The Balance of Modernism, 1904) and *Der Ausgang der Moderne* (The End of Modernism, 1909); Gerhart Hauptmann's *Griechischer Frühling* (Greek Spring, 1908); and Hermann Bahr's *Dalmatinische Reise* (Dalmatian Journey, 1909). Sandberg notes that Mann was influenced by these sources as early as 1895. He also concludes that *Death in Venice* faults Nietzsche's praise of the Dionysian, D'Annunzio's homage to Dionysus, and Hauptmann's use of Greek mythology. The author of *Death in Venice*, Sandberg writes, wanted to set an example of how to treat mythology and the mythical credibly, in a way appropriate to modern thinking. Finally, Sandberg notes that Tchaikovsky, like Aschenbach, died of cholera at the age of fifty-three. In 1995, Albert von Schirnding made similar inquiries into Mann's sources. Mann had known about resistance to Dionysus, von Schirnding notes, from reading Nietzsche, Erwin Rohde, and Jacob Burckhardt. As an opponent of Dionysus, he adds, Aschenbach resembles the ill-fated Pentheus of Euripides' *Bacchae* as well as the Socrates of *Die Geburt der Tragödie*. By rejecting knowledge and psychologism, Aschenbach also opposes this first "theoretical man," as Nietzsche describes Socrates. According to von Schirnding, he thus struggles against untragic decadence in the way Nietzsche thought Wagner did, and his defeat is like Nietzsche's biographic catastrophe. The Socrates of Plato's *Phaedrus,* by contrast, corrects his initial underestimation of eros. In the end, Aschenbach is modeled on Pentheus, von Schirnding concludes, and his demise implies that Mann returns to the Dionysian Wagner. Sandberg and von Schirnding thus come to opposing conclusions about Mann's attitude toward Dionysus.

Two scholars concerned with Mann's sources investigated his allusions to Plato and Euripides, respectively. In 1976, Alice van Buren Kelley argued that studying Plato's *Phaedrus* shows how and why Aschenbach "strays from the Platonic path" (228). While Aschenbach's first recollection of that dialogue is accurate, van Buren Kelley explains, his second directly opposes its conclusions. Mann and Plato, she adds, give equal weight to love and verbal artistry. Both Aschenbach's fear of passion and his love of form, though, are "warped by a suppression of Plato's dark steed" (236). As he "abandons himself more and more to the dark horse of his soul," moreover, "all higher truth slips away from him" (238). When he first cites Socrates' definition of beauty as both intellectual and sensual, van Buren Kelley goes on to say, he adds a reference to the burning of Semele, thereby making beauty seem suspect. The second time he cites that definition, just before he dies, it is given by his own false Socrates. According to van Buren Kelley, Aschenbach never understands the real Socrates' idea of psychic harmony, of a balance between reason and passion in human nature. His writing is accordingly like the oratory that Socrates faults: it emphasizes beauty of form more than ethical content. Van Buren Kelley seems unaware of Schmidt's similar argument of 1974. In 1980, Cedric Watts read *Death in Venice* in light of Euripides' *Bacchae*. This play was Mann's most important source, Watts contends, and allusions to it contribute most to the novella's structure, richness, and resonance. Comparing the two works, he explains, also shows the novella's limitations. Mann "explores the Euripidean theme of Dionysiac impulse which operates to destroy ascetic repression" (154), and Dionysus assumes several forms in his story, as he does in Euripides' play. According to Watts, Aschenbach's artistic career does not pose the general human problems that Euripides treats, however, and the terms of Mann's discussion seem dated, deriving from *fin de siècle* concerns with decadence in art. It is also unclear whether Dionysus punishes Aschenbach for being a bad artist or a good one, that is, for betraying art or for dedicating himself to it. A moral ambivalence is likewise apparent in Mann's wavering between liberal rationality and anti-rationalism. As Watts explains, "Mann is half in love with the writer whom he is endeavouring to criticise" (162). Watts thus thinks that reading the *Bacchae* and *Death in Venice* together stresses a common theme and clarifies Mann's symbols, but also reveals his cultural limitations and unresolved ambivalence.

In 1979, in a monograph on *Death in Venice*, E. L. Marson noted the importance of both the *Phaedrus* and the *Bacchae* for Mann's story. Both are "prefigurative," Marson says, serving as pervasive and structuring literary models. Marson cites twelve ways in which the conflicts, plots, motifs, heroes, and other characters of Mann's and Euripides' texts are alike. Both are about recognizing Dionysus, a god embodied by the painted old dandy as well as by Tadzio, for example, and Aschenbach resembles Pentheus in many ways, being comparably unaware, repressed, and hubristic. Having established this general congruence, Marson interprets the novella as a modern analogue of the play. If Aschenbach's struggle is with Dionysus in the form of Tadzio, for example, one can appreciate his stature and near heroic defense. One can also understand the irony, theories of art and artists, and mythologizing found in Mann's text. How Aschenbach recalls and is misled by his classical learning tells us about his repressed reaction to Tadzio, Marson adds, and how he dies reveals that he is selfish and suicidal. Mann's mythologizing shows how his hero avoids self-knowledge, then, and his irony is so obvious that we pity Aschenbach. As an artist, according to Marson, Aschenbach explains his collapse by recalling the *Phaedrus* in a setting hardly as idyllic as Plato's. His selective memory of the dialogue is ironic and does not help him know himself. As van Buren Kelley had in 1976, Marson finds him to be a false rhetorician like Plato's Lysias. His remarks on beauty differ from those of Diotima in the *Symposium,* Marson goes on to say, and he distorts the Platonic concept of Forms to fit his own needs and to avoid responsibility for his sensual degradation, a state not at all universal among artists. Mann's story, like Plato's dialogue, then, describes the disgrace of a purely literary artist, but it is "an ironic parody of *The Phaedrus*" (126). Aschenbach's suicidal urge is like Frederick the Great's after the battle of Kunersdorf in 1759, according to Marson, but his loneliness as he dies distinguishes and discredits him with regard to both that monarch and Socrates. Marson interprets Aschenbach in light of Orphic religion as well, concluding that his asceticism lacks ethical content and that he is deluded to the very end. Aschenbach's attitudes, however, are not those of Mann's narrator, Marson adds, and Mann achieves the kind of self-knowledge that his protagonist rejects. This summary, of course, mentions only the main points of Marson's extensive and detailed argument.

Marson also considers Aschenbach and Tadzio as purely human fictional characters in a homoerotic situation. Aschenbach lacks emotional experience and is incredibly naïve, Marson argues, but he consciously chooses his lack of self-awareness in an "almost Kierkegaardian and heroic leap into innocence" (15). Writing replaces and represses sexuality for him. The treatise he writes at the beach, in fact, is "a substitute for the act of masturbation" (20), and his worn face even looks like "a nineteenth century classic picture of the . . . effects of onanism" (20). For that matter, Tadzio is no "species of mindless but living marble statuary" (12), but a homosexual boy who is aware of his beauty and knows how to control its effects. Anything but innocent, according to Marson, his behavior is mean, even evil. He tries to entice Aschenbach, not least by succumbing to Jaschu in "a kind of homosexual rape" (25). This psychological analysis of Aschenbach and Tadzio precedes Marson's examination of *The Bacchae* and Plato, and it also seems to determine his reading of those texts. Perhaps that is why Marson wrongly claims that the old dandy on the boat calls Aschenbach "sweetie" (Liebchen). In any case, Marson thinks that Aschenbach takes an obvious sexual interest in that old man and that this embodiment of Dionysus approaches Mann's hero with "an obscene homosexual invitation" (43). Furthermore, referring to Mann's novella and *The Bacchae*, Marson observes that his book "is not the place for either a full-scale comparatist treatment of the two texts, or for amateur depth psychology" (36). The details of Marson's study, however, and the assumptions he makes about the motives of Mann's characters suggest a very full scale indeed, and, at times, just such amateurish psychology. Marson routinely assumes that Mann's characters know more about themselves — or, in the case of Aschenbach, have read more — than *Death in Venice* says they did, for example, and he often measures them according to what he assumes any mature actual person or credible literary character would do or think. Nonetheless, his study is the most thorough and far-reaching comparison of *Death in Venice* to its ancient Greek precursors, and it often provides new insights and perspectives. Marson comments, for example, that Aschenbach is much like the popular German novelist Karl May (1842–1912), whose writings were regarded as

FURTHER DEVELOPMENTS, 1976–95 ◆ 155

ethical models for German youth, but who turned out to have a criminal record and therefore suffered public hostility and disgrace just before Mann began to write *Death in Venice*. Marson also thinks that Yukio Mishima's *Kinjiki* (Forbidden Colors, 1951–53) makes "prefigurative" use of *Death in Venice*. This novel, too, Marson explains, is about male homosexuality and an aging literary artist, and many parallels connect it to Mann's novella.

Two further studies of Mann's sources traced his interest in Socrates to Lukács, rather than directly to Plato. In 1982, Judith Marcus-Tar — like Reed in 1971 and 1974, as well as Schmidt in 1974 — noted the importance of Lukács's essay "Sehnsucht und Form." The essay, which appeared before Mann began the novella, concerns Socrates, eros, beauty, and desire, and contains excerpts from Plato's dialogues. Marcus-Tar finds specific correspondences between the two works, citing Mann's several quotations from the essay in his notes for *Death in Venice*. In his descriptions of Aschenbach's work ethic and the roaring sea of uncertainty to which his laborious life can lead, she also hears echoes of Lukács's essay on Theodor Storm. In 1986, Frank Baron remarked on the influence of these same two essays in greater detail. Lukács had modernized Plato's image of Socrates by connecting it to his own life and to that of Kierkegaard, Baron explains, and Aschenbach is much like the resulting character. Mann, like Lukács, he adds, shows how the ascetic's path to Platonic Forms runs via sensuality. Both authors make Plato's Socrates an ugly seducer, and both write that a lover, rather than a friend, is more divine than the beloved. Mann, however, also heightens the sensuality suggested by Lukács. In Lukács's essays, then, Mann found a Socrates more dramatic than Plato's, a Socrates showing how creativity may come at the expense of moral order. Mann, Baron concludes, questions such creativity more penetratingly that Plato had.

Four researchers found sources for *Death in Venice* in the life or works of Goethe. In an essay dated 1978 and published in 1996, Hans Wysling named six respects in which Goethe was the novella's godfather: (1) Mann's initial intention of writing a novella called *Goethe in Marienbad;* (2) his reading Goethe's *Die Wahlverwandtschaften* while he instead wrote about Aschenbach and himself; (3) Aschenbach's similarity to the hero of Goethe's *Der Mann von fünfzig Jahren;* (4) Mann's attributing to Aschenbach, as well as attempting to realize, Goethean classicality; (5) Goethe's use of Greek mythology in modern plots; and (6) Mann's allusion to Goethe's *Dichtung und Wahrheit* (Poetry and Truth, 1812–33), his autobiography, when noting that the elements of the novella came together as if in a crystal. These six insights were hardly new. In 1995, John S. Angermeier noted details of Goethe's life and their use in *Death in Venice,* above all the poet's love for Ulrike von Levetzow in Marienbad in 1823. The source for these details, Angermeier reports, was Johann Peter Eckermann's *Gespräche mit Goethe* (Conversations with Goethe, 1837–48). Psychological similarities between the poet and Aschenbach abound, according to Angermeier, who names exactly twenty-eight parallels between the novella and Goethe's life. Aschenbach's relaxed response to Tadzio's voice, for example, recalls Goethe's reaction to the piano playing of Maria Szymanowska, another Pole. Because it replaces sexuality, moreover, the page and a half of prose that Aschenbach writes at the beach resembles Goethe's "Marienbader Elegie" (Marienbad Elegy). Unlike Goethe, though, Angermeier writes, Aschenbach never recovers. Many of the other similarities Angermeier cites seem tenuous at best, but he draws distinctions among them and cautiously concludes only that "Mann may have encountered and incorporated many themes from his Goethe studies into his story" (23). In 1992 as well as 1993, Werner Frizen noted that Mann invoked Goethe and Marienbad only after Isemann had panned *Death in Venice* in 1913 and that the real source of the novella was Mann's plan of 1905 to emulate Goethe's *Faust*. Like Faust, Frizen observes, Aschenbach dies an old man, lying in the sand. Indeed, as Frizen put it in 1992, "Faust stürbe demnach ein zweites Mal, nun am Lido von Venedig" (Faust would thus die a second time, now on the Lido of Venice) (140). According to Frizen, the characters, structure, themes, motifs and metaphors, vocabulary, and narrative technique of Mann's story all show how it competes with Goethe's tragedy. The novella begins with a walk and words that recall Goethe's scenes "Osterspaziergang" (Easter Promenade) and "Wald und Höhle" (Forest and Cave), for example, and ends with Tadzio, like Goethe's Gretchen, drawing an admirer up, not down. Frizen notes other similarities and differences between the two texts, but the main point of the reading that results from his linking them is this suggestion that Aschenbach dies in an apotheosis, not in disgrace.

Other scholars likewise compared Goethe's works to *Death in Venice*, but they did not treat them as its source. In 1978, Peter Heller compared it to Goethe's "Wanderers Nachtlied" (Wanderer's Night-Song). Aschenbach and the speaker of that poem, Heller writes, both flee the fallen world and seek peace in death. This problem of civilization is ironic in the novella but direct in the poem, he adds, and Mann is dissonant and grotesque, whereas Goethe is melancholy. The poem is also more general, and thus more timeless, Heller argues, than Mann's story about a specific artist's pathological passion. In 1986, Viktor Žmegač compared that story to Goethe's *Die Wahlverwandtschaften*. He disagrees with Thomas's stylistic comparison of 1955 and gives a socio-historical interpretation that examines the role of eroticism in bourgeois society. Both authors show eroticism to be powerful and destructive, Žmegač writes, but Goethe does not cast his erotic characters out of society. In Mann, by contrast, Aschenbach's homoerotic inclination is a symbolic equivalent of the loneliness and isolation of the artist. Žmegač also argues that public life in Mann's Venice is misleading and that, paradoxically, Aschenbach comes into conflict with the society whose ideology his works supported. Despite their stylistic and narrative similarities, he explains, Goethe and Mann thus have very different concepts of art and society. Ursula Wertheim related *Death in Venice* to Goethe's *Der Mann von fünfzig Jahren* in 1989. Wertheim studies the motifs of mirrors, transitoriness, and rejuvenation in both novellas, maintaining that the two works correspond as well as differ. The motif of rejuvenation is prefigured in both, for example, but the self-estrangement of Goethe's major is temporary, while Aschenbach's is total. According to Wertheim, moreover, Aschenbach's death stands for the isolation of a bourgeois intellectual class. All three of these comparisons of *Death in Venice* to works by Goethe thus stressed problems of civilization or society.

Six scholars compared *Death in Venice* to works by Goethe's German contemporaries. Three focused on Heinrich von Kleist. In 1982, Julie Dyck likened the novella to Kleist's essay *Über das Marionettentheater*. The main theme of both works, Dyck argues, is a yearning and striving for artistic perfection. Such perfection, she adds, is the goal of Aschenbach and Kleist's Herr C. Both works suggest creative people's narcissistic consciousness, and both reach a pessimistic conclusion. Dyck may be right to say that intellect and life are opposed in both. When Mann writes that a god used the form and color of human youth to make the intellectual visible, however, he is not referring to the biblical account of creation. Mann's novella and Kleist's essay were also linked by Andrea Rudolph in 1991. For her, Tadzio is an eroticized Thorn-Puller like the young man Kleist mentions to exemplify unconscious grace lost upon reflection. Only readers who know how the essay is subtly integrated into the novella, Rudolph observes, can understand Mann's artistic interests and his specific aesthetic problem of the possible sublation of beauty. Aschenbach is an artist without a sense of history, she adds, so his neoclassicism must fail. Rudolph thinks several events in Mann's story are reminiscent of Kleist's essay, and she emphasizes her main point: "*Aschenbachs Liebe zur statuarischen Klassizität Tadzios ist eine erotische Variation der Dornauszieherfabel!*" (Aschenbach's love of Tadzio's statuesque classicality is an erotic variation of the tale of the Thorn-Puller!) (140). Rudolph also relates Aschenbach's failure to balance the ethical and the sensual to Goethe's novel *Die Wahlverwandtschaften* and to Schiller's treatise *Über Anmut und Würde* (On Grace and Dignity, 1793). In his second article of 1995, John S. Angermeier drew a different comparison between Mann and Kleist. Seeking a source for the motif of the mythological fruit that Mann uses when he has Aschenbach sip a mixture of pomegranate juice and soda as the street singers perform in chapter 5, Angermeier argues that Mann may have known Kleist's story *Das Erdbeben in Chili* (The Earthquake in Chile, 1807). The lovers whose tale Kleist tells, he notes, find refuge under a pomegranate tree. What is more, sensual desires and illicit love are furthered by disasters that befall a community in both stories. From this evidence, Angermeier concludes that "Mann may have incorporated the pomegranate motif and other themes he encountered in Kleist's *Das Erdbeben in Chili* into his masterful novella" (14).

Three other scholars compared Mann's novella to works by August von Platen and E. T. A. Hoffmann, further contemporaries of Goethe. In 1988, Fred E. Oppenheimer noted Aschenbach's striking similarity to von Platen. Quoting Mann's letters and his lecture on Platen as well as Platen's diaries and his *Sonette aus Venedig* (Sonnets from Venice, 1825), Oppenheimer remarks on Aschenbach's and Platen's aestheticism, ancestors, health, homosexuality, and attraction to Venice. Platen was able to leave that city, however, whereas Aschenbach cannot, Oppenheimer adds, and Mann's novella seems to be a commentary on Platen's poem "Tristan." Many of these resemblances had already been noted, especially by Seyppel in 1959. In 1992, Zoltán Szendi drew on material from Mann's archives to confirm Seyppel's observations and to comment on the ambivalence of Platen's role as a model for Aschenbach. Despite the many analogies between them, Szendi insists, Aschenbach is less quixotic, dying before he loses his dignity. Platen's life and art, he adds, furnished Mann not only with a model but also with a warning. In 1993, Dieter Beyerle, like Petriconi in 1953–54 and Pabst in 1955, saw Mann's series of threatening characters as embodiments of the devil. In this respect, Beyerle adds, *Death in Venice* is like Hoffmann's story *Der Sandmann* (The Sandman, 1816).

Mann's novella was also likened to works by authors writing in German in the early twentieth century. In 1976, Hans Wanner related it to Heinrich Mann's novel *Die Göttinnen,* as Werner had in 1972. The Neoplatonism in Thomas's story, Wanner argues, derives and differs from that in Heinrich's. The Neoplatonic symbolism of the sunrise that opens chapter 4 of *Death in Venice,* he says, contrasts with the theme of the underworld in chapter 5, where the labyrinth of Venice symbolizes an artist's confined existence. Similarly, Aschenbach's Neoplatonic idea of Tadzio as Hermes is an illusion. In truth, seeing him as a mythical reconciliation of mind and matter, of body and soul, is the last stage of alienated European aestheticism. According to Wanner, Thomas thus was skeptical and ironic about the aesthetic vitalism hailed in Heinrich's novel. His objections to that novel also occasioned his parodistic style in *Death in Venice.* Wanner also argues that Thomas rejected Heinrich's treatment of the myth of Persephone. This myth, he explains, was a way of expressing the European intellect's search for identity, for a rebirth of antiquity in the spirit of the Renaissance. It is tied to Aschenbach's attempt to identify with Plato, he adds, and thus to justify his homoeroticism. Aschenbach deludes himself by assuming this Greek identity, yet Thomas does not utterly reject such mythologizing, as Heinrich had. Thomas does criticize it, Wanner remarks, but he leaves open the possibility that his hero attains a mythological standpoint in the end. Wanner also observes that the leading street singer represents Pierrot, the symbol of lost identity, and that Thomas connects this symbol to the myth of Persephone when Aschenbach drinks pomegranate juice while that singer performs. Thomas thus exposes that myth as an illusion. His parodistic intention is similarly apparent, Wanner thinks, in the symbolism of the red and white colors he cites. The theme of his story, then, is the failed attempt of the European intellect to overcome the alienation of nature and culture by reviving Greek antiquity, an attempt recently renewed thanks to Nietzsche. In 1979, W. P. Hanson compared *Death in Venice* to Hofmannsthal's *Brief des Lord Chandos* (Letter of Lord Chandos, 1902). Aschenbach is like the author of that fictional letter, Hanson claims, since both are in crisis after achieving literary renown. Their writings and reflections are similar as well, he adds, though Aschenbach's rejection of his former work is more radical, as is Mann's mistrust of art, compared to Hofmannsthal's. Volker Knüfermann, in 1986, related Mann's novella to Robert Musil's *Die Verwirrungen des Zöglings Törless* (The Confusions of Young Törless, 1906). Both books show the endangerment of Narcissus, Knüfermann argues, that is, the precariousness of the existential equilibrium achieved in the language of literary art. Aschenbach and Törless, he explains, in Tadzio and Basini, both encounter beauty in a manner that calls the sovereignty of the aesthetic attitude into question. Their authors thereby reflect on the ethical and constitutive function of language and form. According to Knüfermann, Aschenbach's attempt to sublimate his existence in style fails — albeit in Mann's successful novella, his own narcissistic work of art.

Further research tied *Death in Venice* to works by more recent authors writing in German. In 1982, Helmut Harald Reuter compared Peter Handke's concept of the autonomous subject to Mann's. Mann writes of self-conscious subjects, Reuter argues, whose supposed identity is threatened by others, and especially by sexual desire. In this sense, according to Reuter, Tadzio makes Aschenbach's studied contemplation impossible. Tadzio's beckoning him at the end of the novella is not to be read as a self-delusion, however, a reading that would presume an individual, bourgeois identity, but rather as a breaking through to the mythic and typical. In 1983, Rainer Stollman provided one of the rare moments of humor in the reception of *Death in Venice*. He wrote about a certain Dr. Noodlekopf, Professor of German, who goes to ridiculous lengths trying to interpret Alexander Kluge's story *Massensterben in Venedig* (Mass Death in Venice, 1973). In the course of explicating Kluge's allusions to Mann, Stollman reports, Noodlekopf finds echoes of Mann's diction, numbers, myths, and notion of death that are hilariously far-fetched. In 1986–87, Jim Jordan and Donal McLaughlin saw links between Mann and Alfred Andersch. Andersch's *Die Rote* (The Red-Head, 1960), a novel set in Venice, invites comparisons and reveals associations with Mann's story, they claim, but also establishes a separate identity. Andersch's manuscript, they add, contains a reference to

Mann excluded in the published version, perhaps in order not to invite comparisons with *Death in Venice*. Andersch alluded to the novella in a speech of 1975, they note, when he refused to "represent," a verb Mann uses to describe Aschenbach's public role. Finally, in 1989, Lene Bollerup compared *Death in Venice* to Max Frisch's novel *Homo Faber* (1957). Both works, Bollerup writes, treat a series of identical themes. Their protagonists have comparable ages, crises, journeys, passions, and illnesses, and their authors describe similar cultural clashes, revivals of myths, and crumbling defenses. There are also many concrete textual correspondences. As Bollerup says, *Homo Faber*, down to the smallest detail, contains all kinds of allusions to *Death in Venice*. Some of the small details of Frisch's story that Bollerup provides seem more like Mann's than others.

Two of the studies comparing Mann's story to other works in German tied it to those of Wolfgang Koeppen. In 1993, John Pizer claimed that Koeppen creates "an intertextual dialogue" (99) with Mann and *Death in Venice*. With his "decontextualized iteration of scenes, motifs and characters" and "ironic reconstellation of elements" (99), Koeppen engages in a "critical ironization" (100). Pizer compares several of Koeppen's works to Mann's novella. His first novel, *Eine unglückliche Liebe* (An Unhappy Love, 1934), for example, alludes to its scenes and borrows its motifs and tableaux. His second, *Die Mauer schwankt* (The Wall Wavers, 1935), alludes to Mann's final episode and contains a partial feminization of Aschenbach as well as a caricature of Tadzio, Pizer remarks, whom Koeppen subverts and demythologizes in a way that confirms his "resolve to turn away from Mann's Platonism and toward 'reality'" (102). In *Der Tod in Rom*, Pizer adds, Siegfried Pfaffrath, a young German avant-garde composer, is an artist and a homosexual like Aschenbach. Gottlieb Judejahn, a former SS general, whose death is described in lines recalling that of Aschenbach, shares Aschenbach's will to persevere. Koeppen's description of postwar German problems likewise suggests a "Germanification of motifs" (104). According to Pizer, Koeppen rejects Mann's aesthetic, idealistic concept of homosexuality, and both his own narration and Pfaffrath's music oppose Mann's early concept of irony. Pizer also remarks on essays by Koeppen and on their "demystifying ironization" (100) and "demystification and deidealization" (101) of Mann and his novella. Such terms tend to obscure as much as they reveal, but Pizer astutely observes that Koeppen seems to overlook the fact that Mann himself took an ironic view of Aschenbach's superficial dignity. Oliver Herwig, in 1995, similarly compared *Death in Venice* to Koeppen's *Der Tod in Rom*. The novel takes the novella as its model, Herwig claims, but only in order to produce a polemical antithesis. Aschenbach's homosexual leanings and his surrender to Dionysian forces are targets of criticism, for example, as they recur in Pfaffrath and Judejahn. The theme of death is likewise shown untransfigured by allegory, and Koeppen's setting is even more threatening. Rejecting aestheticism for a socio-historical conception of the artist, Herwig adds, Koeppen parodies, exaggerates, and pejoratively quotes Mann, ironically varying his motifs and making both his style and themes seem alienated and banal. The word most often used by Herwig to describe this process is "contrafact," a musical term that means setting new words to existing music. In 1980, Koeppen himself recalled reading Mann's story at three different times: in his teens, he admired its Platonism; in the 1930s, his youthful enthusiasm had waned, and Aschenbach's "Durchhalten!" (Persevere!) struck him as the motto of ugly German nationalism; more recently, he admired it again as a beautiful book about a sincere erotic passion. Koeppen appears to regret and retract his sarcastic paraphrase of its final line at the end of *Der Tod in Rom*.

Besides being compared to other writings in German, *Death in Venice* was likened to several works in English. Three of those works are from the late nineteenth or early twentieth centuries. In 1979, Kathy J. Phillips argued that both the novella and Henry James's *The Ambassadors* (1903) multiply their foreshadowings and climaxes, that is, their annunciatory figures and vicarious fulfillments. Mann's series of such figures and foreshadowings starts with the wanderer and ends with Jaschu, Phillips writes, and his series of climaxes starts with Aschenbach's treatise and ends with the fight between Jaschu and Tadzio. Beyond the similarity of their situations and images, the two works share a technique of writing a series of similar episodes, then, a technique tied to their symbolism and thereby to their protagonists' becoming "purely textual existences" (376). Multiple versions of the same character make Aschenbach's change urgent and gradual, Phillips explains, and "echoic" (385) scenes seem increasingly sexual as well as textual. Phillips concludes that "'the word' becomes acceptable currency for sexual expression" (387). In any case, she also incisively writes that "Jaschu is a particularly tempting stand-in for Aschenbach" (380). In 1982, Christopher Butler regarded Aschenbach as an example of a displaced author, comparing *Death in Venice* to Joyce's *Portrait of the Artist as a Young Man*. Both books concern the social status of the artist, Butler claims, and both their protagonists rise to a Platonic appreciation of beauty. Whereas Aschenbach's climatic and erotic perception results in "an abandonment of vocation in death" (63), however, Stephen's leads to its joyful discovery. In 1989, R. D. Stock compared *Death in Venice* to Conrad's *Heart of Darkness* and to Algernon Blackwood's *Ancient Sorceries* (1927). As Stock writes, "Venice is not the Congo, but the heart of darkness comes to *it*, in the form of cholera" (357). In 1993, Ivo Vidan likewise related Mann to Conrad. Criticizing Trilling's article of 1961, Vidan argues that both authors' books express an "oblique diagnosis of the turn-of-the-century crisis of our culture" (265). Aschenbach is motivated by beauty, not power, and nature corrupts culture in Mann, he explains, whereas it is the other way around in Conrad, but the texts share a "deep thematic analogy" and "hidden structural parallelism" (266), and they seem like one narrative in two different codes, since both tell of violence, collapse, and degeneration. Vidan nicely describes "the rough, coarse avatars of Aschenbach's disturbing other, potential self," but the first of them, in Munich, does not appear near an "oriental church" (268).

Death in Venice was also compared to more recent writings in English. In 1984, Margaret Morganroth Gullette related it to Vladimir Nabokov's Lolita (1955). Both their protagonists suffer from pederosis, she explains, a condition caused by resistance to growing older. Both also show sexuality in middle age to be altogether wrong. As Gullette remarks, "The crime that Aschenbach and Humbert have committed is aging. Aging, and wanting nevertheless to have a sexual life" (221). These stories of gloomy passion thus both suggest a fear of adult sexuality. Although Lolita is a girl, Gullette adds, she and Tadzio look alike, and their admirers transgress to a similar degree. Aschenbach is disgusted with himself, moreover, and "nobody in the story — not the barber, not Tadzio's mother, not the narrator — finds natural, graying, leathery Aschenbach attractive" (223). Mann shows Aschenbach's desire that Tadzio die young, thus making his love seem selfish, Gullette goes on to say, and in the end Death in Venice is less forgiving, less potentially elegiac than Lolita. In 1990, Jim Barnes drew parallels between Mann's story and two novels by Malcolm Lowry. Mann's strangers are angels of death, Barnes observes, and such angels appear in Under the Volcano (1947), as does an orgiastic dream prior to death. The hero of Dark as the Grave Wherein My Friend is Laid (1968) deteriorates on a journey, and this novel, too, thus resembles Death in Venice, Barnes adds, even though it ends with an affirmation of life. In 1992–93, Katherine H. Burkman found echoes of Mann's novella in Harold Pinter's 1991 film of Ian McEwan's novel In the Comfort of Strangers (1981). Venice, a beautiful male, and the myth of Dionysus all figure in both the film and the novel, Burkman explains, much as they do in Death in Venice. Drawing a parallel between Aschenbach's release of feelings and that of excrement by one of McEwan and Pinter's characters, she also adds that "The release of feces in his father's study is much like the release that Aschenbach succumbs to in Mann's 1911 story" (39). Actually, Death in Venice was published in 1912.

Other comparisons were drawn between Death in Venice and works in French. Two of those comparisons linked it to Gide's L'immoraliste. In 1981, John Burt Foster, Jr., called both books literary appropriations of Nietzsche, in particular of Die Geburt der Tragödie. The heroes of both, Foster remarks, "turn away from worlds distorted by abstraction and theory only to discover that the Dionysus Nietzsche had invoked as his guide to a better, 'tragic' culture is in reality a savage god" (146). While the books have Nietzschean parallels, then, according to Foster, they radically rework Nietzsche's concept of that god. The fate of their heroes, Foster maintains, raises disturbing questions about liberating the impulses. In Aschenbach's treatise, "Bipolar unity replaces Doric one-sidedness" (167), but Mann's attitude to Apollinian alienation from life is ironic, since he has his hero discover that Apollo, no less than Dionysus, stands for a Nietzschean art drive. Nietzsche is both Mann's model and his rival, Foster argues, undercut but not excluded. The stream of ashes implied by Aschenbach's name, Foster adds, has replaced his fount of inspiration and is externalized in the stagnant water of the canals. Mann addresses not only psychological issues, moreover, but social and political ones as well. According to Foster, he presents excessively Dionysian social feeling, stressing nihilism and class hatred. In that Aschenbach acknowledges Platonic-Christian ideas about art, Foster thinks, Mann also hints at a religious evaluation of Nietzsche's aesthetic naturalism. Foster also mentions D. H. Lawrence's review of the novella in 1913 and Mann's effect on Lawrence's own Nietzschean fiction. In 1988, Kenneth L. Golden likewise compared Mann's story with Gide's. Both portray archetypal forces, Golden notes, that are focused on child projections and fixations, and that activate what C. G. Jung called the "child archetype." According to Golden, Aschenbach steps outside his persona and encounters his contrary self in the wanderer, his vision of the jungle is a precognitive fantasy, and he dies while gazing at Tadzio, "the embodiment of the child archetype and the Dionysian self Aschenbach has for so long repressed" (197). Golden seems to overwork the notion of this archetype when he writes that the Dionysian aspect of experience, as well as Aschenbach's embrace of death, is childlike.

Mann's story was also linked to works by other authors writing in French. In 1991, Bernadette Carrère related *Death in Venice* to *Bruges-la-Morte* (1892), a novel by the Belgian author Georges Rodenbach. The same nostalgia for a legendary past, fascination with endangered beauty, and *fin de siècle* linkage of water, cities, and death occur in both works, Carrère observes. Besides noting profound similarities between these stories, she remarks on how each has been set to music in an opera — Mann's in Britten's *Death in Venice*, Rodenbach's in Korngold's *Die tote Stadt* (The Dead City, 1920). Marie Gribomont compared Mann's story, likewise in 1991, to Frédérick Tristan's *Le Train immobile* (1979). She finds striking similarities as well as significant differences. Both works show a Venice of false appearances and decrepitude, she writes, but Mann's is classic and realistic, while Tristan's is baroque, fantastic, and grotesque.

Three studies compared Mann's novella to Gabriele D'Annunzio's novel *Il Fuoco*. In 1989, Giuliana Giobbi explained their relationship by citing their shared topoi of Venice, art, and death as well as various leitmotifs that they have in common. Both works contain autobiographical elements, Giobbi argues, though D'Annunzio projects his better self into his story, while Mann describes Aschenbach as an artist he did not want to become. Both also refer to Richard Wagner, she adds, though Aschenbach's mind censors the fact that Wagner had died in Venice. Both reveal art to be endangered by corruption, passion, and decay, moreover, though Mann, unlike D'Annunzio, envisages no redemption for it. Also, both their heroes are artists who strive for beauty and transfigure the place and people around themselves, though D'Annunzio's Stelio is of a different age, class, and nationality. Furthermore, Venice is not just a landscape but a character in both, ideas of twilight and pollution permeate both, both describe a momentary epiphany and a sensual urge, and both consist mostly of third-person descriptions and mediations. According to Giobbi, their authors are thus more alike than different. Two other scholars considered them more different than alike. In 1991, Jared M. Becker contrasted the decadence described in Mann's novella with D'Annunzio's and F. T. Marinetti's calls for revitalizing Venice. Nachum Schoffman contrasted Mann's and D'Annunzio's descriptions of Venice again, in 1993, as part of his argument that their views on Wagner were antithetical.

Two studies related *Death in Venice* to works in Spanish. Both of those studies demonstrate disturbing recent trends in its reception. In 1991, Ricardo Gutiérrez Mouat compared Mann's novella to José Donoso's novel *El jardín de al lado* (The Garden Next Door, 1981). It is one of the "implicit subtexts" (60) of that novel, and Gutiérrez Mouat establishes its "intertextual pertinence" (61). Both works, he explains, oppose bohemian pleasure to bourgeois discipline, and textual production to textual reception. Both also show an author in crisis, he adds, and they share incidental details, a motif of passage, ideological contradictions, and a contradiction of ethics and aesthetics. This general argument may be valid, but is often made in bloated jargon. When Aschenbach looks at himself in the mirror, for example, Mann "uses specular tactics" (61). When Aschenbach envisions Tadzio as aesthetic perfection, "the truth according to the universalizing logic of the ideological discourse" (62) is revealed. When he wonders what his stern ancestors would say about his artsy life, "The artist's deviation or degeneration is not outside the genealogical law but is inscribed in it according to the naturalist discourse 'quoted' by the novella's narrator" (63). It is hard to know what, if anything, such jargon means. Gutiérrez Mouat's logic seems fuzzy, moreover, when he writes that Mann's story is "a text whose name is repressed in *El jardín de al lado* but whose blurred image hovers over the novel" (61). One can perhaps say that Aschenbach is "potentially deformed by a responsibility that is not necessarily consubstantial with art," moreover, but it is not true that he becomes a national figure "to whom foreign countries pay homage" (66). Michael G. Paulson, in 1993, made further mistakes when he compared Mann's novella to Reinaldo Arenas's *Otra Vez el Mar* (Farewell to the Sea, 1982). Both books are set at the sea, Paulson argues, and are about lonely writers seeking escape from everyday tedium and partly finding it in a youth at the beach. Those

FURTHER DEVELOPMENTS, 1976–95     ♦     165

books are also linked by their possible intertextuality, he explains, and reveal underlying affinities of human nature. One shows a death in Venice, the other a death in Castro's Cuba of the 1960s. This all sounds fine, though it is hardly accurate to say that Aschenbach travels from Munich to Venice, to the sea and the beach, because he is fleeing everyday monotony or mere boredom. Moreover, Mann's hero is not dissatisfied with Pola, as Paulson claims. He passes through that city on the Istrian peninsula, but it is not the unnamed island where he first, unhappily vacations. Tadzio is not "equated with the Trojan prince, Paris" (21), either. Finally, Paulson sums up Mann's story in terms that are often notably crude. What happens, for instance, when Aschenbach retires at the end of the day? "Nights are spent in a non-resting mode" (21). It is also odd that Paulson gives the date of Mann's novella as 1930, instead of 1912, and that he explains that *Death in Venice* is its title "in most English-language translations" (11). In English, it has never gone by any other name. Whereas Gutiérrez Mouat uses overly theoretical language, Paulson thus seems very poorly informed.

Not all the works in languages other than German that have been compared to *Death in Venice* are prose fiction. In 1984, for example, David Bronsen likened the novella to Ibsen's *The Master Builder* (1892). Both works, he explains, treat the romantic theme of "the artist who is pulled back and forth between his artistic vocation and the call of life" (324–25). Accordingly, Bronsen finds remarkable correspondences between their heroes' minds and between their structures. Both Aschenbach and Ibsen's Solness, for example, are solitary, loveless men and ascetic artists whose art compensates for their dislocated emotional lives. Both also ludicrously try to turn back the clock. Both works treat the unconscious, moreover, with "surface realism and a sub-surface symbolism" (329). According to Bronsen, both works also state a paradox, since their heroes must either kill their instincts to live as artists or die from abandoning themselves to the life force. Bronsen finds Ibsen's view of the artist more modern, though, and thinks that the two works may seem antithetical, partly because they belong to different genres. Mann's is more conscious, cerebral, and resolvable, he also claims, as well as less autobiographical and less cathartic. Bronsen appears to underestimate both the ambiguity of the novella and Mann's personal reasons for writing it.

Three further studies related Mann's novella to works in Japanese. In 1979, Irmela Hijiya-Kirschnereit tied it to Yukio Mishima's *Kinjiki*, as Marson did in the same year. This novel clearly refers to *Death in Venice*, Hijiya-Kirschnereit argues, and the two works contain numerous parallel elements. Both of their protagonists are distinguished authors who seem dignified but who have decadent tastes, for example, Shunsuke Hinoki's appearance corresponds to Aschenbach's, and both of these artists discover a beautiful youth beside the sea. There are also striking correspondences between Tadzio and Yuichi Minami, and Mishima, according to Hijiya-Kirschnereit, alludes to the former in his description of the latter. Dialogues about art, spirit, and beauty occur in both works, she explains, both of which are written on two levels as well. As Hijiya-Kirschnereit adds, Mishima intended parallels not only in scenes that so obviously refer to Mann, but also in the whole plan of his novel, both in its construction as well as in its repeatedly discussed problem of art, spirit, and morality. The content and function of Mishima's Greek references are identical to Mann's, she claims, and the two protagonists are astonishingly alike: just as Mann attributed his own, unfinished essay *Geist und Kunst* to Aschenbach, Mishima wrote a *Treatise on Beauty* and has his hero do the same. In 1994, Linde Keil likewise compared Mishima and Mann. Both of their works treat the theme of beauty as a homoerotic experience, she says, and Mann's may have inspired Mishima's. Among the parallels and similarities Keil cites are references to Plato and contrasts between binary motifs. Finally, in 1990, Jun Ozaki remarked on analogies and differences between *Death in Venice* and Yasunari Kawabata's *Yukiguni* (Snow Country, 1937). The theme of both works is seduction to beauty and death, Ozaki writes, but unlike Mann's, Kawabata's lacks irony.

## Style, Symbols, and Literary History

Another category of research on *Death in Venice* conducted from 1976 to 1995 comprises studies of its style, its symbols, and its literary-historical import. Studies of its style remarked on the workings of its irony, the persona of its narrator and dynamics of its narration, and the deconstruction of its language and linguistic signs. Studies of its symbols stressed the image of the tiger, the symbol of the jungle, recurring turns of phrase, and oceanic animals. Studies of its literary-historical import considered its relationship to the novella as a literary genre and tied it to the larger trends of romanticism, symbolism, decadence, modernism, neoclassicism, and aestheticism. In contrast to the studies cited in the first section of this chapter, which portray Aschenbach as an artist representing such trends, those cited here are more concerned with Mann's story as a whole. The ones cited here also differ from each other in the extent to which they attribute awareness of such trends to Mann himself. While some of the efforts mentioned in this section resemble the earlier ones treated under its heading in the previous chapter — studies that appeared from 1956 to 1975 — others show new scholarly emphases and developments.

Four studies focused on the varieties and significance of Mann's irony. In 1977, Scott Consigny, applying the work of Wayne Booth, considered Mann's rhetoric of irony. Aschenbach's short treatise is quantitatively meager and linked to debauchery, Consigny argues, so it seems ironic rather than ideal. Mann gives stylistic and narrative clues that encourage this reading, he adds, establishing a Socratic context that shows how Aschenbach wrongly favors written language over spoken dialectic. Consigny here alludes to the fact that

Plato's Socrates opposes writing to speaking in the *Phaedrus.* While Consigny regards Mann's irony as stable, Hans Robert Spielmann, in 1982, considered it tragic. Such irony is the key to Mann's novella, Spielmann claims. It reveals how artists are related to their surroundings, he explains, and how Mann uses leitmotifs. Aschenbach is shown to be a failure from the start, he argues, and the end of his story may be tragically ironic, since readers see Tadzio objectively, that is, as unlikely to meet Aschenbach's expectations. The narrative possibilities and the socio-historical implications of irony, Spielmann thinks, might make *Death in Venice* interest German high-school students. In 1987, David Eggenschwiler found several kinds of irony in the novella. Its author explores "the ironic temper itself," he contends, in "spirals of irony, one form playing against another and yet another until irony itself becomes its own object" (65–66). Its forms of irony are philosophical, rhetorical, tragic, and evaluative. According to Eggenschwiler, Aschenbach has turned away from romantic irony; uses stable, rhetorical irony, which is defensive and evasive, when distancing himself from Tadzio by alluding to mythology; and returns to his subjective, dialectical, romantic irony. The narrator, too, uses myths ironically and thus presents "the figure of the ironist ironized" (71). According to Eggenschwiler, Aschenbach accepts the tragic irony of his life and art. Though the narrator is ironic toward Aschenbach, he adds, — and the author toward the narrator, perhaps — his censure of Aschenbach is ambivalent, suggesting an evaluative irony. Eggenschwiler sees a further irony aimed at readers who think Mann's final scene a Platonic fulfillment. Whereas Eggenschwiler emphasizes the ironic complexity of *Death in Venice,* Peter Pütz argued in 1988 that the novella largely avoided irony, which Pütz calls a product of wild thinking that Mann tried to overcome with an ethic of work and effort much like Aschenbach's.

Another aspect of Mann's style that scholars considered was his narration. Five studies distinguished his narrator from his protagonist or from him. In 1977, Eberhard Hermes gave diverse suggestions for interpreting *Death in Venice,* noting that the narrator speaks indirectly and that the various modes of his speech stand in a tense relationship to each other. He is a reporter, a critic, and a philosopher, Hermes explains, and understands his style as a corrective or counterpart to Aschenbach's. In 1978, Dorrit Cohn described the novella as an example of "psycho-narration" (26) in which a narrator remains distanced from the consciousness he narrates. Mann's narrator, Cohn observes, "holds the unwavering stance of a wise and rational psychologist, whose special field is the psychology of creative artists" (26). The distance or dissonance between this narrator and Aschenbach increases, Cohn adds, and is clear from stylistic features such as the narrator's ex cathedra statements and analytical language. Furthermore, she writes, one cannot take the identity of narrator and author for granted. She also notes how both Aschenbach's hallucinatory vision and the one related in Henry

James's *The Beast in the Jungle* (1903) repeatedly use the verb "to see," as well as how quoted monologue after Aschenbach's collapse at the fountain shows "maximal distance between the narrating and the figural voices" (68). In 1982, Gila Ramras-Rauch drew on Cohn's work to contend that the presence of Mann's narrator prevents Aschenbach's psyche from being portrayed or seen from inside, and to conclude that the narrator's moral indignation may not be Mann's own. Aschenbach's mythic regression or undoing, Ramras-Rauch maintains, therefore need not be judged according to Judeo-Christian moralism. Cohn herself argued similarly in 1983, writing that the narrator of *Death in Venice* is not identical with its author. The former is a "seriously perorating monsieur" (224), whose smug, narrow evaluations and ideology result in moralistic overstatement and overkill, especially when he relates Aschenbach's writing scene at the beach and final monologue at the fountain. He does not understand Aschenbach's creative process, Cohn notes, or appreciate the moment of truth conveyed by Aschenbach's last words. His failure to see fantastic characters as such, moreover, confirms that "the author *behind* the work is communicating a message that escapes the narrator he placed *within* the work" (241). Cohn thus amplifies her comments of 1978. In 1992, Franz K. Stanzel cited Cohn's remarks of 1983 to argue that *Death in Venice* has a firmly closed ending connected to the rest of Mann's story by the antagonism or divergence between its narrator and protagonist. It thus exemplifies what Stanzel regards as dissonant closure.

Differences between Mann, his hero, and his narrator similarly figured in studies devoted to other matters in *Death in Venice*. In 1990, Kurt Fickert cited such differences to explain how Mann turned truth into fiction. Mann, he argues, provided "a fictional format for the autobiographical references in *Der Tod in Venedig* and thus evolved a symbolic representation of reality in which its truth or essence could be revealed" (26). The interplay between the author, narrator, and protagonist of the novella, Fickert adds, creates tension in lieu of a plot. The unreliable narrator assumes a "professorial stance" (26), for example, and he and Aschenbach are unaware of Mann's foreshadowing. Fickert's remarks often seem to confuse, rather than clarify, the relationship between Aschenbach, the narrator, and Mann. Fickert also thinks that Aschenbach's initial sighting of Tadzio resembles the way in which Mann first saw his future wife Katia Pringsheim. This similarity, he says, shows how Mann transformed his personal life into art. Lilian R. Furst tied Mann's narrator to his readers' responses. Furst maintained in 1990 that "the act of reading *Death in Venice* and readers' responses to the text evince ethical dilemmas that devolve from the aesthetics of narration" (268). At first, she explains, the narrator seems friendly to readers and to Aschenbach, but the irony inherent in his indirect discourse and rhetorical questions reveals him to be malicious and duplicitous. Readers therefore become unsettled, and "the queasy sense of floating that Aschenbach had felt on the distasteful boat is assimilated into the reading experience" (271). Readers resent the narrator's treachery, malice, and deceitfulness, Furst contends, and distance themselves from him. On the narrational level, they thus experience a conflict between aesthetics and ethics like the one Aschenbach has on the diegetic level of Mann's plot. Furst made this same case again in 1991, when she compared *Death in Venice* to Flaubert's *Madame Bovary* (1857). Readers of both books, she says, are torn between aesthetic admiration and ethical unease, especially with regard to the role of their mean narrators. In 1992, Furst similarly linked Mann's novella and Heinrich von Kleist's *Die Marquise von O . . .* (The Marquise of O . . ., 1808). Tension between assent and resistance felt by their characters, she argues, is projected into the responses of their readers. The characters in and readers of both stories, she explains, experience a sense of derangement, especially at the happy ending of Kleist's and the moralistic conclusion of Mann's. Furst rightly notes how the two stories also differ but incorrectly lodges Aschenbach at the Hotel Excelsior.

Other research on narrative issues in *Death in Venice* raised questions about its motivation, its narrator's knowledge, and its use of mythology and dreams. Three examples of such research focused on Mann's initial chapter. In 1980, Martin Swales observed that one of the central problems posed by the novella concerned motivation and causality. Mann's opening pages, for example, describe events that occur on a realistic, psychological level as well as on a metaphorical, fantastic, or metaphysical one. Swales adds that these two levels coexist throughout Mann's story. In 1985, Dieter Wolfgang Adolphs similarly addressed the problem of narrative motivation. The first chapter of the novella, Adolphs argues, raises but then fails to fulfill expectations about the exact time of Mann's fictional events and about his apparent theme of an artist's existence. The realistic motivation of the story thus comes undone, as it likewise does in contrasts between detailed description and an emphasis on uncertainty. According to Adolphs, Mann's first chapter thereby consciously, even ironically, addresses and rejects the demand for realistic narrative motivation. His text thereby offers a new and double perspective, Adolphs says, an opposition between the banal motif of a trip and the inkling of disaster. In 1988, Bruno Roßbach likewise gave a narrative analysis of the first chapter of *Death in Venice*. Among other things, he explains that the novella's power of fascination is due in part to the opposition between its internal view of Aschenbach and external view of Tadzio. The fact that Tadzio's thoughts are inaccessible to Aschenbach and the narrator, Roßbach observes, cannot mean that he has none. This shared ignorance also shows that the narrator is not omniscient. In the first sentence of the novella, Roßbach adds, the third-person narrator selects and distributes information in a way that launches a plot and creates an elegiac atmosphere. The second sentence shows his strategy of alternately approaching and distancing himself from Aschenbach.

Roßbach thus gives a microanalysis of the first paragraph, an analysis that is followed by only a macroanalytic overview of the rest of the first chapter. He does not pursue his idea that an analysis of the entire novella would concentrate on the narrator's small surplus of knowledge and consciousness in its vertical dimension, the dimension of insight into its characters and events. Finally, in 1995, Ute Heidmann Vischer remarked on how *Death in Venice* combines mythological narration and the narration of a dream. The latter, she explains, integrates the former. Aschenbach's death does not seem violent compared to that of Pentheus, she adds, his mythological double. In his orgiastic dream, however, the narrator relates the violence and brutality that are omitted in the events of the story. Vischer thus elucidates the descriptive procedure Mann chose.

Four further studies presented *Death in Venice* in terms of post-structuralist theory. In 1982, Geoffrey Galt Harpham argued that the novella explores the difficulties and degeneration of writing. Harpham says, "The subject of *Death in Venice* can be conceived as metaphor seizing metonymy and dragging it toward parody" (132). Aschenbach starts in a state of metonymy, he explains, and gravitates toward the origin of language in metaphor. He is replicated, diluted, contaminated, or tempted by characters he meets, Harpham adds, his career thus marked by entropic simplification, his self thus tainted or impure all along. Harpham calls this process a grotesque parody and ties it to the image of sweetness. Sweet things, he observes, delight, dissolve, and rot. "All figures in this narrative rot" (142), moreover, and Aschenbach undergoes a "continual resolution into viscosity" (144). Harpham is mistaken when he tells how Tadzio's identity is likewise subverted. Designating gray the color of metaphor and entropy, he wrongly contends that Tadzio's eyes and Aschenbach's hair are the only gray objects Mann mentions. In fact, Mann often refers to this color. Tadzio's mother, for example, is "grauweiß gekleidet" (dressed in gray and white). Richard W. Barton, in 1985, made a similar argument. That argument, which is both political and deconstructive, addresses "semiosic disorder" (353) in Mann's narrative. Barton's semiotic concepts and diagrams are extremely abstract, as are his conclusions. Caught between Plato's and Freud's ideas of homosexual desire, for example, Aschenbach is "a conflicted, transformed medium of exchange between two foreign discursive economies" (375). Barton also notes that Mann, Freud, and Plato are "enclosed within the same rationalist discourse (logocentrism) in which desire is represented as irrational" (381). In 1987, Dominick LaCapra likewise used post-structuralist terminology. LaCapra argues that Mann's "doubling effects and attempts at transformative reversal" (112) suggest the wonder of a reborn unconstraint that eludes Aschenbach. This wonder results from irony and parody, he explains, rather than from innocence. Offering hope for such a regeneration or renewal, the novella does not fully replicate the problems it describes, then, and does not necessarily imply "an uncontrolled free play of infinite signification" (126). Recalling earlier concepts employed by French structuralists, Betty Rojtman in 1993 distinguished the action of *Death in Venice* from its narration, its hero's teleological obsession from digressions that occur whenever time in his story stands still. The story, Rojtman argues, is slowed down by useless descriptions, insignificant details, and characters and incidents unrelated to Aschenbach's quest. It thus tells of interruption, disorder, and diversion, of and about suspended meaning. One could disagree with her, since Mann's descriptions, details, characters, and incidents are usually highly significant indeed.

In addition to these studies of Mann's irony, narrator, and narration itself, there were four further ones that examined his symbolism. In 1978–79, Ford B. Parkes wrote that Mann uses the image of the tiger not only in Aschenbach's initial vision, but in the rest of the novella as well. At the end, Parkes argues, the "triangular relationship" (73) of the viewer, the birds, and the tiger described in that vision recurs. Aschenbach symbolically dresses like a tiger, he adds, and pursues Tadzio as a tiger does its prey. In these and in other ways, Parkes finds Aschenbach similar to Pentheus in Euripides' *Bacchae*. The tiger recurs when the English clerk tells Aschenbach about the origin of cholera epidemic in India, for example, and Parkes both associates the animal with that plague and concludes that Mann "uses the tiger to portray the latent Dionysian side of Aschenbach's character" (79). This statement recalls Krotkoff's remarks of 1967. Parkes unpersuasively adds that Aschenbach is like the tiger in the end when he tries to follow Tadzio, who is like the imperiled birds of his vision. In 1979, André Cadieux claimed that Mann's central symbol is the jungle of Nietzsche's Dionysus. Aschenbach, Cadieux explains, rejects Nietzsche's idea that the nature of the self is to suffer. A symbol of life in Aschenbach's vision but of death in the English clerk's account of the source of the Asiatic cholera, the jungle represents Nietzsche's Dionysian realm: "It is, in short, the jungle of Dionysus" (59). With his symbols, leitmotifs, and irony, Cadieux adds, Mann avoided Aschenbach's abyss. In Nietzsche's sense, he was thus lyric or tragic. In 1980, Bernhard Meier wrote that Aschenbach's trip symbolizes his decline and that symbols suggested by recurring turns of phrase — most of which are used to describe the series of mysterious men — embody the demonic, lead to Aschenbach's death, and differ from his own and Tadzio's shared attributes. In 1987, Charlotte Rotkin noted "the allegorical significance of sea shells, sea horses, jellyfish, and sidewards-running crabs" (84). Tadzio discovers these animals on the beach, and their interrelationship, Rotkin thinks, reinforces Mann's "criticism of moral lassitude" (84). They suggest pearls, sensuality, weakness, and evasion, she writes, thereby linking Tadzio's mother, Tadzio, and Aschenbach. The terms of most of Rotkin's comparisons are far-fetched. Does Aschenbach actually pursue "a sidewards-running motion away from enlightenment" (87)? Is his seizure by passion really connoted by sea-horses' tails? Do the tentacles of jellyfish truly reinforce the concept of such a seizure and elicit, besides, an image of Medusa and thus of Tadzio's disheveled hair?

Three studies elucidated *Death in Venice* as an example of the novella as a literary genre. According to Josef Kunz in 1977, the fact that Mann's story contains three motifs — the artistic life, eroticism, and Venice — makes it more complicated than the classical novella. The strict parallelism connecting these motifs is nonetheless novelistic, Kunz adds, and they are all variations of the theme of perfection on the basis of death. The conciseness with which Mann treats this theme is characteristic of the novella as a genre, Kunz explains, and everything in his story is related to the same theme in novelistic concentration. Mann's narrative irony reveals and realizes what is paradoxical and dialectic in his motifs and his single theme, Kunz concludes, and in few novellas are form and content so indissolubly one. In 1988, Charlotte Rotkin repeated the argument she made in 1987 about Mann's supposedly allegorical sea animals. She also gave fatuous reasons for Mann's choice of the novella as the literary genre in which he tells Aschenbach's story. In Italian, she explains, the word "novella" means "a little new thing" (498) and that is what Aschenbach thinks he needs. Venerable and popular, she adds, this literary form is like the revered and celebrated author. Finally, the gravity or impropriety of its subject matter, according to Rotkin, makes reference to his sense of responsibility and his homoerotic longing. Rotkin is wrong to draw conclusions about Mann's supposed use of the word "mock" to describe the summer in Munich. This word comes from Lowe-Porter, not Mann, who wrote that the summer was *falsch* (false). In 1993, Helmut Koopmann maintained that the "new classicality" envisioned in Mann's essay of 1911 on Wagner made *Death in Venice* a turning point in the history of the twentieth-century novella, both its high point and the end of an art form. Mann followed literary fashion in writing novellas, Koopmann argues, but that does not mean he had a clear conception of their genre, and there is nothing gained by defining *Death in Venice* as a novella. After finishing it, moreover, Mann bid farewell to the genre, writing mostly novels instead. Its division into chapters is a structural principal of novels, not of novellas, Koopmann adds, a sign of how literary genres can overlap. Nonetheless, the novella was the genre in which classicality seemed most possible. Such classicality is evident in Mann's style, Koopmann notes, and he was ready to use such a style, to practice the neoclassicism that Samuel Lublinski had preached, because he disagreed with his brother Heinrich. As Koopmann explains, *Death in Venice* is nothing less than a declaration of war issued in response to Heinrich's sultry novel *Die Jagd nach Liebe* (The Hunt for Love, 1903). Thomas's story, then, is neoclassical in its more restrained descriptions of love as well.

Other scholars, too, assigned *Death in Venice* a place in literary history. In 1978, Marcel Brion, who in 1930 had contrasted Thomas's aestheticism with Heinrich's political partisanship, related the novella to German romanticism. Brion writes that Aschenbach's voyage is the most perfect itinerary of death furnished by the postromantic period in German literature. All that romantic poetry had expressed, he adds, is realized with rare totality in Mann's story. Brion notes Mann's symbols and Aschenbach's blindness to them, mentioning how the latter fails to recognize the series of sinister men, whose long teeth and short lips form the traditional jaw of a vampire. Aschenbach is the classical author of his generation, in fact, who goes to the most unruly romantic excesses. By showing this regression, Brion thinks, *Death in Venice* is a *Bildungsroman* in reverse. Its hero descends into hell and does so in deathly silence, lured by infernal divinities and escorted by minor demons. Brion likens both Tadzio and the foreign god of Aschenbach's dream to the adolescent embodiment of death that is addressed in the fifth of Novalis's *Hymnen an die Nacht* (Hymns to the Night, 1799). In 1987, in their English revision of a Dutch book published in 1984, Douwe Fokkema and Elrud Ibsch claimed that *Death in Venice* exemplifies "interference between the ironic-Modernist and the Symbolist codes" (295). Its narrator is not often ironic towards its hero, they argue, and its concurrence of narrative voices, its monoperspectivism, its symbolism, and its abandonment of a quest for knowledge and insight all lead them to consider it "part of the current of Aestheticism/Symbolism" (300). In 1992, Naomi Ritter reported on teaching the novella as "a climactic example of the decadent tradition" (88). She does so, she explains, by highlighting its themes of the cult of art, forbidden love and death, and Venice. Gerald Gillespie, also in 1992, concentrated on "the problematics of form as a central modernist concern in *Death in Venice*" (98). The novella, he comments, paradoxically transforms the tragedy of an order-shaping artist into an ambivalently beautiful and dubiously perfect artistic order. Its hero's own life is a form that gets broken, moreover, and his summer house in the mountains refers to Mount Cithaeron, where Pentheus is slain in Euripides' *The Bacchae*. In the final paragraph of Mann's second chapter, Gillespie adds, "the tension between an older naturalistic-positivistic and a newer symbolist literary code reaches a modernist resolution through an abstract logic based on myth" (103), myth that is a timeless paradigm for the European present.

Further research that regarded *Death in Venice* from the standpoint of literary history attributed awareness of its developments to Mann himself. In 1981, Hinrich Siefken noted that Mann, about 1910, perceived a trend toward neoclassicism among his contemporaries. His theme of an aging artist's love for young beauty reflects this trend, Siefken argues, and in the case of Gerhart Hauptmann, Mann had ascertained how rejuvenating or adapting oneself to a current literary fashion could lead to a loss of dignity. Siefken thinks that this insight is reflected by Aschenbach's being made up to look young. As is clear from Mann's essay on Wagner of 1911, moreover, according to Siefken, Mann himself believed a new classicality was necessary.

The problem of artistic existence he treats is thus very similar to his disagreement with his brother Heinrich and with the vogue for a regeneration and renaissance of a classicality and cult of beauty that held charm for him, too, but that he ultimately rejected. Siefken also claims that the scene in which Aschenbach writes his treatise at the beach parodies Goethe's account of composing his "Marienbader Elegie." In 1984, Heinz Gockel argued that *Death in Venice* resulted from Mann's own experience and his exact calculation of his intellectual and historical position. By allowing his hero, an artist infected by decadence, to founder, Gockel writes, Mann passed judgment not only on himself but also on an intellectual epoch, on an age of nihilistic aestheticism. Aschenbach is the "Socratic man" Nietzsche describes in *Die Geburt der Tragödie,* Gockel thinks, and Mann rejects such a detached artist's decadence. In 1986, Bernhard Böschenstein added that *Death in Venice* rejects Stefan George's canonization of antiquity as well as his idea of the poet as *Führer.* According to Böschenstein, the novella also describes the principle at work in the life of Winckelmann. Aschenbach's death in Venice, for example, is analogous to Winckelmann's death in Trieste. Böschenstein also claims that Mann's description of Tadzio's body as a statue alludes to Schiller's poem "Das Ideal und das Leben" (The Ideal and Life). In 1993, Böschenstein noted the eccentric polarity of Mann's story. One example of such polarity, he explains, is its antithesis of naturalism and neoclassicism. Oddly enough, he adds, Mann's naturalistic details illustrate the mythic characters who represent death, while his neoclassical categories suggest Aschenbach's individual personality. Böschenstein also observes, among other things, that Aschenbach's neoclassicism is false and lacks the balance of duty and desire, of life and art, found in Goethe's and Schiller's.

## Philosophy, Politics, and Psychoanalysis

A fourth general category of research on *Death in Venice* conducted from 1976 to 1995 consisted of philosophical, political, and psychoanalytic readings. As in the prior two decades, these three kinds of readings, despite their very different assumptions and concerns, proved similar insofar as they all assessed the novella according to mainly nonliterary criteria. They thus differ in kind from most of the studies cited so far in this chapter: from the ones about aestheticism, artists, and Mann's other works; from those about myth, sources, and comparisons; and from those about style, symbols, and literary history. Philosophical readings described Mann's story in terms that their authors borrow from Nietzsche or Schopenhauer. These readings tend to use such terms more abstractly than research that cites Plato or Nietzsche among Mann's sources or for other purposes. Political readings found fault with Aschenbach as a representative of the bourgeoisie in Germany prior to the First World War, and thus as a precursor of fascism; explained how Mann mixes history and fiction; or raised other issues, among them the role of Poland in *Death in Venice* and the relevance of the novella to political events of the 1980s and 1990s. Psychoanalytical readings included Jungian interpretations of Aschenbach; debates about the date when Mann first knew of Freud; various Freudian insights; a critique of Freud's influence in America; studies of Mann's animosity toward Goethe and of his symbolization of experience for himself and his readers; comments on Dionysus; the thesis that Aschenbach dreams the second half of his story; and remarks on mid-life crises, aging, and repression.

Most of the philosophical readings of *Death in Venice* invoked Nietzsche. In 1977, Ilse Pracht-Fitzell claimed that *Die Geburt der Tragödie* stimulated Mann's love of the theater and that his story bears thematic, linguistic, and structural traits of ancient tragedy. The series of mysterious men form a chorus, Pracht-Fitzell explains, and Aschenbach's vision functions as a prologue. Like tragic heroes, she adds, Aschenbach accepts his guilt, acknowledging his passion for Tadzio. In 1988, Sulamith Sparre likewise cited *Die Geburt der Tragödie* to argue that Aschenbach's Apollinian art conceals his Dionysian sympathy with the abyss. Patrick Reilly, again in 1988, saw in *Death in Venice* a Nietzschean thesis, Nietzschean standpoint, and Nietzschean prescription. "Aschenbach's story, deprived of its Nietzschean key," Reilly contends, "will simply admit the reader into the outer chamber of its almost anecdotal simplicity" (70). On a mythical level, he explains, that story ends in apotheosis, in self-realization in Dionysian rapture. It is a breakthrough, not just the breakdown that occurs in naturalistic terms. Mann suggests these levels, he adds, when his narrator offers competing interpretations, that is, dual explanations of the same event. Reilly compares the novella to Conrad's *Heart of Darkness* and Gide's *L'immoraliste*. He also refers to Aschenbach as a "demoralised boy-stalker" (70) and a "painted, fevered boy-stalker" (85). Keith M. May, yet again in 1988, contended that *Death in Venice* shows civilized values to be mere attitudes. In the novella, he writes, art is a positive value opposed to bestiality and putrefaction. Aschenbach's writing has kept at bay the "slobbering, slavering, rank and fleshly chaos of the natural" (88), in fact, but his ethic of struggle is blind, and he abandons the pursuit of knowledge, having failed to admit his evil. May thus reads Mann's novella according to Nietzsche's idea of going beyond good and evil.

Two further philosophical readings invoking Nietzsche were given in the 1990s. In 1992, Susan von Rohr Scaff wrote about alerting students to the Apollinian and Dionysian elements of Aschenbach's psyche and to "the self-exculpating function of Platonic ideas for Aschenbach" (142). The most cogent Nietzschean reading came from J. M. Hawes in 1993. Hawes begins by noting how, in Aschenbach's initial vision, Mann's association of Dionysus with death radically reinterprets Nietzsche. He explains that there are two opposing, equally Nietzschean, voices in the novella, that it cites the philosopher on two levels, "reckoning with Nietzsche's aesthetic thought — in the light of Nietzsche's psychological-critical thought" (77). Nietzschean aestheticism was still Wagnerian decadence, Hawes adds, and Aschenbach embodies both. Mann's critique of his hero, of Nietzschean aestheticism, sets Nietzsche the psychologist against Nietzsche the aesthete. Alluding to Nietzsche's polemic against Wagner, Hawes says that "the novella could be subtitled *Nietzsche contra Nietzsche*" (87). Mann probably knew that Nietzsche had described the suppression of vulgar language at the court of Louis XIV in *Die fröhliche Wissenschaft* (The Gay Science, 1882), Hawes claims, when Mann described Aschenbach as being like that monarch in this respect. Mann, he writes, probably also knew that Nietzsche linked cholera and pessimism. Finally, Hawes contrasts Mann's Nietzschean analysis of Nietzschean aestheticism with the acceptance of that aestheticism in Hermann Hesse's novel *Rosshalde* (1914).

Other philosophical readings tied *Death in Venice* to Schopenhauer. In an essay dated 1983 and published in 1996, Hans Wysling wrote that Mann knew Schopenhauer's *Metaphysik der Geschlechtsliebe*. Mann's notes for the novella, Wysling adds, cite all the ancient sources that Schopenhauer lists as relevant to the theme of pederasty, though Mann did not reject that kind of love, as Schopenhauer had. As noted in chapter 1, Bruno Frank had related this work to Mann's hero in 1913. In Wysling's case, then, as so often in studies of *Death in Venice*, archival research simply confirmed a connection that critics and scholars had long since surmised. In 1992, Adrian Del Caro, arguing that it applies Schopenhauer's principle of individuation and Nietzsche's idea of the Apollinian, called the account of Aschenbach in Mann's second chapter "a masterpiece of fiction from philosophy" (46). In a monograph on *Death in Venice*, Martina Hoffmann, in 1995, likewise studied Mann's philosophical conceptions. His references to philosophical texts, Hoffmann contends, suggest his protagonist's development on a coherent, abstract-philosophical sublevel. By incorporating Schopenhauer's negation of the will to life, she adds, Mann makes Aschenbach's destruction a condition necessary to achieving a higher state of existence. In the end, Aschenbach has to overcome his individuality, she explains, which is an illusion belonging to the world of appearances. He tries and fails to live according to Plato's Socratic maxims, which for him are mixed with Nietzsche's Dionysian intoxication. His decadent observation of forces he could not resist, moreover, does not prevent the destruction of his former existence. According to Hoffmann, this destruction is not the end of his story, however, since he thereby can negate the will-to-life on the way to nirvana. Mann may not have fully understood Schopenhauer, Hoffmann admits, but his story ends with a positive vision of Hermes Psychopompos pointing to a higher realm, and Aschenbach's death can be interpreted as conforming to Schopenhauer's notion of transcending the illusory world of appearances, of overcoming life in favor of a higher level of consciousness, of retiring to a metaphysical sphere of pure knowledge. That Aschenbach achieves such knowledge only as he dies, Hoffmann adds, suggests that Mann thought it incompatible with affirming life. *Death in Venice*, she concludes, can be interpreted as recommending a way of life whose highest goal is negating the self. The novella thus does not end in a disastrous finale. With this reading, Hoffmann joins the many other critics and scholars who see in Mann's final scene an epiphany and an apotheosis.

Some of the political readings of Mann's story portrayed Aschenbach as a representative of conflicts and contradictions in Wilhelminian Germany. In 1976, Yaak Karsunke disparaged both Mann and his hero as representative of a bourgeoisie that sought feudal protection against the proletariat it exploited. Aschenbach's motto — "Persevere!" — was that of the Nazis, too, he observes, and *Death in Venice* contains at least prefascistic thinking. Karsunke does not seem to know that Mann himself, in the 1930s, saw his hero in this same critical light. Walter H. Sokel, likewise in 1976, wrote that Aschenbach's demise unmasks repressive tendencies of the empire of Wilhelm II. Aschenbach thereby prefigures German history. According to Sokel, he also resembles the title character of Heinrich Mann's *Professor Unrat*, a novel that has astonishing parallels to *Death in Venice*. The heroes of both works, Sokel explains, stand for the same symbiosis of classical-humanistic education and Prussian discipline. Aschenbach is more representative of the German empire, however, and his enemy, unlike Unrat's rebellious schoolboys, Sokel notes, lies within himself. He is threatened by truth, by knowledge of reality, his reason doubts the power of his own creativity, and he represses his sensuality and his wish to speak with Tadzio. He was once an oppositional writer, Sokel continues, but has since become an author who upholds and glorifies the existing order. His empty, formal morality recalls Heidegger's concept of resoluteness, and his musing about a deserted Venice anticipates Hitler's vision of a depopulated earth. In 1977, Walter Falk found Aschenbach typical of his times because he intellectually transcends reality and creates something divine, that is, he turns Tadzio into a god. Aschenbach is also a representative of those times, Falk writes, since Mann shows that wishing for Dionysus means wishing for social chaos. The image of a cholera epidemic expresses such chaos, Falk adds, but it could as easily be an image of revolution or war. Aschenbach, he concludes, represents a wish for war, a wish common in the early years of the twentieth century. In their remarks on the timeless lot of artists, Falk says, neither Mann nor his narrator acknowledges this wish. Helmut Jendreiek, again in 1977, gave a cultural-historical and socio-critical analysis of Aschenbach as the representative of a crisis of the German bourgeoisie. *Death in Venice*, he explains, is a visionary anticipation of the threat to humanity posed by that class. Aschenbach's decline and dissolution, Jendreiek argues, are those of bourgeois culture at the turn of the twentieth century, and Mann's story anticipates his later association of aestheticism and fascism. Jendreiek's comments are rambling and repetitive, and his insights are hardly new. He does observe, though, that Nietzsche, in *Der Fall Wagner* (The Case of Wagner, 1888), described Wagner's music as "Schirokko," the wind that appears to make Aschenbach ill.

Other, similar readings of *Death in Venice* noted further ways in which Mann's fiction conveys historical facts. In 1978, Anni Carlsson mentioned the novella in her study of fantastic realism as historiography. Both beautiful and sick, she observes, Tadzio is characteristic of his epoch. She also links Mann's story to Alfred Kubin's novel *Die andere Seite* (The Other Side, 1909). In 1984, Klaus Vondung drew this same comparison, noting how Aschenbach's orgiastic dream shows his attraction to a vision of death and decline. Such visions were common at the end of the nineteenth century, Vondung explains, but they should not be misunderstood as prophesying a war or expressing a readiness or a wish for it. Vondung thus differs from the many scholars who directly link Aschenbach to the First World War. In 1986, Russell A. Berman read the novella as an indication of tensions in Wilhelmine culture, of "the crisis of liberal individuality and Wilhelmine art and the emergence of the previously suppressed categories of the charismatic community" (265). Aschenbach's internal demise comments on European society prior to the First World War, Berman argues, and, more importantly, on "the labile status of established literary practices" (264). That demise is also tied to the revolt of Aschenbach's "oriental heritage" (63), that is, to Prussia's suppression of his ancestral home of Silesia. *Death in Venice,* Berman suggests, thus undoes the suppression of Poland underlying German literary realism.

The most cogent such historical reading was given by Herbert Lehnert in 1993. Lehnert contrasts authors like Aschenbach with their society, contrasts a writer's striving for timeless authority with historical time. Mann's text, he explains, shows this contrast in many ways. Its very first sentence contains the incomplete date "19..," for example, but alludes to a diplomatic crisis of 1911 as well, when Germany sent a warship to Morocco. The text thus undermines its claim to timeless validity. The ambivalence of timelessness and timeliness is similarly evident, Lehnert adds, in Mann's account of the mortuary chapel, the wanderer, and Aschenbach's tropical vision and national fame. By describing his birthplace only as "L.," moreover, its narrator obscures historical facts about the city of Liegnitz, the site of battles against Mongols and between Prussia and Austria. According to Lehnert, Aschenbach's literary tasks, boat trip, loss of a sense of time, literary language, and social isolation likewise seem ambivalent, both timeless and timely. His self-destructive tendencies are those of European culture, moreover, and as a speaker of German abroad, he represents German foreign policy. When the young clerks from Pola traveling on

Aschenbach's boat toast the Italian troops exercising in Venice, Lehnert adds, they hint at ethnic conflicts in Austria-Hungary. That Aschenbach's national pride distances him from the corrupt capitalistic and democratic West is another historical phenomenon, as is Tadzio's scorn for the Russian family. Throughout the novella, finally, Aschenbach's isolation shows the insufficiency of the European upper classes, and in his Dionysian dream, he represents the individualistic society of modernity that was about to decide its conflicts in a world war. Lehnert's point is that all these signs of the historical horizon of *Death in Venice* undermine its suggestions of an artistic timelessness. In his view, it thus casts doubt on the capacity of literature to offer a timeless-mythical moral exemplarity. The ambivalence between realism and symbolism, between timeliness and timelessness, recurs in Mann's last scene, Lehnert concludes, when Tadzio beckons the dying Aschenbach to a mythical beyond.

A third group of interpretations raised other historical or political issues. In 1987, Robert von Dassanowsky-Harris argued that *Death in Venice* not only exposed an image of Germany in decay, but also revealed Mann's love-hate relationship with its old social order and his accordingly mixed feelings about the new beginning that results from Aschenbach's release of repressed sensuality. According to von Dassanowsky-Harris, Mann liked the barbarism that Aschenbach arrives at but clung to the viability of the bourgeois artist that Aschenbach loses. Von Dassanowsky-Harris also remarks on the role that the "myth of Slavic irrationality" (16) plays in Aschenbach's self-realization, contending that his erotic dream contains the "roots for German repression of Poland before the First World War" (17). In 1988, Bernhard Boschert and Ulf Schramm offered a unique and an odd interpretation of *Death in Venice,* attempting to show how literary scholarship can contribute to peace and to conflict resolution. With an eye to atomic and ecological disasters, Boschert and Schramm ask how the novella develops the motif of catastrophe. They explain that the catastrophe in Mann's story is caused by individuals who repress the truth for private gain instead of thinking about their collective survival. Aschenbach, they note, likewise pursues subjective goals at the expense of the common good. If we wanted to help Mann's Venetians, they add, we would have to break the spell of their repression. Boschert and Schramm are wrong when they argue that Aschenbach wants to leave Venice because he dislikes its greed. In 1992, Herbert O. Smith noted that Mann's story is "a mighty prologue to the Great War" (41). Edward Timms, again in 1992, similarly suggested reading *Death in Venice* as testimony to "the psychohistory of Europe on the eve of World War I" (134). Aschenbach's infatuation with Tadzio, Timms writes, "fits the pattern of psychohistory. Germanic self-control succumbs to the lure of Slavonic sensuousness" (137). By contrast, Timms adds, the English clerk embodies British common sense. In 1995, Rolf Fieguth likewise interpreted the Polish element in *Death in Venice.* On a psychological level, he contends, Tadzio's ethnicity has to do with Aschenbach's Silesian heritage. The Slavic, Fieguth adds, is what Aschenbach wants in his initial vacation spot on the Adriatic coast. That he declines, however, shows how Mann avoids the stereotype of the decadent Pole. Tadzio does not fit the German stereotype of Polish seducers, moreover, though his speech and name satisfy Aschenbach's yearning for Slavic sounds. On a historical level, Fieguth notes, Tadzio's hatred of the Russian family is a sign of the times before the First World War. For the period between 1848 and 1939, he concludes, Mann's story is the most prominent literary treatment of a German-Polish theme. Several articles on political and historical aspects of *Death in Venice* thus paid attention to the role of Poland. Finally, Edward W. Said wrote in 1993 that the plague infecting Europe in Mann's story is Asiatic and that Aschenbach's dread, desire, and degeneration are Mann's way of suggesting that Europe is "no longer invulnerable, no longer able to ignore its ties to its overseas domains" (188).

Like these political readings, psychoanalytic ones came in several varieties. Two psychoanalytic interpretations, like those by Krotkoff and by Hannum in 1967 and 1974, respectively, applied ideas set forth by C. G. Jung. In 1977, Louis Zinkin related *Death in Venice* both to pedophilia and to Jung's concept of individuation. Zinkin reports that he had a number of patients who had read the novella or seen Visconti's film. Two of these patients were pedophiles, and their resemblance to Aschenbach led Zinkin to consider similarities between Mann's story and Jung's writings. In Jung's terminology, he explains, *Death in Venice* relates a crisis of individuation that tells of fragmentation of the self and disintegration of the persona. It ends with the death of the self, but this death could be a rebirth. Zinkin thus acknowledges that the meaning of the novella is ambiguous. The process it describes, he explains, is determined by intensive archetypal activity. The persona becomes an empty shell, and the self appears in a number of archetypal images, the most important of which is the *puer aeternus,* the eternal youth. Aschenbach's life has lost meaning and purpose, Zinkin adds, and his mid-life crisis causes an invasion of archetypal images, starting with the wanderer at the cemetery. Aschenbach's persona is a false self, and it becomes splintered because he has neglected the child within himself. Described as the sea, Venice, and death, according to Zinkin, the mother archetype looms in the background of the story. Almost all the male characters similarly have archetypal properties. The wanderer and the gondolier personify evil aspects of Aschenbach's self, for example, and are shadow figures representing the father, whereas Tadzio embodies Jung's hermaphroditic child archetype. *Death in Venice,* Zinkin concludes, illustrates how pedophiles' formation of disparate partial personalities makes all personal relationships difficult.

In 1984, Heidi M. Rockwood and Robert J. R. Rockwood gave a similar, Jungian reading of the novella. Jung's theory of archetypes, they contend, integrates myth and psychology, the apparently distinct and parallel levels of Mann's story. Aschenbach has completely identified with his persona, they write, and this persona dies, denied nurture from his self. According to them, he also encounters his shadow in the wanderer, the fop, the gondolier, and the street musician. He physically resembles all of them, and they embody his suppressed bohemianism. The Rockwoods think that he is likewise linked to Tadzio, who is both a projection of his feminine anima and the archetype of the child. In him, Aschenbach repudiates, then accepts, but then finally rejects his own maternal, bohemian heritage. Aschenbach is also among the many figures in Mann's story who have attributes of Hermes. The Rockwoods make this argument after stating that no other scholars have read *Death in Venice* solely and consistently in Jungian terms. They seem unaware that Hannum in 1974 and Zinkin in 1977 had done just that. This oversight shows how ignorant most psychoanalysts and literary scholars are of each others' work on *Death in Venice*. Most know only the work of members of their own profession and thus move on parallel, largely independent tracks.

Other psychoanalytic readings discerned the influence of Freud in *Death in Venice*. In 1978, Frederick J. Beharriell, taking issue with Dierks's study of 1972, confirmed his own view of 1962 that the novella showed the influence of psychoanalysis. In 1925, Beharriell notes, Mann himself stated that it came into being under the influence of Freud. Beharriell accepts this statement and explains Freudian aspects of the novella, above all its hero's dynamic unconscious. He cites Aschenbach's death wish, repressed sexuality, rejection of what Mann's story calls "indecent psychologism," and Dionysian dream. The novella, he concludes, is indeed a "Freudian departure" (13) from Mann's earlier work. In 1990, Dierks agreed that *Death in Venice* had been influenced by Freud and argued that in 1911 Mann had read Freud's essay on Wilhelm Jensen's novella *Gradiva*. The essay and the novella, Dierks writes, enabled Mann to understand and formulate the return of his repressed homoerotic feelings. Mann, he adds, borrowed structural and thematic elements from both. Both Jensen's Norbert Hanold and Mann's Aschenbach find themselves unable to work because of their repressed erotic urges, and both flee such urges by traveling south on a trip that is at once psychological and mythical. According to Dierks, Hanold also often encounters honeymoon couples who, like Mann's threatening strangers, seem aggressive reminders of his repressed feelings. Hanold has a dream like Aschenbach's vision, moreover, and in that dream he imagines his beloved Zoe buried by the eruption of Mount Vesuvius in A.D. 79, covered by an "Aschenregen" (rain of ashes), a word recalled by the name of Mann's hero. This dream, Dierks goes on to say, is also like Aschenbach's Dionysian nightmare: in both, emotions stemming from childhood don the garb of antiquity. The importance of ancient mythology and of dreams in *Death in Venice* thus derives from Jensen and Freud, Dierks concludes, and the novella productively appropriates psychoanalytic discoveries. Dierks made this same argument in 1991, stressing that Freud's concept of condensation informs the semantic ambiguity of Mann's narrative style. This is the case in Mann's description of the wanderer, for example, a personification — like Jensen's Gradiva — of Hermes.

Not all Freudian readings of *Death in Venice* were equally cogent. In 1985, for example, Jean Jofen gave a Freudian commentary that amounts to a caricature of such readings. Jofen notes Mann's struggle against his homosexual desires, and Mann's fear that those desires might be revealed. Then come highly speculative remarks on *Death in Venice*. The physical appearance of the wanderer refers to Mann's father, Jofen assumes, a man who, being a German, probably had a snub nose, blond hair, and blue eyes. The wanderer's rucksack can be seen as a deformity of the spine, moreover, a phallic symbol. Aschenbach's desire to travel, Jofen adds, conveys his desire to return to his mother's womb. The white milk blossoms mentioned in his vision are symbols of his mother's breasts; the high-shouldered birds with crooked bills describe Mann, who was high-shouldered, and his brother, both of whom had prominent noses; the knotted bamboo stalks suggest the crib in which the young Thomas witnessed the primal scene, his father represented by the crouching tiger. Jofen also observes that Aschenbach's entertaining the possibility of being hit from behind with the gondolier's oar expresses a wish for homosexual union with a father figure, and that the gondolier's lack of a license symbolically expresses that Mann's father had no right to his mother. By describing Tadzio's high white collar, Jofen adds, Mann separates the head, the seat of guilt, from the body, the seat of desire. That Tadzio comes from the left when he passes Aschenbach's cabana, moreover, indicates that he is not right, not taking the correct and moral course. That Aschenbach, in his dream, hears the *u*-sound that Tadzio's name contains in the vocative case signals homosexual interest in the back, Jofen thinks, *u* being the highest vowel that one forms in the back of the mouth. Red like the strawberries that kill Aschenbach, he goes on to say, the breast-knot on Tadzio's swimsuit indicates that "Mann felt that he drank the poison from the mother's milk" (246). In addition to so speculatively interpreting Mann's tale, Jofen mistakenly claims that the wanderer makes a lewd gesture with his lips, that German papers leak news of the plague one day but deny it the next (it is the Venetian authorities who do the denying), and that as Tadzio moves out to sea at the end of the novella, his gaze is "fastened only on Aschenbach" (246).

A further interpretation of *Death in Venice* related to Freud was given by Allan Bloom in 1987. Bloom is critical of Freud's influence on Mann and on Mann's American readers, and he expresses mixed feelings about Mann's use of Plato. He laments that Freud's psychology neglected the soul and reduced everything higher to something lower, and he calls Mann's novella all that could be expected from such a reduction: "The best a Freudian could do for man's real intellectual longings was *Death in Venice,* clearly not a very rich row to hoe for the finer spirits" (137). Bloom assumes that Mann was a Freudian at the time he told Aschenbach's story. Other scholars have debated this assumption. Bloom also notes the influence of the novella on American consciousness. With "a rather heavy Freudian hand" (230), he says, Mann's story teaches the failure of sublimation. Aschenbach's cultural superstructure collapses when he becomes aware of his real motives for erecting it, Bloom adds, and there is nothing noble or even tolerable he can do with this awareness, since Mann provides no acceptable alternative. *Death in Venice* describes how culture is related to sexual sublimation, then, and shows the crisis of a civilization. Bloom does not think Americans have understood the novella this way. Instead, he argues, they have taken it as a manifesto of sexual liberation, and Aschenbach has struck them as someone who wanted to come out of the closet. Had Mann meant this, Bloom maintains, it would have attested to his own decadence, to a desire for creature, not creator, pleasures. He also notes that there is no place in Freud's system for the satisfaction of the kinds of desires Mann describes. Bloom here resists not only what he considers the corrupting effect of sexual interpretations of literature, but also the way Americans justify sexual lifestyles. Finally, he criticizes Mann's supposedly doctrinaire use of Freudian concepts of sublimation and rationalization in the way Mann presents Plato's *Phaedrus.* To him, Mann makes "Plato's respectable dialogue . . . the intermediary between Aschenbach's good conscience and his carnality" (237). In Mann's story — in its use of Plato, Bloom seems to mean — a tradition of thinking of eros in terms other than Freud's is nonetheless at least present. With what Mann gives us, we might therefore "embark on our own journey and find more interesting prey than is an Aschenbach" (237). In America, however, the thread of that tradition, which is stretched to its limit in Mann, Bloom concludes, is broken. In 1990, Eve Kosofsky Sedgwick took these remarks to mean that Bloom "encapsulates Western culture as the narrative that goes from the *Phaedrus* to *Death in Venice*" (237). She also thinks Bloom sees the crisis of Aschenbach's culture as "the deadeningness of the readings that are performed within its intrinsically explosive canon" (237).

Another two studies explained Mann's psychological motivation and his narrative means of conveying it. In 1978, Peter von Matt claimed that Mann, after the success of *Buddenbrooks,* thought it possible to become the German national author and thereby came into conflict with Goethe. His ambivalence toward this literary father figure, von Matt contends, kept him from carrying out his plans for a novel about Frederick the Great. Instead, he attributed this novel as well the fame it would have won him to Aschenbach. He identified with Schiller, von Matt continues, whose relationship to Goethe had been similarly tense, and his unfinished Schillerian essay *Geist und Kunst* became another of his hero's publications. Then came the execution of Goethe in *Death in Venice.* According to von Matt, the novella enacts the fantasized death of Goethe, whom it transforms into Aschenbach. It also compensates for its author's feelings of guilt. That Mann's own traits recur in Aschenbach, a fact suggesting that Mann himself suffers, for example, is self-punishment for his murderous fantasy. This fact also distracts readers who notice it from perceiving that fantasy. Von Matt argues that the novella presents Aschenbach's point of view, thereby forcing its readers to sympathize with him. It thus steers its own reception, misleading its readers about its actual purpose and reactivating their own Oedipal strategies. In his novella, Mann mastered his aggression toward Goethe, von Matt concludes, then aimed it at competitors: his brother Heinrich and Gerhart Hauptmann. In 1990, Fritz Gesing gave another interpretation of Mann's motivation and means. Gesing is concerned with the technique of symbolization, which, he says, has three aspects: an experience of reality, a cultural frame of reference, and a textual strategy. Mann's symbolic experience, Gesing posits, involved the sight of a beautiful boy and the death of Mahler, recent events perceived in accordance with his attachment to his mother and conflict with his father. Mann's cultural frame of reference, Gesing goes on to say, includes allusions to Greek mythology — to Hermes, for example — and literary intertextuality — passages from Platen, Nietzsche, Rohde, Homer, Plato, Hölderlin, and Goethe — that make that experience psychically manageable and communicable to readers. According to Gesing, Mann's textual strategies alert readers to his symbolic meaning in four ways: derealization, allusion, metaphorizing, and leitmotifs. At issue, then, are the psychodynamics that enabled Mann to have a symbolic experience as well as the means by which he transformed that experience into language and made it possible for readers, too, to feel a sudden gleam of meaning. In the process of symbolization thus defined, Gesing adds, Mann also overcame the regression that engulfs his hero, the chaos that destroys him.

Two further studies explained the psychological significance of Dionysus. In 1980, Lillian Feder called *Death in Venice* the greatest twentieth-century interpretation of this Nietzschean god. In it, she explains, "Mann depicts the continuous cultural and psychic bond of art with irrationality and madness" (232). Mann uses the mythical and cultic background of Aschenbach's dream, for example, to depict his psychological disintegration as "a regression to the primitive roots of civilization and the unconscious sources of art" (219). The novella describes a return to the primordial origins of religion and art, that is, and its hero recognizes that life and the self are tied to lust, cruelty, violence, destruction, and death. Feder also argues that Mann was ambivalent toward both his hero and the experience of the Dionysian. She incisively comments that Aschenbach's defenses start to break down at the outset of his story, when he cannot check his creative impulse, and that his dream about the rite that gave rise to Greek tragedy presents homosexuality as part of that impulse. She may overrate Aschenbach's awareness of his disintegration, however, and she is mistaken when she thinks that his treatise is on "the erotic as intrinsic to the impulse toward creation" (225). Feder here seems to attribute to Aschenbach her own interest in Dionysian sources of art. In 1988, Gary D. Astrachan gave a similar reading of *Death in Venice* (a reading published in a German translation before it appeared, in 1990, in the English version quoted here). Astrachan contends that the novella shows how Dionysian experience, long repressed in Western culture, has degenerated and become corrupted. Aschenbach's dream, he explains, is "the microcosmic, abbreviated recapitulation of his entire degeneration into the bestial impulses and behaviour of his increasingly full-blown psychosis" (69). This dream also exposes "the entire collective psyche and swirling abyss upon which Western civilisation has constructed its house" (72). In his hero, then, Mann foreshadows sadistic outbursts of Germany in the Second World War. Besides referring to the collective psyche, Astrachan finds other Jungian concepts at work in Mann's story. He cites archetypal resonances, images, and drives; he claims that Aschenbach's disintegration derives from the collective unconscious; and he says that Aschenbach is made up in an attempt to restore the persona. Like many psychoanalysts, Astrachan also misperceives some of Mann's details. He repeats Feder's mistake about the subject of Aschenbach's treatise, and he, too, overrates Aschenbach's awareness, writing that Mann's hero records how completely he succumbs to his mania. Astrachan wrongly thinks Aschenbach's work consists "mainly of formal German prose history and biography" (61), moreover, and that the wanderer in Munich stands "in the doorway of a graveyard" (62).

One of the most intriguing interpretations of *Death in Venice* to apply a psychoanalytic concept was given by Cynthia B. Bryson in 1992. Bryson begins with the notion of the daily nap that Mann's first paragraph says Aschenbach needs. Her remarks about his sleep are undercut, however, by her reliance on Lowe-Porter's flawed translation. She explains that this sleep involves "lucid dreaming" (181) and that it starts in the middle of the novella and lasts until the end. Aschenbach awakes only once, she maintains, shortly before he dies. He knows that he is dreaming, she adds, and he does so to restore his psychic balance, trying to resolve his inner conflict and to acquire Tadzio by recalling recent, actual events. In Bryson's view, then, the second half of Mann's story is a dream that recreates and modifies the events of the first. One could argue, she claims, that the plague exists only in that dream, not in Venice. The clerk who explains its source to Aschenbach could likewise be his recreation of the wanderer. Aschenbach's second visit to the deserted fountain, moreover, is an illusion, in his dream-state, that parallels his first. His summer home in the mountains is mentioned twice, too, as is the mortuary chapel he sees in Munich. He also eats strawberries twice, Bryson notes, another event that happens before manifesting itself in his dream. The encounter with the old fop on the boat recurs in the dream when the hotel barber makes Aschenbach look young, she adds, and Tadzio is more revealingly dressed in that dream than he is in Mann's fictional reality. According to Bryson, all these parallels show Aschenbach's creation of a fantasy, of an escape from consciousness that releases his soul. This argument is attractive, but it often rests on evidence provided only in Lowe-Porter's text, not in Mann's. The mythological imagery Bryson thinks marks the beginning of Aschenbach's dream, for example, is not "carefully placed to create a sense of the dream-state" (188) after a break that occurs in the middle of Mann's prose. It comes at the beginning of chapter 4, a fact that Lowe-Porter obscures by not dividing *Death in Venice* into chapters separated by titles, as Mann had done, here by "Viertes Kapitel" (Fourth Chapter). Lowe-Porter's passage ending with the words "three or four weeks of lotus-eating," moreover, cannot be the key to Aschenbach's dream state. Mann makes no such allusion to the "drug-induced state of Odysseus" (183). His Aschenbach imagines merely "eine Siesta von drei, vier Wochen" (a siesta of three, four weeks). Nor does Mann imply all of Bryson's parallels. His Aschenbach does see a "primeval wilderness-world of islands, morasses, and alluvial channels," as Lowe-Porter puts it, but Tadzio is not a similarly "'primeval legend'" (183). Instead, Mann describes him as being "wie Dichterkunde von anfänglichen Zeiten" (like poetic lore about the earliest times). Furthermore, Aschenbach's lips do not become the "colour of ripe strawberries" at the barber's, as Lowe-Porter writes and as Bryson thinks. Mann calls them "himbeerfarben" (raspberry-colored). Finally, Mann hardly believes that "the waking senses prove worthless and insubstantial" (191) in the dream-state. Aschenbach simply finds that his abstract thoughts resemble the whisperings of a dream, which prove shallow and useless on sober reflection. Here Bryson misreads even Lowe-Porter, who wrote of "flattering inventions of a dream, which the waking sense proves worthless and insubstantial." The dream, then, not the waking state, is worthless. Bryson's case is thus severely weakened by her use and her misunderstanding of Lowe-Porter's translation.

Another refreshing psychoanalytical reading of *Death in Venice* was given by Ludwig Haesler in 1993. Haesler is rightly skeptical of psychoanalytic claims such as those made by Kohut in 1957. Instead of exploring biographical links between Mann and his novella, the kind of link uncritically posited in such claims, Haesler focuses on one of the novella's structural aspects, on its "Perversifizierung des Ästhetischen" (perversification of the aesthetic) (160). Aschenbach's psychological development and his relationship to reality and to art are perverse, Haesler contends, insofar as they attest to his denial of death. Precisely this denial leads to death, however. The aesthetic is sexualized, idealized, and idolized, he explains, and helps him deny reality in favor of pleasing appearances. It is not that Aschenbach has seen beauty and is therefore destined to die, Haesler writes, but vice-versa: he has seen death and therefore dedicates himself to beauty. The jungle that Aschenbach envisions is a counter-world to the one of finality and death that he denies, moreover, but a counter-world that is itself threatening and deadly. Increasingly and intoxicatingly delighted by beauty, Haesler contin-ues, Aschenbach loses touch with reality, a fact apparent when he relativizes and denies the existence of the cholera epidemic in Venice. These fictional events may be related to Mann's homoeroticism, but they are presented in a work that is critical and ironic and thus enables its author to deal with and control this eroticism. Mann succeeds where Aschenbach fails, then, writing an aesthetically perfect work, one in which form and desire are reconciled and integrated. In addition to making this argument, Haesler regards Aschenbach's story as a variation on the theme of Orpheus. Like Orpheus, he maintains, Aschenbach is an Apollinian artist who descends into the underworld to recover what he has lost, who encounters Dionysian gods, and whose power is defeated by his sensual desire. Haesler wrongly thinks that Aschenbach's story *Ein Elender* is a novel called *Der Elende*.

A final group of readings raised further psychological issues. Two of those readings concerned Aschenbach's age. In 1976, Leah Davidson saw a mid-life crisis in *Death in Venice*. At the beginning of his own such crisis in 1910, Davidson argues, Mann was rethinking the issues of dignity, crea-tivity, and health in old age. Like Kohut in 1957, with whom she disagrees about details of the longing for father and mother apparent in the novella, Davidson argues that Mann explores psychopathology but seeks psychic health. Aschenbach's work inhibition, she adds, results from realizing that he is aging and from being paralyzed at the prospect of death. In twelve steps, he "reduces himself, through several regressive maneuvers to an en-amoured elderly buffoon" (210). Mann himself had experienced a work inhibition, Davidson claims, but was able to keep being creative because he explored unfulfilled fantasies that, if repressed, might have inhibited his self-expression. More than anything, the novella is thus about "the vicissitudes of narcissism, and idealization of the self" (212). In 1988–89, Kathleen Woodward similarly understood *Death in Venice* as "a parable of the domi-nant discourse of aging in the West" (121). The aging Aschenbach longs for youth, she argues, and his story portrays youthfulness as a masquerade for an aging body in a dark way that reinforces our culture's phobia about aging. When Woodward remembers how Aschenbach's make-up runs down his face, she mistakes Visconti's film for Mann's text, where this event never occurs. In 1983, James R. McWilliams amplified his earlier remarks of 1967. Mann's novella, he explains, represents the failure of his attempt to "subdue and subjugate his feelings by refrigeration and repression" (167). Noting Aschenbach's "overwhelming need for chastisement" (150) and his "subsequent adventures in sin" (151), McWilliams stresses punishment, as he had in 1967. Alluding to the title of his earlier article, he writes that the novella could be subtitled "The Failure of a Repression" (148). Finally, in 1992, Jeffrey B. Berlin wrote about teaching the connections between psychoanalysis and Mann's story. Berlin explains some of Mann's own comments on the novella as well as work by scholars such as Dierks. He also observes that Aschenbach's repudiation of knowledge is conscious *sup*pression, not unconscious *re*pression. Noting that Mann wanted to escape psychologism much as Aschenbach has, Berlin makes a statement that puts many psychoanalytic readings of Mann's novella into perspective: "Although *Death in Venice* provides psychoanalytically oriented critics with a gold mine, the story itself, in keeping with Mann's attitude, sharply repudiates psychoanalysis" (117).

## Homoeroticism and Mann's Biography

A fifth category of research done on *Death in Venice* from 1976 to 1995 comprises books and articles that raise the topic of homoeroticism, often with regard to Mann's biography. Many studies of the novella that were written during these years address this topic, of course. Detering's remarks of 1992 and 1994, for example, are noted earlier in this chapter, in the section about comparisons of the novella to Mann's other writings. The topic of homoeroticism became more prevalent, however, after the publication of Mann's diaries, which contained revelations about its significance to him. As a result, the studies cited in this section treat it more fully — and often more forcefully — than any since the initial reviews of 1913 and 1914. Some of those reviews called Aschenbach's passion, and Mann's description of it, serious, sensitive, symbolic, or idealistic. Others found that passion perverse or pathological and cast its description as repugnant and dangerous. By contrast, studies that appeared in the twenty years at issue here discussed the extent to which homoeroticism is Mann's subject, the function of his Platonic allusions, the role of homosexual love in ancient Greek and in modern German society, the shame or stigma of homosexuality at the time he wrote the novella, bourgeois notions of desire, and the relationship of eros to language. Some of these studies about homoeroticism in the novella are polemical and tendentious, as is clear from their authors' strong words. Other, general studies of Mann's life and work that mention this topic differ in how they assess its importance to his story. Finally, homoeroticism figures in comments on *Death in Venice* by Mann's major biographers.

One group of studies suggested and debated the extent to which homoeroticism is the subject of *Death in Venice*. In 1977, Jeffrey Meyers, contrasting the novella with Gide's *L'immoraliste,* argued that its homosexual theme is not its real subject. "Mann employs homosexuality to symbolize the core of passionate feeling that inspires great art," Meyers writes, "and the theme of his novella is the possibility of self-destruction inherent in creative genius" (43). Meyers thinks Aschenbach's passion teaches him that he cannot control his fate, that his treatise barely hides "the dry rot of its intellectual foundations" (52), and that he dies in a state of absurd, profound degeneration. Aschenbach's quest for Tadzio, "the doomed love of the suspect and anti-social pederast" (53), is symbolic of the artist's quest for perfection, for uniting the real and the ideal. Meyers incisively notes that Mann exaggerates when he writes of the swords and spears that pierce St. Sebastian, who was attacked only with arrows; that the sand used during the purchase of Aschenbach's ticket to Venice, like his parents' hourglass, warns of mortality; and that Tadzio's sickly teeth link the boy to the homosexual fop, who wears dentures. Meyers stretches the idea of parody, though, when he maintains that convulsions caused by cholera "parody the sexual climax" (48) and that the mortuary chapel in Munich is a parody of St. Mark's in Venice. Besides, that chapel stands at the entrance to, not opposite, the North Cemetery. In 1992, Wolfgang Popp wrote that *Death in Venice* thematized Mann's own homosexuality. Aschenbach's trip takes him south, to the Eldorado of homosexual longing, according to Popp, and Tadzio is the idol of his artistically sublimated homosexual desire. His story is thus a pathetic-tragic homosexual novella. By contrast, Hermann Wiegmann, also in 1992, concluded that *Death in Venice* is not just the story of a homoerotic inclination. Its author "literarized" sublimated erotic ideas, he explains, but its themes are art and life, transitoriness and perfection, and Apollo and Dionysus. If it were such a story, its dense literary weaving of symbols, motifs, themes, and reflections would have to be read only as a warning against the dangers of homoeroticism, Wiegmann adds, and this reading would not work. The homoerotic inclination it describes, he contends, is an extreme case of an existential artistic problem, a symbolic expression of the beauty and mortality of human striving against a truly cosmic background. Wiegmann draws these and other conclusions in a style more flowery than the language most scholars had used to describe *Death in Venice* for many years.

    Another group of studies commented on the function of Mann's allusions to Plato and other ancient Greek authors who wrote about homosexuality. In 1979, Leslie A. Fiedler commented that the scene in which Aschenbach visits the hotel barber expresses the self-hatred and obscene joy felt by the author of Mann's "prescient little book" (242). The fact that Aschenbach names Tadzio "Phaedrus," Fiedler adds, reminds us that pederasty was not always thought taboo. In 1982, Ignace Feuerlicht — who had called Mann's novella a *Candide* ambivalently directed at art in 1966, and who had commented on Tadzio's name in 1968 — described *Death in Venice* as "one of the most famous fictional accounts of homoeroticism" (93). Mann could not have published a hymnic "paean to pederasty" (93) in Germany prior to the First World War, Feuerlicht says. For both himself and his readers, his referring to ancient Greeks elevated his emotional experience of a fourteen-year-old boy in Venice in 1911. Contrary to Mann's claim that his Greek material was a refuge for his hero, Feuerlicht thinks it was "more of a help and refuge for Mann, both as the one who had that experience in real life and as the author who had to think of the public's reaction to that experience" (94). Readers' criticism was also reduced, he adds, by the narrator's moralistic tone and by the pessimism that the novella aims at artists in general. Werner Deuse explained the ancient Greek elements of *Death in Venice* differently in 1992. Those elements, he argues, are not a mere ornament. When Aschenbach alludes to Xenophon's *Memorabilia* by calling Jaschu "Kritobulos," for example, he implies both his tendency to play the role of Socrates and the danger that lies merely in looking at beautiful boys. Ironically, this allusion is thus a warning to himself. That Aschenbach eats strawberries after making this allusion foreshadows his later, fatal intake of them, Deuse goes on to say, as well as his failure to get away, as Xenophon's Socrates advises. To claim that Aschenbach's allusion to the *Odyssey* when he calls Tadzio "little Phaecian" implies not only easy living but also being ferried to the underworld is valid, Deuse adds, because Mann could have known that Phaecians ferried the dead from reading Rohde's *Psyche*, as we know he did. Furthermore, Aschenbach's last glimpse of Tadzio walking on the sandbank reads like Rohde's account of Elysium. According to Deuse, such allusions suggest the multi-dimensionality of Mann's text. His notes for the novella also contain an excerpt about Dionysus that comes from Jacob Burckhardt's *Griechische Kulturgeschichte*, Deuse argues, a fact that weakens Dierks's thesis of 1972 that Mann had modeled his plot on Euripides' *Bacchae*. Deuse also remarks on Aschenbach's rediscovery of Platonism. Taking issue with Schmidt's argument of 1974, which holds that Aschenbach turns Platonism into an alibi for pagan sensuality, Deuse claims that Aschenbach omits Plato's mention of a transcendent world of ideas and that ontology thus becomes psychology. For Aschenbach, Deuse concludes, this psychologizing paradoxically protects his passion against the "indecent psychologism," as Mann calls it, of his times. Deuse does not seem to know that Hans-Joachim Sandberg, in 1991, had already listed Burckhardt among Mann's sources for his knowledge of Dionysus.

Two studies compared concepts of homosexual love in Plato's Greece and Mann's Germany. In 1985, Bernd Effe explained Mann's account of pederasty and his reception of Plato, relating the way in which these two authors thematize pederasty to their biographies and to the attitudes of their respective societies. *Death in Venice* differs from Mann's other fiction, Effe remarks, in that its author directly consulted ancient sources while writing it, rather than simply relying on modern authors' commentaries. He was drawn to such sources, Effe adds, especially to Plato, by his pederastic theme. That theme occasioned the Greek style of his prose as well — as when he describes Helios's chariot at the outset of chapter 4. Effe is not breaking new ground when he writes that the theme of pederasty is motivated by Mann's own experience or that its pessimistic treatment results from Mann's reading of Lukács's *Die Seele und die Formen.* He says something original, however, when he notes how both Mann and Plato treat that theme in accordance with societal attitudes. Both authors oppose those attitudes, he explains, but also conform to them: Plato condemns actual pederasty but tries to preserve it through philosophical sublimation, while Mann opposes such condemnation but discredits such sublimation. Effe adds that Plato criticizes a practice widely accepted in his time, whereas Mann's skepticism corresponds to the rejection of homosexuality by most of his society. This societal rejection, Effe argues, is the actual reason for the anti-Platonic turn taken by Mann's pederastic theme. In 1986, George Bridges similarly examined the problem of pederastic love in *Death in Venice* and the *Phaedrus.* Both works trace the development of such love from beginning to end, Bridges argues, and describe three periods: before, during, and after the encounter with the loved one. In each of these periods, he explains, social reality sets parameters. The extensive preparation for Tadzio's appearance, for example, reflects the fact that Aschenbach's society proscribes his desire and that his mental defenses against that desire must be overcome. Through his narrator, Mann brings "the full weight of society's prohibition of pederastic love to bear on Aschenbach's deteriorating condition" (42). According to Bridges, even Aschenbach sees himself through the disapproving eyes of society. Constraints placed on his story by social reality, moreover, prevent him and Tadzio from doing more than exchange glances. Bridges thus demonstrates the influence of society on literature, though he also writes that the conflict between spirit and flesh, a conflict within an emotion itself, does not seem determined by time or place. This conflict is a constant, he adds, despite the different values that Plato's and Mann's societies assigned to pederastic love.

Two other studies stressed the shame and the stigma attached to homosexuality in Mann's day. Hermann Kurzke mentioned shame in his overview of *Death in Venice* in 1985. Kurzke remarks on many other aspects of the novella as well: its neoclassicism, place in Mann's oeuvre, tragic form, leitmotifs, use of sources, opposition of the Apollinian and Dionysian, and its hero's role as an artist. Kurzke comments incisively on all of these subjects. According to him, Mann allows his search for classicality to fail, for example, and thus formulates the problems of classicism. Kurzke also observes that the novella marks the end of Mann's early work; that its five chapters correspond to the acts of an ancient tragedy, though its narrator's seriousness seems almost parodied; and that its leitmotifs suggest its mythic substructure. Knowledge of Mann's sources is sobering, Kurzke adds, since it shows how limited and ad hoc his acquaintance with mythology was. Finally, Kurzke notes that Mann's patriotism during the First World War replaced his pessimistic view of aestheticism. Kurzke is at his most incisive, however, when he comments on Aschenbach the lover. The strong sense of shame felt in Mann's day lends his story a tension it would not have now, Kurzke writes, in an age of sexual directness. Back then, bourgeois barriers to physical contact made yearning, rather than fulfillment, the decisive factor. Tadzio can assume mythical proportions only in such wordless yearning. As Kurzke describes Aschenbach's failure to break the boy's spell by talking to him, "Den Mythos fragt man nicht, wie spät es ist" (One does not ask a myth the time of day) (126). In 1991, Karl Werner Böhm similarly noted that Mann's novella bears traces of the stigma attached to homosexuality. *Death in Venice,* he argues, is a provocation that went unnoticed. It treats the theme of pederasty with artistic daring, Böhm explains, and it invites an autobiographical reading, but Mann concealed its connection to his personal life. He did so both in a public relations campaign and in a narrative strategy, both by cultivating his image as a family man and respectable citizen and influencing the reception of the novella, and by reversing the motive for Aschenbach's suffering, referring to myths and a classical canon, and objectifying the "hymn" he initially planned. As an established author, a husband and father, a member of Munich's board of censors, and an analyst of decadence, Böhm continues, Mann masked himself with the truth. By citing Goethe's heterosexual affair in Marienbad as the source of his story, according to Böhm, he likewise masked his own homosexuality. He also made Aschenbach seem to die *in* homosexual love, rather than *of* it, making such love seem merely a symbol or symptom of a general decadence. He also legitimated his story by means of its hieratic style, elevated diction, Platonism, and allusions to ancient sources, thereby neutralizing Tadzio's sexuality. Finally, Böhm notes, Mann seems pessimistic about pederasty, or at least about passion, and Aschenbach becomes increasingly aware of its stigma. Böhm thus shows how *Death in Venice* reflects and reacts to the anti-homosexual climate in which it arose.

Another two studies explained the novella as one of the many literary representations of homosexuality that were written in Wilhelmine Germany and one of many homosexual fantasies set in the Mediterranean. In 1990, James W. Jones called *Death in Venice* the best known and most artistically successful literary account of homosexuality in Wilhelmine Germany. Jones's interest is in the link between homosexual and artistic impulses, and he finds in Mann's story "a well-developed theory on the relationship between the artist and the homosexual" (278). Mann shows both to be egocentric, he says, and Aschenbach's self-orientation proves unfruitful as well as dangerous. Mann's presentation of homosexuality as narcissistic, pathological, and repressed seems to show the influence of Freud, he adds, but Schopenhauer's theory of it is even more clearly evident. The novella also bears at least some traces of medical notions of homosexuality. Its motifs of the artist, ancient Greece, and Italy are found in much of the German fiction that treats this subject, Jones observes, but it is fascinating because it describes homosexuality in a contradictory and an ambiguous way, both as a disease and as a path to higher values. About an artist and a homosexual, *Death in Venice* suggests a "dual Otherness" (290). In 1993, Robert Aldrich cited the novella as a paradigm of northern European homosexuals' attraction to the Mediterranean. He also discusses Visconti's and Britten's treatments of "the 'Aschenbach phenomenon'" (4), not to mention other works associated with "the Aschenbach theme" (6). As so often, such generalizations about Mann's hero reflect inaccurate reading. It may certainly be true that *Death in Venice* is "a parable about longing and obsession and a *mise-en-scène* of the homosexual condition in a certain historical epoch, even if Aschenbach himself fails to act on his repressed desires and remains only a voyeur" (4). It coarsens Mann's story, however, to say that Aschenbach longs for companionship and sexual comfort from its outset and that he is instantly lovestruck and lusts after Tadzio from afar. Furthermore, Aldrich's remarks are riddled with mistakes. Aschenbach is not searching for a new or manly kind of hero, for example, nor does he decide to go to Venice while he is still in Munich or intend to spend a quiet summer there. He does not spy Tadzio on the beach soon after arriving at his hotel either, and he hardly "stumbles onto the beach" (2) for a final look at the boy. For that matter, Visconti did not add the street musicians' performance. Mann had already described it. In any case, Aldrich also notes that Tadzio and Jaschu have a sexually ambivalent relationship and that Aschenbach's death in Venice was inspired by Platen's in Syracuse.

Two further studies explained *Death in Venice* by criticizing bourgeois notions of desire. In 1989, Tom Hayes and Lee Quinby examined the novella as modernist art showing such aporetic notions in its "connections between representations of homoeroticism and masculinist assumptions implicit in the patriarchal ideology that produces and is produced by bourgeois art" (160). Mann's story questions assumptions about sexual difference only to reaffirm them, according to Hayes and Quinby, who argue that the binary oppositions found in bourgeois discourse reflect and reinforce patriarchal values such as misogyny and homophobia. Aschenbach's infatuation with Tadzio at once is comic and has tragic consequences that "reinforce the homophobic strictures and repressions of bourgeois morality" (168). Hayes and Quinby's reading of *Death in Venice* is highly theoretical and deconstructive. Since they quote the novella in Lowe-Porter's deficient translation, moreover, that reading is also often mistaken. They contend that Aschenbach is "'quite unmanned'" (163), for example, when he whispers that he loves Tadzio. This phrase, they think, shows his fear of emasculation. In German, however, Aschenbach is "überwältigt," that is, overwhelmed. They also associate the hooked nose of the Apollinian horse in Plato's *Phaedrus* with Aschenbach's "'aristocratically hooked nose'" (167). In German, though, that nose is "edel gebogen," that is, nobly curved. Finally, they claim that the narrator refers to art as feminine when using the pronoun "she" to describe it. In German, though, the word for "art" — *Kunst* — is simply a feminine noun, one that takes the pronoun *sie* for purely grammatical reasons. In such a case, one renders this pronoun into English as "it." Hayes and Quinby thus cite evidence that Mann never gives. Eugene Goodheart made a similar, sounder case in 1991. *Death in Venice*, he argues, is about the disintegration of Aschenbach's power, of his social and political authority, under the pressure of desire. His art is one of repression and containment of desire, one that supports bourgeois society, Goodheart writes, but art is an enemy of bourgeois order, and a fatal desire for the illimitable destroys him. Unlike him, moreover, Mann experiences ambivalence as a form of control and writes it into his story: "Ambivalence for Mann becomes a condition for the cathartic exorcism of the demons of desire" (52). Goodheart is mistaken when he mentions Aschenbach's "abortive decision to go to Trieste" (47). In fact, Aschenbach goes there by train, from Munich, en route to Pola and an unnamed Adriatic island.

Three authors mentioned homoeroticism in Mann's novella in the course of reflecting on androgyny and other sexual identities. In 1984, Richard Exner argued that *Death in Venice*, like many of Mann's other writings, suggests androgyny, a psychological concept to which hermaphrodism and bisexuality are subordinate. Tadzio has soft and tender features, Exner remarks, while his sisters appear manly. Exner's point is that one-sidedness is inhuman and that Mann's hero, for the sake of life as well as art, must abandon his celibacy. According to Exner, his encounter with Tadzio is a hieroglyph and cipher of androgynous harmony and perfection, and his homoerotic inclination is the first step on his way to becoming human. In 1990, Camille Paglia defined Tadzio's and Aschenbach's sexual personae. Tadzio exemplifies what she calls "the beautiful boy" (118). Like Exner, Paglia also calls him androgyne. He is Apollinian, silent, sexually self-complete, narcissistic, and destructive. Aschenbach is an example of "the depraved Decadent aesthete" (429), and becomes "the deranged fan of the star-god" (597). The jungle he imagines is "the female swamp of generation, the chthonian miasma against which the beautiful boy dreamily protests" (595). It, too, thus seems to have a sexual persona. Some of Paglia's statements are more accurate than others. While Tadzio may have a radical visibility, as she claims, he does not make Delphic utterances. Some of the sources she names and comparisons she draws similarly seem more likely than others. *Death in Venice* is Mann's homage to Oscar Wilde, she says, and deeply indebted to his *Picture of Dorian Gray*. She also thinks Goethe's *Venezianische Epigramme* (Venetian Epigrams, 1795) is its ancestor. Aschenbach's vision in Munich is clearly inspired by Huysmans, she writes, and corresponds to the similar setting of Melville's *The Paradise of Bachelors and the Tartarus of Maids* (1855). Tadzio is more solipsistic than Melville's Billy Budd, moreover, and his mother may have been inspired by Hawthorne's Hester Prynne. Finally, Paglia contends that Aschenbach does not want sex and that, "It trivializes *Death in Venice* to reduce it, as has been done, to a homosexual chronicle of coming out of the closet" (597). In 1991, Claus Tillmann noted that the novella resembles several of Mann's other writings insofar as it shows its hero torn between male and female traits, contrary characteristics inherited from his father and his mother.

Two authors discussed the relationship of eros to language. In 1983, Claus Sommerhage linked the erotic and the poetic when he told how Aschenbach identifies with Socrates. He does so, Sommerhage explains, in his daydreams of Socrates' speeches to Phaedrus. In psychoanalytic terms, both of these dreams show appropriation, regression, and wish-fulfillment. Sommerhage contends that Socrates' homoeroticism must hold a specific attraction for Mann's hero. That homoeroticism was sublimated but not repressed, he adds, and Socrates put it to use in his art of philosophical midwifery. Aschenbach's artistic crisis and erotic conflict, moreover, both result from identifying with his mother. He wants to be like Socrates, Sommerhage thinks, and the latent content of his daydreams amounts to the following text:

> Ich möchte, wie Sokrates, Jünglinge lieben und von ihnen geliebt werden, genauso wie ich von der Mutter geliebt werden wollte. Wie Sokrates möchte ich meine Kunst befreit wissen von den vom Vater mir auferlegten Pflichten, um, wie Sokrates, mich frei zu dem Ursprung meiner Kunst und meiner damit verknüpften Vorliebe für Knaben und Jünglinge bekennen zu können.
>
> [Like Socrates, I would like to love boys and be loved by them, just as I wanted to be loved by my mother. Like Socrates, I would like to know my art is freed from the duties my father imposed on me, so that I, like Socrates, can freely acknowledge the origin of my art and of my preference for boys and young men that is connected to it.] (96)

Sommerhage, then, analyzes not only Aschenbach's life and dreams but also the biography of Socrates. Sommerhage also notes the enormous tension between Aschenbach's real and ideal selves, the narcissism inherent in his love for Tadzio, and the partial identity of the erotic and the poetic object when he writes his treatise, stimulated by the boy and knowing that eros is in the word. In 1985, Frederick Alfred Lubich gave a similar reading of *Death in Venice,* stressing its dialectic of logos and eros. At the start of the novella, Lubich writes, Aschenbach's language has reached an artistic freezing point. This fact is evident in the linguistic anemia of Mann's second chapter. When Tadzio appears, he adds, that language changes from prosaic description to lyrical praise. In Aschenbach's treatise, an artistic union with the boy, logos and eros are fused and his ethics of achievement turns into an aesthetics of pleasure. Lubich interprets this event in terms borrowed from Roland Barthes's *Le*

*Plaisir du Texte* (The Pleasure of the Text, 1973). In the subsequent disintegration of Aschenbach's language, he notes, such pleasure becomes agony.
Eros and logos come apart and dissolve into a vision of chaos and into unintelligible sounds, respectively. In Aschenbach's dream, for example, there is
just orgiastic noise. Furthermore, Aschenbach's encounter with Tadzio enacts
Mann's emblem of the arrow and the lyre. Like this symbolic emblem, Lubich
goes on to say, that encounter represents self-knowledge as well as ecstasy, art
as well as criticism. It also corresponds to Mann's relationship with his hero.
In both instances, for example, an author recoils from a narcissistic projection
of himself. In Mann's work, Lubich continues, *Death in Venice* is a high point
in the dialectic of logos and eros. It is also a turning point, for his later fiction
develops that dialectic in new ways. Lubich thus joins the many critics and
scholars who see Aschenbach's treatise as the brief achievement of a balance
between intellect and the senses. He made this same argument in 1986, adding remarks on Aschenbach's erotic gaze and stressing the "structural equation
of the act of love and the act of writing" (9).

Several studies that discuss homoeroticism are remarkably polemical and
tendentious. Their authors often use provocative vocabulary. In 1992, Robert
K. Martin not only noted the "sexual geography" (63) of Aschenbach's trip
to the south and the east, but also argued that his "tightly grasped fist . . . is
also to be understood as the tightly closed sphincter" (65). In 1993, Gerhard
Härle, remarking on Mann's homosexual aesthetics, wrote that the threat
posed by homosexual desire was less important to Mann than the enormous
productive energies its sublimation released. Härle claims that Aschenbach is
destroyed by a wish-fulfillment "als sich ein riesiges Glied, das den Namen des
Knaben Tadzio trägt, im Traum in ihn einsenkt" (when a huge member that
bears the name of the boy Tadzio sinks into him in his dream) (119). Robert
Tobin, also in 1993, wrote that Mann's story consists simply of Aschenbach's
homosexual love. Mann's rhetoric of concealment and revelation, Tobin adds,
links homosexuality and disease. Both are terrible secrets. Aschenbach's masochism, moreover, results from Mann's assigning him a feminine role that is
negatively defined. Tobin made similar remarks in 1994. Calling the connection between suffering and literature the central issue of *Death in Venice,* he
examines discourses of homosexuality, homosexual desire in Mann's life, and
the theme as well as the meaning of homosexuality in the novella. In an experimental reading of Mann's first three chapters, Tobin notes homosexual
connections: the first has "a subtext about a botched homosexual encounter
in a park" (220), not least because the wanderer is strange, odd, and thus
"queer"; in the second chapter, the passage about St. Sebastian, which Mann
quotes from Samuel Lublinski's comments on Thomas Buddenbrook, is "a
kind of homosexual penetration of one man's text by another man's words"
(222); and Aschenbach's trip to Venice in the third chapter recalls Mann's
earlier novella set there, *Enttäuschung,* in which two men engage in "a kind

of attempted pick-up" (225). Tobin knows that his experimental reading is a stretch. He often stretches its textual evidence, in fact, to the breaking point. He also concludes that the closeting of cholera and man-boy love makes Mann's novella a story of secrets. In 1995, Sue Vice thought Aschenbach an erotomaniac, an addicted lover. Mann emphasizes the male gaze, she contends, a voyeuristic impulse with "penetrative origins" (120). Vice incorrectly thinks that readers cannot tell whether Tadzio sees or knows that Aschenbach looks at him. It is clear from Mann's text that he does. Ursula W. Schneider, again in 1995, argued that Aschenbach's debasement includes sadomasochism. Compared to the claims made by the other authors just cited, her remark that Mann "does not take pederasty lightly" (196) is an elegant understatement.

Homoeroticism in *Death in Venice* is also mentioned in more general studies of Mann's life and works. The authors of those studies reached various conclusions about its importance. In 1982, Hans Rudolf Vaget remarked that the novella hinted at tension in Mann's marriage. Aschenbach's tragedy is a sign of Mann's ambivalent relationship to homoeroticism, Vaget explains, a sign of his own bisexuality, which he had not yet reconciled with normality. *Death in Venice* rejects homoeroticism decisively, Vaget writes, but only pro forma. In 1984, Vaget's commentary on all Mann's stories included astute remarks on the genesis of the novella, on Mann's interpretations of it, on its literary-historical context, and on its reception. Vaget stresses Mann's critique of his literary career, his interest in Goethe, and his skepticism about German neoclassicism. He does not accept T. J. Reed's suggestion, first made in 1971, that *Death in Venice* began as a homoerotic hymn. In further remarks on the novella in 1990, Vaget added that it at once rejects and celebrates homoeroticism. After its publication, he notes, Mann's struggle with his own, ambivalent sexuality was largely confined to his diaries. Only there, as a secret, according to Vaget, could it continue to spur his creativity. Reinhard Baumgart reached different conclusions in 1989. In an article, Baumgart wrote that only twice, in *Tonio Kröger* and *Death in Venice,* did Mann not project the erotic allure and terrors he wanted to narrate onto heterosexual relationships. The resulting abstraction nearly ruined his stories. The closer he comes to the autobiographical core of his recurring motif of erotic affliction, Baumgart adds, the more strongly his sublimation elevates him. Baumgart also notes that Mann later made female characters suffer the kind of erotic catastrophe that sweeps away Aschenbach. In a book, Baumgart also commented on other aspects of *Death in Venice.* Mann may have attributed his own unfinished works to Aschenbach so as not to exhaust himself by writing them, he thinks, and Aschenbach is the first of Mann's fictional authors whose reception is part of his story. According to Baumgart, Mann also liquidates him in the execution of an alter ego. Mann's prose is suspiciously beautiful, though, an artistic counterpoint to the dissolution it describes. The moral of his story may thus be "Fiat ars pereat poeta" (150). In addition to making these and several other remarks, Baumgart comments on Aschenbach's sexuality. The feminine "Frau von Aschenbach" (40), he says, is confused about it. Aschenbach also often folds his hands in his lap. How suggestive and obscene this gesture is, Baumgart writes, since it can signify rest, fatigue, piety, and the womb, but also readiness and defense of the male sexual organ.

Other scholars who mention homosexuality in studies of Mann's life and work were more insistent about its importance in *Death in Venice*. In 1988, Gerhard Härle said that Mann's struggle with homosexual feelings was staged in the novella as the problem of the artist. Mann, he adds, described writing a later Italian novella, *Mario und der Zauberer*, on the beach at the Baltic sea, thereby indicating that he was identical to the erotically confused Aschenbach who writes about Tadzio on the Lido. The bad conscience implied by such writing, Härle argues, suggests divergent aspects of such identification. Like Aschenbach, moreover, Mann traveled to Italy, a favorite destination of German homosexuals. Mann, unlike his hero, however, had a round-trip ticket. Härle also explains Mann's remark that his story is marzipan "auf eine tiefere Weise" (in a deeper sense) (XI, 393), as Mann put it in the essay *Lübeck als geistige Lebensform*. This remark, Härle claims, alludes to the deeper and lower senses that sparked the content and are contained in the form of *Death in Venice*. According to him, Mann's erotic experience underlying the motif of marzipan is suggested when the novella alludes to Aschenbach's first trip to Venice. Building upon Kohut's psychoanalytical reading of 1957, which notes that Mann's wife was away while he wrote *Death in Venice*, Härle also contends that the novella reflects Mann's sublimated homosexual love for his five-year-old son Klaus. In 1991, Marianne Krüll likewise wrote that, as Mann's diaries show, he once looked at Klaus in the way Aschenbach looks at Tadzio, with the same erotic feelings. Krüll also observes that Mann's mood during his trip to Venice in 1911, and while he wrote *Death in Venice*, may have been affected by the death of his sister Carla, who had been present on his last trip there in 1908. The extraordinary intensity of the novella's final scene may also be explained by her death, according to Krüll, who imagines that this death awakened memories of that of Mann's father. Like Aschenbach, she says, he died at a beach. In any case, Krüll bluntly sums up the novella she thinks Mann fashioned out of the love he felt for a beautiful boy in Venice: "War dies nicht wie ein grandioses Comingout, ein Öffentlich-Machen seiner homoerotischen Gefühle?" (Was this not like a grandiose coming out, a making public of his homoerotic feelings?) (225).

Finally, homoeroticism also figured in comments on *Death in Venice* by Mann's major biographers. Those scholars' opinions of its importance to the novella differed. In 1977, Peter de Mendelssohn did not mention it at all when repeating remarks made in his biography of 1975. De Mendelssohn did add that the novella was a turning point and a change of direction for Mann, who soon came to believe that his personal, autobiographical confessions could have public, pedagogical effects — a pretension that he criticized in Aschenbach. In 1981, Richard Winston noted that Mann allotted to Aschenbach his own "special tenderness for prepubescent boys" (268). Winston also writes that homosexual proclivities were neither rare nor unmentionable in Germany when Mann wrote his story, and that they were actually in vogue thanks to the poet Stefan George. In a photograph taken when Mann was writing *Death in Venice,* Winston finds "not the slightest resemblance to the deteriorating character his mind is dwelling on" (275). Three full biographies of Mann appeared in 1995. Donald Prater wrote then that Aschenbach's homosexual love reflects Mann's intense infatuation with the boy he called Tadzio. The novella was the first of Mann's works to express his innate homosexuality, Prater notes, "the nearest he ever came to public revelation of his tendency to inversion" (89). According to Prater, it also reflected his ambivalence, though, and after its publication Mann stressed its essential morality. Also in 1995, Klaus Harpprecht wrote that the novella had left no doubt about Mann's passion for members of his own sex. Its charm, secret, and lasting magic, in Harpprecht's opinion, come from the dangerous and heartbreaking game it plays with forbidden desire, a game merely veiled by its classicality. Harpprecht also wonders if Mann is dropping a hint to his own monarch when he ennobles Aschenbach. Furthermore, Harpprecht disagrees with Lukács, arguing that Aschenbach's demise may show a tragic triumph, not the defeat, of the Prussian ethos. Ronald Hayman, again in 1995, wrote that none of Mann's characters tells us more about him than Aschenbach. Like Aschenbach, Hayman writes, Mann was cold yet passionate, a stylistic perfectionist who carefully managed his fame. Both authors, Hayman adds, succumb to temptation in *Death in Venice.* Mann there seems to equate spontaneity with homosexuality, he adds, to question having given success priority over sexual passion. Both he and Aschenbach also seem to regret sins of omission they committed by living heterosexual lives. Reassessing his own experience of love, he was "warning himself, in the story, against the dangers of reining himself in too tightly" (259). He came close to revealing his darkest secret in it, Hayman argues, but then turned critical of Aschenbach, maintaining order in the novella and in his own life. Hayman rightly praises David Luke's 1988 translation of Mann's story for restoring the last sentence of its penultimate paragraph, a sentence Lowe-Porter omits. He also thinks *Death in Venice* Mann's "best love story" (601). In any case, the novella is more important to his assessment of Mann's career than it is to those of his fellow biographers.

## Other Approaches and Themes

A further kind of research done on *Death in Venice* from 1976 to 1995 took approaches and treated themes other than the ones considered so far in this chapter. Four studies discussed its reception or its rereading, for example, and four shed light on Tadzio's teeth, name, or real-life model. Four others explained miscellaneous aspects of Mann's style: his use of a French phrase; the dramatic form and narrative method used in his story; the hexameters that occur in his prose, and derision as a form of his satire. One speculated that he may have known photographs related to the theme of his story, and another stressed the nymphs that he mentions when he alludes to the setting of the *Phaedrus*. One combined politics, philosophy, and music in a reading of the novella that related Mann to Nietzsche and Mahler. Several studies explained that Germans had long been drawn to Venice, or remarked on how that city figures in much modern fiction. Some of these studies about Mann's setting are superficial and incorrect, but others are more reliable and incisive. Finally, one study described the novella as showing the call of a corporeal abyss. All the varieties of research discussed in this section can be revealing, for they often view *Death in Venice* from new perspectives.

Four studies discussed the reception or rereading of Mann's story. In 1976, Walther Kindt wrote a pedantic critique of Seidlin's essay of 1947. Seidlin had given the first sentence of Mann's second chapter a close reading that Kindt criticizes for its supposed theoretical vagueness, pathetic tone, use of terms it does not define, and imprecise and metaphorical language. Kindt accuses Seidlin of subjectivity and speculation. In 1978, Nigel Hamilton wrote that Heinrich Mann was the greatest admirer of *Death in Venice* and that his review of it was perhaps the most moving one the novella ever received. That review, analyzed above, in chapter 1, hardly seems to support Hamilton's statements. In 1987, Hinrich Siefken recalled the nasty remarks that Theodor Haecker made on *Death in Venice* in 1914. Haecker failed to see, Siefken observes, that the novella itself criticizes Aschenbach's hieratic and heroic pretension. In 1981, Claus B. Schröder cryptically hinted at the powerful effect of rereading the novella in Venice seven decades after Mann wrote it there.

Four other studies mention the fictional Tadzio or his historical model. In 1976, Theodore Ziolkowski commented that Mann ironically inverts the topos of healthy teeth when he has Aschenbach notice Tadzio's pale and brittle ones. Such use of dental imagery is "psychodontic" (17), indicating weakness and disease in an individual debilitated by art or beauty. Norbert Honsza, again in 1976, wrote that Mann used Polish motives in *Death in Venice* sixteen years before he first visited Poland. Not only the model for Tadzio, Władisław Moes, Honsza adds, but also that of his teacher still lives there. In the novella, Mann calls this teacher a companion and a governess. Dietmar Grieser, in 1977, visited von Moes, whose role as the historical model for Tadzio had been widely known since 1965 and described by de Mendelssohn in 1975. Moes had been taken to Venice to calm his young nerves, Grieser remarks, and Mann erred when writing that Tadzio would not grow old. Michael Winkler, also in 1977, argued that the Polish name "Tadzio" can be understood as a form of "Anastasios." This Greek name, according to Winkler, implies the destruction and the renewal that permeate the novella. Four further studies mention various stylistic matters. In 1981, Heidi M. Rockwood noted the symbolic significance of the liftboy's remark "Pas de chance, monsieur." Addressed to Aschenbach when he returns to the hotel from the train station, Rockwood explains, this phrase implies not only that he has had no luck leaving Venice but also that he has no hope of ever doing so. In 1984, Volkmar Hansen thought *Death in Venice* a prose tragedy that parodically meets the requirements established in Gustav Freytag's *Die Technik des Dramas* (The Technique of Drama, 1863). Hansen adds that Mann's account of cholera is comparable to famous descriptions of plagues in world literature, despite his using a newspaper article about it as one of his sources. This was an example of his "Montagetechnik" (montage-method) (63). In 1987–88, Peter Geiser reported that Mann's novella contains over three hundred hexameters, an average of four to five per page. Mann consciously composed them, Geiser remarks, to evoke ancient Greece. In 1991, Burghard Dedner wrote that derision, an aspect of Mann's satire, is important in the pivotal scenes of *Death in Venice*. Aschenbach is one of Mann's many fictional heroes, Dedner writes, who are the object of ridicule.

Two other studies commented on Mann's possible knowledge of photographs of young men and on his interpretation of the nymphs his story mentions. In 1989, John Margetts suggested a possible pictorial source of *Death in Venice*. Mann, Margetts suggests, may have seen photographs by Wilhelm von Gloedens (1856–1931). Those photographs are often of young men nude or in classical poses, he explains, and they were shown in a gallery in Munich that Mann visited. Mann was also in Berlin when they were published in magazines there. Mann never mentions these homoerotic and somewhat pornographic photographs, Margetts admits, but their themes and their subjects are important in his novella, and they helped shape its cultural context. Aschenbach's association of Tadzio with the *Spinario* — the ancient statue of a boy pulling a thorn from his foot — is accordingly ambivalent, Margetts thinks, both evoking an ancient ideal of beauty and indicating homosexuality. The camera abandoned on the beach, Margetts adds, must be Mann's invention, a voyeuristic monument to an absent artist like Aschenbach and a symbolic piece of equipment that, like him, no longer functions. In 1993, Antje Syfuß commented on the nymphs mentioned when Mann alludes to the setting of the *Phaedrus* in his account of one of Aschenbach's Platonic visions. Mann profoundly interprets those nymphs' loveliness, Syfuß believes, by associating it with mediation between the sensual and the intellectual.

One scholar regarded *Death in Venice* as a story about a character whose political views are like the young Nietzsche's, a story told by a narrator whose style is like Mahler's. In 1984, Geoffrey Sweet noted the political ideologies at work in the novella and in *Die Geburt der Tragödie*. "Both the young Nietzsche and the mature Aschenbach," Sweet argues, "write in the interests of their country's national cause" (26). He wonders if Mann may have thought that Nietzsche was motivated by a desire, like Aschenbach's, for official status. Aschenbach has risen high in the state hierarchy, Sweet claims, and his career reflects the conservative and patriotic climate. He has sold his artistic soul to the state, in fact, his clipped speech seems military, and his relationship with his public is "not unlike that of a General to his troops, or of a Kaiser to his subjects" (19). He is part of the establishment, Sweet adds, and his works promote authoritarian values. His Dionysian death is purely personal, however, with none of the collective virtues that Nietzsche imagined, and his fate suggests that we should distrust Dionysus. Sweet also observes that Mann's narrator is critical but fair and that this narrator lets readers judge Aschenbach for themselves. The narrator's criticism, he writes, defeats Aschenbach's conformism. According to Sweet, that criticism also involves Mahler. Mann may have been wounded and angered by the injustice of Mahler's low status, he thinks, and may have attacked the opposite in Aschenbach, who is not a truly great artist and who gets more approval than he deserves. In the description of Aschenbach's dream, moreover, Mann may have been trying to reproduce the sound of the flutes and piccolos in Mahler's *Das Lied von der Erde*. In any case, according to Sweet, differences between Wagner and Mahler are analogous to those between Nietzsche and Mann's narrator. Whereas Wagner's music directly appeals to organs of sensual perception, Mahler's includes irony and parody, for example, and it appeals to the intellect. The narrator's economy and control are similar, Sweet thinks, to the restraint of Mahler's music. "This narrator's awareness of the various distances between himself and Aschenbach," Sweet says, "is analogous to Mahler's ironic handling of various degrees of passionate involvement in the emotional effect of music" (33). Sweet's argument thus recalls both all the others that cast Aschenbach as a Prussian representative of Wilhelminian Germany and all those that compare Mann's style to music. It differs from the latter insofar as it regards Mahler, rather than Wagner, as his stylistic model.

Several miscellaneous studies remarked on Mann's setting of Venice. A number of them are cursory, derivative, and often mistaken. In 1976, Karl Ipser wrote about the many German-speaking merchants, bankers, artists, musicians, and poets who had visited Venice since the Middle Ages. Ipser incorrectly claims that Mann began writing *Death in Venice* after a trip there in 1910. He criticizes Visconti's handling of the author who is its hero, moreover, but himself calls Mann's Aschenbach a musician. In 1987, Christiane Schenk examined treatments of Venice in decadent literature of the *fin de siècle,* noting that Mann's description of Venice differs from Maurice Barrès's because it is directly tied to events of Mann's plot. Schenk's remarks are seldom more than a string of quotations, and they are sometimes mistaken. Contrary to her claims, the Istrian island Aschenbach visits remains unnamed, and he is not given the same room when he returns to his hotel after trying to leave Venice. In 1992, Tony Tanner described Aschenbach as Mann's "quintessential German" artist and an "uptight Germanic writer" (353). Mann, Tanner adds, shows the "cracking of his Teutonic carapace" (354). Such comments seem to border on nationalistic clichés when Tanner also writes about Aschenbach's "Apollonian-Germanic principles of discipline and control" (355). Not only does Aschenbach stop writing, Tanner concludes; for ten years, Mann himself wrote no more fiction. Tanner seems unaware of the fact that Mann wrote part of *Felix Krull* and began *Der Zauberberg* then. Michael L. Ross, in 1994, compared *Death in Venice* to Charles Dickens's *Little Dorrit* (1857). Dickens's focus is public, he explains, whereas Mann probes the depths of the self. Ross calls Venice an antidote to Prussia for Aschenbach, apparently ignoring that Aschenbach's family comes from Silesia and that he lives in Munich, in Bavaria. Such geographical distinctions are often lost on authors writing in English about Mann's story. Ross more plausibly remarks that "Adgio," as Aschenbach mishears Tadzio's name, appropriately sounds just like *agio,* the Italian word for "ease." His main argument is mistaken, though, because he relies on Lowe-Porter's flawed translation. He thinks Aschenbach's collapse is caused by "a consuming Venetian lust of the eye" (137) and that he indulges in "visual hedonism" (138) and turns into "Venetian voyeurism incarnate" (139). Aschenbach's "libidinous peering" (139) is thus part of a larger Venetian disease, a "malignant affection of the retina" (141). Much of Ross's evidence for such claims comes from Lowe-Porter but was never written by Mann. When Aschenbach looks at Tadzio, for example, Lowe-Porter writes that "the delight of his eye was unending," but Mann writes that he finds "der zarten Sinneslust kein Ende" (no end of delicate sensual pleasure). Similarly, Lowe-Porter tells how Aschenbach's heart "leaped at the sight" of his reflection after the barber rejuvenates him, but Mann tells how he looks at himself "mit Herzklopfen" (with heart-pounding). Lowe-Porter also describes how Aschenbach tries "not to lose sight of the figure after which his eyes thirsted," but Mann describes how he tries "das sehnlich verfolgte Bild nicht aus den Augen zu verlieren" (not to lose sight of the yearningly pursued image). Mann thus places less stress on seeing than Lowe-Porter does, and when one consults Mann's German, much of Ross's case collapses.

Other studies that discussed the setting of Mann's novella are both more reliable and more persuasive. In 1978, Richard Carstensen, noting historical links between Venice and Mann's hometown of Lübeck, wrote that Venice, thanks to its symbolic associations, became the dream-land of the German soul for Mann in *Death in Venice*. In 1981, Burton Pike called the novella "the high-water mark of the city as an emblem of cultural decay mirroring the decay of an isolated artist-figure" (107). This statement refers to cities in general, but Pike also writes that Mann's Venice is the meeting point of a European West and an Indian East. Tadzio, he observes, hovers between these extremes. Venice is a geographical place for Aschenbach, he adds, and a mythic one for Mann's narrator. In 1989, Jacques Darmaun described Mann's Venice similarly. Far from playing its traditional literary role as a marvelous and alluring city, Darmaun writes, Venice gives rise to a feeling of disquieting strangeness in Mann's story. Mann does not tell of a city risen from the sea or of its powerful republic, nor does his narrator describe it in detail. Instead, Darmaun adds, his Venice transfigures the real, which it elevates beyond space and time. Mann's description of the city as equivocal and duplicitous, Darmaun also observes, anticipates and goes beyond Georg Simmel's analysis of Venetian art. Aschenbach does not go to any museums, he explains. Instead, Aschenbach encounters a living work of art: Tadzio. In his dream, moreover, Venice is no longer Athens or Byzantium, but the sinful city of Babylon. Indeed, according to Darmaun, Venice is an oriental Circe who subjugates Aschenbach.

Bernard Dieterle gave the fullest such interpretation of Mann's setting in 1995. Dieterle puts *Death in Venice* into literary-historical perspective. In contrast to Maurice Barrès, he explains, Mann narrates the end of the romantic myth of an artist in Venice. He does so, Dieterle adds, by integrating various Venetian motifs into his story. Mann translates the motifs of the swamp and of illness into action, for example, and he likewise integrates the motif of the gondola. He thereby lends such motifs symbolic value. Aschenbach's gondola, according to Dieterle, is a modality of sitting and a concretization of comfort. It both suggests his relaxed Venetian way of life and is related to all the other chairs in which he sits, including the one in which he dies. Aschenbach's leisurely existence in Venice, Dieterle adds, is related to other literary accounts of aestheticism there. *Death in Venice,* for example, is an implicit critique of the Dionysian aestheticism of D'Annunzio's *Il Fuoco.* Dieterle also observes that Mann integrates Venice into his story, via Tadzio, who is analogous to it. Like him, Venice is near, related to water, beautiful, and foreign. In Mann's story, Dieterle adds, the city regains its earlier position as a threshold between Europe and Asia. Finally, Dieterle ties that story to Wagner's *Tristan und Isolde,* Byron's *Childe Harold* (1812), and Platen's sonnets on Venice. According to him, Aschenbach's recollection of those sonnets, the Homeric hymns he hears when Tadzio emerges from the sea, and the antiphonal calls of the gondoliers exemplify a motif of song. By linking those calls to the cries emitted in Aschenbach's dream, he explains, Mann again heightens a traditional literary motif long associated with the city of Venice.

Finally, in 1990, the Peruvian novelist Mario Vargas Llosa argued that *Death in Venice* presents the calling of an abyss. He admires the formal perfection of the novella as well as its fascinating plot and its many symbolic associations. He also observes that it tells of individual self-determination at

odds with social norms and conventions. Aschenbach is a model of bourgeois respectability, he says, but nonetheless succumbs to the temptation of
the abyss, to passions and to drives prompted by his body. Ideas seem less
important to Aschenbach than feelings, sensations, and desires, Vargas Llosa
adds. The cholera epidemic, moreover, is symbolic in several ways. It stands
for irrational forces of sexuality as well as for a primitive and an exotic world
and way of life, and possibly for the social and political decline of Europe.
According to Vargas Llosa, Mann is no less a moralist than Aschenbach once
was, for he, too, fears sensual desire and sexual euphoria. Many of Mann's
allegories and symbols now seem quaint, he says, but readers are still deeply
moved by his account of the abyss of lust, violence, and dreams that is part
of human nature and that lies just below the surface of civilization. Vargas
Llosa thus takes *Death in Venice* to be a powerful statement about civilization and its discontents.

# Music, Film, Opera, Art; Plays and Ballets; Texts and Translations

A final category of research done on *Death in Venice* from 1976 to 1995
consists of studies concerned with various media. As in the two decades after
Mann's death in 1955, scholars writing about such media in the next twenty
years approached his story from several angles. Some thought it exemplified
the ideas and the influence of Richard Wagner. Others noted the similarities
of, and differences between, Mann's hero and Gustav Mahler, the model for
the musical Aschenbach of Visconti's film. Still others reached ambivalent
conclusions about that film, both in articles that treat its links to Mann's text
briefly and in books that do so at greater length. Studies of Visconti's life
and works included further remarks on the relationship between the novella
and the film. Preoccupied with Visconti's images, such studies often misconstrued Mann's words. Further research linked other elements of the film and
the novella, above all their shared reliance on Nietzsche. A few studies analyzed Britten's opera along with Mann's novella and Visconti's film. Like
others that treat the opera and the novella only, these studies usually show
how — and how well — Britten tells Mann's story in music. Further remarks
on the opera and the novella reveal additional nuances of Britten's interpretation. One study regarded music more generally, as part of the acoustic
spectrum Mann's story describes. That story was also illustrated as well as
acted in plays and danced in ballets. Furthermore, Mann's text was published
in German together with his working notes for it, as well as in three new
English translations. Studies of the earlier two English translations, the two
from the 1920s, confirm that new ones were urgently needed.

Several scholars read *Death in Venice* in light of the life and works of
Richard Wagner. In 1976, Ernest Bisdorff recalled traces of Wagner's life in

Aschenbach's. Steven Paul Scher, also in 1976, took issue with Vaget's study of 1975, which held that Mann turned away from Wagner and toward Goethe while he wrote the novella. Scher contends that Mann was always ambivalent about the composer. In 1978, T. E. Apter added that *Death in Venice* reveals Mann's mistrust of the emotions and the impulses presented in Wagner's works. Aschenbach's story, Apter writes, is similar to one of "Wagnerian contagion" (50), though Wagner never shows sensuousness as crude and as primitive as his. The effect of Tadzio's smile is like that of Wagner's music, Apter adds, but the boy lacks a Wagnerian innocence, and Aschenbach's passion for him is not the love of Tristan and Isolde. Apter seems too critical of that passion when he explains that its point is destruction of the social order. One might also disagree with the conclusion that Aschenbach's failure reveals "the defeat of Mann's own imagination" (57). In 1982, Dieter Borchmeyer numbered *Death in Venice* among Mann's Wagner-novellas. Borchmeyer relies on Vortriede's study of 1958, adding that Mann's critical view of decadence pertains to Wagner's works and influence. Mann nonetheless composed his story, Borchmeyer writes, by using leitmotifs in the way Wagner had. Raymond Furness, also in 1982, noted Mann's allusions to Wagner. The black cloth on the camera at the beach, he claims, alludes to a black flag that Wagner mentioned in a letter to Liszt in 1854. Aschenbach's rejection of Wotan's ravens, Furness adds, parallels the composer's abandoning work on *Der Ring des Nibelungen* (The Ring of the Nibelungen, 1876) to write *Tristan und Isolde*. Mann also thought, he argues, the aestheticism of Venice matched only by the example of Wagner.

Further links to Wagner were forged by other scholars. In 1984, Paul Gerhard Klussmann explained how Mann's use of leitmotifs derives from Wagner's music-dramas, noting how all the death-figures in *Death in Venice* are related by their similar appearances and by identical or synonymous words used to describe them. This series of characters lends the novella meaning, he adds, and makes Aschenbach's trip and death seem mythical. James Northcote-Bade, again in 1984, described the novella as "possibly the best known example of the 'Liebestod' pattern" (13), a type of plot that involves a tragic death after the experience of love and that derives most notably from *Tristan und Isolde*. Luc Wagner, in 1985, similarly argued that Mann's myth of love is that of Tristan. Aschenbach's itinerary is an ironic travesty, he adds, of the mystical one described in Richard Wagner's music-drama. Hermann Fähnrich, in 1986, wrote that Mann's story is about a voluptuousness of decline found in Wagner's operas. Mann's use of leitmotifs shows his proximity to Wagner, Fähnrich argues, while the classical form of his story, the form of a symphony in four movements, indicates his distance from him. Fähnrich analyzes each of those "movements" (Mann's first and second chapter count as the opening one), noting their themes and motifs. He also likens Mann's prose to Wagner's music, says that both men lent their works mythical dimensions, and insists that the musical elements in the novella are more powerful than those that recall the fine arts. Mann's last lines, Fähnrich concludes, are a final coda. Fähnrich, then, draws the most sustained analogy between *Death in Venice* and music since Hermann Broch's of 1913. In 1989, Jürgen Hillesheim added that the novella was the high point and summation of Mann's Wagner-crisis. Mann disliked the decadence of Wagner's art, Hillesheim explains, and therefore flirted with neoclassicism. Aschenbach's work habits are like Wagner's as described in Nietzsche's *Der Fall Wagner*. Aschenbach is also like Nietzsche insofar as he tries to overcome decadence by repressing knowledge. This attempt fails, Hillesheim continues, so Mann is critical of Nietzsche, too, rejecting his aestheticism and vitalism. In the end, he argues, Mann cannot resolve the antithesis of life and intellect, and remains a decadent himself. Like his hero — and like Wagner, in Nietzsche's view — he produces artifacts, works that are consciously constructed instead of spontaneously organic. According to Hillesheim, then, *Death in Venice* is pessimistic.

Other scholars, writing about Visconti's film, explained how Aschenbach is — or is not — like Mahler. Those scholars often contrasted the hero of that film with his forerunner of the same name in Mann's story. In 1978, Anthony J. Mazzella found Aschenbach's evolution from a writer to a composer necessary and effective. With Mahler's music, he says, Visconti successfully renders Aschenbach's creative process and inner world in the medium of film, a medium that radically differs from Mann's fiction. Indeed, Mahler's music on Visconti's soundtrack is "the film's equivalent of the novella's seamless web of words" (188). Mazzella likewise demonstrates differences between the media of film and fiction when noting how Visconti changes the themes of Mann's story. In an essay from 1975 that was published in 1980, by contrast, Hans Mayer remarked favorably on the film but added that Mann's protagonist is not Mahler, not an ailing musician like Visconti's. His spiritual art cannot be conveyed, Mayer argues, by Mahler's sensual music. As a result, the film shows an aging man's loss of dignity, not the artist's tragedy that Mann had in mind. In the film, Mayer adds, Mahler's music hardly sounds spent and thus contradicts Mann's thesis regarding the roles of decadence and eroticism.

Mahler likewise figured in other research on Visconti's film. In 1986, Neil Sinyard called the mixture of Mann, Mahler, and Visconti in the film "a well-nigh indigestible cultural pudding" (126). Contrary to Sinyard's claims, Mahler's life and death were not the prime inspiration for Mann's story, and the details that Mann uses from the life of the composer do not include the death of one of his children. Sinyard seems to confuse Mann and Visconti, for it is the Aschenbach of the film, not of the novella, who has lost a daughter. Perhaps Sinyard's misunderstanding of Mahler's importance for Mann's story explains his statement that Visconti's identifying Aschenbach with the composer is fully justifiable. In 1987, Philip Reed more astutely wrote that Visconti's use of Mahler's music demonstrates "the naivety of Visconti's conception and his confusion of Mahler and Aschenbach" (182). The allusion to Mahler, Reed adds, is undoubtedly the most regrettable of the film's deficiencies. Another was that Dirk Bogarde played Aschenbach with an "air of an absent-minded provincial professor" (182). A number of Visconti's alterations of Mann's text were analyzed by Douglas Radcliff-Umstead in 1988. By using Mahler's setting of Nietzsche's "Sound of the Night-Wanderer" (the poem beginning "O Mensch! Gib acht . . ."), he explains, Visconti demonstrates his understanding of Mann's story. Radcliff-Umstead also observes that "the filmic Aschenbach resembles Brahms more than Mahler in his desire to compose music of Olympian serenity" (206). It is true that the film does not present the mythical dimension of the novella, as Radcliff-Umstead also says, but neither does the film correspond to the novella in relating Aschenbach's "fantasy of caressing Tadzio's golden hair" (203). Instead, Mann has him imagine placing his hand on Tadzio's head and turning away. In 1989, Kurt von Fischer wrote that Visconti's transformation of Aschenbach into Mahler was a kind of decoding, a clarification of Mann's allusion to the composer's first name in that of his hero. Accordingly, von Fischer approves of Visconti's using in his soundtrack the Adagietto from Mahler's Fifth Symphony.

Other scholars similarly expressed mixed views about Visconti's achievement as a whole. In 1976, Irving Singer described both the failures and the successes of the film. Its sights and sounds, Singer argues, make Aschenbach's love of beauty apparent to us in a way that Mann cannot. Visconti, however, distorts and diminishes the symbolism of Mann's final scene. According to Singer, Visconti alters the nature of Aschenbach's despair as well, making it seem that he has loved and lost, not that he has never loved at all. Singer also observes that Visconti's images do not convey Mann's irony, concepts, or ambiguity. Visconti's scene with the barber may lose literary value, Singer adds, but it makes us realize what Mann only implies. If one knows the novella while watching the film, moreover, one may achieve a "stereoscopic enrichment" (1353). Like Singer, Hans Rudolf Vaget, in 1980, expressed ambivalence toward the film. Vaget notes glaring omissions in the film but does not fault Visconti for the inability of film in general to translate narration such as Mann's into moving pictures. The film contains enough of Mann's material to justify its title, he adds, and Visconti's use of music is an acceptable and even admirable solution to the problem of conveying Mann's symbols and allusions. Visconti's flashbacks are less successful, however, and the link with Mahler changes Aschenbach, a neoclassicist in Mann, into a late romantic. According to Vaget, the film also emphasizes homosexuality to an extent that changes the meaning of Mann's story. It reduces and simplifies Mann's case against his hero. While he calls the film a new interpretation of Mann's novella, Vaget also observes that it "not only tells the story differently, it also tells a different story" (172). Thomas Bleicher, also in 1980, thought Visconti's metamorphosis of the novella approximated it by distancing itself from it. By omitting Mann's first chapter, which is set in Munich rather than Venice, Bleicher remarks, the film, thanks to spatial limitation, gains atmospheric cohesion. This cohesion is further motivated by Visconti's flashbacks. Via Alfried, the fellow composer with whom he argues, for example, Aschenbach's psyche is extroverted into the optical. Visconti's other changes, variations, and additions likewise illuminate and enrich the novella, Bleicher contends. Bleicher wrongly claims that Mann indirectly mentions the heart attack that Visconti's Aschenbach has suffered. In 1983, David Glassco took a dim view of the changes Bleicher praised. He disliked the flashbacks and the looseness of the film, for example, which he calls banal, silly, trite, obvious, superficial, and reductive. Visconti condescendingly travesties Mann, he adds, producing "a film mortally weakened by its intellectual shallowness" (173). By contrast, in 1990, Rolf G. Renner hailed the film as a productive transformation of the novella. It visually condenses everything Mann narrates, he explains, and it sets new standards precisely because it departs so originally from Mann's text.

Mixed reactions also characterized more extended and detailed discussions of Visconti's film. In 1977, Werner and Ingeborg Faulstich drew an admirably thorough and literate comparison between it and Mann's story. They note the nearly identical structure of immediate events in both works as well as major differences on the level of motifs. The film conveys such motifs in flashbacks, they say, but omits the mythological ones because the medium of film cannot narrate allegorically, as such abstract motifs require. The Faulstichs trace other major differences between Mann's story and the film to Visconti's individual interpretation and to his specific filmic means of presentation. Both the story and the film are related from Aschenbach's perspective, they say, but Mann's authorial narrative voice is lost, and Aschenbach's decline accordingly seems more personal, without larger meaning. In the film, Aschenbach also appears one-dimensional, becoming increasingly passive. His decline is more concrete and corporeal, and less intellectual than in the novella. According to the Faulstichs, the narrator's absence in the film causes the loss of any kind of speech but direct discourse. The film also makes Aschenbach's demise seem to happen faster. Through its commentaries, reflections, and explanations, the Faulstichs add, Mann's text makes its meaning clearer, requiring its readers to think; Visconti's film appeals to the emotions. In its reception, then, the film invites a reduction of critical consciousness. Visconti nonetheless creates a new myth in the Faulstichs' view: the myth of decline in general. In 1979, Gabriele Seitz wrote that the film not only differs substantially from Mann's text but is also, in itself, flawed and contradictory. The film does not treat Mann's theme of the opposition of art to life, she explains, and it lacks the irony and parody evident in his story. Visconti's intention of remaining true to his model thus fails. Seitz praises Visconti's use of music and colors, but she finds other aspects of his film reductive and trivial. As she is in her remarks on the reception of the novella — remarks cited above, in the introduction — Seitz is especially interested in political matters. She adds that the film met with far more success among critics than the novella had sixty years earlier. By contrast, in 1994, Béatrice Delassalle wrote that the reception of the film was highly contentious. She also asks how well Visconti translates Mann's text. She examines the filmmaker's omissions, substitutions, and additions; she also compares the portrayal of Aschenbach, function of Tadzio, symbols and leitmotifs, critique of the *fin de siècle*, and crisis of art in the film to the corresponding parts of the novella. Delassalle concludes that Visconti's reductions, substitutions, inserts, and equivalents are legitimate and justified, as are his characters of Aschenbach and Tadzio and his elaboration of Mann's symbols and leitmotifs. He stresses the *fin de siècle* mood more than Mann, she adds, and fails in his treatment of the crisis of art, but both of these shortcomings can be attributed at least in part to the limitations of film in general. Visconti has captured the spirit of the novella, she thinks, which he loosely but successfully translates. Like Mann, Delassalle contends, he has thus created a masterpiece.

Further remarks on the novella and the film occur in studies of Visconti's life and works. The authors of those studies often conflate the two versions of Aschenbach's tale, wrongly thinking that what Visconti shows is what Mann tells. In 1979, for example, Monica Stirling garbled Mann's text in several ways. She writes that Mann's hero has suffered a heart attack, that he goes to Venice to convalesce, that the Kaiser has ennobled him, that his child is dead, and that his hotel is the Excelsior. In fact, only the Aschenbach of the film has a heart attack and has lost a child. In the novella, he has been made *von* Aschenbach by an unnamed German prince, and he stays at the "Bäderhotel," that is, the Hôtel des Bains. The Excelsior is a different hotel on the Lido. Stirling's account of Aschenbach's story also confuses Visconti's images with Mann's words, switching back and forth between them even though the film and the novella treat the scenes she mentions in markedly different ways. Furthermore, she misrepresents Mann's story when she writes about how Visconti's Aschenbach finds himself walking behind Tadzio on the path to the beach. The boy glances at the man, almost speaks to him, and then swings slowly around one of the poles supporting an awning. This part of the film is not unduly provocative, Stirling adds, for "there is not a detail in this little scene that is not in Mann's text" (217). In fact, the opposite is the case: none of the details just mentioned *is* in Mann's text. Such mistakes in Stirling's understanding of Mann's story are amusing when she attributes Aschenbach's bad temper to tension. Mann, she writes, has a friend say of him, "'You see, Aschenbach has always lived like this,' contracting the fingers of his left hand into a fish [*sic*]" (212). In 1981, Gaia Servadio wrote that Visconti tells the story of himself in the film. He does so by making Aschenbach a famous upper-class aesthete like Mahler, Servadio observes, and could not have forged the same autobiographical link to Mann's "middle-class unknown writer" (198). It seems strange to call Mann's hero middle-class, since he has been ennobled and is extremely well-off. His prose is quoted in schoolbooks, moreover, and he receives letters from all over the world, so he hardly seems unknown. Claretta Tonetti avoided such blunders in 1983. She argues that Visconti's flashbacks add ambiguity to a story with enough complications of its own, and that Mahler's music does not fill the vacuum left by the absence of Mann's philosophical insights. The film presents Tadzio more sensually than Mann, she adds, but it is neither tasteless nor pedestrian. Visconti's direction, Tonetti writes, is a tour de force.

Other elements of the film and the novella were examined in additional studies. In 1980, Friedrich Wolfzettel analyzed Visconti's Aschenbach psychologically, as an aging father figure. He is pathetic and anachronistic in the film, Wolfzettel maintains, a failed father rather than a tragic artist. Tadzio's family lacks a father, and Aschenbach seems incapable of being one. Wolfzettel adds that Aschenbach identifies with the father more intensely in the film than in the novella. He also observes that Visconti demythologizes Mann's story. In 1985, Carolyn Galerstein described images of decadence in Visconti's film. Visconti strikingly captures Mann's description of the street musicians, she thinks, though Aschenbach's dream was too obscene for him to include. That may be true, but this dream is not Mann's "vision of hell" (33). In 1992, John Francis Fetzer recalled Visconti's deletions and distortions but wrote that the novella and film both show "threshold situations" (146) when Aschenbach sees Tadzio for the first and the last times. These situations are metaphoric as well as literal, Fetzer argues, showing Aschenbach poised between Apollo and Dionysus, life and death, the finite and the infinite. They show ambivalence, he adds, as well as the ambiguity expressed in the dual tonality of Mahler's Adagietto. Mann's story, Visconti's film, and Mahler's music thus convey a "tripartite thresholdism appropriate to our age of ambiguity" (152).

Four studies tied the novella and the film to Nietzsche. In 1985, Willy Michel maintained that Visconti's reception of Nietzsche in the film makes a new approach to their own intellectual traditions possible for its German viewers. Angus Fletcher, in 1986, similarly argued that the film derives from Nietzsche in every way and that its alterations of Mann's story reveal "Nietzschean dimensions of Mann's 'musicology'" (310). Fletcher thus understands music as the key to a worldview and to a metaphysical distance in Mann, Nietzsche, and Visconti. In 1988, Roger E. Wiehe noted that Visconti deletes or alters the figures that represent death in Mann's novella. Accordingly, Wiehe explains, the film is about sensuousness and decadence, and it differs from Mann's account of a hero who finally attains Nietzschean insights into the proper role of art. Wiehe's notion of that role often seems more informed by Nietzsche's ideas than by Mann's. Aschenbach hardly seems to learn, for example, that human beings need artistic illusions. Wiehe made a similar argument in 1992, claiming that the *danse macabre* in the novella communicates a Nietzschean conception of art. The head of the street singers leads that dance, he explains, which has a different meaning in the film. He also observes that Visconti's Tadzio acts insinuatingly coy and looks at Aschenbach like an "accomplished hustler," and that Visconti's dialogue is pretentious, consisting of "Nietzschean apothegms reduced to intellectual kitsch" (96). As Wiehe puts it, the film presents only the "superannuated dotage of an overwrought Puritan" (99). Finally, in 1994, Alexander J. Marshall III argued that Visconti's changes work because Nietzsche influenced Mahler as well as Mann. According to Marshall, Visconti heightens and dramatizes the tension that Mann posits between Apollo and Dionysus.

A few studies compared Mann's novella not only with Visconti's film but also with Britten's opera. In 1990, Ernest W. B. Hess-Lüttich and Susan Liddell considered differences in how these three works, in different media, present and interpret the relationship between Aschenbach and Tadzio. That Visconti's Tadzio has a more active role than Mann's, they note, may be due to the nature of Visconti's cinematic medium. The boy's swinging around the poles of an awning, though, is a dance that suggests an ambivalence between abstraction and lasciviousness, they think, and this ambivalence is in the spirit of Mann's story. Similarly, Visconti's colors are visual leitmotifs that correspond to Mann's verbal ones. Hess-Lüttich and Liddell know that Visconti shows few equivalents of Mann's allusions to ancient mythology and that Aschenbach and Tadzio's relationship is accordingly different, more sensual and sexually concrete. They conclude that Visconti transforms Mann's text according both to the different semiotic code of film in general and to particular aesthetic procedures of his own filmic art. Hess-Lüttich and Liddell also consider Britten's opera, noting the emphasis it lays on Aschenbach's inability to speak to Tadzio. In contrast to the novella as well as the film, they argue, it inserts less distance between Aschenbach and his audience, but more between him and Tadzio. Rather than Mann's narrator, Britten's music comments on Aschenbach, they add, and through dance Britten accentuates mythological associations more than even Mann himself. According to Hess-Lüttich and Liddell, then, Visconti and Britten tell their own stories, each in his own way and each in his own medium. In 1991, Hess-Lüttich and Liddell made this argument again. In 1992, Roger Hillman drew a similar comparison between the novella, the film, and the opera. He explains that the film conveys neither Mann's abstraction nor his irony and that its Tadzio no longer seems the product of Aschenbach's imagination. Its equation of Aschenbach and

Mahler is uneasy, he adds, and its flashbacks are realistic but mundane. Its lack of a mythological dimension, Hillman notes, is apparent in its final scene. Visconti thus reduces Mann's concerns to an individual case. Hillman likes Britten's opera better. Its subtle musical narrative, he claims, contains equivalents of the ambiguity, irony, and uses of point of view that are present in Mann's prose. In 1993, Hillman made this same argument about the narrative characteristics of the three artists' genres.

Studies that compared the opera and the novella, but not the film, showed just how well Britten's music conveys Mann's story. In 1977, Gary Schmidgall rightly wrote that Britten was a more discreet commentator on that story than many a scholar. Though he had to simplify it, Schmidgall argues, his opera actually "ennobles Mann's story; it increases the fictional amplitude and heightens the dramatic impact of the original through the added dimension of music" (324). Visconti captured Mann's least important, realistic level, he adds, but Britten focused on its most important one, that of its hero's psychic distress. By responding to Mann's universal intellectual and philosophical level, too, Britten avoids telling merely "a moral tale for pederasts" (338). According to Schimdgall, the opera not only captures the essentials of the novella, but also fills gaps that even Mann's fine prose cannot fill. In 1987, Patrick Carnegy wrote that Britten and Piper's libretto sometimes strays from Mann's idiom and can be clumsy. Their ballet scenes, however, realize a mythopoeic aspect of the novella, he adds, and Britten's music creates a world of oriental and seductive beauty as surprising and as powerful as Mann's. Britten thus emphasizes that Mann's story can be read as showing "a Western Platonic psyche undone by the Orient" (176). Carnegy also mentions Mann's verbal music and his description of the "Venetian soundscape" (170), and he concludes that Britten articulates the musical dimension implicit in the novella, though differently than Mann may have intended or recognized. In 1988, Steven R. Cerf called the opera faithful to Mann not only since it renders almost all of his story line, but also since it shows "the ability of the composer and librettist to capture and even enrich the profound interiority of Mann's complex work" (124). Britten and Piper's adaptation of Mann's novella, Cerf explains, contains stylistic characteristics of literary modernism and is therefore akin to Mann's prose. Their work is therefore an operatic equivalent of Mann's modernist account of his hero's internal reality. In 1989, Sandra and Larry Corse similarly cited nonreferential ways in which Britten's music, like Mann's language, creates meaning. Britten's musical structures and devices are analogous to Mann's and Piper's literary ones, they argue, and though the opera differs from the novella, its cumulative effect on its audience is similar. When they attribute a lack of sympathy to Aschenbach, the Corses incorrectly maintain that Mann has discussed his hero's "attitude toward the unfortunate individuals of the world" (354). They also claim that the esteem accorded Aschenbach's prose is a sign that its quality is suspect and that Mann uses ideas from folk literature.

Further aspects of Britten's interpretation of Mann were revealed in other remarks on the opera and the novella. In 1979, Myfanwy Piper told of reorganizing Mann's story in a way that balanced the erotic and the symbolic, retained the order of his fictional events, and rendered the different levels of his prose. Her reasons for having Tadzio and the other children dance at the beach and for having a single singer perform the roles of all Mann's death-figures, of the hotel manager and the barber, and of Dionysus likewise show her remaining true to the spirit of that story even when she changes its letter. In 1983, Eric Walter White wrote that the success of Mann's story as an opera depended on Britten's ability to write a convincing part for Aschenbach. In 1984, Christopher Palmer recalled many other writers and composers inspired by Venice. Palmer notes that the literary lineage of Mann's story includes Ibsen's *When We Dead Awaken* (1899–1900) and Walter Pater's *Apollo in Picardy*. Mann himself, he adds, unwittingly adumbrated Britten's opera in the essay that he composed at the Lido in 1911, an essay that calls for an un-Wagnerian masterpiece. It is ironic, Palmer concludes, that the opera is based on the work that was taking shape in Mann's mind as he wrote that essay, sitting in sight of the real-life Tadzio. In 1986, John Evans added that Mann and Britten made Aschenbach in their own image. "Britten, Mann, and Aschenbach," he says "were all susceptible to the touching beauty of the adolescent male form" (107). That Aschenbach, a highly articulate writer, Evans observes, cannot communicate with Tadzio is one of the ironies of Mann's novella. In 1990, Clifford Hindley argued that the changes Britten made to Mann's story suggest Britten's intention to show "not only the obsession which destroyed Aschenbach but also the positive possibility of a sublimated love of youthful male beauty along the lines of Platonic philosophy" (511). The turning point in the novella is the loss of Aschenbach's luggage, Hindley maintains, but in the opera, this point occurs after the Games of Apollo, when Aschenbach fails to develop a genuine, if sublimated, relationship with Tadzio. Affirmative where Mann was at best ambivalent, then, Britten interprets Aschenbach's story differently. In 1992, Hindley added that Britten, in contrast to Mann, may have regarded a physical consummation of Platonic love as a source of artistic inspiration. Unlike Mann, Hindley writes, he may even have thought this consummation could be Apollinian. In 1992, Humphrey Carpenter was mistaken when he maintained that the operatic Aschenbach's rejection of his youthful aesthetic in favor of form and beauty is not based on anything in Mann's text.

In addition to all these studies that read *Death in Venice* with regard to Wagner, Mahler, or Britten, a further one related the novella to music in a more general sense. In 1987, Marc A. Weiner argued that its psychological, aesthetic, and social dimensions are illuminated through their association with the acoustical realm of silence, sound, and song. Aschenbach works in silence, Weiner explains, while the masses of society around him are noisy. Music can be either noise or art, he adds, either threatening or aesthetic. Sound and social stature are thus linked in the novella. Aschenbach's receptiveness to sound changes, however. At first, Weiner writes, music and sound are both tied to what Aschenbach tries to repress, to his irrational impulses. Later, musical and acoustic motifs suggest his loss of control over himself and his surroundings. When Tadzio appears, Aschenbach begins to accept the acoustical realm and to distinguish between sound and music. This transformation, Weiner continues, also occurs in his encounters with Mann's various Dionysian figures, and it represents his recognition of his repressed sexuality. In his dream, music and sound again both represent the Dionysian. Mann polarizes the implications of music and writing to heighten the irony of his final lines, Weiner argues. In those lines, Aschenbach is glorified for his silent art by a world that knows nothing of his internal acceptance of music. In sum, Mann's "polarization of artistic forms — music and writing — for extra-aesthetic reasons operates both within Aschenbach's psychological make-up and in his world" (149). In Weiner's view, that world judges different kinds of art according to their relationship to sound. Music lies between the extremes of silence and cacophony, he writes, and is aurally ambiguous. Weiner made similar remarks in 1993, when he related the novella to social and political issues raised by the conservative composer Hans Pfitzner. Like Pfitzner's polemics, Weiner explains, *Death in Venice* demonstrates the "social iconography of music at the end of the Wilhelminian Empire" (75). Weiner notes similarities between the novella and Pfitzner's works, and he argues that Mann's musical narrative technique invites readers to reflect on the polarized aesthetic forms of music and writing. The form of the novella thereby implies, Weiner concludes, a political and social orientation that is more liberal than its content suggests — and than Mann may have intended.

Besides being filmed by Visconti and set to music by Britten, Mann's story inspired several visual artists. In 1978, Hans-G. Sperlich and Herbert Albrecht introduced drawings, watercolors, and paintings of Mann's scenes by Jörg Madlener and Jan Vanriet. Sperlich notes Visconti's influence and the treatment of time in Madlener's works, while Albrecht stresses Vanriet's sensitivity to nature and to landscapes, the vividness and transparency of his colors, and his fundamental antinaturalism. In 1991, Klaus W. Jonas gave an overview of illustrated editions of *Death in Venice*. He mentions art created by Wolfgang Born in 1921, by Felix Hoffmann and by Alfred Hrdlicka, both in 1972, by Vanriet in 1978, and by Rosario Morra and by Helmut Werres, both in 1990. He especially likes the edition illustrated by Werres, calling it the most beautiful one not only of *Death in Venice,* but also of any of

Mann's works. With the exception of *Felix Krull,* Jonas also observes, none of those works have been as popular among illustrators as this novella.

Death in Venice also inspired two plays and two ballets. The first of the plays, by Lee Breuer, was called *A Prelude to Death in Venice.* In 1978 and 1979, parts, reworkings, and revisions of this play were performed in New York, Los Angeles, and Amsterdam. In 1980, it premiered in New York, then was also given in San Francisco, Los Angeles, Brussels, Paris, and Milan. According to Breuer's stage directions in a text published in 1979–80, one of the two actors in it reads selections from Lowe-Porter's translation "in a German accent and a tone reminiscent of Peter Lorre." Those stage directions also call for an image of Tadzio, "with 'punk' overtones" such as a black motorcycle jacket. In a review from 1980, Alan M. Brown found this strange take on Mann's novella "a stark existential telephone drama" (5). Death in Venice likewise assumed dramatic form in England. In 1993, Gabriele Annan reviewed an adaptation done by Jonathan Holloway and performed by the company Red Shift. Annan notes that this version included a role for Aschenbach's wife, who, in contrast to the little Mann tells us about her, "informs us that she had only a stillborn child, then tells her husband that she doesn't want him inside her any more" (18). Such feminist touches lead Annan to consider Holloway's work more a judgment on Mann than a recreation of Mann's novella, a story one needs to know in order to understand the events on stage. The first of the two ballets was given in Munich and reviewed in newspapers there. On 3 November 1986, for example, Charlotte Nennecke reported that the Canadian choreographer Norbert Vesak had created a ballet of *Death in Venice* for the Bavarian State Opera. Vesak, like Visconti, she notes, used excerpts from Mahler's symphonic music. The same dancer played the fop, the barber, and the leader of the street singers, so Vesak seems to have combined these roles in a way reminiscent of Britten's opera. On 13 November 1986, the reviewer "Mz.," writing for a newspaper in Zurich, reported that Vesak had been booed at the première and that the critics found the work very problematic at best. At its second performance, his Aschenbach seemed miscast, being about the same age as his Tadzio. That this performance was nonetheless successful, "Mz." writes, is because the ballet has little besides its setting and social milieu in common with Mann's novella. Flemming Flindt's *Death in Venice,* a ballet of 1991, has already been noted above, in the introduction.

Death in Venice also appeared in an important new German edition and in three new English translations. The German edition was prepared by T. J. Reed and published in 1983. It includes a list of words and passages that shows how the limited luxury edition of 1912 differed from the text that had appeared when the novella was published in serial form earlier that year. More importantly, it includes Mann's handwritten working notes. Those notes contain many kinds of information, among them details about Tadzio's name and about Aschenbach's age, birthplace, and the dates of his journey; definitions of ideas such as eros, mania, and pedophilia among the ancient Greeks; stories of figures from Greek mythology; excerpts from Plato, Lukács, Virgil, Homer, Erwin Rohde's *Psyche,* Friedrich Nösselt's handbook of Greek and Roman mythology, Plutarch, and Schiller; comments on the history, symptoms, and treatment of Asiatic cholera; and a photograph of Mahler. Reed remarks on Mann's juxtaposition of medical and mythological items, on his distribution of his own contradictory impulses among the various stages of Aschenbach's career, and, taking issue with White's argument of 1950, on his distillation of keywords for the motifs treated in his last chapter. Reed also draws on Mann's notes in his own footnotes and commentary, using them to prove that Mann became critical of Platonic love only in the course of the emotional experiment of writing his story. According to Reed, Mann's stylistic mastery is both an aesthetic achievement and a moral problem. This argument is similar to the one Reed had made 1971 and 1974. Here, besides panning Visconti's film, he also notes that Schopenhauer's *Metaphysik der Geschlechtsliebe,* the forty-fourth chapter of the second volume of *Die Welt als Wille und Vorstellung,* is the source of Mann's knowledge of Plato and Plutarch. In 1988, David Luke's new translation of *Death in Venice* appeared. In his introduction, Luke calls the novella Mann's greatest story and "the most artistically perfect and subtle of all his works" (vii). One of its most remarkable features, he adds, is how subtly it shows the process of falling in love. Its ambiguous presentation of Aschenbach, moreover, reflects Mann's ambivalence and his "schizoid cerebral dread of instinctual disorder" (xxxviii). Disagreeing with Reed, Luke regards its combination of contrasting elements as "iridescent interweaving" (xli). He also faults Lowe-Porter's translation in no uncertain terms, citing its poor quality, linguistic inadequacies, factual mistakes, lexical failure, and incorrect readings of German grammar and syntax, not to mention its omission of the last sentence in Mann's penultimate paragraph: "And as so often, he set out to follow him" (xlix). *Death in Venice* was also translated into English by Clayton Koelb in 1994 and by Stanley Appelbaum in 1995. Koelb's edition includes an English rendering of Mann's working notes as well as scholarly articles cited elsewhere in the present study.

Three studies of the earlier translations into English show why new ones were necessary. In 1985, John Whiton evaluated Lowe-Porter's translation of 1928. Whiton cites four levels of felicity in her rendering of Mann's meaning. He even discerns strokes of genius on her part and shining examples of her art of translating. She does not always convey the motifs of life and death, though, he adds, sometimes missing Mann's sexual and erotic connotations. Noting her prudishness and uneven talent, Whiton also observes that she makes "gross errors that would be unworthy of a pupil in a grammar school" (254), as he put it in 1991. Her translation seems weak,

# 5: Recent Trends, 1996–2001

## Introduction

RESEARCH ON *Death in Venice* conducted in the last few years falls into categories like the ones established in the previous two chapters to order the scholarly efforts made in the preceding four decades. First, there are remarks on aesthetics and artists, including insights into Aschenbach's significance for modernity and decadence. Second, there are studies of the myths at work in Mann's story and comparisons drawn between it and fiction by other writers. Third, there are analyses of his style, especially of his narrator's irony. Fourth, there are readings that invoke philosophers, cite political history or cultural differences, or apply psychoanalytic concepts. Fifth, there are comments on homoeroticism. These comments often involve Mann's biography, which has figured in other interpretations as well. Sixth, there are articles that take other approaches or treat other themes: readings of the novella, its setting, its Orphic mysticism, its hero's gaze, its motif of travel, and its characters' clothes. Seventh and last, there are books and articles on Visconti's film, Britten's opera, Flemming Flindt's ballet, and editions of Mann's text. These seven categories do not contain all the kinds of research done in earlier years. No new studies of the novella seriously treat Mann's other writings, sources, or symbols, for example, and none sheds much new light on his story with regard to literary history or to music. Such omissions may be only apparent, though, since some recent research on the novella has doubtless not yet been entered into bibliographies or catalogues and thus not yet become known. The conclusions drawn in this chapter must therefore remain tentative, subject to revision as such new sources surface. Nonetheless, one new trend is already evident: the emphasis now laid upon how the novella presents conflicting cultures. This emphasis reflects a recent theoretical fashion for the concepts of colonialism and orientalism. Many other such fashions have come and gone in the reception of *Death in Venice*. One may well wonder how long this one will last, what will happen next, and which of the issues and ideas that seem so urgent today will still be of interest tomorrow. In any case, the number of books and articles mentioned in each of the seven categories just named is too small to warrant introductions to the individual sections of this last chapter. Because current research is still ongoing and open-ended, moreover, there is no conclusion at the end of it.

## Aesthetics and Artists

Two scholars working on Mann's novella in the last few years stressed Aschenbach's role as an artist. They reached differing conclusions about it. In 1996, Peter Mudford linked Aschenbach's passion and decadence to his renewed artistic creativity. *Death in Venice* directs irony at that passion, according to Mudford, but it also shows how Aschenbach's sexual inclination inspires his art and his life. Indeed, the entire novella is a "memorial reconstruction of the last weeks of Aschenbach's life" (142–43), an elegy made possible by the narrator's intimate understanding of Aschenbach's soul. The narrator also relates Aschenbach's tale "from an Olympian perspective, . . . as though one god were writing about another" (143). In the memory of the narrator, Mudford adds, who does not exist apart from Mann's hero, Aschenbach's death even achieves mythic status. This death — a death like Wagner's — is one that Mann imagined in an "Olympian vision of himself" (144). Mudford seems to overlook the narrator's distance from Aschenbach and to overrate how closely Mann identified with his hero. At any rate, he sees Aschenbach in a very favorable light. Describing his orgiastic dream, for example, Mudford maintains that Aschenbach discovers in excess the route to self-transcendence. Indeed, Aschenbach also becomes "a mythological being, inspired by daemonic power, in the service of creativity" (152). In sum, Mudford contends that *Death in Venice* is preoccupied with "passion as a form of degeneracy which leads to a renewal of the artist's life, and the particular value of spiritual beauty which the work of art represents" (151). Contrary to Mudford's claim, Mann gives no hint that Aschenbach is making notes for his next work at the time of his death, notes that Mudford says are for *Death in Venice* itself, for a work that forges spiritual beauty out of an illicit passion. This mistake appears consistent with Mudford's insistence on Aschenbach's progress and on both the narrator's and Mann's own approval of it. By contrast, in 1997, Rita A. Bergenholtz wrote that Aschenbach is not a tragic character. His story is a parody of a tragedy, she says, and he is a parody of a romantic artist-hero. Like Venice, he is a "fallen queen" (146). Whereas Mudford describes the story as elegiac, Bergenholtz assumes it is satirical.

Two other researchers raised more general issues of art and aesthetics. In 2001, Ulrike Prechtl-Fröhlich wrote that Aschenbach ends badly because he avoids and denies his melancholic consciousness. He fails to acknowledge the melancholy inherent in all art, she claims, and he suppresses "das melancholische Andere seiner Natur" (the melancholic Other of his nature) (153). Erich Meuthen, likewise in 2001, called *Death in Venice* a milestone in the history of the German *Künstlerroman,* a genre of novels about historical or fictional artists. According to him, Mann shows a process of disintegration apparent in that genre, a loss of faith in the Western notions of an autonomous subject and recognizable truth. Meuthen explains that the novella treats the problem of an artist's dignity, a concept that he relates to the idealistic aesthetics of Friedrich Schiller, in particular to Schiller's treatise *Über Anmut und Würde*. Aschenbach founders on the contradictions inherent Schiller's aesthetic philosophy, he adds, above all on its untenable dichotomy of body and mind. Mann discredits beautiful appearances, moreover, and lets readers know that they result from rhetoric. In chapter 4, those appearances include a sunrise and Tadzio. The phrase wrongly attributed to Cicero in Mann's opening paragraph underscores this rhetorical aspect, Meuthen argues, as does the fact that Hermes, a god embodied by several of Mann's characters, was the patron of oratory. Even Mann's account of Aschenbach's story *Ein Elender*, he claims, shows moral resolve to be a matter of stylistic refinement. Mann cites Plato's philosophy and Schiller's aesthetics, then, to show why they fail — that is, to expose their hermetic character — and to make clear that the truth of the texts he cites lies solely in their rhetorical effect. Remarking on Aschenbach's "Übertragung" (transferal, translation) of Tadzio's physical beauty into the realm of intellect, Meuthen stresses what he calls the metaphorical quality of poetic production. It thus comes as no surprise that, when he explains Aschenbach's unsettling view of the boy, he also quotes Jacques Derrida.

Another two scholars tied Aschenbach's problems as an artist to the larger issues of modernity and decadence. In 1996, Hideo Tateno wrote that the crisis of Mann's hero is the crisis of modernity. Like Aschenbach, modernity is frail, Tateno observes, and its crisis, like his, is that of formalism, of intellectual emptiness and a loss of a will to life. Like Aschenbach, moreover, modernity, in its rationalism, excludes the Other. Their shared formalism, according to Tateno, also occurs in the spirit of capitalism as described by Max Weber. Aschenbach is an ascetic, furthermore, who seeks the Other and flees modern European life. That life no longer includes the irrational and has become solipsistic, Tateno adds, and Aschenbach sets out to find the unconscious. For him, the unconscious, unknown, and Other are Tadzio, whose body he cannot comprehend. Both he and modernity suffer a loss and relativization of the subject, Tateno concludes, and Mann flees modernity, as his hero does. These generalities often sound just as empty as the formalism that Tateno decries. Similarly, in 1997, Bernd M. Kraske discussed *Death in Venice* as a novella about an artist whose decadence characterizes an entire intellectual epoch. As Kraske explains, Mann analyzes, criticizes, and rejects this decadence, which was a development in European aesthetics, a development symbolized by Venice. Kraske also fears the novella may have a narcotic effect on people who prefer sects, drugs, and apocalyptic concepts — which he calls symptoms of a new decadence — to reason. We should avoid, he thinks, Aschenbach's sympathy with the abyss. Kraske, like Tateno, thus suggests that *Death in Venice* is still relevant to our current concerns and dissatisfactions.

# Myths and Comparisons

Three recent studies examined Mann's use of Greek myths. These studies display varying levels of sophistication. In 1996, Andrée Shalabi interpreted elements of Greek thought in *Death in Venice,* in other words, Greek culture and mythology. In Aschenbach's development, Shalabi posits an alliance of Dionysus, Pan, Eros, Aphrodite, Ares, Poseidon, and Apollo. Apollo's displacement by Dionysus, Shalabi argues, is the result of this Olympian conspiracy, and Greek myth is a medium conveying the problem of achievement attained at the expense of life. This is hardly news, and Shalabi's remarks are often vague and rambling. Wendelin Schmidt-Dengler noted in 1997 the various transfigurations of Hermes in the novella. They include Tadzio and Aschenbach, he explains, and they attest to Mann's use of myth to transcend time. The individual assumes a mythical identity, and myth thus creates unity and conveys timelessness. The narrative innovation of *Death in Venice,* Schmidt-Dengler concludes, lies in this integration of ancient mythology into a realistic context. The mythical and mundane, he adds, are likewise combined in Max Frisch's novel *Homo Faber.* Pierre Brunel, again in 1997, similarly read the novella with regard to Hermes. Tadzio resembles this god at the end of the novella, he explains, and so does the wanderer at the beginning. Both of these characters are Aschenbach's shadow and double, according to Brunel, as are the fop and the gondolier. In Nietzsche's *Der Wanderer und sein Schatten* (The Wanderer and His Shadow, 1880) and in Freud's concept of the uncanny, Brunel finds support for his argument that the three strangers, figures of death that have been repressed, represent Aschenbach's self. Aschenbach cannot become Tadzio, Brunel adds, who is his divine double and the child he once was. Aschenbach's first shadow, moreover, may be the rational Socrates described in Nietzsche's *Die Geburt der Tragödie.* In Aschenbach, Mann allows this Socrates to succumb to desire for Phaedrus and thus to Dionysus. Brunel suggests that Mann shares Nietzsche's skepticism about Socrates and Socratic discourse. He also wrongly contends that *Death in Venice* first appeared as a book and that Pola is the island where Aschenbach vacations before going to Venice. His argument is intriguing, however, and he notes suggestive details like the fact that the fop's drunkenness anticipates Aschenbach's wildest dream.

A dozen further studies compared *Death in Venice* to fiction by other writers. These studies, too, vary in quality. Three of them connect the novella to works by Henry James. In 1996, Ilona Treitel compared it to James's *The Beast in the Jungle.* These two stories, she argues, are linked by their shared dialectic between the presence and absence of a beast: the tiger. According to her, the tiger represents, or is represented by, almost everyone and everything in Mann's novella. It is a metaphor of creativity, of Oedipal conflict and narcissism, and of "'doubling by multiplication'" (141), a term used by Robert Rogers in 1970. The tiger is also an image of both life and death, Treitel adds, both Apollo and Dionysus. It stands for Aschenbach's suppressed emotions, his identity as an artist, his pursuit of beauty, and the obscene symbol hoisted in his final dream. According to Treitel, it is at once a product of his imagination and a representation of his imagination at work. Last but not least, the tiger signifies a "flaw in the interpretive process itself that implicates the interpreter" (148). Treitel also finds traits of the tiger in all Mann's strange men — the wanderer, fop, gondolier, and street singer — not to mention in Aschenbach and in Tadzio. Treitel thus posits the tiger in many places other than the jungle envisioned by Aschenbach in Munich. That it may not be everywhere she thinks is suggested by her mistaken notion of the setting of that vision. According to her, Aschenbach sees "'apocalyptic *beasts*'" (144) at the mortuary chapel. The word "beast," though, which she italicizes for emphasis, is only Lowe-Porter's. In German, Mann mentions apocalyptic "Tiere" (animals). In 1999, Sergio Perosa likened *Death in Venice* to James's *Roderick Hudson* (1876). Both works show an oxymoron, Perosa argues, an anomalous situation due to the historical and artistic contradictions that constitute Venice. Perosa calls literary yearnings for death there, yearnings prompted by the overwhelming force of this oxymoron, "a Ruskin or an Aschenbach syndrome" (126). Andreas Mahler, again in 1999, found Mann's story similar to James's *The Wings of the Dove* (1902). Like James, he thinks, Mann shows Venice to be a place where characters engage in make-believe by exchanging illusions. When Tadzio sees Aschenbach pursuing him, for example, but does not betray him, Aschenbach briefly has the illusion of being loved. In this way, Mahler writes, the two of them "perform" Venice.

As so often before, *Death in Venice* was also compared to Gide's *L'immoraliste*. Martin Halliwell drew this comparison in 1999. In a review of Albert Guérard's book on Gide in 1951, Halliwell begins, Mann did not acknowledge how disturbing a tale of decadence Gide had told. Preoccupied with harmony and balance, he explains, Mann overlooked the loss of artistic control that Gide describes. Mann's understanding of decadence was too narrow, so he misread Gide. Halliwell interprets Mann's story, too, as a strong misreading of Gide's. The two works examine similar impulses, he argues, but these impulses have different consequences. Halliwell's primary concern is the idea of abjection, and he cites four themes showing how Gide and Mann treat it: travel, doublings, homosexuality, and illness. All these themes, according to him, involve spatial, psychic, and corporeal limits or borders. Both works, he writes, describe travel beyond Europe that destabilizes their protagonists in an encounter with a cultural Other. Both also show doublings, that is, recurring characters or reversals, and thereby criticize Nietzschean individualism. In both, homosexuality is a shock, a challenge, and a symbolic site. Finally, both works show how illness and corporeality intersect. Halliwell goes on to say that Aschenbach and Michel suffer psychic disturbance, a disruption of the self. Aschenbach cannot contend with the resulting abjection, and his abject demise thus differs from Michel's abject nihilism. While Aschenbach does not or cannot face his abjection, Gide's Michel acknowledges and accepts an abject life. Halliwell thus shows how Mann and Gide treat abject decadence differently. He also observes that both of their protagonists' ruined lives are symbolized by ruined language. In making this case, he invokes not only Harold Bloom's notion of strong misreadings but also Julia Kristeva's theory of abjection. In applying this theory to *Death in Venice,* Halliwell seems to assume that David Luke was right to translate the title of Aschenbach's story *Ein Elender* as *A Study in Abjection.* In other English versions of the novella, this title is rendered differently. Lowe-Porter similarly translates it as *An Abject,* but for Burke it is *A Wretch,* for Neugroschel it is *A Wretched Man,* for Chase it is *A True Wretch,* for Koelb it is *A Man of Misery,* and for Appelbaum it is *A Miserable Man.* In any case, Halliwell is mistaken when he speaks of Aschenbach's "German clergyman father" (161).

Three comparative studies mostly concerned sex. In 1997, R. F. Fleissner said that Mann was indirectly influenced by Shakespeare's *Merchant of Venice.* The evidence Fleissner cites is shaky, consisting mainly of the fact that both works, apart from mentioning Venice in their titles, address the theme of homoeroticism. Robert K. Martin, also in 1997, read Tennessee Williams's stories *The Mysteries of the Joy Rio* and *Hard Candy* (1954) as reworkings of *Death in Venice* and *Tonio Kröger.* Both of these stories, Martin notes, involve elderly men who seek sex with other men. The first is a "modern, and less sentimental, *Death in Venice*" (62), he claims, and the collapse of the principal character in the second recalls and rewrites that of Aschenbach. In 1998, Vladimir Troubetzkoy explained how Mann's novella and Nabokov's *Lolita* treat the topic of pedophilia. Mann does so in a way that is simpler and more direct, Troubetzkoy says, since Aschenbach desires but never transgresses. *Death in Venice* also caused less scandal, he adds, because in it pedophilia is part of the theme of decadence. According to him, moreover, Aschenbach and Nabokov's Humbert Humbert both want to violate Narcissus, and both prefer felinity to femininity. Troubetzkoy incorrectly thinks that Tadzio is thirteen years old and that Mann had once imagined his hero in love with a girl of this age.

Other comparative studies raised various other issues. Two of those studies related *Death in Venice* to detective fiction. In 1997, Edward Sackey linked it to Kwame Anthony Appiah's *Another Death in Venice* (1995). Appiah's motif of death, setting of Venice, and character Peggy Aschenheim are all allusions to Mann, Sackey explains, all part of an intertextual project. He improbably adds that Mann's novella reintegrates scattered or repressed parts of its hero's self and that Aschenbach succumbs not only to physical, but also to spiritual desires. He also calls Tadzio "a beautiful polite youth" (246). Sackey seems to mean "a beautiful Polish youth." In 1999, Indira Ghose cited *Death in Venice* to interpret another detective novel, Michael Dibdin's *Dead Lagoon* (1994). With its orientalized site of Venice, she says, this novel evokes shades of Mann's story. Ghose mistakenly believes that Aschenbach "walks to his death in the sea" (221). Two other comparative studies stressed the idea of parody. In 1999, Judith Seaboyer read Robert Coover's *Pinocchio in Venice* (1991) with regard to Mann's novella. Mann parodically rereads Plato's *Phaedrus,* Seaboyer argues, and Coover parodies Mann's version of this dialogue in turn. Both *Death in Venice* and Carlo Collodi's story of Pinocchio include repression, she adds, and Coover interweaves Aschenbach's discovery of Dionysiac passion with a reversal of that children's story. He thereby engages, through parody, Mann's ambivalence toward art and artists. By accepting, when he dies, Seaboyer concludes, the part of himself that he has denied, Coover's Pinocchio suggests the positive something that Mann could not allow Aschenbach. Rosella Mamoli Zorzi, once again in 1999, wrote that the doings of Professor Eschenbaum in Robert Dessaix's *Night Letters* (1996) seem to be a parody of Mann's novella. "Eschenbaum's homosexual frequentations," she explains, "are a debased version of Aschenbach's passion for Tadzio" (234). Finally, yet again in 1999, George B. von der Lippe compared *Death in Venice* to Daphne du Maurier's *Don't Look Now* (1971) and to Ian McEwan's *In the Comfort of Strangers,* considering the film versions of these works as well. In all three of the works, he writes, a northern visitor is trapped in the labyrinth of Venice, where rebirth of the erotic ends in a *Liebestod.* What makes Visconti's film so effective, he adds, is the shock and humiliation it arouses by showing Aschenbach's disintegration without Mann's irony and mediation. In sum, von der Lippe thinks that Mann has furthered a long artistic tradition.

# Style

Remarks on Mann's style focused on how he turned real life into fiction and on how he employed his ironic narrator. In 1996, Urszula Kawalec wrote that Mann remained faithful to elements of reality he experienced in Venice yet transferred them to a fictional literary world. Circumstances surrounding the young Władisław Moes, she argues, the model for Tadzio, are thereby neutralized. Mann's description of him is accurate, she adds, but augmented by commentary that lends the fictional Tadzio symbolic dimensions. Relieved of individual traits, Tadzio is an incarnation of beauty and a dematerialized symbol. He is representative, not real. Kawalec's further remark that such transformation of Mann's memories into fiction has no consequences for interpreting his story seems to disregard the links often noted between the events of that story and his life. In 1996, Patrick O'Neill similarly claimed that Aschenbach's world is constructed, not merely reported, by the discourse of Mann's ironic narrator. According to O'Neill, this discourse determines readers' understanding of that world, and it is distinct from both the events and the characters they find there. Applying the concept of "narrative setting" (19), O'Neill discusses Mann's descriptions of physical locations and characters in seven "hermeneutic series" (22) that structure and develop that discourse: the labyrinth of Venice, the journey into the heart of darkness, messengers of death, allusions to classical myths, hexametric diction, epithets for Aschenbach, and textual leitmotifs and other devices that demonstrate the narrator's ironic attitude to Aschenbach and the reader. *Death in Venice* is thus predominately the story of its setting, which O'Neill considers extremely rich. Indeed, he describes the novella as "one of the fixed stars in the canon of modern German literature" (17). In 1998, André Brink said that the dialectic between Aschenbach and the narrator demonstrates a "problematising view of language" (173). Tadzio and the tiger in Aschenbach's vision, in fact, take revenge that is "*the revenge of human language* (when relegated to silence) on the pretensions of art" (176). The narrator uses such language, Brink says, which Aschenbach has silenced and betrayed in pursuit of beauty. This is the case in the narrator's accounts of the jungle and Tadzio, when Aschenbach is mum or quotes ancient rhetoric. Brink also ties such language to femininity, which he thinks Aschenbach suppresses. In the end, Aschenbach is killed by discovering "the impossibility of original articulation" (187). Unfortunately, Brink relies on Lowe-Porter's poor translation when he tells how the written word informs Aschenbach's understanding of dawn in Mann's fourth chapter. He stresses what Lowe-Porter calls a "'*a winged word*'" (186), whereas Mann had written "eine beschwingte Kunde," a poetic expression for news or knowledge that could just as well be spoken. It is not true that the gondolier is sent off by the hotel staff, moreover, and Mann never says that most guests at the hotel are American, English, or Russian. These mistakes suggest and compound the unconvicingness of Brink's essay.

## Philosophy, History, and Psychoanalysis

Only one new philosophical reading of *Death in Venice* has been given in the last few years. In 1997, Werner Hickel read the novella mainly as a confrontation between Schopenhauer and Nietzsche. He thinks the former more important than the latter. Mann, Hickel explains, seems to warn against lapsing into Nietzsche's vitalism. Aschenbach must die not because he becomes Dionysian, however, but because he does so only half-heartedly. He does so only in thought, not in deed, and remains an Apollinian, pseudo-Platonic voyeur. By combining Wagner and Schopenhauer, moreover, Mann identifies death with nirvana and salvation. His several messengers of death lead Aschenbach to a salvation that is a misunderstood and "Wagnerized" version of Schopenhauer, Hickel argues, not to unlimited Dionysian life. In sum, Mann's synthesis of Wagner and Schopenhauer, he says, preserves Aschenbach's dignity. Since Aschenbach's looking at Tadzio is not truly erotic, he adds, Mann falsifies both the composer and the philosopher. In 1999, Martina Hoffmann assessed Aschenbach's progress in the same philosophical terms she had used in 1995, adding a chapter on the narrator's ironic commentary. The narrator notes Aschenbach's delusion, she explains, and Mann thereby guides his readers. Aschenbach's changes become apparent against the backdrop of the narrator's stable normative values, she adds, but these same values cause Aschenbach's problems, so the narrator actually elicits sympathy for him. Mann compromises his own narrator, in other words, and suggests a concept of dialectic contrast that operates on the philosophical sublevel of his novella as well, between the Apollinian and Dionysian. In this addendum to her old argument, Hoffmann relies heavily on Cohn's remarks from 1983.

Readings that stressed historical elements of *Death in Venice* often invoked ideas of community and culture together with the issues of colonialism and orientalism. In 1998, Russell A. Berman read the novella from the perspective of new historicism. Berman relates personal to political time, that is, Aschenbach's doings to the European developments that later resulted in the First World War. The presence of a naval base in Pola, for example, shows the imperialist character of the Habsburg regime. According to Berman, there is also mythic time. The nationalism of the Italian clerks on the boat to Venice, for example, emerges as music and with the aid of wine, and thus seems Dionysian. The text is not sympathetic to such a desire for national liberation, Berman adds, neither as it is shown by those drunken clerks, nor as it is suggested by Tadzio's scorn for the Russian family. That these hints of international tension are not mentioned again is one sign of how Aschenbach represses politics, Berman thinks, and even of his "ideological involvement with the agenda of German imperialism" (269). Colonialism, moreover, emerges in the English clerk's story of how the cholera epidemic began in India, a land ruled by his fellow Britons. Besides displacing politics with aesthetics, Berman argues, Aschenbach displays Prussian soldierliness and a Protestant work ethic like the one studied by Max Weber. It is surprising, given these statements, that Berman does not condemn Mann's hero. Instead, he says that Aschenbach's restraint in not acting immorally keeps his story from being one of decay. In the end, in fact, his "transfiguring salvation" (275) suggests "a utopian hope for human community" (277). The Prussian ethic, it seems, is not always wrong. Another interpretation of *Death in Venice* in 1998, by John Burt Foster, Jr., applied the ideas of culture and cultural multiplicity. The novella advocates contact across the borders of its "cultural geography" (198), Foster remarks, in particular between Germans and Slavs. Foster rejects critiques of Eurocentrism that neglect such boundaries within Europe, and — explaining Aschenbach's attraction to Tadzio — he judiciously adds that "lifting the taboos surrounding the discussion of homosexuality . . . can also obscure other issues that deserve attention" (199). That attraction, he explains, includes recognition of Aschenbach's mixed, partly Bohemian heritage. His "troubled flirtation with cultural multiplicity" (201), moreover, suggests criticism of elite, narrow, and nationalistic German *Kultur*. It also casts doubt, Foster writes, on venerating classical Greek culture. Finally, Foster thinks that the novella orientalizes the East, including Venice, where cosmopolitanism and Italian nationalism clash. According to him, this story about an outbreak of repressed cultural links and the importance of cross-cultural communication anticipates the development of Mann's later and less patriotic political views.

In 1997 and again in 2000, Yahya A. Elsaghe took a historical and cultural approach to *Death in Venice* more critical than those of Berman and Foster. In 1997, Elsaghe published an article about sexualization of the foreign in the novella. In his essay on Frederick the Great, Elsaghe notes, Mann thought of the Seven Years' War as a battle of the sexes between that Prussian monarch and Maria Theresia of Austria. Frederick's perseverance and toughness, which Aschenbach emulates, were thus directed, in Mann's mind, against a woman. Accordingly, Aschenbach's patriarchal lineage is opposed to his matriarchal traits, which seem corporeal, foreign, and Dionysian. The border separating Germany and Bohemia, the land of his mother's father, Elsaghe adds, is ethnographic insofar as it marks the difference between Germans and Slavs, maybe even the one between Germans and Jews. Mann also locates sickness and death beyond the borders of Germany, placing them in Venice or at least Vienna. According to Elsaghe, in fact, the topography of his tale is that of Freud's colonialistic orientalism. When Aschenbach becomes ill and dissolute, Elsaghe continues, he no longer belongs to the German linguistic community. Finally, Elsaghe says that Mann's description of Venice as a dubious beauty harboring unclean internal processes is misogynistic (his German grammar implies that the city is female). To put it crudely — though not much more crudely than Elsaghe does — Mann's novella displays sexism, racism, anti-Semitism, and xenophobia. Compared to such claims, Elsaghe's statement that Aschenbach's snobbery is linked with the neofeudal tendencies of Wilhelminian Germany sounds almost tame. In 2000, Elsaghe amplified this argument in a book about Mann and the German nation as he imagined it. Mann's departures from the photograph of Mahler on which he based his description of Aschenbach's face, Elsaghe maintains, show him coming close to using the terminology of racist biology. Elsaghe adds that the border between Germany and Bohemia, as Mann imagined it, has a hygienic dimension. Noting

Mann's combination of the modern and mythological, Elsaghe writes that Aschenbach infects himself by drinking soda and pomegranate juice, soda being made of regular drinking water. Furthermore, Mann never mentions the unsanitary living conditions in northern European cities favorable to the outbreak of cholera. Attributing this disease to Asia, according to Elsaghe, he turns a social problem into an intercultural conflict, a fact with an ideological function. Associating Austria with illness and death — that is, imagining the German border with Austria as a *cordon sanitaire* — Mann justifies the otherwise indefensible division between the two empires of Wilhelm and the Habsburgs. *Death in Venice,* Elsaghe concludes, thus reflects the endangered modern German identity. Elsaghe also comments on the function of German as the language of the super-ego. With these new ideas, Elsaghe again argues that Mann describes the foreign as feminine.

Laura Otis made similar remarks in 1999, stressing the idea of membranes and metaphors of invasion in scientific, literary, and political writings. Otis explains how both Mann and the German bacteriologist Robert Koch associated the origin of cholera with the tiger, an animal that represents imperial conquest as well as erotic drives. Both Mann and Koch, she thinks, thus show concern with the violation of borders and boundaries used to construct identity. Mann's "discourse of disease" (149) reflects a coincidence of germ theory and imperialism, moreover, and it reveals European fears and fantasies of Asia. By means of its irony, though, his story also shows that the many meanings assigned to bacteria are European projections and that corruption and decay are indigenous to Europe. According to Otis, Aschenbach and the Venetians still subscribe to the miasmatic theory of disease, linking the cholera to foul vapors, while the English clerk explains the epidemic according to the more recent bacteriological theory. The conflict between these two theories reflects scientific controversies that were current in Mann's day and were reported in German newspapers he may have read. His story compromises between the two, she adds; it relies on the older notion of individual disposition in stressing Aschenbach's affinity for cholera. Otis also claims that Aschenbach's membranes, which she says have to do with his sexual terrors, are penetrated and dissolve, and that he can no longer function like a self-contained cell. In his Dionysian dream, he is pierced, violated, and subjected to rape, she contends, and thus submits to a "senescent deflowering" (164). Mann thereby suggests that "identity based on exclusion can end only in chaos as the 'hungry life' one has rejected overwhelms one's defenses" (156). The parallels that Otis draws between Mann's metaphors of disease and geopolitical aspects of his story sometimes seem forced. *Death in Venice* may undermine stereotypes and the association of eastern and southern racial types with disease, and Aschenbach's encounter with the foreign certainly seems to be an encounter with his self. It is less clear that Mann was implying Germans' xenophobia and desire for a colonial empire, or that he was writing about the decline of national boundaries and the decay of such empires. Otis's claims seem plausible, however, when she supports them by citing Mann's diction. She notes that Mann uses the word "üppig" (luxuriant, voluptuous) to describe bacteria as well as Aschenbach's writing and his vision of the jungle, and she argues that Mann thereby hints how disease, art, and eroticism are related. Otis similarly remarks that Mann uses the word "kauern" (crouch, cower) to describe not only the tiger Aschenbach envisions, but also second-class passengers on the boat to Venice and a beggar in that city. He thus suggests, she writes, a connection between the disease that the tiger represents and the lower social classes. She also oddly says that Aschenbach gets to Venice by traveling north. Otis made her case more concisely in 2000, again noting the "bacteriological dimension of Mann's story" (244).

Another reading of *Death in Venice* that raised political issues was given by Jochen Strobel, once again in 2000. Strobel argues that the novella addresses the problem of national representativeness. He means that it describes the decline and fall of a national author. Aschenbach becomes such an author, and in this way "represents" the German nation, but only by suppressing his modernity. Mann tells how he stops playing his public role, Strobel claims, and thus shows how he loses his national stature. Aschenbach enjoys such stature, Strobel says, thanks to his novel about Frederick the Great and to the fact that his texts are included in German schoolbooks. These literary texts encourage social integration, and Aschenbach mediates between the state and its citizens. Strobel also writes that he tries to reconcile representative Wilhelminian culture with the consciousness typical of modernity, the requirements of a national mythology with his ascetic work ethic. He can no longer be both a national author and a modern artist, though, and he accordingly loses his representativeness. According to Strobel, this loss begins with his inability to write, and it is suggested by his anonymity in Munich and Venice, by the fact that the wanderer and other such figures meet his gaze with aggression instead of the proper respect, by his rejecting the thought of returning to his summer house in Germany, and by his following Tadzio rather than educating him. Aschenbach attempts to avoid this loss by reviving ancient myths, Strobel notes, but he fails. At the end of the novella, Aschenbach is representative again, but at the expense of his physical destruction. He could never be a national author like Goethe, and he resembles false representatives such as Gerhart Hauptmann, who aspired to be a symbol of the German nation and whose *Griechischer Frühling*, Strobel maintains, *Death in Venice* discredits. Strobel overstates his case when he claims that Aschenbach was striving for popularity when he simplified his critical literary attitude, that he tries to unify the German nation, that the entire nation honors his mastery, that he is a pillar of the German state, and that he deceives his public. Strobel also says Aschenbach ignores conflicts between nationalities, but he confuses two separate scenes in the novella when he explains that Aschenbach dismisses Tadzio's wrestling with his Russian rival as childish fanaticism. In fact, Aschenbach attributes such fanaticism to Tadzio when the boy is scornful of the relaxed Russian family, not when he wrestles with his friend Jaschu. Besides, Jaschu is his fellow Pole.

Psychoanalytic readings of *Death in Venice* given from 1996 to 2001 took various views of its hero's mental life. In 1997, Carrie Zlotnick-Woldenberg gave an object-relational interpretation that stresses Aschenbach's intrapsychic as well as his interpersonal splitting, his problematic relationship with his parents, and his paranoid/schizoid character. Unable to accept ambivalence, she explains, Aschenbach sees polar opposites in himself and in others. His self consists of two parts, which do not communicate with each other, and he demonizes or idealizes other people, to whom he has trouble relating. His parents pushed him to succeed, Zlotnick-Woldenberg guesses, and he wants Tadzio to meet the needs they neglected. Like the red knot on the breast of the boy's suit, the strawberries Aschenbach eats represent his mother's nipples, and the fact that those strawberries are overripe suggests she withheld her nipples when he needed them most. That he licks blood in his dream, instead of sucking his mother's milk, similarly suggests that she may have withheld the breast or that he experienced her as destructive. According to Zlotnick-Woldenberg, his strawberries evoke the penis, too, and demonstrate the close association of love, disease, destruction, and death. What is more, Aschenbach himself symbolically brings the epidemic to Venice. By putting Tadzio in danger, failing to tell the boy's family to leave that city, he also risks annihilating the artistic, passionate side of himself. In sum, Zlotnick-Woldenberg thinks Mann says that one must relate to whole objects, not parts, and that artists need to integrate their impulses and their restraint. She also observes that splitting, which destroys Aschenbach, worked successfully for Mann in his projection of himself onto his hero. It seems, she concludes, that Mann struck a better balance between passion and discipline. These conclusions do not break new ground. Furthermore, Tadzio's scorn for the Russian family has political causes. It is not an idealized "demonstration of snobbishness" (545). Rudolph Binion, also in 1997, argued that *Death in Venice* shows how culture is grounded in repression and thus carries a risk of regression. Mann tells how creativity is prone to self-destruct, he maintains, and how "culture is the more tenuous the higher it is pitched" (139). Aschenbach's consciousness shapes physical reality in the novella, moreover, thanks to Mann's expressionistic, dreamlike narrative technique. It is not the case, as Binion thinks, that the revelers in Aschenbach's dream feast on each other's flesh.

Two further psychoanalytic readings were more comprehensive. In 1998, Rodney Symington discussed various psychoanalytic approaches to *Death in Venice,* applying, above all, concepts proposed by Jacques Lacan.

Aschenbach's adherence to Apollinian ideals, Symington says, provides "a near-perfect case history to illustrate Lacanian theory" (135). Aschenbach, he explains, suppresses knowledge of the Other and of the conflict between the Imaginary and the Symbolic. These terms, he adds, suggest what might also be called the unconscious, an ideal ego, and language. Symington concludes that the decline and fall of Mann's hero confirm that we can never know the Real. In 1999, Susanne Widmaier-Haag gave another such interpretation. Widmaier-Haag's summary of other psychoanalytic comments on Mann's story has been noted above, in the introduction. Her own analysis of the work relates Aschenbach's experiences, conflicts, and desires to Mann's biography, especially to his relationship with his mother. For example, she writes that the wanderer both symbolizes Aschenbach's suicidal tendencies and embodies a partial ego of his author. In Aschenbach, she sees Mann's psychological defenses against his own fear of aging and against his homosexual tendencies. Aschenbach regresses, she adds, merging with the sea, an act that suggests a union of mother and child. His vision of the jungle, moreover, is a metaphor for the wish for pre-Oedipal symbiosis with the mother. Mann's mother came from a country across the sea, after all, a tropical landscape like the one that his hero imagines. Venice, too, bears symbolically maternal traits, at once attracting and rejecting. Through Aschenbach, Widmaier-Haag continues, Mann liberates himself from his ambivalent feelings for his attractive yet cool mother and his distant and feared dead father. Neither Mann nor Aschenbach can fully approach the object of his love, according to her, that is, Mann's mother and Tadzio, respectively. Tadzio is also Aschenbach's idealized alter ego, and his defeat when he wrestles with Jaschu, she says, symbolically prepares the way for Aschenbach's own demise. Widmaier-Haag also remarks on Mann's narcissistic personality and on the fact that, from the perspective of ego-psychology, the treatise Aschenbach writes is a sublimation that temporarily stabilizes his self. In contrast to the many psychoanalysts who have interpreted *Death in Venice* in literary ignorance, she is careful to formulate these conclusions as hypotheses and questions rather than as pronouncements.

# Homoeroticism and Mann's Biography

Studies of homoeroticism in *Death in Venice* differed in their insights and tendentiousness. In 1996, Anthony Heilbut contended that "no previous artist had spoken so boldly for homosexuals" (251). Mann's story, he adds, is "a revolutionary breakthrough in the expression of gay desire" and even "a virtual Baedeker's guide to homosexual love" (261). These strong claims are undercut by Heilbut's account of Mann's plot, which he often describes or distorts in ways that make it seem more overtly or more crudely sexual than it is. Heilbut believes the wanderer at the cemetery in Munich is "red-bearded" and has "throbbing neck muscles" (252), for example, but Mann says that he is beardless and that his neck is haggard. Heilbut thinks Aschenbach's story *Ein Elender* tells of a sexual encounter between its hero and his younger rival, and shows its author renouncing sympathy with the abyss for "engagement in the world of normal men" (252), but Mann hardly hints at such an encounter and such a world. Heilbut thinks Aschenbach "swoons" (254) at the sight of Tadzio running out of the water, but Mann says nothing of the kind. Moreover, Plato's *Phaedrus* is not — and Mann does not describe it as — "a Socratic dialogue in which ugly wise men court handsome youths" (255). Heilbut also observes that Aschenbach writes his treatise "within embracing distance of Tadzio's almost-nude body" (255), while Mann notes only that he writes in Tadzio's presence, in sight of his idol. Perhaps Heilbut's tendency to overstatement accounts for his claim that Aschenbach's love for Tadzio is bound up with venereal infections caused by the vice of homosexual prostitution as Aschenbach becomes "a highbrow john teased by his little Polish tramp" (257). In any case, Heilbut calls the females in Aschenbach's dream "women fondling snakes" (257), whereas Mann writes only that these women held them. Heilbut also maintains that whenever Jaschu assaults Tadzio, "the attack borders on rape" (251), but the boys fight only once, when they wrestle at the end of the story, and Mann writes that Tadzio's attempts to shake off Jaschu are convulsive at first, then twitching, not that Aschenbach sees both "their bodies twitching convulsively" (258). Finally, in Mann's last scene, when Tadzio looks over his shoulder at the beach, Heilbut thinks he "turns to view his lover," who has "invisibly embraced him" (258). In the end, in Heilbut's words, "the sexual prowl is revealed as a death trek" (258). The extremely tendentious slant of these remarks discredits Heilbut's entire reading of the novella.

Other studies of *Death in Venice* and homoeroticism sometimes came to less skewed conclusions. In 1996, T. J. Reed argued that the concept of taboo helps explain the reception, genesis, final form, and crucial details of the novella. Reed repeats his earlier claim that Mann's initially drunken song became a moral fable, as Mann himself stated in his *Gesang vom Kindchen* (Song of a Child, 1919). In addition to recalling this "astounding repudiation of an acclaimed work" (126), however, Reed now writes that the novella not only *was* hymnic in origin but also still *is* so in character. Its inner core is hymnic, he explains, a fact that suggests a covert act of defiance behind Mann's overt conformity to public morals. Its fourth chapter ends with the words "I love you," he notes, and its fifth with Aschenbach's being raised to tragic dignity. Mann still labored under the constraint of a taboo, though, as have many of his critics, Reed adds, and his novella is "the story of a frustrated poet" (133). In 1998, Robert Tobin described Mann's life and work from a gay perspective, as he had in 1993 and 1994. Some of his statements about *Death in Venice* are less provocative than the ones he made then, but he still maintains that its initial setting hints at "a gay-friendly story" (222), that its hero "sings the productivity of the closet" (232), and that it shows sexuality to be a linguistic and cultural construct. Searching for its homosexual signifiers, Tobin notes, among other things, that Aschenbach's encounters with homosexual loners lead him to the strange, and thus the queer, Venice. Mann's linking cholera and homosexuality, he adds, suggests an awareness of medical discourses that considered the latter an illness. Klaus Peter Luft, also in 1998, loosely tied the idea and the motif of androgyny to Aschenbach's artistic and homoerotic traits, to Tadzio's sexuality, to the relationship between these characters, and to death.

Further readings of Mann's novella that stressed homoeroticism raised still other issues. In 1998, Gregory Woods wrote that *Death in Venice* shows how men can hero-worship boys. Mann's story frames sexuality, Woods argues: Tadzio is pre- and Aschenbach post-sexual. Woods contrasts the fop with both of them. This grotesque old man shows that Aschenbach is "not a libidinous old queen" (322), but he also shows what Aschenbach might have become. What is more, he foreshadows what Tadzio might become, once his beauty has faded. Both the fop and the boy are coquettish, Woods observes, and the former's repulsive mouth serves to highlight the latter's kissable lips. Aschenbach thinks he sees a Platonic ephebe, Woods adds, but Tadzio is just a kid. Woods also calls Tadzio's "fragile translucency" (322), however, the angelic beauty of a sickly child. Finally, Woods does not think *Death in Venice* especially daring, assuming that its autobiographical revelations are inadvertent. He asks if Mann knew that Aschenbach deceives himself about the purity of his feelings for Tadzio. Scholars better acquainted with Mann's remarks on his tale and with the role of his narrator have answered this question in the affirmative. In 1999, Edward S. Brinkley commented on homoerotic elements in the novella, above all on the series of figures who function as Aschenbach's nemesis. Brinkley reads Mann's story as "culturally contestatory" (4), and his main point seems to be that it is a "social-critical *and* deconstructive take on *Dorian Gray*" (21). Like many other such attempts to offer or combine abstract theoretical approaches to *Death in Venice*, Brinkley's article is often nearly unintelligible. It might conceivably make sense to call the nemesis figures "a collective antifetish" (10), to speak of Mann's "synoptic structurings of epistemology, sexuality, and artistic production" (11), or even to mention Aschenbach's "theorization of Tadzio as *pure form,* as phallic plenitude" (14). It is less than clear, however, that Aschenbach wants "not simply to follow but to *open* Tadzio" (16) or that Mann describes how "the *uses* of form, through whatever theoretical vehicle, *effect* the subjection of *the writing,* of that which is *post*-ulated as subject" (19). In Mann's wording that there is something wild ("etwas . . . Wildes") in the wanderer's attitude, moreover, Brinkley sees a thinly veiled reference to Oscar Wilde. This is an unusually free association. For that matter, Mann neither indicates that the wanderer is young, nor places him "in the graveyard" (9). At the beach, finally, contrary to Brinkley's claim, Aschenbach writes a treatise in Tadzio's presence, not a story. In 2000, Gerald N. Izenberg wrote that *Death in Venice* shows manliness struggling with a feminine passion for transcendence. Writers like Aschenbach battle their own passion, he says, their temptation to surrender and submit. Aschenbach betrays a feminine masochism in his behavior toward Tadzio, moreover, and his style is a lie. By contrast, Mann was aware that his own style was "parasitical upon the 'feminine' temptation of loss of control" (143). Mann's story, Izenberg concludes, highlights the tension between feminine passion and a desire for traditional masculinity.

Homoeroticism also figured, albeit in various ways, in readings of *Death in Venice* given with regard to Mann's biography. In 1996, Doris Alexander wrote that the novella showed Mann coming to terms with the recent suicide of his sister Carla, a provincial actress. Alexander accordingly links Carla and Mahler, whose face was Mann's model for Aschenbach's. The sore throat the composer had while dying, Alexander says, must have been linked in Mann's mind with Carla's gargling after she swallowed cyanide. The facial features of wanderer, gondolier, and street singer, moreover, recall the death's head that Carla kept on her dresser. According to Alexander, the symptoms of cholera, as Mann describes them, are also those of cyanide poisoning. Even the made-up fop on the boat is like his deceased sister, she thinks, who similarly used rouge and cosmetics to accentuate her person. These links between Mann's life and fiction seem tenuous at best, but Alexander concludes that Carla's suicide taught him that art is not always on the side of life and that his homoerotic tendency, too, came from the pull of death. "At the finale of *Death in Venice*," Alexander argues, "Mann stood side by side with Carla" (19). In 1997, Manfred Dierks gave a fictional account of Mann's writing the novella, a paraphrase and pastiche of its events and its language. This account includes snippets from Mann's letters, and it hints at both his homosexual longings and at Dierks's contention, from 1990, that he knew Jensen's *Gradiva* and Freud's interpretation of it while composing his story. Gary Schmidgall added, again in 1997, that Mann later remained excited by the prospect of meeting a real-life Tadzio. A rehearsal or retelling of *Death in Venice* occurred in 1950, Schmidgall says, when Mann was seventy-five and met Franz Westermeier, a young waiter in Zurich. In Schmidgall's view, this episode is an instance of life imitating literature, and the entries in Mann's diaries about it constitute "an important commentary on Mann's masterly novella" (298). Those diaries and the novella, he writes, are both acts of opening and of coming out. Finally, in the most recent major biography of Mann, Hermann Kurzke noted in 1999 that Aschenbach's story of love for a boy could hardly come closer to Mann's own experience. Kurzke is more reserved about this circumstance than scholars who take the story to be its hero's and its author's unambiguous coming out. According to him, it is not improbable that the success of *Death in Venice* can be attributed to the re-admittance of the repressed theme of homoeroticism. The word "success" here refers not to praise or profit, but rather to the novella's having turned out well.

## Other Approaches and Themes

Studies that took other approaches or treated other themes raised a range of further issues. Two considered readings of *Death in Venice*. In 1996, Andrew Harrison and Richard Hibbitt pointed out two mistakes D. H. Lawrence made in his review in 1913. Lawrence wrongly wrote that Mann was then fifty-three, they observe, and that Aschenbach fell ill in Vienna at this same age, instead of at thirty-five. These mistakes show what was on Lawrence's mind at the time, they claim, and facilitate his "rejection of Mann's Flaubertian aesthetic" (443). His other errors are noted in chapter 1. In 1998, Lilian R. Furst stressed other readers' responses to Mann's story, just as she had in 1990, 1991, and 1992. Aschenbach's readers may misunderstand his writing, she argues, and he himself misreads Plato's *Phaedrus*. *Death in Venice* shows "the potential deceptiveness of reading" (162), then, and its readers should construe its meaning more accurately. According to Furst, they can use clues it gives to connect its details and to detect its narrator's sometimes cruel irony. They thus learn to read the novella in a "supralinear manner" (166), and they can experience its theme of deception and betrayal.

Other miscellaneous studies considered various other topics. In 1996, Don Meredith retraced Aschenbach's steps in Venice, visiting the actual sites of Mann's "most perfect work" (45). In 1997, Nicole Meiners related Aschenbach's passive heroes, the stages of his artistic creation, and the androgynous Tadzio to mysticism. The cathartic effect of beauty and nature, Meiners believes, enables Aschenbach, who is mystically inclined, to recognize his Orphic depths, which transport him into creative ecstasy. Meiners always misspells Tadzio's name as "Tazido." Visual perception and communication in the novella were analyzed by Angelika Schaller, again in 1997. Schaller's remarks on the role of eyes in Aschenbach's silent encounter with Tadzio, and her conclusions about how the gaze structures *Death in Venice*, barely go beyond the ones Frey made and drew in 1968. She notes that Aschenbach's looking at Tadzio leads to falling in love, that his desirous staring alternates with Apollinian visions, that Tadzio flirts by raising or lowering his eyes as women would, that visual lust substitutes for verbal or physical contact, and that looking even takes the place of living. She also observes that Aschenbach averts his eyes from characters who represent Charon and that the novella both begins and ends with a visual encounter. More originally, Schaller adds that *Death in Venice* displays Hellenistic notions of visual bliss, especially those found in Plato's *Phaedrus* and *Symposium*, and that eyes function as a mirror in Aschenbach's and Tadzio's shared narcissism. She faults Visconti's film for its less subtle handling of ocular language. She also notes the many objects in the novella that are gray, which she calls the color of nothingness and death.

Two such miscellaneous readings raised the issue of semiotics. In 1999, Olaf Schwarz argued that Aschenbach's trip is semiotic insofar as it depicts his becoming conscious of what he has repressed. This trip, Schwarz argues, is the external, topographical equivalent of an internal, psychological process leading to self-knowledge. Aschenbach's spatially concrete change of location, in other words, corresponds to a spatially metaphorical expansion of awareness. Schwarz discusses similar trips in Jensen's *Gradiva* and in Musil's *Die Vollendung der Liebe* (The Consummation of Love, 1911). Holger A. Pausch and Diana Spokiene, again in 1999, analyzed the language of fashion in Mann's story. The clothes worn by Tadzio, his mother, and his sisters, Pausch and Spokiene explain, correspond to their high social status. Aschenbach's suits signal such status and his intelligence, they add, and he dresses less conservatively in order to attract Tadzio. Mann's language of fashion is thus a semiotic system.

## Film, Opera, Ballet, and Texts

Like their predecessors in earlier periods, scholars writing about Visconti's film between 1996 and 2001 differed in their opinions of how it treats Mann's story. In 1996, Jeanne-Marie Clerc commented on how the film deviates from Mann in its use of the myth of Faust. In flashbacks showing an hourglass and discussing beauty, Clerc writes, Visconti both expands and transforms themes present in the novella. He rereads it in light of Mann's *Doktor Faustus,* that is, which is a fundamental intertext in the film. According to Clerc, Visconti's hourglass, unlike the one Mann mentions, introduces the theme of Faustian dissatisfaction and a sense of tragic fatality foreign to the novella. His discussion of beauty, moreover, is Faustian, not Platonic. In Clerc's view, that discussion is even the dialogue with the devil reported in *Doktor Faustus.* The themes of death and of artistic creativity, Clerc concludes, thereby acquire new meanings in the film. In 1997, Natalya Todd argued that the medium of film enables one to grasp Aschenbach's sensual aestheticism better than Mann ever could have dreamed. Mann's symbolic colors achieve their full potential only in film, Todd explains, and Visconti's images and soundtrack correspond to Aschenbach's sensitivity to the visual and the auditory. Giorgio Bertellini, in 1997 as well, discussed Mann's and Visconti's versions of decadence. According to him, Mann's novella is "a major decadent literary work" (17). Mann's portrayal of artists' problematic status in bourgeois society is both "an act of ideological resistance" (13), moreover, and a "radicalization of post-Romantic aesthetics and artistry" (15). Bertellini's choice of words seems even trendier when he writes that Aschenbach is "engaged in research" (14) within the agony of bourgeois probity and has been "theorizing" (14) himself as a disciplined and dignified hero. According to William van Watson, again in 1997, both Mann and Visconti use modernist discourses legitimizing the taboo of homosexual pederastic desire. Both, he explains, exploit the aesthetic to validate the erotic. Van Watson's article is riddled with mistakes that seem to result from reading the novella in this way. The bacchanal that occurs in Aschenbach's dream, for example, includes women, not just "satyrs and male youths" (335). When Aschenbach says "It must be kept quiet," as Lowe-Porter writes, he is speaking about news of the cholera epidemic, not about homosexuality, and there is no "it" at all in Mann's German, which says "Man soll schweigen" (One should keep silent). What is more, Mann did not project his homosexuality onto Mahler, nor did he have difficulty deciding whether Aschenbach looked like Mahler or himself. Van Watson thinks he did, arguing that Mann describes Aschenbach in one passage as having red hair and light skin and being of medium height, but in another as short and dark. In fact, only the second of these passages is about him. The first describes the wanderer at the cemetery in Munich. For that matter, contrary to what van Watson writes, Katia Mann was Thomas Mann's wife, not his daughter. Finally, in 1998, Michael Wilson wrote that Visconti's use of the zoom lens is equivalent to Mann's free indirect style (a narrative mode that oscillates between a character's and a narrator's point of view). Like Mann, Wilson says, Visconti conveys an attitude toward Aschenbach that is ambivalent, an attitude that combines sympathy and irony.

Three scholars commented on Mann's story and Britten's opera, and one mentioned Flemming Flindt's ballet. Each of the three thought Britten changed that story in an important way. In 1997, Daniel Fischlin claimed that the opera obscures, diminishes, and poeticizes the political and historical context Mann indicates. That context, though, is not as explicit as Fischlin seems to think when he explains that the novella articulates a sense of the fanatic, frenzied, irrational, and inhuman German self, or that Aschenbach's homoerotic desires "proclaim him as the 'liberal-decadent' threatening fascist purity, transparency, and homogeneity" (219). Mann clearly hints at historical circumstances, though, and Fischlin is on firmer ground when he does not try so hard to write "post-fascist criticism" (216). It is true, for example, that "Aschenbach's interiority always has a cultural context" (224). What is more, Fischlin is not the only scholar who thinks Mann links his hero's homoeroticism to a German nationalist ideology. Historical conditions do not appear to have shaped Aschenbach's sexual identity, however, to the extreme political extent Fischlin at times suggests. In 1999, Daniel Kempton noted that there is no basis in Mann's story for the representation of sport, for the five athletic contests Britten stages in the scene he entitled "The Games of Apollo." The physical delicacy essential to Mann's Tadzio, Kempton says, "ill assorts with the athletic prowess Britten bestows on him" (56). This prowess, he adds, was meant to calm cultural anxieties caused in Britten's England by Aschenbach's homoeroticism. Edward W. Said, again in 1999, argued that Britten omits Mann's irony, both the irony that separates Mann from his narrator and the irony that separates this narrator from Aschenbach. Said makes the mistake of relying on Lowe-Porter's translation when he explains how Mann's narrator refers to Aschenbach as "our adventurer." As noted above, in connection with Bouson's misinterpretation of the novella in 1989, Mann does not use the possessive pronoun "our" here. Said also seems sure that Aschenbach dies in his chair at the beach. In fact, Mann says only that he collapses there, adding that he is then carried to his room and that his death is announced on the same day. What is more, Said wrongly thinks that Mann wrote nothing in the ten years after *Death in Venice* was published. Like many critics and scholars who have only a passing acquaintance with the novella and its author, he also misstates the year in which *Death in Venice* appeared, giving that year as 1911 instead of 1912. In 1998, Diane Solway wrote that Rudolf Nureyev could identify with Aschenbach's obsession with a beautiful boy when he danced the leading role in Flemming Flindt's ballet *Death in Venice*. The ballet was first performed in Verona, Italy, in May 1991.

A final category of research done on *Death in Venice* from 1996 to 2001 concerned its text. In 1996, Terence James Reed reported that Fischer, Mann's German publisher, had recently used for its paperback editions of the novella an earlier version of the text than the one that initially appeared in *Die neue Rundschau* in October and November of 1912, then again in the trade edition published by Fischer in 1913, and then in every edition ever since. This other, earlier version, Reed discovered, was the one contained in the limited luxury edition published by Hans von Weber and dated, perhaps inaccurately, 1912. Reed tells how these two different texts came about, arguing that the one published by von Weber is both inferior and inadmissible. Mann may have been interested in publishing *Death in Venice* in von Weber's bibliophile edition, according to Reed, because he had doubts about how well it would be received. In any event, Reed explains that he first sent his text to von Weber, then made a few significant revisions in passages that von Weber had already printed. The text he later sent to *Die neue Rundschau* contained these revisions, and this second or revised text was published first. Its most important emendations, Reed adds, occur in Mann's descriptions of Aschenbach's vision in Munich. They eliminate the presence of the narrator, he explains, and thus show Mann's attempt to convey the power and the immediacy of that vision, and to do so in a single sentence. A further result of these emendations is that Aschenbach's vision

# Conclusion

I N THE NINETY YEARS since it was published, Thomas Mann's *Death in Venice* has been taken, and sometimes made, to mean many things. The wide variety of all the reviews, articles, books, and other sources surveyed in the foregoing five chapters, in fact, not to mention their large number, make the reception of Mann's story too complex to be summed up in a single narrative. Like any great work of fiction, that story is far richer than any one critical approach or scholarly method. When passed through the force field of its prose, so to speak, almost any such approach or method lights up, but none illuminates more than part of it. Similarly, an account of its reception that emphasizes only its homoerotic, psychoanalytical, or political aspect — the aspects treated by the most extensive studies of that reception to date — must necessarily neglect other issues that critics and scholars have raised. Those issues include its concepts of aesthetics and artists, its links to Mann's other writings, the myths and sources it incorporates, its similarity to works by other writers, its style and symbols and its place in literary history, its philosophical import, its miscellaneous details, its adaptations in other media, and its editions as well as its translations. Any full account of how the novella has been received needs to include all of these other issues. The foregoing chapters do so. This concluding chapter recalls how such issues persist and how the various periods in the reception of *Death in Venice* differ. It also remarks on the quantity and quality of the criticism and scholarship that raise those issues and constitute that reception. Finally, though it avoids simplifying the variety of responses to *Death in Venice* in a single, limited narrative, this conclusion ends with a retelling of the novella, a retelling that combines the critics' and scholars' mistakes noted throughout this book. The result is a single narrative after all, then, but a narrative that is — or at least once was — Mann's own. In a nutshell, this retelling suggests the many ways in which *Death in Venice*, to judge from what has been written about it, has been read.

Many of the issues raised and approaches taken in the long and complex reception of *Death in Venice* have remained more or less the same over the years. Studies that focus on aesthetics, artists, and Mann's other writings routinely relate the events of the novella to decadence, modernism, or Platonic concepts of beauty. They also tell how Aschenbach is and is not like Mann's other heroes — above all, Tonio Kröger — or how he resembles or differs from Mann himself, for better or worse. Studies that discuss the myths and

sources Mann used or that draw comparisons between his story and fiction by
other writers often note his allusions and indebtedness to ancient Greek or
modern German authors, especially to Homer, Plato, Euripides, Platen, and
Goethe. These studies also compare or contrast *Death in Venice* with Conrad's
*Heart of Darkness,* Gide's, *L'immoraliste,* D'Annunzio's *Il Fuoco,* and Yukio
Mishima's *Kinjiki,* to name only four of the many titles they mention. Studies
about the style, symbols, or structure of Mann's novella help explain its syntax,
diction, images, irony, characters, and leitmotifs. They also connect it to the
tradition of its genre and to movements in literary history such as naturalism
and neoclassicism. At times, such studies claim that *Death in Venice* contains
some of the most beautiful German ever written. They also often distinguish
Aschenbach from his author. Studies approaching Mann's story from philosophical, political, or psychoanalytic angles, by contrast, tend to apply less
strictly literary concepts. Nietzsche has never gone out of style in philosophical
readings of that story. Political readings, which were often nationalistic at first,
now invoke Max Weber more often than Karl Marx, but they still almost
always portray Aschenbach as the ugly German, that is, as Prussian, bourgeois,
and even proto-fascist. Psychoanalytic readings cite Freud, Adler, Jung, Klein,
and Lacan in remarks on the mental life of Mann, his hero, and his readers.
The authors of these readings are sometimes actual psychoanalysts, and these
doctors regularly fail to appreciate that Mann's story is literary fiction. Studies
that concentrate on homoeroticism have attacked, defended, ignored, down-
played, and defined it. Some of these studies can be extremely polemic. Homoeroticism also figures in remarks that link *Death in Venice* to Mann's
biography and to other issues. Further studies treat other themes or take other
approaches. These studies are frequently innovative, and their themes include
Venice and Tadzio's name, among many others. Studies that discuss Visconti's
film, Britten's opera, other artistic adaptations of Mann's story, or the editions
and translations of Mann's text show how *Death in Venice* has been transformed in other arts, other media, and other languages. Related studies raise
the issue of music, most notably in comments on how Aschenbach is and is
not like Wagner or Mahler. All these many issues seem to be perennial.

 Each of the five chronological periods into which the reception of *Death
in Venice* has been divided in this book nonetheless differs from the others.
Each of those periods has its own distinct profile, so to speak, one that
shows the emphases and developments peculiar to it. The initial reactions of
1913–14 were marked by several literary disputes and by attacks on Aschenbach and his author. Reviewers' personal and political motivations often
informed their remarks, and those remarks made *Death in Venice* an object
of controversy. The novella was critically as well as commercially successful,
but it was not universally praised or recommended. Its increasing acceptance
from 1915 to 1955 is reflected in many social, political, and cultural interpretations; in the great interest scholars took in its symbolism; in reviews of

its English and French translations; and in the often conflicting remarks on it by Mann himself that were published or otherwise public during his lifetime. Posthumous praise of *Death in Venice* in the twenty years after its author died, from 1956 to 1975, resulted partly from access to his archives and correspondence and from the popularity it enjoyed thanks to Visconti's film and, to a lesser extent, Britten's opera. The further developments occurring from 1976 to 1995 included a renewed emphasis on its homoerotic component, an emphasis that coincided with, and can partly be attributed to, the publication of Mann's diaries. The most notable of the recent trends observable between 1996 and 2001 has been the rise of culturally sensitive studies that apply the concepts of colonialism and orientalism. While much in the reception of *Death in Venice* has remained constant, then, much has also changed along with the times, tastes, and documents that have affected critics' and scholars' concerns. Whether the historical-critical edition of Mann's works that is now being published will occasion new interpretations remains to be seen.

Meanwhile, the current state of scholarship on *Death in Venice* can be judged from four articles in *The Cambridge Companion to Thomas Mann*, a book that has just appeared in 2002. The authors of these articles interpret the novella under the rubrics of history, literary techniques, gender and sexuality, and classicism. T. J. Reed describes its place in history, both social and political. Regarding the first, he calls the novella a classic of homosexual passion, one that has "probably done more to edge homosexuality into the common culture than any other single work of art" (5). Regarding the second, Reed adds that Aschenbach's solutions to his artistic conundrum later struck Mann himself as a clear "proto-fascist syndrome" (6). Michael Minden notes Mann's literary techniques, remarking that *Death in Venice* displays a "liminal quality" (50), a balance of two opposing value systems. Minden seems to mean the ambiguity of form, which is said in the novella to be both moral and immoral. Andrew J. Webber wrote that Mann combines the performance of gender and sexual identity with Freudian strategies of representing unconscious desires. Aschenbach and the old fop both engage in a "masquerade of aberrant sexuality," he argues, and in a "burlesque theater of sexual performance" (77). What is more, Webber relates Mann's vocabulary to Freud's: "Triebwerk" (engine, mechanism) to sexual drives, "Entstellung" (disfigurement) to distortion, and "das Verworfene" (the rejected) to the repressed. What Mann refers to as Aschenbach's "Traumlogik" (dream-logic) is thus Freudian. Webber also contends that Mann conflates Nietzsche and Freud in a strategic contamination of "Rausch" (intoxication) and "Rauschen" (the rushing sound of the sea). The camera abandoned on the beach at the end of Mann's story, he adds, is an apparatus of reproduction that recalls the vain attempt of the young Baltic woman, the one on the beach with the Russian family, to capture the sea in a painting.

The sea is an archetypal object that stands for the morally unspeakable subject of Mann's story, moreover, and its incommensurability suggests resistance to articulating that subject. Mann's final image of Tadzio gesturing toward the transcendent, though, is an allegory of the representability of homosexual passion. While Webber calls Aschenbach a "rearguard classicist" (73), Ritchie Robertson points out the strengths, weaknesses, and pitfalls of his classicism. Aschenbach is a "devotee of classicism" (97), Robertson claims, and thus part of a German literary tradition represented by Winckelmann, Goethe, and Platen. This German fascination with ancient Greece and its sculpture, Robertson adds, includes sensual desire as well as aesthetic appreciation, and Aschenbach's classicism has an unacknowledged underside in his romantic affinities and his repressed emotions. With their various emphases — and with their occasional lapses into academic jargon — these four articles attest to innovation as well as continuity in the reception of Mann's novella.

Looking back on how the many issues raised in the reception of *Death in Venice* both have and have not changed, literary scholars may be moved to reflect on their profession, especially if they are Germanists. This is because they may be struck by the enormous quantity of research on the novella as well by its sometimes poor quality. They may also note that this research is now written mostly in English. The number of studies of *Death in Venice* is so vast that few such scholars seem able to keep up with it. Perhaps this is why many of them do not bother to do their homework, that is, to see what has already been written about the novella, and why many simply rediscover or repeat what was already known. In any case, much research on the novella is unnecessary or redundant. A good deal of it is mediocre, moreover, and some of it is nonsense. This state of affairs seems to have many causes. Some scholars do not get the facts of Mann's plot straight. Others are unduly convinced that those facts prove one or another pet theory. Some speak in jargon that would baffle general readers and probably most colleagues, too. Others take an interest in Mann's biography that borders on the prurient and the sensational. One may perhaps be consoled by knowing how quickly the most inaccurate and tendentious readings of *Death in Venice* age. Such readings seem dated after only a short time. One may also notice that most research on the novella is more or less solid. It is sometimes even original. In rare instances, it can be a pleasant surprise. Telling the wheat from the chaff can be difficult at first, but one can start to do so by observing the following rule: Beware of any book or article in which Aschenbach's first name is "Gustave." This spelling — with an *e* at the end — is not Mann's, and it hints that the author of such a book or article has read *Death in Venice* in English translation, probably in Lowe-Porter's. The egregious errors that can result from relying on such a translation have often been noted in this book. This misspelling of "Gustav" may well also mean that such an author is ignorant of all the studies of the novella that are written in German. The relative number of those studies, however, has been declining. Compare the first and last periods studied here, for example, the initial reactions of 1913–14 and the recent trends of 1996–2001. The proportion of studies written in German has shrunk dramatically. Ninety percent of the earlier ones were in German, but less than thirty percent of the more recent ones are. In the later period, moreover, over twice as many books and articles on *Death in Venice* appeared in English as in German. The reasons for this striking shift are complex, of course, and reflect more than a change in Mann's audience. At least part of this shift, though, can be attributed to the appeal of his story itself and to the way in which its fame has spread. That appeal has long been international, thanks to Mann's tale and to how well he tells it. Its fame now seems to precede it, moreover, coming from preconceived ideas of its message rather than from careful reading of its words. While *Death in Venice* may be known ever more widely, then, it is not always known very well. Literary scholars, alas, sometimes not only disseminate but also distort it.

One way to sum up the extensive and imperfect reception of *Death in Venice* is to retell it according to some reviewers', critics', and scholars' mistaken notions of its fictional facts. These authors misstate more than a few of those facts, and their reasons for doing so are revealing. The many mistakes they make about Aschenbach have to do with his name, his vision of a tropical landscape, his writings, his professional and his personal life, his thoughts, his actions, his orgiastic dream, his visit to the barber, and his death. Tadzio's name, age, mother, and reaction to Aschenbach have all likewise been misconstrued. The treatise Aschenbach writes in sight of Tadzio at the beach has also been misunderstood, as have many other details of Mann's story. These mistakes seem to occur for several reasons. Some critics and scholars are careless, foolish, or ignorant. Others are overly zealous when defaming or defending Mann's story. Still others appear to have been misled by adhering to an abstract theory or doctrine. This is the case especially often among psychoanalysts, Marxist critics, and true believers in deconstruction. Further mistakes result from mistranslations. Sometimes, the fault for such mistakes lies with the author of a particular review, book, or article. More often, it lies with the translation that such an author cites. In both cases, the letter and spirit of *Death in Venice* become distorted. While general readers understandably rely on translations, moreover, it is hard to believe that serious scholars do, for more than a few of their arguments simply fall apart because they quote Lowe-Porter's words, which are often not the equivalent of Mann's. Even Mann's German is sometimes taken to mean things it does not say — or does not say as crudely or crassly as some critics and scholars think. Finally, some mistakes come from the many changes to *Death in Venice* made in Visconti's film. Some readers wrongly think that Mann tells what Visconti shows, or that he does so in just the same manner. In Mann's story, for example, Aschenbach has Mahler's facial features but is also a composite figure whose career, art, and homoeroticism mix traits of Frederick the Great, Goethe, Platen, Wagner, and Mann himself, at the very least. Like Lowe-Porter's translation, Visconti's film thus seems to be a mixed blessing. Both have made *Death in Venice* known to a larger audience than the one that presumably could — and would — read it in German. Both take considerable liberties with it, however, creating and leaving many impressions that Mann does not. This trade-off may be acceptable, but ignoring it leads to misunderstandings.

So how does *Death in Venice* sound when told in the erroneous way that some reviewers, critics, and scholars seem to prefer, in other words, when one retells it by combining their mistakes? Well, it sounds like this:

*Chapter One*

In April 1909, Georg Achenbach met a wanderer in a mausoleum near an oriental church in the doorway of a graveyard opposite the North Cemetery. This man had a red beard, strawberry-colored eyes, and throbbing neck muscles. He was young, and he made a lewd gesture with his lips. Achenbach envisioned a rank African scene. He was searching for a new and a manly kind of hero. He decided to go to Venice, where he planned to spend a quiet summer. At home, he dyed his beard and hair. He was in his fortieth year.

*Chapter Two*

Achenbach was an unknown middle-class writer, a national figure to whom foreign countries paid homage. As an artist and an author, before he got so tired and deviant, he had tried to please, and had been inspired by, the feminine sex. His rejection of knowledge and his subsequent moral resoluteness were a clear victory of ethics over doubt and intellectualism. He taught his readers (and himself) not to dwell in the abyss of superficial psychological understanding. He lived life like a clenched fish.

Achenbach's work consisted primarily of formal German prose history and biography. It included a novel called *Der Elende*. His writings were excerpted in German schoolbooks because he enunciated noble ethical principles. He castigated immorality by writing stories fit for school syllabuses and for making children decent citizens. His writing was also folksy *Heimatkunst*.

Achenbach had been ennobled by an emperor who considered him one of the most representative minds of his country, by the German Kaiser, actually, who thus rewarded him for supporting the reactionary ideas of the Hohenzollerns. After being knighted, he moved from Silesia to Bavaria. He had also won a distinguished literary award.

Achenbach was an old professor, a historian, and a musician. He was still married. He and his wife had been childless, and his child was dead. His mother had been the daughter of a composer. His father was a German clergyman.

Achenbach had an aristocratically hooked nose. He had red hair and light skin and was of medium height. He was also short and dark.

### Chapter Three

Achenbach made an abortive decision to go to Trieste. On his journey south, he yearned for the north. In fact, he got to Venice by traveling north from Munich. Before arriving in that Italian city, he vacationed on the island of Pola, which he left because he was bored to the point of extinction.

He went to the other side of the boat carrying him to Venice from Trieste, trying to avoid a flirtatious old man who had been mingling with a crowd of young Poles. This man talked to him about love for a woman, teased him about his mistress, and called him "sweetie."

Achenbach thought of a poet who had earlier arrived in Venice and who had sung its praises. That poet was Byron and Dante.

Achenbach's gondolier made no concession and was sent off by the hotel staff.

Achenbach was disappointed by the cloudy sky when he got to his hotel, the Hotel Excelsior. Most of the guests there were American, English, or Russian.

Soon after arriving at that hotel, he spied Tazido, Tadzin, Tandzio, Taju, or Adgio, a Polite boy of twelve, thirteen, or fifteen, on the beach. The boy's mother was mildly tolerating and even reluctantly encouraging in the ways of the woman eternally divided against herself. The only thing gray besides the boy's eyes was Achenbach's hair.

Achenbach dismissed Tazido's, Tadzin's, Tandzio's, Taju's, or Adgio's wrestling with a Russian rival as childish fanaticism. He once saw him swimming completely undressed. The boy was a primeval legend and made Delphic utterances.

Achenbach had suffered a heart attack and went to Venice to convalesce. Once there, he was in a drug-induced state like that of Odysseus among the lotus-eaters.

Achenbach wanted to leave Venice because he disliked its greed. After returning from its train station, he was given the same room at his hotel.

### Chapter Four

Struck by Tazido's, Tadzin's, Tandzio's, Taju's, or Adgio's beauty, which spoke to him in the language of pictures, Achenbach wrote two pages about the fatal power of eros, a treatise about art and taste that liberated the boy into words, a book that translated him into an enraptured essay on aesthetic theory. With his image of the boy in that story about how the erotic is intrinsic to the impulse toward creation, Achenbach tried to grasp the boy's beauty and to seize and possess him in a frankly pornographic eulogy.

Achenbach would not admit that Tazido, Tadzin, Tandzio, Taju, or Adgio was internally unsound. When he once found himself walking behind him on the path to the beach, the boy glanced at him, almost spoke to him, and then swung slowly around one of the poles supporting an awning.

After Tazido, Tadzin, Tandzio, Taju, or Adgio came home one night and smiled at him, Achenbach threw himself on the darkened beach in an absurd, abject frenzy and mumbled a fervent declaration of love at the boy's door. Whispering that he loved him, Achenbach was quite unmanned.

*Chapter Five*

German papers leaked news of the plague in Venice one day but denied it the next.

Tazido, Tadzin, Tandzio, Taju, or Adgio responded with a sigh to Achenbach's glance after a group of street musicians had entertained the hotel guests. Achenbach liked their music because passion makes people relax.

Achenbach then dreamed of phallic women and instances of cannibalism. In fact, the revelers in his dream feasted on each other's flesh.

Our traveler, our solitary, and our adventurer was seventy-three years old, and his hair had turned white by the time he went to the barber. His lips, by contrast, became the color of ripe strawberries.

Achenbach stumbled onto the beach for a final look at Tazido, Tadzin, Tandzio, Taju, or Adgio. As the boy moved out to sea, he fastened his gaze only on Achenbach, whose make-up was running down his face.

Achenbach stayed in Venice after Tazido, Tadzin, Tandzio, Taju, or Adgio had left. Just when his passion for the boy would have made them better acquainted, he committed suicide by walking to his death in the sea. He was at the height of his powers and, at the time of his death, he was making notes for his next work, *Death in Venice*.

# Bibliography

## 1913

Alberts, Wilhelm. *Thomas Mann und sein Beruf.* Leipzig: Xenien, 1913.

Bab, Julius. "Dem Dichter Thomas Mann." *Die Schaubühne* 9.6 (6 February 1913): 167–71.

Benn, Joachim. "Thomas Mann und 'Der Tod in Venedig.'" *Die Rheinlande* 23 (1913): 307–11.

Braun, Felix. "Rundschau: Deutsche Prosa." *Österreichische Rundschau* 37.5 (1 December 1913): 426–33.

Broch, Hermann. "Philistrosität, Realismus, Idealismus der Kunst." *Der Brenner* 3.9 (1 February 1913): 399–415. Reprinted in his *Gesammelte Werke,* vol. 10, *Die unbekannte Grösse und frühe Schriften,* edited by Ernst Schönwiese, 237–50. Zurich: Rhein, 1961. Also in *Hermann Broch: Kommentierte Werkausgabe,* edited by Paul Michael Lützeler, vol. 9/1, *Schriften zur Literatur 1: Kritik,* 13–29. Frankfurt am Main: Suhrkamp, 1991.

Bródy, Sándor. "Egy könyvről." *Az Újság* 11.142 (15 June 1913): 37–38. Translated by Irene Kolbe as "Über ein Buch" in *Thomas Mann und Ungarn,* edited by Antal Mádl and Judit Győri, 272–74. Cologne: Böhlau, 1977.

Brüll, Oswald. "Thomas Manns neues Buch." *Der Merker* 4.10 (2. Mai-Heft 1913): 375–80. Reprint, Scarsdale, NY: Schnase, 1970.

———. "Eine Schmähschrift gegen Thomas Mann: Erwiderung von Oswald Brüll." *Der Merker* 4.24 (2. Dezember-Heft 1913): 945–53. Reprint, Scarsdale, NY: Schnase, 1970.

Busse, Carl. "Neues vom Büchertisch." *Velhagen & Klasings Monatshefte* 27.10 (June 1913): 309–13.

Dallago, Carl. "Gegenüberstellung." *Der Brenner* 3.10 (15 February 1913): 442–49.

Dohm, Hedwig. "'Der Tod in Venedig': Novelle von Thomas Mann." *Der Tag,* 23 February 1913.

Eckardt, Johannes. "Thomas Manns Novelle 'Der Tod in Venedig.'" *Über den Wassern* 6.5 (May 1913): 263–72.

Ehrenstein, Albert. "Der Tod in Venedig." *Der Sturm* 4.164–65 (June 1913): 44. Reprint, Nendeln, Liechtenstein: Kraus, 1970.

F[ischer], Ödön Halasi. "Thomas Mann." *Világ,* 31 August 1913, 33–34. Translated by Irene Kolbe as "Thomas Mann" in *Thomas Mann und Ungarn,* edited by Antal Mádl and Judit Győri, 276–80. Cologne: Böhlau, 1977. Translation reprinted in Hansen and Heine, 1983, 28–34.

Frank, Bruno. "Thomas Mann: Eine Betrachtung nach dem 'Tod in Venedig.'" *Die Neue Rundschau* 24 (1913): 656–69. [N.B. Other remarks by Frank, made at about the same time that this review appeared, are included, in English, in Neider, 1947, 119–23, and entitled "Death in Venice." The English text is not a translation of this review, though Neider's acknowledgments say that it is. Those acknowledgments also say that the review had originally appeared in the *Wuerttemberger Zeitung* in 1913. The English text may thus be a translation of a different and an earlier review that Frank had written for this German newspaper. The translation is by E. B. Ashton.]

Freksa, Friedrich. "Thomas Mann der Epiker." *Die Zeit im Bild* 11 (1913): 772–73.

Friedrich, Paul. *Thomas Mann.* Berlin: Borngräber/Neues Leben, 1913.

"Goethe und Fräulein Lade." *Frankfurter Zeitung,* 7 October 1913, 1. Reprinted in Hansen and Heine, 1983, 40 n. 5.

Goth, Ernst. *"Der Tod in Venedig:* Novelle von Thomas Mann." *Pester Lloyd,* 30 March 1913, 28.

Götz [Bruno Goetz]. "Literar. Neuerscheinungen: Anlässlich Thomas Manns 'Tod in Venedig.'" *Die Aktion* 3 (28 May 1913): 559–60. Reprint, Stuttgart: J. G. Cotta'sche Buchhandlung Nachf., 1961.

Hamann, E. M. "Aus neuer Erzählliteratur." *Paul Kellers Monatsblätter: Die Bergstadt* 1.12 (September 1913): 1090–94.

Heilborn, Ernst. "Sterbens-Orgie." *Das literarische Echo* 15 (1913): 1039–41.

Hellpach, Willy. "Der Dichter und sein Werk: Um Thomas Manns 'Der Tod in Venedig.'" *Berliner Tageblatt,* 22 October 1913, 1–2.

Herwig, Franz. "Neue Romane." *Hochland* 10 (July 1913): 488–91.

Heymel, Alfred Walter. "Gespräch über den 'Tod in Venedig.'" *Frankfurter Zeitung,* 3 August 1913, 1–2.

Hofmiller, Josef. "Thomas Manns neue Erzählung." *Süddeutsche Monatshefte* 10 (May 1913): 218–32. Reprinted as "Thomas Manns 'Tod in Venedig'" in *Merkur* 9.6 (June 1955): 505–20. Also in *Interpretationen,* edited by Jost Schillemeit, vol. 4, *Deutsche Erzählungen von Wieland bis Kafka,* 303–18. Frankfurt am Main: Fischer, 1966. Also in Hofmiller's *Ausgewählte Werke,* 326–43. Rosenheim: Rosenheimer Verlagshaus, 1975.

Huebner, Friedrich Markus. "Der Fall Bernd Isemann." *Der Sturm* 4.173–74 (August 1913): 87.

Hübner, Fritz. "Der Tod in Venedig: Novelle von Thomas Mann." *Der Bücherwurm* 3.7 (April 1913): 213–14.

Hülsen, Hans von. "Der Tod in Venedig: Novelle von Thomas Mann." *Münchner Neueste Nachrichten,* 10 March 1913, 3.

Isemann, Bernd. *Thomas Mann und Der Tod in Venedig: Eine kritische Abwehr.* Munich: Bonsels, 1913.

Joelsohn, Hermann. "Vom Künstler und vom Bürger: Anläßlich Thomas Manns Novelle 'Der Tod in Venedig.'" *Wiecker Bote* 1.1 (1913): 6–10.

Kerr, Alfred. "Tagebuch." *Pan* 3.27 (11 April 1913): 635–41. Reprint, Nendeln, Liechtenstein: Kraus, 1975.

Korrodi, Eduard. "Thomas Mann: Der Tod in Venedig." *Wissen und Leben* 12 (1 April–15 September 1913): 690–94.

Lawrence, D. H. "German Books." *The Blue Review* 1.3 (July 1913): 200–206. Reprinted in *Phoenix: The Posthumous Papers of D. H. Lawrence,* edited by Edward D. McDonald, 308–13. London: Heinemann, 1936. Also in *D. H. Lawrence: Selected Literary Criticism,* edited by Anthony Beal, 260–65. London: Heinemann; New York: Viking, 1956.

M., F. "Zwei Erzähler." *Neue Zürcher Zeitung,* 31 August 1913, Blatt 1.

Mann, Heinrich. "Der Tod in Venedig: Novelle von Thomas Mann." *März* 7.13 (29 March 1913): 478–79. Reprinted in *Thomas Mann im Urteil seiner Zeit: Dokumente 1891–1955,* edited by Klaus Schröter, 65–66. Hamburg: Wegner, 1969. Translated by Don Reneau in *Letters of Heinrich and Thomas Mann, 1900–1949,* edited by Hans Wysling, 269–71. Berkeley: U of California P, 1998.

Martens, Kurt. "Bücher-Besprechungen: 'Der Tod in Venedig,' Novelle von Thomas Mann." *Der Zwiebelfisch* 5.1 (1913): 62–63.

Meyer, Richard M. "Literarische Kunst." In *Das Jahr 1913: Ein Gesamtbild der Kulturentwicklung,* edited by D. Sarason, 465–79. Leipzig: Teubner, 1913.

r. "Das neue Buch Arthur Schnitzlers." *Neue Freie Presse,* 22 June 1913, 31.ˉ

Schumann, Wolfgang. "Zwei Novellen." *Kunstwart und Kulturwart* 27.4 (Zweites Novemberheft 1913): 305–8.

Stieve, Friedrich. "Ein offenes Wort an Herrn von Aschenbach." *Die Gegenwart* 42, vol. 84, no. 49 (6 December 1913): 774–76.

"Thomas Mann: A Világ irodalmi estélye." *Világ,* 7 December 1913, 15–17. Translated by Irene Kolbe as "Thomas Mann: Literaturabend der Zeitung 'Világ'" in *Thomas Mann und Ungarn,* edited by Antal Mádl and Judit Györi, 284–86. Cologne: Böhlau, 1977.

"Thomas Mann-nál: Az író új novellájáról és a modern magyar líráról." *Pesti Napló,* 14 September 1913, 8. Excerpted and translated as "Goethe und 'Der Tod in Venedig'" in *Frankfurter Zeitung,* 5 October 1913, 1–2. Translated in full by Géza Engl as "Bei Thomas Mann: Der Schriftsteller über seine neue Novelle und über die moderne ungarische Lyrik" in Hansen and Heine, 1983, 35–41.

Tóth, Vanda. "Disputa: Levél a szerkesztőhöz." *Nyugat* 6.13 (1 July 1913), vol. 2, 62–69. Translated by Irene Kolbe as "Disput" in *Thomas Mann und Ungarn,* edited by Antal Mádl and Judit Györi, 274–76. Cologne: Böhlau, 1977.

Wendriner, Karl Georg. "Thomas Mann: 'Der Tod in Venedig.' Novelle." *Berliner Tageblatt,* 23 April 1913, Literarische Rundschau, 1.

z., p. [Zifferer, Paul.] "Der Tod in Venedig." *Neue Freie Presse,* 8 June 1913, 31–32.

# 1914

Bertaux, Félix. "*Der Tod in Venedig* par Thomas Mann." *La Nouvelle Revue Française* 6.68 (1 August 1914): 338–42.

Haecker, Theodor. "Die müde Nazarenerseele." *Der Brenner* 4.13 (1 April 1914): 611–14.

———. "Vorworte/von Sören Kierkegaard." *Der Brenner* 4.14–15 (1 May 1914): 666–70.

Hiller, Kurt. "Wo bleibt der homoerotische Roman?" *Jahrbuch für sexuelle Zwischenstufen* 14.3 (July 1914): 338–41.

Müller-Freienfels, Richard. "Genialität und Fleiß." *Das literarische Echo* 16.22 (15 August 1914): 1531–38.

Pache, Alexander. "Verschiedenes." Review of *Thomas Mann und sein Beruf,* by Wilhelm Alberts, and of *Thomas Mann und der Tod in Venedig: Eine kritische Abwehr,* by Bernd Isemann. *Die schöne Literatur: Beilage zum Literarischen Zentralblatt für Deutschland* 15.6 (14 March 1914): 118–21.

Sachs, Hanns. "Das Thema 'Tod.'" *Imago* 3.5 (October 1914): 456–61.

Zimmermann, Richard. "Der Tod in Venedig: Novelle. Von Thomas Mann." *Preußische Jahrbücher* 156.2 (May 1914): 356–57.

# 1915

Hankamer, Paul. "Thomas Mann: Die Schicksalsidee und ihr Verhältnis zur Form seiner Kunst." *Mitteilungen der Literarhistorischen Gesellschaft Bonn* 10.7 (1915/16): 157–86.

Hitschmann, E. "'Der Tod in Venedig': Novelle von Thomas Mann." *Internationale Zeitschrift für ärtzliche Psychoanalyse* 3.2 (1915): 124–26.

Kuh, Anton. "Die vorahnende Literatur: Ein Versuch." *Pester Lloyd,* 11 January 1915, 1–2.

Leppmann, Franz. "Der Tod in Venedig." In his *Thomas Mann,* 121–38. Berlin: Juncker, [1915].

# 1917

Müller, Robert. "Thomas Mann." In his *Europäische Wege: Im Kampf um den Typus,* 22–39. Berlin: Fischer, 1917.

# 1919

Praetorius, Numa. "Die Bibliographie der homosexuellen Belletristik aus den Jahren 1913–1918." *Jahrbuch für sexuelle Zwischenstufen* 19.1–2 (January and April 1919): 75–81.

# 1920

Braun, Felix. "Gedanken zu den neuen Büchern Thomas Manns." *Österreichische Rundschau* 64 (July-September 1920): 180–82.

Neumann, Alfred. "Gespräch mit Thomas Mann." *Neues Wiener Journal,* 22 June 1920. Reprinted in Hansen and Heine, 1983, 45–49.

# 1922

Helbling, Carl. "Thomas Mann und der Kreis um Stefan George." In his *Die Gestalt des Künstlers in der neueren Dichtung: Eine Studie über Thomas Mann,* 51–87. Bern: Seldwyla, 1922.

# 1925

Bertaux, Félix. Introduction to *La mort à Venise,* by Thomas Mann, translated by Félix Bertaux and Ch. Sigwalt, 7–15. Paris: Kra, 1925.

Bjorkman, Edwin. "The Revenge of Life: Death in Venice, and Other Stories. By Thomas Mann." *New York Evening Post,* 28 February 1925, Literary Review, 3.

Boyd, Ernest. "A Great German Novelist: Thomas Mann, Author of 'Buddenbrooks,' Charts an Artist's Life in 'Death in Venice.'" *New York World,* 8 February 1925, 7M.

———. "Within the Quota." *Bookman* 61.3 (May 1925): 352–54.

"Death in Venice." *Independent,* 21 March 1925, 331.

"Death in Venice." *Open Shelf* 7–8 (July-August 1925): 81.

Drake, William A. "The Growing Fame of Thomas Mann." *New York Herald Tribune,* 1 February 1925, Books, 7.

Eloesser, Arthur. "Der Tod in Venedig." In his *Thomas Mann: Sein Leben und sein Werk,* 168–81. Berlin: Fischer, 1925.

———. "Zur Entstehungsgeschichte des 'Tods in Venedig.'" *Die Neue Rundschau* 36 (1925): 611–16.

"Germany's 'Weltschmerz' in Mr. Mann." *New York Times Book Review,* 22 February 1925, 9.

Jaloux, Edmond. "L'esprit des livres." *Les nouvelles littéraires* 4.166 (19 December 1925): 3. Reprinted as "La Mort à Venise" in *Revue Rhénane — Rheinische Blätter* 6.4 (January 1926): 51–52.

Kronenberger, Louis. "Finely-Wrought Fiction." *Saturday Review of Literature,* 27 June 1925, 851.

Krutch, Joseph Wood. "Swan Song." *The Nation,* 25 March 1925, 330–31.

"Mann, Thomas: Death in Venice." *Booklist* 21.9 (June 1925): 340–41.

Wright, Cuthbert. "Eros." *Dial* 78.5 (May 1925): 420–25.

Zarek, Otto. "Neben dem Werk." *Die Neue Rundschau* 36 (1925): 616–24. Excerpted as "Thomas Mann in einem Gespräch mit Otto Zarek" in *Dichter über ihre Dichtungen: Thomas Mann, Teil I: 1889–1917,* edited by Hans Wysling and Marianne Fischer, 411–12. Munich: Heimeran; Frankfurt am Main: Fischer, 1975.

# 1926

Oppenheim, D. E. "Thomas Mann's Novelle: Der Tod in Venedig." In Oppenheim's *Dichtung und Menschenkenntnis: Psychologische Streifzüge durch alte und neue Literatur,* 142–71, 246–62. Munich: Bergmann, 1926.

# 1927

Havenstein, Martin. *Thomas Mann: Der Dichter und Schriftsteller.* Berlin: Wiegandt & Grieben, 1927.

Thalmann, Marianne. "Thomas Mann, Tod in Venedig." *Germanisch-Romanische Monatsschrift* 15 (1927): 374–78.

# 1928

Hirsch, Arnold. "Thomas Mann: 'Der Tod in Venedig.'" In his *Der Gattungsbegriff "Novelle,"* 135–45. Berlin: Ebering, 1928.

Soergel, Albert. *Dichtung und Dichter der Zeit: Eine Schilderung der deutschen Literatur der letzten Jahrzehnte.* Leipzig: Voigtländer, 1928.

Spann, Meno. *Der Exotismus in Ferdinand Freiligraths Gedichten.* Dortmund: Strauch, 1928.

# 1929

Bianquis, Geneviève. "Thomas Mann: romancier de la bourgeoisie allemande." *Revue des Deux Mondes* 99 (1 August 1929): 697–709.

Keller, Helen Rex. "Death in Venice." In her *Reader's Digest of Books,* 1044–45. Rev. ed. New York: Macmillan, 1929.

Roberts, Cecil. "A Trio." *Bookman* 449.75 (February 1929): 293–94.

# 1930

Brion, Marcel. "*La Mort à Venise,* par Thomas Mann. — *Les Pauvres, Mère Marie,* par Heinrich Mann." *Cahiers du Sud* 17.118 (February 1930): 636–39.

Lewisohn, Ludwig. Preface to *Death in Venice,* by Thomas Mann, translated by H. T. Lowe-Porter, v–xv. New York: Knopf, 1930. Reprinted as "Death in Venice" in Neider, 1947, 124–28. (Quoted in Neider.)

# 1931

Burke, Kenneth. "Thomas Mann and André Gide." In his *Counter-Statement,* 116–35. New York: Harcourt, Brace, 1931. Reprinted in Neider, 1947, 253–64.

Eloesser, Arthur. *Die deutsche Literatur vom Barock bis zur Gegenwart.* Vol. 2. *Von der Romantik bis zur Gegenwart.* Berlin: Cassirer, 1931. Translated by Catherine Alison Phillips as *Modern German Literature.* London: Hamilton; New York: Knopf, 1933. Translation excerpted as "A Note on Thomas Mann" in Neider, 1947, 416–28.

Hotes, Leander. *Das Leitmotiv in der neueren deutschen Romandichtung.* Bückeburg: Prinz, 1931.

# 1932

Baer, Lydia. *The Concept and Function of Death in the Works of Thomas Mann.* Philadelphia: n.p., 1932.

Kasdorff, Hans. "Der Tod in Venedig." In his *Der Todesgedanke im Werke Thomas Manns,* 86–97. Leipzig: Eichblatt, 1932.

# 1933

Cleugh, James. "The Adventure of Beauty." In his *Thomas Mann: A Study,* 136–51. London: Secker, 1933.

Obenauer, K. J. *Die Problematik des ästhetischen Menschen in der deutschen Literatur.* Munich: Beck, 1933.

# 1934

Bennett, E. K. *A History of the German Novelle.* Cambridge: Cambridge UP, 1934.

Nolte, Fritz. *Der Todesbegriff bei Rainer Maria Rilke, Hugo von Hofmannsthal und Thomas Mann.* Heidelberg: Lippl, 1934.

Peacock, Ronald. *Das Leitmotiv bei Thomas Mann.* Bern: Akademische Buchhandlung, 1934. Reprint, Nendeln, Liechtenstein: Kraus 1970.

# 1935

Lion, Ferdinand. *Thomas Mann in seiner Zeit.* Zurich: Niehans, 1935.

Rosenfeld, Hellmut. *Das deutsche Bildgedicht.* Leipzig: Mayer & Müller, 1935.

Schriftgiesser, Karl. "Communistic Gain Due, Says Thomas Mann." *Washington Post,* 1 July 1935, 1 and 6. Translated as "Kommunistischer Erfolg zu erwarten, sagt Thomas Mann" in Hansen and Heine, 1983, 214–18.

# 1937

Seuffert, Thea von. *Venedig im Erlebnis deutscher Dichter.* Cologne: Petrarca-Haus; Stuttgart: Deutsche Verlags-Anstalt, 1937.

# 1938

McLean, Helen V. "Freud and Literature." *Saturday Review of Literature,* 3 September 1938, 18–19.

Menninger, Karl. *Man Against Himself.* New York: Harcourt, Brace & World, 1938. Reprint, New York: Harcourt Brace Jovanovich, 1985.

Venable, Vernon. "Poetic Reason in Thomas Mann." *Virginia Quarterly Review* 14 (Winter-Autumn 1938): 61–76. Reprinted as "Death in Venice" in Neider, 1947, 129–41. Also reprinted as "Structural Elements in *Death in Venice*" in *Thomas Mann,* edited by Harold Bloom, 23–34. New York: Chelsea House, 1986.

# 1939

Colomba. "Thomas Mann väntar omsvängning." *Dagens Nyheter,* 1 September 1939, 5. Translated as "Thomas Mann erwartet Umschwung" in Hansen and Heine, 1983, 247–49.

# 1942

Brennan, Joseph Gerard. *Thomas Mann's World.* New York: Columbia UP, 1942.

Waddell, Joan. "Two Illustrations for Death in Venice: With an Introductory Letter From Thomas Mann." *Trend* 1.2 (February 1942): 15–17.

# 1944

Lukács, Georg. "Preußentum in der deutschen Literatur." *Internationale Literatur* 14.5 (1944). Reprinted as "Über Preußentum" in his *Schicksalswende: Beiträge zu einer neuen deutschen Ideologie,* 68–94. Berlin: Aufbau, 1948.

# 1945

Hoffman, Frederick J. *Freudianism and the literary mind.* Baton Rouge: Louisiana State UP, 1945. 2d. ed. 1957.

Lukács, Georg. "Auf der Suche nach dem Bürger." *Internationale Literatur* 15.6–7 (1945): 58–75. Quoted in his *Thomas Mann,* 9–48. Berlin: Aufbau, 1949. Reprinted in his *Werke,* vol. 7, *Deutsche Literatur in zwei Jahrhunderten,* 505–34. Neuwied: Luchterhand, 1964. Translated by Stanley Mitchell as "In Search of Bourgeois Man" in Lukács's *Essays on Thomas Mann,* 13–46. London: Merlin Press, 1964; New York: Grosset & Dunlap, 1965. Reprint, New York: Fertig,

1978. Translation reprinted in *Critical Essays on Thomas Mann*, edited by Inta M. Ezergailis, 24–47. Boston: Hall, 1988.

———. "Die deutsche Literatur im Zeitalter des Imperialismus." *Internationale Literatur* 15.3 (1945): 53–65.

Zerner, Marianne. "Thomas Mann in Standard English Anthologies." *German Quarterly* 18.4 (November 1945): 178–88.

# 1946

Bauer, Arnold. *Thomas Mann und die Krise der bürgerlichen Kultur*. Berlin: Verlag der deutschen Buchvertriebs- und Verlags-Gesellschaft, 1946.

Gustafson, Lorraine. "Xenophon and *Der Tod in Venedig*." *Germanic Review* 21.3 (October 1946): 209–14.

# 1947

Fougère, Jean. *Thomas Mann ou la séduction de la mort: essai*. Paris: Pavois, 1947. Translated by Eva Kowalski as *Thomas Mann oder die Magie des Todes*. Baden-Baden: Bühler, 1948.

Grothe, Wolfgang. "Tod in Venedig." *Das goldene Tor* 2.8–9 (1947): 756–58.

Lion, Ferdinand. *Thomas Mann: Leben und Werk*. Zurich: Oprecht 1947.

Neider, Charles, ed. *The Stature of Thomas Mann*. New York: New Directions, 1947.

Rosenthal, M. L. "The Corruption of Aschenbach." *University of Kansas City Review* 14.1 (Fall 1947): 49–56.

Seidlin, Oskar. "Stiluntersuchung an einem Thomas Mann-Satz." *Monatshefte* 39.7 (November 1947): 439–48. Reprinted in his *Von Goethe zu Thomas Mann*, 148–61. Göttingen: Vandenhoeck & Ruprecht, 1963. Also in *Die Werkinterpretation*, edited by Horst Enders, 336–48. Darmstadt: Wissenschaftliche Buchgesellschaft, 1967.

# 1948

Thalmann, Marianne. *J. W. Goethe: "Der Mann von fünfzig Jahren."* Vienna: Amandus, 1948.

# 1949

Blume, Bernhard. *Thomas Mann und Goethe*. Bern: Francke, 1949.

Lukács, Georg. "Die Tragödie der modernen Kunst." In his *Thomas Mann*, 49–113. Berlin: Aufbau, 1949. Reprinted in his *Werke*, vol. 7, *Deutsche Literatur in zwei Jahrhunderten*, 535–82. Neuwied: Luchterhand, 1964. Translated by Stanley Mitchell as "The Tragedy of Modern Art" in Lukács's *Essays on Thomas Mann*, 47–97. London: Merlin Press, 1964; New York: Grosset & Dunlap, 1965. Reprint, New York: Fertig, 1978.

# 1950

Martini, Fritz. "Thomas Manns Kunst der Prosa: Versuch einer Interpretation." In *Form und Inhalt: Kunstgeschichtliche Studien*, edited by Hans Wentzel, 311–31. Stuttgart: Kohlhammer, [1950].

Mayer, Hans. *Thomas Mann: Werk und Entwicklung.* Berlin: Volk und Welt, [1950].

Michael, Wolfgang F. "Thomas Mann auf dem Wege zu Freud." *Modern Language Notes* 65.3 (March 1950): 165–71.

Schlappner, Martin. "Venedig — Symbol der Wende." In his *Thomas Mann und die französische Literatur: Das Problem der Décadence*, 239–63. Saarlouis: Hausen, 1950.

White, James F. "Some Working Notes of Thomas Mann." *Yale University Library Gazette* 25.2 (October 1950): 73–80.

# 1951

Guérard, Albert J. *André Gide.* Cambridge, MA: Harvard UP, 1951.

Hatfield, Henry. *Thomas Mann.* Norfolk, CT: New Directions, 1951; *Thomas Mann. An Introduction to His Fiction.* London: Owen, 1952.

Luke, F. D. "Kafka's 'Die Verwandlung.'" *Modern Language Review* 46.2 (April 1951): 232–45.

# 1952

Mautner, Franz H. "Die griechischen Anklänge in Thomas Manns 'Tod in Venedig.'" *Monatshefte* 44.1 (January 1952): 20–26. Reprinted in his *Wort und Wesen: Kleinere Schriften zur Literatur und Sprache*, 178–86. Frankfurt am Main: Insel, 1974.

# 1953

Böckmann, Paul. "Die Bedeutung Nietzsches für die Situation der modernen Literatur." *Deutsche Vierteljahrsschrift für Literaturwissenschaft und Geistesgeschichte* 27.1 (1953): 77–101.

Eichner, Hans. *Thomas Mann: Eine Einführung in sein Werk.* Munich: Lehnen, 1953.

Lamprecht, Helmut. "Besuch bei Thomas Mann." *Diskus: Mitteilungsblatt von Freunden und Förderern der Johann Wolfgang Goethe Universität* 3.3 (April 1953): 5–6. Reprinted in Hansen and Heine, 1983, 344–49.

Petriconi, Hellmuth. "*La mort de Venise* und *Der Tod in Venedig.*" *Romanistisches Jahrbuch* 6 (1953–54): 133–51. Reprinted in his *Das Reich des Untergangs: Bemerkungen über ein mythologisches Thema*, 67–95. Hamburg: Hoffmann und Campe, 1958.

# 1954

Gerster, Georg. "Thomas Mann an der Arbeit." *Die Weltwoche,* 3 December 1954, 21. Reprinted in Hansen and Heine, 1983, 387–91.

Klein, Johannes. "Der Tod in Venedig." In his *Geschichte der deutschen Novelle von Goethe bis zur Gegenwart,* 412–14. Wiesbaden: Steiner, 1954. Zweite verbesserte und erweiterte Auflage, 423–25. Wiesbaden: Steiner, 1954.

Martini, Fritz. "Thomas Mann: Der Tod in Venedig." In his *Das Wagnis der Sprache: Interpretationen deutscher Prosa von Nietzsche bis Benn,* 176–224. Stuttgart: Klett, 1954.

# 1955

Faesi, Robert. *Thomas Mann: Ein Meister der Erzählkunst.* Zurich: Atlantis, 1955.

Hirschbach, Frank Donald. *The Arrow and the Lyre: A Study of the Role of Love in the Works of Thomas Mann.* The Hague: Nijhoff, 1955.

Lukács, Georg. "Das Spielerische und seine Hintergründe." *Aufbau* 11.6 (June 1955): 501–24. Reprinted in his *Thomas Mann,* 5. verm. und verb. Aufl., 86–119. Berlin: Aufbau, 1957. Also in his *Werke,* vol. 7, *Deutsche Literatur in zwei Jahrhunderten,* 583–617. Neuwied: Luchterhand, 1964. Translated by Stanley Mitchell as "The Playful Style" in Lukács's *Essays on Thomas Mann,* 98–134. London: Merlin Press, 1964; New York: Grosset & Dunlap, 1965. Reprint, New York: Fertig, 1978.

Nicholls, R. A. "Death in Venice." In Nicholls's *Nietzsche in the Early Work of Thomas Mann,* 77–91. Berkeley: U of California P, 1955.

Pabst, Walter. "Satan und die alten Götter in Venedig: Entwicklung einer literarischen Konstante." *Euphorion* 49 (1955): 335–59.

Thomas, R. Hinton. *"Die Wahlverwandtschaften* and Mann's *Der Tod in Venedig." Publications of the English Goethe Society,* n.s., 24 (1955): 101–30.

Tindall, William York. *The Literary Symbol.* New York: Columbia UP; Bloomington: Indiana UP, 1955.

Ulshöfer, Robert. "Die Wirklichkeitsauffassung in der modernen Prosadichtung: Dargestellt an Thomas Manns 'Tod in Venedig'[,] Kafkas 'Verwandlung' und Borcherts 'Kurzgeschichten'[,] verglichen mit Goethes 'Hermann und Dorothea.'" *Der Deutschunterricht* 7.1 (1955): 13–40. Reprinted in his *Theorie und Praxis des Deutschunterrichts Sekundarstufe II,* 198–218. Frankfurt: Lang, 1997.

Wiese, Benno von. "Bild-Symbole in der deutschen Novelle." *Publications of the English Goethe Society,* n.s., 24 (1955): 131–58.

# 1956

Gronicka, André von. "'Myth Plus Psychology': A Style Analysis of *Death in Venice.*" *Germanic Review* 31.3 (October 1956): 191–205. Reprinted in *Thomas Mann: A Collection of Critical Essays,* edited by Henry Hatfield, 46–61. Englewood Cliffs, NJ: Prentice-Hall, 1964. Also in Koelb, 1994, 115–30.

Heller, Erich. "Psychoanalyse und Literatur." In *Jahresring 56/57,* edited by Rudolf de le Roi et al., 74–83. Stuttgart: Deutsche Verlags-Anstalt: 1956.

Jens, Walter. "Der Gott der Diebe und sein Dichter: Ein Versuch über Thomas Manns Verhältnis zur Antike." *Antike und Abendland* 5 (1956): 139–53. Reprinted as "Der Gott der Diebe und sein Dichter: Thomas Mann und die Welt der Antike" in his *Statt einer Literaturgeschichte,* 87–107. Pfullingen: Neske, 1957. Reprinted under this second title in his *Zur Antike,* 117–35. Munich: Kindler, 1978.

Pongs, Hermann. *Im Umbruch der Zeit.* 2. erw. Auflage. Göttingen: Göttinger Verlagsanstalt, 1956.

Shuster, George N. "Art at War With the Good (Thomas Mann: *Death in Venice*)." In *Great Moral Dilemmas in Literature, Past and Present,* edited by R. M. Mac-Iver, 25–36. New York: Institute for Religious and Social Studies, 1956.

Thomas, R. Hinton. "Death in Venice." In his *Thomas Mann: The Mediation of Art,* 59–84. Oxford: Clarendon, 1956.

Wiese, Benno von. "Thomas Mann: Der Tod in Venedig." In his *Die deutsche Novelle von Goethe bis Kafka,* 304–24. Düsseldorf: Bagel, 1956.

# 1957

Kaufmann, Fritz. *Thomas Mann: The World as Will and Representation.* Boston: Beacon, 1957. Reprint, New York: Cooper Square Publishers, 1973.

Kohut, Heinz. "'Death in Venice' by Thomas Mann: A Story About the Disintegration of Artistic Sublimation." *Psychoanalytic Quarterly* 26.2 (1957): 206–28. Reprinted in *Psychoanalysis and Literature,* edited by Hendrik M. Ruitenbeek, 282–302. New York: Dutton, 1964. Also in *The Search for the Self: Selected Writings of Heinz Kohut: 1950–1978,* vol. 1, edited by Paul H. Ornstein, 107–30. New York: International Universities Press, 1978. Translated by Käte Hügel as "'Tod in Venedig' von Thomas Mann: Über die Desintegration künstlerischer Sublimierung" ["Thomas Manns 'Tod in Venedig': Zerfall einer künstlerischen Sublimierung"] in *Psycho-Pathographien I: Schriftsteller und Psychoanalyse,* edited by Alexander Mitscherlich, 142–67. Frankfurt am Main: Suhrkamp, 1972. Translation reprinted in *Psycho-Pathographien des Alltags: Schriftsteller und Psychoanalyse,* edited by Alexander Mitscherlich, 137–59. Frankfurt am Main: Suhrkamp, 1982. Translated by Juan José Utrilla as "'La muerte en Venecia' de Thomas Mann" in *Psicoanálisis y literatura,* edited by Hendrik M. Ruitenbeek, 397–423. Mexico: Fondo de Cultura Económica, 1973. Translated by Catherine Alicot as "'La Mort à Venise' de Thomas Mann: histoire d'une désagrégation de la sublimation artistique." *Revue française de psychanalyse* 62.4 (October-November 1998): 1233–45.

Lockemann, Fritz. *Gestalt und Wandlungen der deutschen Novelle*. Munich: Hueber, 1957.

Mileck, Joseph. "A Comparative Study of 'Die Betrogene' and 'Der Tod in Venedig.'" *Modern Language Forum* 42.2 (December 1957): 124–29.

Seyppel, Joachim H. "Two Variations on a Theme: Dying in Venice (Thomas Mann and Ernest Hemingway)." *Literature and Psychology* 7.1 (February 1957): 8–12. Translated and condensed as "Zwei Variationen zum Thema: Tod in Venedig" in his *Umwege nach Haus: Nachtbücher über Tage 1943 bis 1973*, 139–40. Berlin: Aufbau, 1974.

Wolff, Hans M. *Thomas Mann: Werk und Bekenntnis*. Bern: Francke, 1957.

# 1958

Heimann, Heidi. "Thomas Manns 'Hermesnatur.'" *Publications of the English Goethe Society*, n.s., 27 (1958): 46–72.

Heller, Erich. *Thomas Mann: The Ironic German*. Boston: Little, Brown; London: Secker & Warburg, 1958. Translated and revised as *Thomas Mann: Der ironische Deutsche*. Frankfurt am Main: Suhrkamp, 1959. Quoted in *Thomas Mann: The Ironic German*. South Bend, IN: Regnery/Gateway, 1979.

Mautner, Franz H. "Thomas Mann über 'Tod in Venedig.'" *Monatshefte* 50.5 (October 1958): 256–57. Reprinted in his *Wort und Wesen: Kleinere Schriften zur Literatur und Sprache*, 187–88. Frankfurt am Main: Insel, 1974.

Rey, W. H. "Tragic Aspects of the Artist in Thomas Mann's Work." *Modern Language Quarterly* 19.3 (September 1958): 195–203.

Urdang, Constance. "Faust in Venice: The Artist and the Legend in 'Death in Venice.'" *Accent* 18 (1958): 253–67.

Vortriede, Werner. "Richard Wagners 'Tod in Venedig.'" *Euphorion*, Dritte Folge, 52 (1958): 378–96.

# 1959

Diersen, Inge. *Untersuchungen zu Thomas Mann*. Berlin: Rütten & Loening, 1959.

Michael, Wolfgang F. "Stoff und Idee im 'Tod in Venedig.'" *Deutsche Vierteljahrsschrift für Literaturwissenschaft und Geistesgeschichte* 33 (1959): 13–19.

Seyppel, Joachim. "Adel des Geistes: Thomas Mann und August von Platen." *Deutsche Vierteljahrsschrift für Literaturwissenschaft und Geistesgeschichte* 33 (1959): 565–73.

# 1960

Fourrier, Georges. "L'aventurier de Venise." In his *Thomas Mann: Le message d'un artiste-bourgeois (1896–1924)*, 193–216. Paris: Belles Lettres, 1960.

Hellersberg-Wendriner, Anna. "Der Tod in Venedig." In her *Mystik der Gottesferne: Eine Interpretation Thomas Manns*, 67–76. Bern: Francke, 1960.

Root, John G. "Stylistic Irony in Thomas Mann." *Germanic Review* 35.2 (April 1960): 93–103.

Stephan, Doris. "Thomas Manns 'Tod in Venedig' und Brochs 'Vergil.'" *Schweizer Monatshefte* 40.1 (April 1960): 76–83.

Tramer, Hans. "Umgenannte und Umgetaufte: Gustav Mahler und seine Zeit." *Bulletin fuer die Mitglieder der Gesellschaft der Freunde des Leo Baeck Instituts* 10 (1960): 130–50.

Yamamoto, Atsushi: "Über das mythische Element in 'Der Tod in Venedig.'" *Doitsu Bungaku* 24 (May 1960): 28.

# 1961

Soergel, Albert, and Curt Hohoff. *Dichtung und Dichter der Zeit: Vom Naturalismus bis zur Gegenwart.* Vol. 1. Düsseldorf: Bagel, 1961.

Trilling, Lionel. "On the Modern Element in Modern Literature." *Partisan Review* 28.1 (January-February 1961): 9–35.

# 1962

Beharriell, Frederick J. "Psychology in the Early Works of Thomas Mann." *PMLA* 77.1 (March 1962): 149–55.

Church, Margaret. "'Death in Venice': A Study of Creativity." *College English* 23.8 (May 1962): 648–51.

Gross, Harvey. "Aschenbach and Kurtz: The Cost of Civilization." *The Centennial Review* 6.2 (Spring 1962): 131–43.

Luckow, Marion. "Thomas Mann: Der Tod in Venedig (1911)." In Luckow's *Die Homosexualität in der literarischen Tradition: Studien zu den Romanen von Jean Genet,* 58–63. Stuttgart: Enke, 1962.

McNamara, Eugene. "'Death in Venice': The Disguised Self." *College English* 24.3 (December 1962): 233–34.

Schmidt, R. "Das Ringen um die Überwindung der Dekadenz in einigen Novellen von Thomas Mann." *Wissenschaftliche Zeitschrift der Ernst-Moritz-Arndt-Universität Greifswald* 11 (1962), Gesellschafts- und sprachwissenschaftliche Reihe, nos. 1–2, pp. 141–53.

Stavenhagen, Lee. "The Name Tadzio in *Der Tod in Venedig.*" *German Quarterly* 35.1 (January 1962): 20–23.

Weisstein, Ulrich. *Heinrich Mann.* Tübingen: Niemeyer, 1962.

# 1963

Hepworth, James B. "Tadzio — Sabazios: Notes on 'Death in Venice.'" *Western Humanities Review* 17.2 (Spring 1963): 172–75.

Martin, John S. "Circean Seduction in Three Works by Thomas Mann." *Modern Language Notes* 78.4 (October 1963): 346–52.

Pütz, Heinz Peter. *Kunst und Künstlerexistenz bei Nietzsche und Thomas Mann.* Bonn: Bouvier, 1963.

Seidler-von Hippel, Elisabeth. "Der Tod in Venedig: Novelle, 1913." In *Handbuch zur modernen Literatur im Deutschunterricht,* edited by Paul Dormagen et al., 71–73. Frankfurt am Main: Hirschgraben, 1963.

Stresau, Hermann. *Thomas Mann und sein Werk.* Frankfurt am Main: Fischer, 1963.

# 1964

Amory, Frederic. "The Classical Style of 'Der Tod in Venedig.'" *Modern Language Review* 59.3 (July 1964): 399–409.

Baumgart, Reinhard. "'Tod in Venedig.'" In his *Das Ironische und die Ironie in den Werken Thomas Manns,* 116–23. Munich: Hanser, 1964.

Lehnert, Herbert. "Thomas Mann's Early Interest in Myth and Erwin Rohde's *Psyche*." *PMLA* 79.3 (June 1964): 297–304.

———. "Thomas Mann's Interpretations of *Der Tod in Venedig* and their Reliability." *Rice University Studies* 50.4 (Fall 1964): 41–60.

McClain, William H. "Wagnerian Overtones in *Der Tod in Venedig.*" *Modern Language Notes* 79.5 (December 1964): 481–95. Excerpted in *German Literature: A Library of Literary Criticism,* vol. 2, edited by Agnes Körner Domandi, 146. New York: Ungar, 1972.

Novey, Riva. "The Artistic Communication and the Recipient: 'Death in Venice' as an Integral Part of a Psychoanalysis." *Psychoanalytic Quarterly* 33.1 (1964): 25–52.

Petri, Horst. *Literatur und Musik.* Göttingen: Sachse & Pohl, 1964. Excerpted as "Die musikalische Form in der Literatur" in *Sprache, Dichtung, Musik,* edited by Jakob Knaus, 76–86. Tübingen: Niemeyer, 1973.

Stelzmann, Rainulf A. "Thomas Mann's *Death in Venice: Res et Imago.*" *Xavier University Studies* 3.3 (December 1964): 160–67.

Van der Schaar, P. J. *Dynamik der Pseudologie: Der pseudologische Betrüger versus den großen Täuscher Thomas Mann.* Munich: Reinhardt, 1964.

Weiss, Walter. *Thomas Manns Kunst der sprachlichen und thematischen Integration.* Beiheft zur Zeitschrift "Wirkendes Wort" 13. Düsseldorf: Schwann, 1964.

# 1965

Berendsohn, Walter A. *Thomas Mann: Künstler und Kämpfer in bewegter Zeit.* Lübeck: Schmidt-Römhild, 1965.

Dettmering, Peter. "Die Problematik der Suizide im Werk Thomas Manns." *Psyche* 19.9 (December 1965): 547–69.

Doegowski [*sic*], Andrzej. "Ich war Thomas Manns Tadzio." *Twen* 7.8 (August 1965): 10. Translated by Martin Cooper as "I was Thomas Mann's Tadzio" in *Benjamin Britten: Death in Venice,* edited by Donald Mitchell, 184–85. Cambridge: Cambridge UP, 1987.

Gray, Ronald. *"Tonio Kröger; Death in Venice."* In his *The German Tradition in Literature 1871–1945,* 137–56. Cambridge: Cambridge UP, 1965

Hilscher, Eberhard. *Thomas Mann: Leben und Werk.* Berlin: Volk und Wissen, 1965.

Hoffmeister, Werner. *Studien zur erlebten Rede bei Thomas Mann und Robert Musil.* The Hague: Mouton, 1965.

Lehnert, Herbert. "Note on Mann's *Der Tod in Venedig* and the *Odyssey.*" *PMLA* 80.3 (June 1965): 306–7.

———. "Untersuchungen zum 'Tod in Venedig.'" In his *Thomas Mann: Fiktion, Mythos, Religion,* 99–139. Stuttgart: Kohlhammer, 1965.

Martini, Fritz. Nachwort (Afterword) to *Klassische Deutsche Dichtung,* edited by Fritz Martini and Walter Müller-Seidel. Vol. 22, *Wegbereiter der modernen Prosa,* 589–650. Freiburg im Breisgau: Herder, 1965.

Sandberg, Hans-Joachim. *Thomas Manns Schiller-Studien.* Oslo: Universitetsforlaget, 1965.

Sørensen, Bengt Algot. "Die symbolische Gestaltung in den Jugenderzählungen Thomas Manns." *Orbis Litterarum* 20.2 (1965): 85–97.

Traschen, Isadore. "The Uses of Myth in 'Death in Venice.'" *Modern Fiction Studies* 11.2 (Summer 1965): 165–79. Reprinted in *Thomas Mann,* edited by Harold Bloom, 87–101. New York: Chelsea House, 1986.

Trilling, Lionel. "On the Teaching of Modern Literature." In his *Beyond Culture: Essays on Literature and Learning,* 3–27. New York: Harcourt Brace Jovanovich, 1965.

Welter, Marianne. "Späte Liebe." *Spektrum: Mitteilungsblatt für die Mitarbeiter der Deutschen Akademie der Wissenschaften zu Berlin* 11.5 (1965): 210–15.

Wysling, Hans. "Aschenbachs Werke: Archivalische Untersuchungen an einem Thomas Mann-Satz." *Euphorion* 59.3 (1965): 272–314. Revised and expanded as "Zu Thomas Manns 'Maya'-Projekt," "'Ein Elender': Zu einem Novellenplan Thomas Manns," and "'Geist und Kunst': Thomas Manns Notizen zu einem 'Literatur-Essay'" in Paul Scherrer's and Wysling's *Quellenkritische Studien zum Werk Thomas Manns,* 23–47, 106–22, and 123–233. Thomas-Mann-Studien 1. Bern: Francke, 1967.

# 1966

Daemmrich, Horst S. "Mann's Portrait of the Artist: Archetypal Patterns." *Bucknell Review* 14.3 (December 1966): 27–43.

Feuerlicht, Ignace. *Thomas Mann und die Grenzen des Ich.* Heidelberg: Winter, 1966.

Heller, Peter. "Mann: Spheres of Ambiguity." In his *Dialectics and Nihilism: Essays on Lessing, Nietzsche, Mann, and Kafka,* 149–226. Amherst: U of Massachusetts P, 1966.

Kirchberger, Lida. "'Death in Venice' and the Eighteenth Century." *Monatshefte* 58.4 (Winter 1966): 321–34.

Lander, Jeannette [Joachim Seyppel?]. "Von der fünffachen Wurzel des Todes: Zu Thomas Manns 'Tod in Venedig.'" *Die Diagonale* 1.1 (1966): 23–30.

Moeller, Hans-Bernhard. "Thomas Manns venezianische Götterkunde, Plastik und Zeitlosigkeit." *Deutsche Vierteljahrsschrift für Literaturwissenschaft und Geistesgeschichte* 40.2 (June 1966): 184–205.

Reed, T. J. "'Geist und Kunst': Thomas Mann's Abandoned Essay on Literature." *Oxford German Studies* 1 (1966): 53–101.

Santoli, Vittorio. Introduction to *Racconti*, by Thomas Mann, 25–59. Milan: Mondadori, 1966. Translated by K.-Richard Bausch as "Drei Erzählungen Thomas Manns" in Santoli's *Philologie und Kritik*, 162–87. Bern: Francke, 1971.

Woodward, Anthony. "The Figure of the Artist in Thomas Mann's *Tonio Kröger* and *Death in Venice*." *English Studies in Africa* 9.2 (September 1966): 158–67.

# 1967

Conley, John. "Thomas Mann on the Sources of Two Passages in *Death in Venice*." *German Quarterly* 40.1 (January 1967): 152–55.

Hofman, Alois. "Die Tragödie des Künstlers im 'Tod in Venedig' in Beziehung zu Tolstois und Tschechows Schaffenskrisen." In his *Thomas Mann und die Welt der russischen Literatur*, 249–57. Berlin: Akademie-Verlag, 1967.

Krotkoff, Hertha. "Zur Symbolik in Thomas Manns 'Tod in Venedig.'" *Modern Language Notes* 82.4 (October 1967): 445–53.

Lehnert, Herbert. "Another Note on 'motus animi continuus' and the Clenched-Fist-Image in *Der Tod in Venedig*." *German Quarterly* 40.3 (May 1967): 452–53.

Linn, Rolf N. *Heinrich Mann*. New York: Twayne, 1967.

McWilliams, J. R. "The Failure of a Repression: Thomas Mann's *Tod in Venedig*." *German Life and Letters*, n.s., 20.3 (April 1967): 233–41.

Pike, Burton. "Thomas Mann and the Problematic Self." *Publications of the English Goethe Society*, n.s., 37 (1967): 120–41.

Rasch, Wolfdietrich. *Zur deutschen Literatur seit der Jahrhundertwende*. Stuttgart: Metzler, 1967.

# 1968

Cox, Catherine. "Pater's 'Apollo in Picardy' and Mann's *Death in Venice*." *Anglia* 86.1–2 (1968): 143–54.

Durzak, Manfred. "Tod in Venedig." In his *Hermann Broch: Der Dichter und seine Zeit*, 54–63. Stuttgart: Kohlhammer, 1968.

Egri, Peter. "The Function of Dreams and Visions in *A Portrait* and *Death in Venice*." *James Joyce Quarterly* 5.2 (Winter 1968): 86–102.

Feuerlicht, Ignace. "Beauty and the Abyss." In his *Thomas Mann*, 117–26. Boston: Twayne, 1968.

Frey, John R. "'Die stumme Begegnung': Beobachtungen zur Funktion des Blicks im *Tod in Venedig*." *German Quarterly* 41.2 (March 1968): 177–95.

Nicklas, Hans W. *Thomas Manns Novelle "Der Tod in Venedig": Analyse des Motivzusammenhangs und der Erzählstruktur.* Marburg: Elwert, 1968.

# 1969

Dettmering, Peter. "Suizid und Inzest im Werke Thomas Manns." In his *Dichtung und Psychoanalyse*, 9–79. Munich: Nymphenburger Verlagshandlung, 1969.

Dittmann, Ulrich. "Die Sprache des Künstlers in ihrer Entsprechung zum Menschlichen." In his *Sprachbewußtsein und Redeformen im Werk Thomas Manns*, 84–93. Stuttgart: Kohlhammer, 1969.

Jonas, Ilsedore B. "*Der Tod in Venedig* (1911)." In her *Thomas Mann und Italien*, 53–59. Heidelberg: Winter, 1969. Revised as "Death in Venice (1912)" in Jonas's *Thomas Mann and Italy*, translated by Betty Crouse, 34–41. University, AL: U of Alabama P, 1979.

Lehnert, Herbert. "'Tristan,' 'Tonio Kröger' und 'Der Tod in Venedig': Ein Strukturvergleich." *Orbis Litterarum* 24.3 (1969): 271–304.

———. *Thomas-Mann-Forschung: Ein Bericht.* Stuttgart: Metzler, 1969.

Myers, David. "Sexual Love and *Caritas* in Thomas Mann." *Journal of English and Germanic Philology* 68.4 (October 1969): 593–604.

Pumpian-Mindlin, E. "Thomas Mann's *Death in Venice*." *Journal of Nervous and Mental Disease* 149.2 (August 1969): 236–39.

Slochower, Harry. "Thomas Mann's *Death in Venice*." *American Imago* 26.2 (Summer 1969): 99–122. Reprinted in *American Imago* 46.2–3 (Summer-Fall 1989): 255–79.

Tarbox, Raymond. "*Death in Venice*: The Aesthetic Object as Dream Guide." *American Imago* 26.2 (Summer 1969): 123–44.

Vanggaard, Thorkil. "Gustav von Aschenbachs sammenbrud." In his *Phallós*, 167–85. Copenhagen: Gyldendal, 1969. Translated by Vanggaard as "The Breakdown of Gustav von Aschenbach" in his *Phallós: A Symbol and its History in the Male World*, 183–204. London: Cape; New York: International Universities Press, 1972.

Wysling, Hans. "*Mythos und Psychologie*" *bei Thomas Mann.* Zurich: Polygraphischer Verlag, 1969. Reprinted as "'Mythus und Psychologie' bei Thomas Mann," in his *Dokumente und Untersuchungen: Beiträge zur Thomas-Mann-Forschung*, 167–80. Thomas-Mann-Studien 3. Bern: Francke, 1974.

# 1970

Baron, Frank. "Sensuality and Morality in Thomas Mann's *Tod in Venedig*." *Germanic Review* 45.2 (March 1970): 115–25.

Braverman, Albert, and Larry David Nachman. "The Dialectic of Decadence: An Analysis of Thomas Mann's *Death in Venice*." *Germanic Review* 45.4 (November 1970): 289–98.

Gronicka, André von. *Thomas Mann: Profiles and Perspectives*. New York: Random House, 1970.

Heller, Erich. "Autobiography and Literature." In *Thomas Mann: Death in Venice*, translated by Kenneth Burke, 101–27. Rev. ed. New York: Modern Library, 1970.

Hinxman, Margaret. "Death in Venice." *Sight and Sound* 39.4 (Autumn 1970): 198–200.

Noble, C. A. M. "Der Tod in Venedig." In Noble's *Krankheit, Verbrechen und künstlerisches Schaffen bei Thomas Mann*, 119–35. Bern: Lang, 1970.

Rogers, Robert. *A Psychoanalytic Study of the Double in Literature*. Detroit: Wayne State UP, 1970.

Schweckendiek, Adolf. "Gustav Aschenbach in Thomas Manns 'Der Tod in Venedig.'" In his *Könnt ich Magie von meinem Pfad entfernen: Neurosenkundliche Studien an Gestalten der Dichtung*, 82–92. Leimen: Hans Lungwitz-Stiftung, 1970.

Stelzmann, Rainulf A. "Eine Ironisierung Nietzsches in Thomas Manns 'Der Tod in Venedig.'" *South Atlantic Bulletin* 35.3 (May 1970): 16–21.

# 1971

Améry, Jean. "Venezianische Zaubereien: Luchino Visconti und sein 'Tod in Venedig.'" *Merkur* 25 (1971): 808–12.

Berger, Willy R. "Thomas Mann und die antike Literatur." In *Thomas Mann und die Tradition*, edited by Peter Pütz, 52–100. Frankfurt am Main: Athenäum, 1971.

Dyson, A. E. "The Stranger God: 'Death in Venice.'" *Critical Quarterly* 13.1 (Spring 1971): 5–20. Reprinted as "The Stranger God: Mann's *Death in Venice*" in Dyson's *Between Two Worlds: Aspects of Literary Form*, 81–99. London: Macmillan, 1972.

Geiser, Christoph. "Der Tod in Venedig." In his *Naturalismus und Symbolismus im Frühwerk Thomas Manns*, 66–74. Bern: Francke, 1971.

Grossvogel, David I. "*Death in Venice*: Visconti and the Too, Too Solid Flesh." *Diacritics* 1.2 (Winter 1971): 52–55.

Günther, Joachim. "'Der Tod in Venedig': Randbemerkungen zu Film und Buch." *Neue deutsche Hefte* 18.4 (1971): 89–99.

Hollingdale, R. J. *Thomas Mann: A Critical Study*. Lewisburg, PA: Bucknell UP, 1971.

Jenny, Urs. "Luchino Visconti: Der Tod in Venedig." *Filmkritik* 15 (July 1971): 378–80.

Josipovici, Gabriel. *The World and the Book.* London: Macmillan; Stanford, CA: Stanford UP, 1971.

Limmer, Wolfgang. "Genialer Schwanengesang: 'Tod in Venedig' von Luchino Visconti." *Fernsehen und Film* 9.7 (July 1971): 32–33.

Mann, Michael. "Der verfilmte *Tod in Venedig:* Offener Brief an Lucchino [*sic*] Visconti." *Süddeutsche Zeitung,* 20–21 November 1971, SZ am Wochenende: Feuilleton-Beilage der Süddeutschen Zeitung. Translated by Louise Servicen as "Le film tiré de 'la Mort à Venise' (Lettre ouverte de Michaël Mann, fils cadet de Thomas Mann, à Lucchino Visconti, auteur du film)." *Allemagne d'aujourd'hui,* n.s., 32 (March-April 1972): 52–56.

Mellen, Joan. "Death in Venice." *Film Quarterly* 25.1 (Fall 1971): 41–47.

Pringsheim, Klaus. "Protest gegen 'Tod in Venedig': Der Schwager hält nicht viel davon." *Abendzeitung* [Munich], 20–21 November 1971, 10.

Reed, T. J. Introduction to *Der Tod in Venedig,* by Thomas Mann, edited by T. J. Reed, 9–51. Oxford: Oxford UP, 1971.

Schmeier, Bernd. "Viscontis 'Tod in Venedig' — ein Sakrileg." *Lübeckische Blätter* 131.20 (2 October 1971): 244.

Schmidt, Christian. "Die Todesverbundenheit der Gestalten und Elemente der östlichen Welt in der Erzählung 'Der Tod in Venedig.'" In his *Bedeutung und Funktion der Gestalten der europäisch östlichen Welt im dichterischen Werk Thomas Manns,* 71–92. Munich: Sagner, 1971.

# 1972

Anton, Herbert. *Die Romankunst Thomas Manns.* 2., erweiterte Auflage. Paderborn: Schöningh, 1972. [N.B. The 1. Auflage (first printing) — the title page of which, like that of this 2. Auflage, lists 1972 as a copyright date — does not include Anton's remarks on *Death in Venice* .]

Bance, A. F. "*Der Tod in Venedig* and the Triadic Structure." *Forum for Modern Language Studies* 8.2 (April 1972): 148–61.

Brann, Eva. "The Venetian Phaedrus." *The College* 24.2 (July 1972): 1–9.

Dierks, Manfred. "Untersuchungen zum *Tod in Venedig,*" "Die Übertragung des *Tod-in-Venedig*-Modells," and "Anhang I: Ausgewählte Notizen aus den Vorarbeiten zum *Tod in Venedig.*" In his *Studien zu Mythos und Psychologie bei Thomas Mann,* 13–59, 188–92, and 207–10. Thomas-Mann-Studien 2. Bern: Francke, 1972. Translated and edited by John M. Jeep in Koelb, 1994, 130–49.

Good, Graham. "The Death of Language in *Death in Venice.*" *Mosaic* 5.3 (Spring 1972): 43–52.

Heller, Erich. "Autobiographie und Literatur: Über Thomas Manns *Tod in Venedig.*" In *Essays on European Literature: In Honor of Lieselotte Dieckmann,* edited by Peter

Uwe Hohendahl, Herbert Lindenberger, and Egon Schwarz, 83–100. St. Louis: Washington UP, 1972. Reprinted as "Thomas Mann in Venedig: Zum Thema Autobiographie und Literatur" in Heller's *Die Wiederkehr der Unschuld,* 167–88. Frankfurt am Main: Suhrkamp, 1977.

Hellmann, Winfried. "'Der Tod in Venedig.'" In Hellmann's *Das Geschichtsdenken des frühen Thomas Mann (1906–1918),* 54–55. Tübingen: Niemeyer, 1972.

Jonas, Ilsedore B. "Sehnsucht nach dem Süden: Gedanken zu Thomas Manns Novelle 'Der Tod in Venedig.'" *Lübeckische Blätter* 132.2 (22 January 1972): 32–34; 133.3 (5 February 1972): 45.

Kane, B. M. "Thomas Mann and Visconti." *Modern Languages* 53.2 (June 1972): 74–80.

Neumeister, Erdmann. *Thomas Manns frühe Erzählungen.* Bonn: Bouvier, 1972.

Noble, C. A. M. "Erkenntnisekel und Erkenntnisfreude: Über Thomas Manns Verhältnis zu Sigmund Freud." *Revue des langues vivantes/Tijdschrift voor levende talen* 38.2 (1972): 154–63.

Plank, Robert. "Death in Venice: Tragedy or Mishap?" *Hartford Studies in Literature* 4.2 (1972): 95–103.

Werner, Renate. "Heinrich Manns Roman 'Die Göttinnen' und eine Replik." In her *Skeptizismus, Ästhetizismus, Aktivismus: Der frühe Heinrich Mann,* 117–44. Düsseldorf: Bertelsmann, 1972.

# 1973

Evans, Peter. "Britten's 'Death in Venice.'" *Opera,* June 1973, 490–96. Expanded as "Death in Venice" in his *The Music of Benjamin Britten,* 523–47. Minneapolis: U of Minnesota P; London: Dent, 1979.

Finck, Jean. *Thomas Mann und die Psychoanalyse.* Paris: Belles Lettres, 1973.

Frühwald, Wolfgang. "Repräsentant des Zeitalters: Zu Thomas Manns Erzählung 'Der Tod in Venedig.'" *Analele Universitatii Bucaresti,* Limbi Germanice, 22 (1973): 51–59.

Koppen, Erwin. "Aschenbach und Wagner." In his *Dekadenter Wagnerismus: Studien zur europäischen Literatur des Fin de siècle,* 225–37. Berlin: de Gruyter, 1973.

Mitchell, Donald. "*Death in Venice:* The Dark Side of Perfection." Radio broadcast transmitted by the BBC on 21 June 1973. Edited version printed in *The Britten Companion,* edited by Christopher Palmer, 238–49. Cambridge: Cambridge UP, 1984.

Nowell-Smith, Geoffrey. *Luchino Visconti.* Rev. ed. New York; Viking, 1973.

Reed, T. J. "Thomas Mann's 'Death in Venice.'" In *The 26th Aldeburgh Festival Programme Book* (1973), 5–6. Reprinted as "Mann and his Novella 'Death in Venice'" in *Benjamin Britten: Death in Venice,* edited by Donald Mitchell, 163–67. Cambridge: Cambridge UP, 1987.

Székely, Lajos. "Thomas Manns 'Tod in Venedig.'" Translated by Käte Hügel. *Psyche* 27.7 (July 1973): 614–35.

Vaget, Hans Rudolf. "Thomas Mann und die Neuklassik: 'Der Tod in Venedig' und Samuel Lublinskis Literaturauffassung." *Jahrbuch der deutschen Schillergesellschaft* 17 (1973): 432–54. Reprinted in *Stationen der Thomas-Mann-Forschung: Aufsätze seit 1970,* edited by H. Kurzke, 41–60. Würzburg: Königshausen + Neumann, 1985.

Wolf, Ernest M. "A Case of Slightly Mistaken Identity: Gustav Mahler and Gustav Aschenbach." *Twentieth Century Literature* 19.1 (January 1973): 40–52. Reprinted as "A Case of Slightly Mistaken Identity: Gustav Mahler and Gustav Aschenbach in Visconti's Film *Death in Venice*" in Wolf's *Magnum Opus: Studies in the Narrative Fiction of Thomas Mann,* 209–23. Bern: Lang, 1989.

# 1974

Girard, René. "The Plague in Literature and Myth." *Texas Studies in Literature and Language* 15.5 (Special Classics Issue 1974): 833–50. Reprinted in his *"To double business bound": Essays on Literature, Mimesis, and Anthropology,* 136–54. Baltimore: Johns Hopkins UP, 1978.

Hannum, Hunter G. "Archetypal Echoes in Mann's *Death in Venice.*" *Psychological Perspectives* 5.1 (Spring 1974): 48–59.

Hutchison, Alexander. "Luchino Visconti's *Death in Venice.*" *Literature/Film Quarterly* 2.1 (Winter 1974): 31–43.

Leibrich, Louis. *Thomas Mann: Une recherche spirituelle.* Paris: Aubier Montaigne, 1974.

Leppmann, Wolfgang. "Kein Tod in Venedig." *Frankfurter Allgemeine Zeitung,* 21 March 1974, 21. Reprinted in his *In Zwei Welten zu Hause: Aus der Lebensarbeit eines amerikanischen Germanisten,* 122–26. Munich: Drei Ulmen, 1989.

Porter, Andrew. "Musical Events: *Death in Venice.*" *New Yorker,* 28 October 1974, 166–70. Reprinted in his *Music of Three Seasons,* 14–19. London: Chatto & Windus; New York: Farrar Straus Giroux, 1978. Revised as "The last opera: *Death in Venice*" in *The Operas of Benjamin Britten,* edited by David Herbert, 59–62. New York: Columbia UP, 1979.

Reed, T. J. "The Art of Ambivalence." In his *Thomas Mann: The Uses of Tradition,* 144–78. Oxford: Clarendon, 1974. Excerpted in Koelb, 1994, 150–78.

———. "'Der Zauberberg': Zeitenwandel und Bedeutungswandel 1912–24." In *Besichtigung des Zauberbergs,* edited by Heinz Sauereßig, 81–139. Biberach: Wege und Gestalten, 1974.

Schmidt, Ernst A. "Künstler und Knabenliebe: Eine vergleichende Skizze zu Thomas Manns *Tod in Venedig* und Vergils zweiter Ekloge." *Euphorion* 68.4 (1974): 437–46.

———. "'Platonismus' und 'Heidentum' in Thomas Manns 'Tod in Venedig.'" *Antike und Abendland* 20.2 (1974): 151–78.

Theobaldy, Jürgen. "Die Erdbeeren in Venedig." In his *Blaue Flecken: Gedichte: Mit Zeichnungen von Berndt Höppner,* 50. Reinbek bei Hamburg: Rowohlt, 1974.

Wiese, Epi. "Visconti and Renoir: Shadowplay." *Yale Review* 64.2 (December 1974): 202–17.

# 1975

Banuls, André. "Schopenhauer und Nietzsche in Thomas Manns Frühwerk." *Études Germaniques* 30.2 (April-June 1975): 129–47.

Diersen, Inge. "'Der Tod in Venedig.'" In her *Thomas Mann: Episches Werk[,] Weltanschauung[,] Leben*, 100–120. Berlin and Weimar: Aufbau, 1975.

Ezergailis, Inta Miske. "An Early View of the Male Realm: Gustave Aschenbach." In her *Male and Female: An Approach to Thomas Mann's Dialectic*, 47–71. The Hague: Nijhoff, 1975.

Farrelly, D. J. "Apollo and Dionysus Interpreted in Thomas Mann's *Der Tod in Venedig*." *New German Studies* 3.1 (Spring 1975): 1–15.

Fried, Erich. "Ein veraltetes Thema." In his *Fast alles Mögliche*, 45–50. Berlin: Wagenbach, 1975.

Gandelman, Claude. "Abstraction et empathie: Présence d'un thème esthétique dans l'œuvre de Thomas Mann." *Études Germaniques* 30.2 (April-June 1975): 179–92.

Koeppen, Wolfgang. ["Die Beschwörung der schweren Stunde."] *Frankfurter Allgemeine Zeitung*, 31 May 1975. Reprinted in *Thomas Mann: Ein Kolloquium*, edited by Hans H. Schulte and Gerald Chapple, 140–42. Bonn: Bouvier, 1978. Also reprinted as "Die Beschwörung der schweren Stunde" in Koeppen's *Die elenden Skribenten: Aufsätze*, edited by Marcel Reich-Ranicki, 107–110. Frankfurt am Main: Suhrkamp, 1981. And in his *Gesammelte Werke in sechs Bänden*, edited by Marcel Reich-Ranicki, Dagmar von Briel, and Hans-Ulrich Treichel, vol. 6, *Essays und Rezensionen*, 193–95. Frankfurt am Main: Suhrkamp, 1986.

Koopmann, Helmut. "Hanno Buddenbrook, Tonio Kröger und Tadzio: Anfang und Begründung des Mythos im Werk Thomas Manns." In *Gedenkschrift für Thomas Mann: 1875–1975*, edited by Rolf Wiecker, 53–65. Copenhagen: Text & Kontext, 1975. Reprinted in *Thomas Mann: Erzählungen und Novellen*, edited by Rudolf Wolff, 86–99. Bonn: Bouvier, 1984. Also in Koopmann's *Der schwierige Deutsche: Studien zum Werk Thomas Manns*, 3–12. Tübingen: Niemeyer, 1988.

———. "Der Tod in Venedig." In his *Thomas Mann: Konstanten seines literarischen Werks*, 31–45. Göttingen: Vandenhoeck & Ruprecht, 1975.

Leppmann, Wolfgang. "Time and Place in *Death in Venice*." *German Quarterly* 48.1 (January 1975): 66–75. Reprinted in his *In Zwei Welten zu Hause: Aus der Lebensarbeit eines amerikanischen Germanisten*, 127–39. Munich: Drei Ulmen, 1989.

McIntyre, Allan J. "Psychology and Symbol: Correspondences Between *Heart of Darkness* and *Death in Venice*." *Hartford Studies in Literature* 7.3 (1975): 216–35.

Marzinek, Otto. ["Der Tod in Venedig"]. *Medaillenkabinett* 1 (1975): 1–4.

Mendelssohn, Peter de. "Landschaft mit Kindern." In his *Der Zauberer: Das Leben des deutschen Schriftstellers Thomas Mann. Erster Teil 1875–1918*, 867–974. Frankfurt am Main: Fischer, 1975.

Mertz, Wolfgang, ed. *Thomas Mann: Wirkung und Gegenwart*. Frankfurt am Main: Fischer, 1975.

Northcote-Bade, James. "Thomas Manns Wagner-Krise 1909–1911." In his *Die Wagner-Mythen im Frühwerk Thomas Manns*, 81–91. Bonn: Bouvier, 1975.

Richner, Peter. *Thomas Manns Projekt eines Friedrich-Romans*. Zurich: Juris, 1975.

Schütte, Wolfram. "Morte a Venezia." In *Luchino Visconti*, edited by Peter W. Jansen and Wolfram Schütte, 117–22. Munich: Hanser, 1975.

Smith, Duncan. "The Education to Despair: Some Thoughts on *Death in Venice*." *Praxis* 1.1 (Spring 1975): 73–80.

Springer, Mary Doyle. "Degeneration in Mann's *Death in Venice*." In her *Forms of the Modern Novella*, 102–5. Chicago: U of Chicago P, 1975.

Ternes, Hans. "Das Groteske in 'Tod in Venedig.'" In his *Das Groteske in den Werken Thomas Manns*, 45–49. Stuttgart: Heinz, 1975.

Tyroff, Siegmar. *Namen bei Thomas Mann in den Erzählungen und den Romanen Buddenbrooks, Königliche Hoheit, Der Zauberberg*. Bern: Lang, 1975.

Uhlig, Ludwig. *Der Todesgenius in der deutschen Literatur von Winckelmann bis Thomas Mann*. Tübingen: Niemeyer, 1975.

Vaget, Hans Rudolf. "'Goethe oder Wagner': Studien zu Thomas Manns Goethe-Rezeption 1905–1912." In his and Dagmar Barnouw's *Thomas Mann: Studien zu Fragen der Rezeption*, 1–81. Bern: Lang, 1975.

Wagner, Geoffrey. "Death in Venice (1971)." In his *The Novel and the Cinema*, 338–47. Rutherford, NJ: Fairleigh Dickinson UP; London: Tantivy, 1975.

Wyatt, Frederick. "The Choice of the Topic in Fiction: Risks and Rewards: A Comparison of André Gide's *The Immoralist* and Thomas Mann's *Death in Venice*." In *Janus: Essays in Ancient and Modern Studies*, edited by Louis L. Orlin, 213–41 and 243–50. Ann Arbor: Center for Coördination of Ancient and Modern Studies, University of Michigan, 1975. Translated by Ulla Renner-Henke as "Zur Themenwahl in der Literatur: Gefahren und Gewinne. Ein Vergleich von André Gides 'Der Immoralist' und Thomas Manns 'Der Tod in Venedig'" in *Freiburger literaturpsychologische Gespräche* 3, edited by Johannes Cremerius et al., 113–44. Frankfurt am Main: Lang, 1984.

# 1976

Baumgart, Reinhard. "Betrogene Betrüger: Zu Thomas Manns letzter Erzählung und ihrer Vorgeschichte." In *Thomas Mann*, edited by Heinz Ludwig Arnold, 99–107. Munich: Text + Kritik, 1976. Zweite erweiterte Auflage, 1982, 123–31.

Bisdorff, Ernest. "Musik bei Thomas Mann." In his *Von Schiller zu Thomas Mann*, 69–107. Luxembourg: Institut Grand-Ducal, 1976.

Davidson, Leah. "Mid-Life Crisis in Thomas Mann's 'Death in Venice.'" *Journal of the American Academy of Psychoanalysis* 4.2 (1976): 203–14.

Heller, Erich. "Thomas Mann in Venice." In his *The Poet's Self and the Poem: Essays on Goethe, Nietzsche, Rilke and Thomas Mann*, 73–91. London: Athlone, 1976.

Hill, Reginald. *Another Death in Venice*. London: Collins, 1976; New York: New American Library, 1987.

Honsza, Norbert. "Thomas Mann und Polen." *Wissenschaftliche Zeitschrift der Friedrich-Schiller-Universität Jena, Gesellschafts- und Sprachwissenschaftliche Reihe*, no. 25.3 (1976): 403–7.

Ipser, Karl. "'Viel Tag für Dichter' in der Civitas metaphysica." In his *Venedig und die Deutschen*, 81–97. Munich: Markus, 1976.

Karsunke, Yaak. "'. . . von der albernen Sucht, besonders zu sein': Thomas Manns 'Der Tod in Venedig' — wiedergelesen." In *Thomas Mann*, edited by Heinz Ludwig Arnold, 61–69. Munich: Text + Kritik, 1976. Zweite erweiterte Auflage, 1982, 85–93.

Kindt, Walther. "Überlegungen zu Oskar Seidlin 'Stiluntersuchung an einem Thomas Mann-Satz.'" In *Interpretationsanalysen: Argumentationsstrukturen in literaturwissenschaftlichen Interpretationen*, edited by Walther Kindt and Siegfried J. Schmidt, 56–92. Munich: Fink, 1976.

Luft, Hermann. *Der Konflikt zwischen Geist und Sinnlichkeit in Thomas Manns "Tod in Venedig."* Bern: Lang, 1976.

Miller, R. D. "Thomas Mann." In his *Beyond Anarchy: Studies in Modern Literature*, 182–223. Harrogate: Duchy, 1976. Reprinted as *"Death in Venice": An Essay on Thomas Mann's Novella*. Harrogate: Duchy, 1983.

Scher, Steven Paul. "Kreativität als Selbstüberwindung: Thomas Manns permanente 'Wagner-Krise.'" In *Rezeption der deutschen Gegenwartsliteratur im Ausland*, edited by Dietrich Papenfuss and Jürgen Söring, 263–74. Stuttgart: Kohlhammer, 1976.

Singer, Irving. "*Death in Venice*: Visconti and Mann." *Modern Language Notes* 91.6 (December 1976): 1348–59.

Sokel, Walter H. "Demaskierung und Untergang wilhelminischer Repräsentanz: Zum Parallelismus der Inhaltsstruktur von *Professor Unrat* und 'Tod in Venedig.'" In *Herkommen und Erneuerung: Essays für Oskar Seidlin*, edited by Gerald Gillespie and Edgar Lohner, 387–412. Tübingen: Niemeyer, 1976.

Van Buren Kelley, Alice. "Von Aschenbach's *Phaedrus*: Platonic Allusion in *Der Tod in Venedig*." *Journal of English and Germanic Philology* 75.1–2 (January-April 1976): 228–40.

Wanner, Hans. "Im Labyrinth des platonischen Erotikers: Zu Thomas Manns 'Der Tod in Venedig'" and "Auf der Suche nach der verlorenen Identität: Zu Thomas Manns 'Tod in Venedig.'" In his *Individualität, Identität und Rolle: Das frühe Werk Heinrich Manns und Thomas Manns Erzählungen "Gladius Dei" und "Der Tod in Venedig,"* 102–13 and 203–15. Munich: Tuduv, 1976.

Ziolkowski, Theodore. "The Telltale Teeth: Psychodontia to Sociodontia." *PMLA* 91.1 (January 1976): 9–22.

# 1977

Anton, Herbert. "Die Rettung des Narziß: Eine 'transzendente Linie' im Werk Thomas Manns." In *Thomas Mann 1875–1975: Vorträge in München — Zürich — Lübeck*, edited by Beatrix Bludau, Eckhard Heftrich, and Helmut Koopmann, 207–21. Frankfurt am Main: Fischer, 1977.

Consigny, Scott. "Aschenbach's 'Page and a Half of Choicest Prose': Mann's Rhetoric of Irony." *Studies in Short Fiction* 14.4 (Fall 1977): 359–67.

Falk, Werner. "Thomas Mann: Der Tod in Venedig (1911–12)." In his *Der kollektive Traum vom Krieg: Epochale Strukturen der deutschen Literatur zwischen "Naturalismus" und "Expressionismus,"* 216–26. Heidelberg: Winter, 1977.

Faulstich, Werner, and Ingeborg Faulstich. "Luchino Visconti: 'Tod in Venedig' — Ein Vergleich von Film und literarischer Vorlage." In their *Modelle der Filmanalyse,* 14–60. Munich: Fink, 1977. Excerpted as "Der Tod in Venedig: Ein Vergleich von Film und literarischer Vorlage" in *Literaturverfilmung,* edited by Wolfgang Gast, 113–25. Bamberg: Buchner, 1993.

Grieser, Dietmar. "Venedig — der Nerven wegen." *Börsenblatt für den Deutschen Buchhandel,* 23 December 1977, 10–14. Reprinted as "Venedig — Der Nerven wegen: Wie Thomas Manns 'Tadzio' sich treu geblieben ist." In his *Piroschka, Sorbas & Co.: Schicksale der Weltliteratur,* 19–30. Munich: Langen-Müller, 1978.

Hermes, Eberhard. "Thomas Mann: 'Der Tod in Venedig' (1912) — Anregungen zur Interpretation." *Der Deutschunterricht* 29.4 (August 1977): 59–86.

Jendreiek, Helmut. "Kunst und Tod als mythische Universalisierung und Verfall: 'Der Tod in Venedig.'" In his *Thomas Mann: Der demokratische Roman,* 220–65. Düsseldorf: Bagel, 1977.

Kunz, Josef. "Der Tod in Venedig." In his *Die deutsche Novelle im 20. Jahrhundert,* 150–61. Berlin: Schmidt, 1977.

Kurzke, Hermann. *Thomas-Mann-Forschung 1969–1976: Ein kritischer Bericht.* Frankfurt: Fischer, 1977.

Mendelssohn, Peter de. "Bekenntnis und Autobiographie." In *Thomas Mann 1875–1975: Vorträge in München — Zürich — Lübeck,* edited by Beatrix Bludau, Eckhard Heftrich, and Helmut Koopmann, 606–27. Frankfurt am Main: Fischer, 1977.

Meyers, Jeffrey. "Mann and Musil: *Death in Venice* and *Young Törless.*" In his *Homosexuality and Literature 1890–1930,* 42–57. London: Athlone, 1977.

Pracht-Fitzell, Ilse. "*Die Geburt der Tragödie* und *Der Tod in Venedig.*" *Germanic Notes* 8.1/4 (1977): 10–17.

Schmidgall, Gary. "Death in Venice." In his *Literature as Opera,* 321–55. New York: Oxford UP, 1977.

Winkler, Michael. "Tadzio-Anastasios: A Note on *Der Tod in Venedig.*" *Modern Language Notes* 92.3 (April 1977): 607–9.

Zinkin, Louis. "'Death in Venice' — A Jungian View." *Journal of Analytical Psychology* 22.4 (October 1977): 354–66. Translated by Doris Baldus as "'Der Tod in Venedig': Ein *Jung*scher Aspekt." *Analytische Psychologie* 13.3 (August 1982): 165–82.

# 1978

Albrecht, Herbert. "Jan Vanriet und die Illustration: Eine kritische Untersuchung." In *Der Tod in Venedig: Hommage à Thomas Mann et Luchino Visconti: Zeichnungen, Aquarelle und Gemälde von Jörg Madlener [und] Jan Vanriet*. Darmstadt: Kunstverein Darmstadt, 1978.

Albright, Daniel. *Personality and Impersonality: Lawrence, Woolf, and Mann*. Chicago: U of Chicago P, 1978.

Apter, T. E. *Thomas Mann: The Devil's Advocate*. London: Macmillan, 1978; New York: New York UP, 1979.

Beharriell, Frederick J. "'Never without Freud': Freud's Influence on Mann." In *Thomas Mann in Context: Papers of the Clark University Centennial Colloquium*, edited by Kenneth Hughes, 1–15. Worcester, MA: Clark UP, 1978.

Brion, Marcel. "Les itinéraires initiatiques de la mort: Thomas Mann." In his *L'Allemagne romantique*, vol. 4, *Le voyage initatique II*, 261–313. Paris: Michel, 1978.

Carlsson, Anni. *Teufel, Tod und Tiermensch: Phantastischer Realismus als Geschichtsschreibung der Epoche*. Kronberg/Ts.: Athenäum, 1978.

Carstensen, Richard. "Lübeck und Venedig: 'Schwestern' an Ostsee und Adria." In *Der Wagen: Ein Lübeckisches Jahrbuch*, edited by Rolf Saltzwedel, 138–54. Lübeck: Hansisches Verlagskontor, 1978.

Cohn, Dorrit. *Transparent Minds: Narrative Modes for Presenting Consciousness in Fiction*. Princeton: Princeton UP, 1978.

Hamilton, Nigel. *The Brothers Mann*. London: Secker & Warburg, 1978; New Haven: Yale UP, 1979.

Heller, Peter. "Der *Tod in Venedig* und Thomas Manns *Grund-Motiv*." In *Thomas Mann: Ein Kolloquium*, edited by Hans H. Schulte and Gerald Chapple, 35–83. Bonn: Bouvier, 1978. Also as "'Der Tod in Venedig' und Manns Grundmotiv" in Heller's *Probleme der Zivilisation: Versuche über Goethe, Thomas Mann, Nietzsche und Freud*, 59–121. Bonn: Bouvier, 1978.

———. "Vergleiche." In his *Probleme der Zivilisation: Versuche über Goethe, Thomas Mann, Nietzsche und Freud*, 122–31. Bonn: Bouvier, 1978.

Leibrich, Louis. "Politique, culture et métaphysique chez Thomas Mann." *Études Germaniques* 33.1 (January-March 1978): 42–52.

Matt, Peter von. "Zur Psychologie des deutschen Nationalschriftstellers: Die paradigmatische Bedeutung der Hinrichtung und Verklärung Goethes durch Thomas Mann." In *Perspektiven psychoanalytischer Literaturkritik*, edited by Sebastian Goeppert, 82–100. Freiburg m Breisgau: Rombach, 1978. Reprinted in von Matt's *Das Schicksal der Phantasie: Studien zur deutschen Literatur*, 242–56. Munich: Hanser, 1994.

Mazzella, Anthony J. "*Death in Venice:* Fiction and Film." *College Literature* 5.3 (Fall 1978): 183–94.

Northcote-Bade, James. "*Der Tod in Venedig* and *Felix Krull:* The Effect of the Interruption in the Composition of Thomas Mann's *Felix Krull* Caused by *Der Tod in Venedig.*" *Deutsche Vierteljahrsschrift für Literaturwissenschaft und Geistesgeschichte* 52.2 (June 1978): 271–78.

Parkes, Ford B. "The Image of the Tiger in Thomas Mann's *Tod in Venedig.*" *Studies in Twentieth-Century Literature* 3 (1978–1979): 73–83.

Sontag, Susan. *Illness as Metaphor.* New York: Farrar, Straus ,& Giroux, 1978. Remarks on *Death in Venice* reprinted in her *Illness as Metaphor and AIDS and Its Metaphors.* New York: Doubleday, 1990.

Sperlich, Hans-C. "Madleners malerische Integrationen." In *Der Tod in Venedig: Hommage à Thomas Mann et Luchino Visconti: Zeichnungen, Aquarelle und Gemälde von Jörg Madlener [und] Jan Vanriet.* Darmstadt: Kunstverein Darmstadt, 1978.

Stewart, Walter K. "*Der Tod in Venedig:* The Path to Insight." *Germanic Review* 53.2 (Spring 1978): 50–55.

Vaget, Hans Rudolf. "Georg Lukács, Thomas Mann, and the Modern Novel." In *Thomas Mann in Context: Papers of the Clark University Centennial Colloquium,* edited by Kenneth Hughes, 38–65. Worcester, MA: Clark UP, 1978.

# 1979

Breuer, Lee. *A Prelude to Death in Venice.* New York: Plays in Process, 1979–80.

Cadieux, André. "The Jungle of Dionysus: The Self in Mann and Nietzsche." *Philosophy and Literature* 3.1 (Spring 1979): 53–63.

Fiedler, Leslie A. "Eros and Thanatos: Old Age in Love." In *Aging, Death, and the Completion of Being,* edited by David D. Van Tassel, 235–54. Philadelphia: U of Pennsylvania P, 1979.

Hanson, W. P. "The Achievement of Chandos and Aschenbach." *New German Studies* 7.1 (Spring 1979): 41–57.

Hijiya-Kirschnereit, Irmela. "Thomas Mann's Short Novel *Der Tod in Venedig* and Mishima Yukio's novel *Kinjiki:* a Comparison." In *European Studies on Japan,* edited by Ian Nish and Charles Dunn, 312–17. Tenterden, Kent: Norbury, 1979.

Marson, E. L. *The Ascetic Artist: Prefigurations in Thomas Mann's "Der Tod in Venedig."* Bern: Lang, 1979.

Phillips, Kathy J. "Conversion to Text, Initiation to Symbolism, in Mann's *Der Tod in Venedig* and James' *The Ambassadors.*" *Canadian Review of Comparative Literature/Revue Canadienne de Littérature Comparée* 6.4 (Fall/Automne 1979): 376–88.

Piper, Myfanwy. "Writing for Britten." In *The Operas of Benjamin Britten,* edited by David Herbert, 8–21. New York: Columbia UP, 1979.

Seitz, Gabriele. "Die Erzählung 'Der Tod in Venedig'" and "Der Film 'Der Tod in Venedig.'" In her *Film als Rezeptionsform von Literatur*, 186–327 and 498–582. Munich: Tuduv, 1979.

Stirling, Monica. *A Screen of Time: A Study of Luchino Visconti*. New York: Harcourt Brace Jovanovich, 1979.

# 1980

Bleicher, Thomas. "Zur Adaptation der Literatur durch den Film: Viscontis Metamorphose der Thomas Mann-Novelle 'Tod in Venedig.'" *Neophilologus* 64.4 (October 1980): 479–92.

Brown, Alan M. "Existential Bunraku." *Artweek*, 13 September 1980, 4–5.

Feder, Lillian. "The Return of the Dionysiac." In her *Madness in Literature*, 204–47. Princeton: Princeton UP, 1980.

Koeppen, Wolfgang. "Eine schwerblütige, wollüstige Erregung: Über Thomas Manns *Der Tod in Venedig*." *Frankfurter Allgemeine Zeitung*, 7 February 1980, 23. Reprinted as "Die Beschwörung der Liebe" in Koeppen's *Die elenden Skribenten: Aufsätze*, edited by Marcel Reich-Ranicki, 110–18. Frankfurt am Main: Suhrkamp, 1981. Also as "Die Beschwörung der Liebe" in his *Gesammelte Werke in sechs Bänden*, edited by Marcel Reich-Ranicki, Dagmar von Briel, and Hans-Ulrich Treichel, vol. 6, *Essays und Rezensionen*, 196–203. Frankfurt am Main: Suhrkamp, 1986. Also as "Eine schwerblütige, wollüstige Erregung: Wolfgang Koeppen über Thomas Mann: *Der Tod in Venedig* (1913) in *Romane von gestern — heute gelesen*, vol. 1., 1900–1918, edited by Marcel Reich-Ranicki, 187–94. Frankfurt am Main: Fischer, 1989.

Kurzke, Hermann. "Ästhetizistisches Wirkungsbewußtsein und narrative Ethik bei Thomas Mann." *Orbis Litterarum* 35.2 (1980): 163–84.

Mayer, Hans. "'Der Tod in Venedig.' Ein Thema mit Variationen." In his *Thomas Mann*, 370–85. Frankfurt am Main: Suhrkamp, 1980. Reprinted in *Literaturwissenschaft und Geistesgeschichte: Festschrift für Richard Brinkmann*, edited by Jürgen Brummack et al., 711–24. Tübingen: Niemeyer, 1981.

Meier, Bernhard. "Gustav von Aschenbachs Verfall: Studien zur Symbolik in Thomas Manns Erzählung 'Der Tod in Venedig.'" *Blätter für den Deutschlehrer* 24.1 (March 1980): 3–14.

Swales, Martin. *Thomas Mann: A Study*. London: Heinemann, 1980.

Vaget, Hans Rudolf. "Film and Literature: The Case of 'Death in Venice': Luchino Visconti and Thomas Mann." *German Quarterly* 54.2 (March 1980): 159–75.

Watts, Cedric. "The Protean Dionysus in Euripides' *The Bacchae* and Mann's *Death in Venice*." *Studi dell'Istituto Linguistico* [Florence, Italy], 3 (1980): 151–63.

Wolfzettel, Friedrich. "Familien- und Fremdenthematik im Werk Viscontis: Zu einer psychologisch-thematisierenden Sicht des Adaptionsproblems." In *Literatur in Film und Fernsehen: Von Shakespeare bis Beckett*, edited by Herbert Grabes, 57–80. Königstein/Ts.: Scriptor, 1980.

# 1981

Foster, John Burt, Jr. "From Nietzsche to the Savage God: An Early Appropriation by the Young Gide and Thomas Mann." In his *Heirs to Dionysus: A Nietzschean Current in Literary Modernism*, 145–79. Princeton: Princeton UP, 1981.

Pike, Burton. *The Image of the City in Modern Literature*. Princeton: Princeton UP, 1981.

Rockwood, Heidi M. "Mann's *Death in Venice*." *Explicator* 39.4 (Summer 1981): 34.

Schröder, Claus B. "Eines Tages, sieben Jahrzehnte später: Über Thomas Manns Novelle 'Der Tod in Venedig.'" Radio broadcast written for the series "Literatur aus aller Welt" of the Stimme der DDR and transmitted on 27 December 1981. Printed in *Das unbestechliche Geheimnis: Schriftsteller über Weltliteratur*, edited by Helmut Baldauf, 116–19. Berlin: Aufbau, 1984.

Servadio, Gaia. *Luchino Visconti: A Biography*. London: Weidenfeld & Nicholson, 1981; New York: Franklin Watts, 1983.

Siefken, Hinrich. *Thomas Mann: Goethe — "Ideal der Deutschheit."* Munich: Fink, 1981.

Winston, Richard. "Death in Venice." In his *Thomas Mann: The Making of an Artist 1875–1911*, 264–80. New York: Knopf, 1981.

# 1982

Borchmeyer, Dieter. *Das Theater Richard Wagners*. Stuttgart: Reclam, 1982. [N.B. The section containing Borchmeyer's comments on *Death in Venice* is not included in the English translation of his book by Stewart Spencer — *Richard Wagner: Theory and Theater*. Oxford: Clarendon Press, 1991.]

Butler, Christopher. "Joyce and the Displaced Author." In *James Joyce and Modern Literature*, edited by W. J. McCormack and Alistair Stead, 56–73. London: Routledge, 1982.

Dyck, Julie. "*Über das Marionettentheater* und *Der Tod in Venedig*." In *Der Instinkt der Verwandtschaft*, by J. W. Dyck, 121–29. Bern: Lang, 1982.

Feuerlicht, Ignace. "Thomas Mann and Homoeroticism." *Germanic Review* 57.3 (Summer 1982): 89–97. Translated by Karl Werner Böhm as "Thomas Mann und die Homoerotik." *Forum Homosexualität und Literatur* 3 (1988): 29–50.

Furness, Raymond. *Wagner and Literature*. Manchester: Manchester UP; New York: St. Martin's Press, 1982.

Harpham, Geoffrey Galt. "Metaphor, Marginality, and Parody in *Death in Venice*." In his *On the Grotesque: Strategies of Contradiction in Art and Literature*, 122–45. Princeton: Princeton UP, 1982.

Marcus-Tar, Judith. *Thomas Mann und Georg Lukács*. Cologne: Böhlau, 1982. Translated as *Georg Lukács and Thomas Mann*. Amherst: U of Massachusetts P, 1987.

Otto, Susanne. "'Tod in Venedig.'" In her *Literarische Produktion als egozentrische Variation des Problems von Identitätsfindung und -stabilisierung: Ursprung, Grundlagen und Konsequenzen bei Thomas Mann*, 228–38. Frankfurt am Main: Lang, 1982.

Ramras-Rauch, Gila. "Aschenbach in *Death in Venice*." In her *The Protagonist in Transition*, 115–55. Bern: Lang, 1982.

Reuter, Helmut Harald. *Der Intellektuelle und die Politik*. Frankfurt am Main: Lang, 1982.

Seeba, Hinrich C. "Johann Joachim Winckelmann: Zur Wirkungsgeschichte eines 'unhistorischen' Historikers zwischen Ästhetik und Geschichte." *Deutsche Vierteljahrsschrift für Literaturwissenschaft und Geistesgeschichte* 56 (September 1982): 168–201. (Sonderheft "Kultur. Geschichte und Verstehen.")

Spielmann, Hans Robert. "Die Ironie der Ironie: Ein gescheiterter (?) Unterrichtsversuch zu Thomas Manns 'Der Tod in Venedig.'" *Diskussion Deutsch* 13.66 (August/September 1982): 330–48.

Vaget, Hans Rudolf. *Goethe: Der Mann von 60 Jahren: Mit einem Anhang über Thomas Mann*. Königstein/Ts.: Athenäum, 1982.

# 1983

Cohn, Dorrit. "The Second Author of 'Der Tod in Venedig.'" In *Probleme der Moderne: Studien zur deutschen Literatur von Nietzsche bis Brecht. Festschrift für Walter Sokel*, edited by Benjamin Bennett, Anton Kaes, and William J. Lillyman, 223–45. Tübingen: Niemeyer, 1983. Reprinted in *Critical Essays on Thomas Mann*, edited by Inta M. Ezergailis, 124–43. Boston: Hall, 1988. Also in Koelb, 1994, 178–95.

Glassco, David. "Films Out of Books: Bergman, Visconti and Mann." *Mosaic* 16.1–2 (Winter/Spring 1983): 165–73.

Hansen, Volkmar and Gert Heine, eds. *Frage und Antwort: Interviews mit Thomas Mann 1909–1955*. Hamburg: Knaus, 1983.

McWilliams, James R. "Death in Venice." In his *Brother Artist: A Psychological Study of Thomas Mann's Fiction*, 147–58. Lanham, MD; London: UP of America, 1983.

Reed, T. J., ed. *Thomas Mann: Der Tod in Venedig*. Munich: Hanser, 1983.

Sommerhage, Claus. "Exkurs: Einige Bemerkungen zu Gustav von Aschenbachs Sokrates-Identifikation." In his *Eros und Poesis: Über das Erotische im Werk Thomas Manns*, 90–97. Bonn: Bouvier, 1983.

Stollman, Rainer. "Reading Kluge's *Mass Death in Venice*." Translated by Jeffrey S. Librett. *New German Critique* 30 (Fall 1983): 65–95.

Tonetti, Claretta. "*Death in Venice*: Rational Man Among the 'Devils.'" In her *Luchino Visconti*, 141–51. Boston: Twayne, 1983.

White, Eric Walter. "Death in Venice." In his *Benjamin Britten: His Life and Operas*, 2d ed., edited by John Evans, 268–81. Berkeley: U of California P, 1983.

# 1984

Bronsen, David. "The Artist against Himself: Henrik Ibsen's *Master Builder* and Thomas Mann's *Death in Venice.*" *Neohelicon* 11.1 (1984): 323–44.

Exner, Richard. "Das berückend Menschliche oder Androgynie in der Literatur: Im Hauptbeispiel Thomas Mann." *Neue deutsche Hefte* 31 (1984): 254–76.

Fokkema, Douwe, and Elrud Ibsch. *Modernisme in de Europese Letterkunde.* Amsterdam: Arbeiderspers, 1984. Translated by the authors as *Modernist Conjectures: A Mainstream in European Literature 1910–1940.* London: Hurst, 1987.

Gockel, Heinz. "Aschenbachs Tod in Venedig." In *Thomas Mann: Erzählungen und Novellen,* edited by Rudolf Wolff, 27–41. Bonn: Bouvier, 1984.

Gullette, Margaret Morganroth. "The Exile of Adulthood: Pedophilia in the Midlife Novel." *Novel* 17.3 (Spring 1984): 215–32.

Hansen, Volkmar. *Thomas Mann.* Stuttgart: Metzler, 1984.

Heller, Erich. "Observations on Psychoanalysis and Modern Literature." In his *In the Age of Prose: Literary and philosophical essays,* 177–91. Cambridge: Cambridge UP, 1984.

Klussmann, Paul Gerhard. "Die Struktur des Leitmotivs in Thomas Manns Erzählprosa." In *Thomas Mann: Erzählungen und Novellen,* edited by Rudolf Wolff, 8–26. Bonn: Bouvier, 1984.

Northcote-Bade, James. "The Background to the 'Liebestod' Plot Pattern in the Works of Thomas Mann." *Germanic Review* 59.1 (Winter 1984): 11–18.

Palmer, Christopher. "Towards a Genealogy of *Death in Venice.*" In *The Britten Companion,* edited by Christopher Palmer, 250–67. Cambridge: Cambridge UP, 1984.

Rockwood, Heidi M., and Robert J. R. Rockwood. "The Psychological Reality of Myth in *Der Tod in Venedig.*" *Germanic Review* 59.4 (Fall 1984): 137–41.

Sonner, Franz Maria. *Ethik und Körperbeherrschung: Die Verflechtung von Thomas Manns Novelle "Der Tod in Venedig" mit dem zeitgenössischen intellektuellen Kräftefeld.* Opladen: Westdeutscher Verlag, 1984.

Sweet, Geoffrey. *Kratos, Ethos, Music (Nietzsche, Mann, Mahler).* Oxford: Polmus, 1984.

Thornton, Lawrence. "The Closed Circle: *Death in Venice* and the Passions of the Mind." In his *Unbodied Hope: Narcissism and the Modern Novel,* 169–85. Lewisburg, PA: Bucknell UP; London and Toronto: Associated University Presses, 1984.

Vaget, Hans Rudolf. "Der Tod in Venedig." In his *Thomas Mann — Kommentar zu sämtlichen Erzählungen,* 170–200. Munich: Winkler, 1984.

Vondung, Klaus. "Träume von Tod und Untergang: Präludien zur Apokalypse in der deutschen Literatur und Kunst vor dem Ersten Weltkrieg." In *Von kommenden Zeiten: Geschichtsprophetien im 19. und 20. Jahrhundert,* edited by Joachim H. Knoll and Julius H. Schoeps, 143–68. Stuttgart: Burg, 1984.

# 1985

Adolphs, Dieter Wolfgang. "Der Anfang der Novelle 'Der Tod in Venedig' und das Problem seiner erzählerischen Motivierung." In his *Literarischer Erfahrungshorizont: Aufbau und Entwicklung der Erzählperspektive im Werk Thomas Manns,* 23–30. Heidelberg: Winter, 1985.

Barton, Richard W. "Plato/Freud/Mann: Narrative structure, undecidability, and the social text." *Semiotica* 54.3–4 (1985): 351–86.

Effe, Bernd. "Sokrates in Venedig: Thomas Mann und die 'platonische Liebe.'" *Antike und Abendland* 31.2 (1985): 153–66.

Galerstein, Carolyn. "Images of Decadence in Visconti's *Death in Venice.*" *Literature/Film Quarterly* 13.1 (1985): 29–34.

Jofen, Jean. "A Freudian Commentary on Thomas Mann's *Death in Venice.*" *Journal of Evolutionary Psychology* 6.3–4 (August 1985): 238–47.

Kurzke, Hermann. "Der Tod in Venedig." In his *Thomas Mann: Epoche — Werk — Wirkung,* 118–28. Munich: Beck, 1985.

Lubich, Frederick Alfred. "Die Entfaltung der Dialektik von Logos und Eros in Thomas Manns 'Tod in Venedig.'" *Colloquia Germanica* 18.2 (1985): 140–59.

Michel, Willy. "Literaturverfilmung — Funktionswandel eines Genres." *Universitas* 40, no. 472, Heft 9 (September 1985): 1015–27.

Renner, Rolf Günter. "Nichtsprachliche Kommunikation und familiale Phantasien: 'Der Tod in Venedig' und andere Novellen." In his *Lebens-Werk: Zum inneren Zusammenhang der Texte von Thomas Mann,* 38–55. Munich: Fink, 1985.

Schmitz, Walter. "'Der Tod in Venedig': Eine Erzählung aus Thomas Manns Münchner Jahren." *Blätter für den Deutschlehrer* 29.1 (March 1985): 2–20.

Wagner, Luc. "'La Mort à Venise': Mythe et Passion." *Impacts: Revue de l'Université Catholique de l'Ouest* 15.1 (March 1985): 49–55.

Whiton, John. "H. T. Lowe-Porters *Death in Venice.*" *Mannheimer Berichte aus Forschung und Lehre* 27 (1985): 3–11. Translated as "H. T. Lowe-Porter's *Death in Venice*" in Whiton's *Faith and Finality: Collected Essays in German Literature,* 235–59. New York: Lang, 1991.

# 1986

Baron, Frank. "Das Sokrates-Bild von Georg Lukács als Quelle für Thomas Manns *Tod in Venedig.*" In *Im Dialog mit der Moderne: Zur deutschsprachigen Literatur von der Gründerzeit bis zur Gegenwart: Jacob Steiner zum sechzigsten Geburtstag,* edited by Roland Jost and Hansgeorg Schmidt-Bergmann, 96–105. Frankfurt am Main: Athenäum, 1986.

Berman, Russell A. *The Rise of the Modern German Novel: Crisis and Charisma.* Cambridge, MA: Harvard UP, 1986.

Böschenstein, Bernhard. "Apoll und seine Schatten: Winckelmann in der deutschen Dichtung der beiden Jahrhundertwenden." In *Johann Joachim Winckelmann 1717–68*, edited by Thomas W. Gaehtgens, 327–42. Hamburg: Meiner, 1986.

Bridges, George. "The Problem of Pederastic Love in Thomas Mann's *Death in Venice* and Plato's *Phaedrus*." *Selecta* 7 (1986): 39–46.

Evans, John. "*Death in Venice:* The Apollonian/Dionysian Conflict." *Opera Quarterly* 4.3 (Autumn 1986): 102–15.

Fähnrich, Hermann. "Der Tod in Venedig (Novelle), Juli 1911 — Juli 1912." In his *Thomas Manns episches Musizieren im Sinne Richard Wagners*, edited by Maria Hülle-Keeding, 163–79. Frankfurt am Main: Herchen, 1986.

Fletcher, Angus. "Music, Visconti, Mann, Nietzsche: *Death in Venice*." *Stanford Italian Review* 6.1–2 (1986): 301–12.

Frank, Bernhard. "Mann's *Death in Venice*." *Explicator* 45.1 (Fall 1986): 31–32.

Jordan, Jim, and Donal McLaughlin. "'Inmitten des quälenden Geschreies der Dummheit': A New Assessment of the Relationship between Alfred Andersch and Thomas Mann." Parts 1, 2. *New German Studies* 14.1, 14.2 (1986/7): 55–72, 101–14.

Knüfermann, Volker. "Die Gefährdung des Narziß oder: Zur Begründung und Problematik der Form in Thomas Manns *Der Tod in Venedig* und Robert Musils *Die Verwirrungen des Zöglings Törleß*." In *Im Dialog mit der Moderne: Zur deutschsprachigen Literatur von der Gründerzeit bis zur Gegenwart: Jacob Steiner zum sechzigsten Geburtstag*, edited by Roland Jost und Hansgeorg Schmidt-Bergmann, 84–95. Frankfurt am Main: Athenäum, 1986.

Lubich, Frederick Alfred. "'Der Tod in Venedig.'" In his *Die Dialektik von Logos und Eros im Werk von Thomas Mann*, 24–73. Heidelberg: Winter, 1986.

Mz. "Ästhetischer Schein: 'Der Tod in Venedig' als Ballett in München." *Neue Zürcher Zeitung*, 13 November 1986, 39.

Nennecke, Charlotte. "Liebesqualen in der Lagunenstadt: Norbert Vesaks 'Der Tod in Venedig' nach Thomas Manns Novelle im Nationaltheater." *Süddeutsche Zeitung*, 3 November 1986, 13.

Rasch, Wolfdietrich. "Thomas Mann und die Décadence." In his *Die literarische Décadence um 1900*, 159–69. Munich: Beck, 1986.

Sinyard, Neil. "Death in Venice." In his *Filming Literature: The Art of Screen Adaptation*, 126–30. New York: St. Martin's Press, 1986.

Žmegač, Viktor. "Zu einem Thema Goethes und Thomas Manns: Wege der Erotik in der modernen Gesellschaft." *Goethe Jahrbuch* 103 (1986): 152–67. Reprinted in his *Tradition und Innovation: Studien zur deutschsprachigen Literatur seit der Jahrhundertwende*, 180–98. Cologne: Böhlau, 1993.

# 1987

Bloom, Allan. *The Closing of the American Mind.* New York: Simon and Schuster, 1987.

Carnegy, Patrick. "The Novella Transformed: Thomas Mann as Opera." In *Benjamin Britten: Death in Venice,* edited by Donald Mitchell, 168–77. Cambridge: Cambridge UP, 1987.

Dassanowsky-Harris, Robert von. "Thomas Mann's *Der Tod in Venedig:* Unfulfilled 'Aufbruch' from the Wilhelminian World." *Germanic Notes* 18.1–2 (1987): 16–17.

Eggenschwiler, David. "The Very Glance of Art: Ironic Narrative in Mann's *Novellen.*" *Modern Language Quarterly* 48.1 (March 1987): 59–85.

Geiser, Peter. "En hexametro tono." *Blätter der Thomas Mann Gesellschaft Zürich* 22 (1987–88): 19–27.

LaCapra, Dominick. "Mann's *Death in Venice:* An Allegory of Reading." In his *History, Politics, and the Novel,* 111–28. Ithaca: Cornell UP, 1987.

Luijs, John. "Der Tod in Venedig von Thomas Mann: Rezeption des homoerotischen Elements." Utrecht, 1987.

Reed, Philip. "Aschenbach becomes Mahler: Thomas Mann as film." In *Benjamin Britten: Death in Venice,* edited by Donald Mitchell, 178–83. Cambridge: Cambridge UP, 1987.

Renner, Rolf Günter. *Das Ich als ästhetische Konstruktion: "Der Tod in Venedig" und seine Beziehung zum Gesamtwerk Thomas Manns.* Freiburg im Breisgau: Rombach, 1987.

Rotkin, Charlotte. "Oceanic Animals: Allegory in *Death in Venice.*" *Papers on Language & Literature* 23.1 (Winter 1987): 84–88.

Schenk, Christiane. "Thomas Mann, Der Tod in Venedig (1911)." In her *Venedig im Spiegel der Décadence-Literatur des Fin de siècle,* 380–410. Frankfurt am Main: Lang, 1987.

Siefken, Hinrich. "Thomas Mann und Theodor Haecker." In *Internationales Thomas-Mann-Kolloquium 1986 in Lübeck,* 246–70. Thomas-Mann-Studien 7. Bern: Francke, 1987.

Vogt, Karen Drabek. "'Death in Venice.'" In her *Vision and Revision: The Concept of Inspiration in Thomas Mann's Fiction,* 27–54. New York: Lang, 1987.

Weiner, Marc A. "Silence, Sound, and Song in *Der Tod in Venedig:* A Study in Psycho-Social Repression." *Seminar* 23.2 (May 1987): 137–55.

# 1988

Astrachan, Gary D. "Dionysos in Thomas Manns Novelle 'Der Tod in Venedig.'" Translated by A. J. Ziegler. *Gorgo* 14 (1988): 45–62. Printed in English as "Dionysos in Thomas Mann's Novella, 'Death in Venice'" in *Journal of Analytical Psychology* 35.1 (January 1990): 59–78.

Boschert, Bernhard and Ulf Schramm. "Literatur und Literaturwissenschaft als Medium der Bearbeitung von Verdrängung: Beobachtungen an Thomas Manns 'Der Tod in Venedig' — ein Beitrag zur Germanistik als Friedens- und Konfliktforschung." In *Politische Aufgaben und soziale Funktionen von Germanistik und Deutschunterricht,* edited by Norbert Oellers, 19–34. Tübingen: Niemeyer, 1988.

Cerf, Steven R. "Benjamin Britten's *Death in Venice:* Operatic Stream of Consciousness." In *Criticism, History, and Intertextuality,* edited by Richard Fleming and Michael Payne [*Bucknell Review* 31.1], 124–38. Lewisburg, PA: Bucknell UP, 1988.

Golden, Kenneth L. "Archetypes and 'Immoralists' in André Gide and Thomas Mann." *College Literature* 5.2 (Spring 1988): 189–98.

Goldman, Harvey. "The Death in Life of the Artistic Personality: *Death in Venice.*" In his *Max Weber and Thomas Mann: Calling and the Shaping of the Self,* 187–208. Berkeley: U of California P, 1988.

Härle, Gerhard. *Männerweiblichkeit: Zur Homosexualität bei Klaus und Thomas Mann.* Frankfurt am Main: Athenäum, 1988.

Luke, David. Introduction to *Death in Venice and Other Stories by Thomas Mann,* translated by David Luke, vii–li. New York: Bantam, 1988. Excerpted in Koelb, 1994, 195–207.

May, Keith M. *Nietzsche and Modern Literature.* London: Macmillan, 1988.

Mennemeier, Franz Norbert. *Literatur der Jahrhundertwende II: Europäisch-deutsche Literaturtendenzen 1870–1910.* Bern: Lang, 1988.

Oppenheimer, Fred E. "Auf den Spuren Gustav Aschenbachs: Schlüsselfiguren zu Gustav Aschenbach in Thomas Manns Der Tod in Venedig." In *Studies in Modern and Classical Languages and Literature (I),* edited by Fidel López Criado, 145–53. Madrid: Orígenes, 1988.

Pütz, Peter. "Der Ausbruch aus der Negativität: Das Ethos im *Tod in Venedig.*" *Thomas Mann Jahrbuch* 1 (1988): 1–11.

Radcliff-Umstead, Douglas. "The Journey of Fatal Longing: Mann and Visconti." *Annali d'Italianistica* 6 (1988): 199–219.

Reilly, Patrick. "*Death in Venice:* the Boons of Chaos." In his *The Literature of Guilt,* 69–91. Iowa City: U of Iowa P, 1988.

Roßbach, Bruno. "Der Anfang vom Ende: Narrative Analyse des ersten Kapitels der Novelle 'Der Tod in Venedig' von Thomas Mann." In *Sprache in Vergangenheit und Gegenwart,* edited by Wolfgang Brandt in Verbindung mit Rudolf Freudenberg, 237–49. Marburg: Hitzeroth, 1988.

Rotkin, Charlotte. "Form and Function: The Art and Architecture of *Death in Venice.*" *Midwest Quarterly* 29.4 (Summer 1988): 497–505.

Sparre, Sulamith. "Gustav Aschenbachs Sympathie mit dem Abgrund — Thomas Mann und Nietzsche." In her *Todessehnsucht und Erlösung: 'Tristan' und 'Armer Heinrich' in der deutschen Literatur um 1900,* 25–28. Göppingen: Kümmerle, 1988.

Wiehe, Roger E. "Of Art and Death: Film and Fiction Versions of *Death in Venice.*" *Literature/Film Quarterly* 16.3 (1988): 210–15.

Woodward, Kathleen. "Youthfulness as a Masquerade." *Discourse* 11.1 (Fall-Winter 1988–1989): 119–42.

# 1989

Baumgart, Reinhard. "Der erotische Schriftsteller." In *Thomas Mann und München: Fünf Vorträge von Reinhard Baumgart, Joachim Kaiser, Kurt Sontheimer, Peter Wapnewski, Hans Wysling,* 7–24. Frankfurt am Main: Fischer, 1989.

————. *Selbstvergessenheit: Drei Wege zum Werk: Thomas Mann, Franz Kafka, Bertolt Brecht.* Munich: Hanser, 1989.

Bollerup, Lene. "Allerlei Sonstiges durch Thomas Mann: Eine vergleichende Lektüre von Max Frisch: *Homo Faber* und Thomas Mann: *Der Tod in Venedig.*" *Text & Kontext* 17.2 (1989): 266–78.

Bouson, J. Brooks. "Defensive Aestheticism and Self-Delusion: The Demise of the Artist in Mann's *Death in Venice.*" In his *The Empathic Reader: A Study of the Narcissistic Character and the Drama of the Self,* 105–17. Amherst: U of Massachusetts P, 1989.

Corse, Sandra and Larry Corse. "Britten's *Death in Venice:* Literary and Musical Structures." *Musical Quarterly* 73.3 (1989): 344–63.

Darmaun, Jacques. "Aspects de l'Italie chez T. Mann: L'image de Venise de la 'Mort à Venise.'" In *Études allemandes et autrichiennes: Hommage à Richard Thieberger,* 103–13. Paris: Belles Lettres, 1989.

Engelberg, Edward. "*Death in Venice:* Narcissus by the Seaside." In his *Elegiac Fictions: The Motif of the Unlived Life,* 96–103. University Park: Pennsylvania State UP, 1989.

Fischer, Kurt von. "Gustav Mahlers Adagietto und Luchino Viscontis Film *Morte a Venezia.*" In *Verlust und Ursprung: Festschrift für Werner Weber,* edited by Angelika Maass and Bernhard Heinser, 44–52. Zurich: Ammann, 1989.

Giobbi, Giuliana. "Gabriele D'Annunzio and Thomas Mann: *Venice, Art and Death.*" *Journal of European Studies* 19, pt. 1, no. 73 (March 1989): 55–68.

Hayes, Tom, and Lee Quinby. "The Aporia of Bourgeois Art: Desire in Thomas Mann's *Death in Venice.*" *Criticism* 31.2 (Spring 1989): 159–77.

Hillesheim, Jürgen. "'Der Tod in Venedig.'" In his *Die Welt als Artefakt: Zur Bedeutung von Nietzsches "Der Fall Wagner" im Werk Thomas Manns,* 82–98. Frankfurt am Main: Lang, 1989.

Lesér, Esther H. "An Artist's Call and Fate: The Nature of Beauty: 'Death in Venice' ('Der Tod in Venedig')." In her *Thomas Mann's Short Fiction,* edited by Mitzi Brunsdale, 161–80. Rutherford, NJ: Fairleigh Dickinson UP; London and Toronto: Associated University Presses, 1989.

Margetts, John. "Die 'scheinbar herrenlose' Kamera: Thomas Manns 'Tod in Venedig' und die Kunstphotographie Wilhelm von Gloedens." *Germanisch-Romanische Monatsschrift* 39.3 (1989): 326–37.

Sheppard, Richard. "*Tonio Kröger* and *Der Tod in Venedig:* From Bourgeois Realism to Visionary Modernism." *Oxford German Studies* 18–19 (1989–90): 92–108.

Stock, R. D. *The Flutes of Dionysus: Daemonic Enthrallment in Literature.* Lincoln: U of Nebraska P, 1989.

Wertheim, Ursula. "Goethe-Motive im Wandel oder ein Goethe-Motiv bei Thomas Mann." *Goethe Jahrbuch* 106 (1989): 160–68.

# 1990

Barnes, Jim. "*Death in Venice* and *Under the Volcano*" and "*Death in Venice* and *Dark as the Grave Wherein My Friend is Laid.*" In his *Fiction of Malcolm Lowry and Thomas Mann*, 107–16, 117–20. Kirksville, MO: Thomas Jefferson UP, 1990.

Dierks, Manfred. "Thomas Mann und die Mythologie." In *Thomas-Mann-Handbuch*, edited by Helmut Koopmann, 301–6. Stuttgart: Kröner, 1990.

———. "Der Wahn und die Träume in 'Der Tod in Venedig': Thomas Manns folgenreiche Freud-Lektüre im Jahr 1911." *Psyche* 44.3 (March 1990): 240–68.

Fickert, Kurt. "Truth and Fiction in *Der Tod in Venedig*." *Germanic Notes* 21.1–2 (1990): 25–31.

Furst, Lilian R. "The Ethics of Reading in *Death in Venice*." *LIT* 1.4 (1990): 265–74.

Gesing, Fritz. "Symbolisierung. Voraussetzungen und Strategien: Ein Versuch am Beispiel von Thomas Manns 'Der Tod in Venedig.'" *Freiburger literaturpsychologische Gespräche* 9, *Die Psychoanalyse der literarischen Form(en)*, edited by Johannes Cremerius et al., 226–53. Würzburg: Königshausen & Neumann, 1990.

Hess-Lüttich, Ernest W. B., and Susan A. Liddell. "Medien-Variationen: Aschenbach und Tadzio in Thomas Manns 'Der Tod in Venedig,' Luchino Viscontis 'Morte a Venezia,' Benjamin Brittens 'Death in Venice.'" In *Code-Wechsel: Texte im Medienvergleich*, edited by Ernest W. B. Hess-Lüttich and Roland Posner, 27–54. Opladen: Westdeutscher Verlag, 1990. Revised in *Kodikas/Code: Ars semeiotica* 14.1–2 (1991): 145–61.

Hindley, Clifford. "Contemplation and Reality: A Study in Britten's 'Death in Venice.'" *Music & Letters* 71.4 (November 1990): 511–23.

Jones, James W. *"We of the Third Sex": Literary Representations of Homosexuality in Wilhelmine Germany.* New York: Lang, 1990.

Ozaki, Jun. "Über die zwei Werke, 'Das Schneeland' und 'Der Tod in Venedig.'" *Gengo Bunkabu kiyåo* 18 (1990): 199–201.

Paglia, Camille. *Sexual Personae.* London and New Haven: Yale UP, 1990.

Renner, Rolf G. "Verfilmungen der Werke von Thomas Mann." In *Thomas-Mann-Handbuch*, edited by Helmut Koopmann, 799–822. Stuttgart: Kröner, 1990.

Sedgwick, Eve Kosofsky. *Epistemology of the Closet.* Berkeley: U of California P, 1990.

Vaget, Hans R. "Die Erzählungen." In *Thomas-Mann-Handbuch*, edited by Helmut Koopmann, 524–618. Stuttgart: Kröner, 1990.

Vargas Llosa, Mario. "La muerte en venecia: El llamado del abismo." In his *La verdad de las mentiras: Ensayos sobre literatura,* 21–29. Barcelona: Seix Barral, 1990. Reprinted in his *La verdad de las mentiras: Ensayos sobre la novela moderna,* 19–25. Lima: Peisa, 1993. Translated as "Der Ruf des Abgrunds: *Der Tod in Venedig*" in Vargas Llosa's *Die Wahrheit der Lügen: Essays zur Literatur,* translated by E. Wehr, 21–27. Frankfurt am Main: Suhrkamp, 1994.

White, Richard. "Love, Beauty, and Death in Venice." *Philosophy and Literature* 14.1 (April 1990): 53–64.

# 1991

Bahr, Ehrhard. *Erläuterungen und Dokumente: Thomas Mann: Der Tod in Venedig.* Stuttgart: Reclam, 1991.

Becker, Jared M. "Life in Venice: D'Annunzio, Marinetti and Thomas Mann." *Italian Culture* 9 (1991): 231–41.

Böhm, Karl Werner. "Geschichte eines Themas: Ein kritischer Forschungsbericht" and "Die unbegriffene Provokation: *Der Tod in Venedig.*" In his *Zwischen Selbstsucht und Verlangen: Thomas Mann und das Stigma Homosexualität,* 17–57, 321–35. Würzburg: Königshausen & Neumann, 1991.

Carrère, Bernadette. "Envoûtements et sortilèges de la ville morte au tournant du siècle: *Bruges-la-Morte* et *Mort à Venise.*" *Litteratures* 24 (Spring 1991): 105–13.

Colin, René-Pierre. *Les privilèges du chaos: "La Mort à Venise" et l'esprit décadent.* Tusson, Charente: Du L'érot, 1991.

Dedner, Burghard. "Satire Prohibited: Laughter, Satire, and Irony in Thomas Mann's Oeuvre." In *Laughter Unlimited: Essays on Humor, Satire, and the Comic,* edited by Reinhold Grimm and Jost Hermand, 27–40. Madison: U of Wisconsin P, 1991.

Dierks, Manfred. "Traumzeit und Verdichtung: Der Einfluß der Psychoanalyse auf Thomas Manns Erzählweise." In *Thomas Mann und seine Quellen: Festschrift für Hans Wysling,* edited by Eckhard Heftrich and Helmut Koopmann, 111–37. Frankfurt am Main: Klostermann, 1991.

Furst, Lilian R. "Reading 'Nasty' Great Books." In *The Hospitable Canon: Essays on Literary Play, Scholarly Choice, and Popular Pressures,* edited by Virgil Nemoianu and Robert Royal, 39–51. Philadelphia: Benjamins, 1991. Reprinted in Furst's *Through the Lens of the Reader: Explorations of European Narrative,* 39–50. Albany: State U of New York P, 1992.

Goodheart, Eugene. "The Art of Ambivalence: Mann's *Death in Venice.*" In his *Desire and Its Discontents,* 45–57. New York: Columbia UP, 1991.

Gribomont, Marie. "*Le train immobile* de Frédérick Tristan et *La Mort à Venise* de Thomas Mann." *Les Lettres Romanes* 45.3 (August 1991): 231–35.

Gutiérrez Mouat, Ricardo. "Aesthetics, Ethics, and Politics in Donoso's *El jardín de al lado.*" *PMLA* 106.1 (January 1991): 60–70.

Jonas, Klaus W. "Illustrierte Thomas-Mann-Ausgaben: Ein Überblick." *Aus dem Antiquariat* 5 (1991) [*Börsenblatt für den Deutschen Buchhandel*, 31 May 1991], A177–A184.

Krüll, Marianne. "'Der Tod in Venedig.'" In her *Im Netz der Zauberer: Eine andere Geschichte der Familie Mann*, 224–28. Zurich: Arche, 1991.

Rudolph, Andrea. "'Der Tod in Venedig': Das klassische Gleichgewicht und der erotisierte Dornauszieher Tadzio." In her *Zum Modernitätsproblem in ausgewählten Erzählungen Thomas Manns*, 128–46. Stuttgart: Heinz, 1991.

Sandberg, Hans-Joachim. "'*Der fremde Gott*' und die Cholera: Nachlese zum *Tod in Venedig*." In *Thomas Mann und seine Quellen: Festschrift für Hans Wysling*, edited by Eckhard Heftrich and Helmut Koopmann, 66–110. Frankfurt am Main: Klostermann, 1991.

Suzuki, Junichi. "Narziß und Narzißmus im 'Tod in Venedig.'" *Doitsu Bungaku* 87 (Fall 1991): 94–95.

Tillmann, Claus. *Das Frauenbild bei Thomas Mann*. Wuppertal: Deimling, 1991.

# 1992

Berlin, Jeffrey B., ed. *Approaches to Teaching Mann's "Death in Venice" and Other Short Fiction*. New York: Modern Language Association, 1992.

———. "Psychoanalysis, Freud, and Thomas Mann." In Berlin, 1992, 105–18.

Bruhn, Gert. *Das Selbstzitat bei Thomas Mann*. New York: Lang, 1992.

Bryson, Cynthia B. "The Imperative Daily Nap; Or, Aschenbach's Dream in *Death in Venice*." *Studies in Short Fiction* 29.2 (Spring 1992): 181–93.

Burkman, Katherine H. "Harold Pinter's Death in Venice: *The Comfort of Strangers*." *The Pinter Review* (1992–93): 38–45.

Carpenter, Humphrey. *Benjamin Britten: A Biography*. New York: Scribners, 1992.

Del Caro, Adrian. "Philosophizing and Poetic License in Mann's Early Fiction." In Berlin, 1992, 39–48.

Detering, Heinrich. "'Der Litterat als Abenteurer': *Tonio Kröger* zwischen *Dorian Gray* und *Der Tod in Venedig*." *Forum Homosexualität und Literatur* 14 (1992): 5–22.

Deuse, Werner. "'Besonders ein antikisierendes Kapitel scheint mir gelungen': Griechisches in *Der Tod in Venedig*." In *"Heimsuchung und süßes Gift": Erotik und Poetik bei Thomas Mann*, edited by Gerhard Härle, 41–62. Frankfurt am Main: Fischer, 1992.

Fetzer, John Francis. "Visconti's Cinematic Version of *Death in Venice*." In Berlin, 1992, 146–52.

Frizen, Werner. "Der 'Drei-Zeilen Plan' Thomas Manns: Zur Vorgeschichte von *Der Tod in Venedig*." *Thomas Mann Jahrbuch* 5 (1992): 125–41.

Furst, Lilian R. "Assent and Resistance in *Die Marquise von O* — and *Der Tod in Venedig.*" In her *Through the Lens of the Reader: Explorations of European Narrative,* 53–66. Albany: State U of New York P, 1992.

Gillespie, Gerald. "Mann and the Modernist Tradition." In Berlin, 1992, 93–104.

Goldman, Harvey. *Politics, Death, and the Devil: Self and Power in Max Weber and Thomas Mann.* Berkeley: U of California P, 1992.

Hillman, Roger. "Deaths in Venice." *Journal of European Studies* 22, pt. 4, no. 88 (December 1992): 291–311.

Hindley, Clifford. "Platonic Elements in Britten's 'Death in Venice.'" *Music & Letters* 73.3 (August 1992): 407–29.

Martin, Robert. K. "Gender, Sexuality, and Identity in Mann's Short Fiction." In Berlin, 1992, 57–67.

Popp, Wolfgang. "Thomas Mann." In his *Männerliebe: Homosexualität und Literatur,* 386–98. Stuttgart: Metzler, 1992.

Ritter, Naomi. "*Death in Venice* and the Tradition of European Decadence." In Berlin, 1992, 86–92.

Rohr Scaff, Susan von. "Plato and Nietzsche in *Death in Venice.*" In Berlin, 1992, 140–45.

Smith, Herbert O. "Prologue to the Great War: Encounters with Apollo and Dionysus in *Death in Venice.*" *Focus on Robert Graves and His Contemporaries* 1.13 (Winter 1992): 36–42.

Stanzel, Franz K. "Consonant and Dissonant Closure in *Death in Venice* and *The Dead.*" In *Neverending Stories: Toward a Critical Narratology,* edited by Ann Fehn, Ingeborg Hoesterey, and Maria Tatar, 112–23. Princeton: Princeton UP, 1992.

Szendi, Zoltán. "Platen, der 'Kronzeuge': Philologische Bemerkungen zu Thomas Manns Erzählung *Der Tod in Venedig.*" *Jahrbuch der ungarischen Germanistik* (1992): 127–37.

Tanner, Tony. *Venice Desired.* Cambridge, MA: Harvard UP, 1992.

Timms, Edward. "*Death in Venice* as Psychohistory." In Berlin, 1992, 134–39.

Travers, Martin. "Liebestod: Death in Venice." In his *Thomas Mann,* 48–59. New York: St. Martin's Press, 1992.

Wiegmann, Hermann. "Der Tod in Venedig." In his *Die Erzählungen Thomas Manns,* 186–201. Bielefeld: Aisthesis, 1992.

Wiehe, Roger. "The *Danse macabre* as the Crucial Moment in Story and Film Versions of *Death in Venice.*" In *The Symbolism of Vanitas in the Arts, Literature, and Music,* edited by Liana DeGirolami Cheney, 85–99. Lewiston, NY: Mellen, 1992.

# 1993

Aldrich, Robert. *The Seduction of the Mediterranean: Writing, art and homosexual fantasy.* London: Routledge, 1993.

Annan, Gabriele. "Missing the Sexual Undertow." *Times Literary Supplement*, 24 September 1993, 18.

Beyerle, Dieter. "Thomas Mann und der Teufel." In *Literaturhistorische Begegnungen: Festschrift zum sechzigsten Geburtstag von Bernhard König*, edited by Andreas Kablitz and Ulrich Schulz-Buschhaus, 1–16. Tübingen: Narr, 1993.

Böschenstein, Bernhard. "Exzentrische Polarität: Zum *Tod in Venedig*." In *Thomas Mann: Romane und Erzählungen*, edited by Volkmar Hansen, 89–120. Stuttgart: Reclam, 1993.

Frizen, Werner. "Fausts Tod in Venedig." In *Wagner — Nietzsche — Thomas Mann: Festschrift für Eckhard Heftrich*, edited by Heinz Gockel, Michael Neumann, and Ruprecht Wimmer, 228–53. Frankfurt am Main: Klostermann, 1993.

———. *Thomas Mann: Der Tod in Venedig: Interpretation von Werner Frizen*. Munich: Oldenbourg, 1993.

Härle, Gerhard. "Lust, Angst und Provokation: Homosexuelle Ästhetik bei Platen, Mann und Fichte." In *Lust, Angst und Provokation: Homosexualität in der Gesellschaft*, edited by Helmut Puff, 104–28. Göttingen: Vandenhoeck & Ruprecht, 1993.

Haesler, Ludwig. "Gustav Aschenbach und sein Idol: Über die Perversifizierung des Ästhetischen in Thomas Manns Novelle 'Der Tod in Venedig.'" *Zeitschrift für psychoanalytische Theorie und Praxis* 8.2 (1993): 158–75.

Hawes, J. M. "The Aesthete Going Under (Thomas Mann: *Death in Venice*)." In his *Nietzsche and the End of Freedom*, 73–96. Frankfurt am Main: Lang, 1993.

Heftrich, Eckhard. "Dionysisch — apollinisch." In his *Geträumte Taten: "Joseph und seine Brüder,"* 200–212. Frankfurt am Main: Klostermann, 1993.

Hillman, Roger. "Literatur — Film — Musik: *Der Tod in Venedig*." In *Übersetzen, verstehen, Brücken bauen: Geisteswissenschaftliches und literarisches Übersetzen im internationalen Kulturaustausch*, Teil 2, edited by Armin Paul Frank et al., 469–78. Berlin: Schmidt, 1993.

Koopmann, Helmut. "Ein grandioser Untergang: Thomas Mann: *Der Tod in Venedig* (1912)." In *Deutsche Novellen: Von der Klassik bis zur Gegenwart*, edited by Winfried Freund, 221–35. Munich: Fink, 1993.

Lehnert, Herbert. "Historischer Horizont und Fiktionalität in Thomas Manns *Der Tod in Venedig*." In *Wagner — Nietzsche — Thomas Mann: Festschrift für Eckhard Heftrich*, edited by Heinz Gockel, Michael Neumann, and Ruprecht Wimmer, 254–78. Frankfurt am Main: Klostermann, 1993.

Lubich, Frederick A. "Probleme der Übersetzung und Wirkungsgeschichte Thomas Manns in den Vereinigten Staaten." *Weimarer Beiträge* 39.3 (1993): 464–77.

Paulson, Michael G. *The Youth and the Beach: A Comparative Study of Thomas Mann's "Der Tod in Venedig" (Death in Venice) and Reinaldo Arenas' "Otra Vez el Mar" (Farewell to the Sea)*. Miami, FL: Universal, 1993.

Pizer, John. "From a Death in Venice to a Death in Rome: On Wolfgang Koeppen's Critical Ironization of Thomas Mann." *Germanic Review* 68.3 (Summer 1993): 98–107.

Rojtman, Betty. "Les trous du temps: à propos de 'La mort à Venise.'" *Rivista di Letterature moderne e comparate,* n.s., 46.3 (July-September 1993): 237–47.

Said, Edward W. *Culture and Imperialism.* New York: Knopf, 1993.

Schoffman, Nachum. "D'Annunzio and Mann: Antithetical Wagnerisms." *Journal of Musicology* 11.4 (Fall 1993): 499–524.

Syfuß, Antje. "'Der Tod in Venedig' (1912): Zu Ehren der Nymphen." In her *Zauberer mit Märchen: Eine Studie zu Thomas Mann,* 173–74. Frankfurt am Main: Lang, 1993.

Tobin, Robert. "Das offene Geheimnis der Sexualität: Verhüllung und Enthüllung von Krankheit und Faschismus in den Schriften Thomas Manns." In *Verschwiegenes Ich: Vom Un-Ausdrücklichen in autobiographischen Texten,* edited by Bärbel Götz, Ortrud Gutjahr, and Irmgard Roebling, 207–18. Pfaffenweiler: Centaurus, 1993.

Vidan, Ivo. "Conrad and Thomas Mann." In *Contexts for Conrad,* edited by Keith Carabine, Owen Knowles, and Wiesław Krajka, 265–85. Boulder, CO: East European Monographs, 1993.

Wells, G. A. "The Morality of the Artist: An Aspect of Thomas Mann's *Tonio Kröger* and *Der Tod in Venedig.*" *Trivium* 28 (1993): 83–92. [*Essays in Germanic Studies,* edited by Anthony Bushell.]

Weiner, Marc A. "Music and Repression: *Death in Venice.*" In his *Undertones of Insurrection,* 73–99. Lincoln: U of Nebraska P, 1993.

# 1994

Delassalle, Béatrice. *Luchino Viscontis "Tod in Venedig": Übersetzung oder Neuschöpfung.* Aachen: Shaker, 1994.

Detering, Heinrich. *Das offene Geheimnis: Zur literarischen Produktivität eines Tabus von Winckelmann bis zu Thomas Mann.* Göttingen: Wallstein, 1994.

Heller, Joseph. *Closing Time.* New York: Simon & Schuster, 1994.

Keil, Linde. "Beauty as a Homoerotic Aspect in *Forbidden Colors* (1951) and *Death in Venice* (1912): An East-West Encounter Between Yukio Mishima and Thomas Mann." In *Gender and Culture in Literature and Film East and West: Issues of Perception and Interpretation,* edited by Nitaya Masavisut, George Simson, and Larry E. Smith, 135–40. Honolulu: U of Hawaii P, 1994.

Koelb, Clayton, ed. and trans. *Thomas Mann: Death in Venice.* New York: Norton, 1994.

Marshall, Alexander J., III. "The Lure of Eros: Nietzschean Intertextuality in Visconti, Mahler, and Mann." *Post Script* 13.3 (Summer 1994): 30–38.

Reed, T. J. *Death in Venice: Making and Unmaking a Master.* New York: Twayne, 1994.

Ross, Michael L. "The Abyss: Death in Venice." In his *Storied Cities: Literary Imaginings of Florence, Venice, and Rome,* 133–41. Westport, CT: Greenwood, 1994.

Sixel, Friedrich W. "What is a Good Translation? Some Theoretical Considerations Plus a Few Examples." *Meta: Journal des Traducteurs/Translators' Journal* 39.2 (June 1994): 342–61.

Stock, Irvin. "Death in Venice." In his *Ironic Out of Love: The Novels of Thomas Mann,* 32–35. Jefferson, NC: McFarland, 1994.

Tobin, Robert. "Why is Tadzio a Boy? Perspectives on Homoeroticism in *Death in Venice.*" In Koelb, 1994, 207–32.

Weiller, Edith. "Gesichter der Askese: Max Weber und Thomas Mann." In her *Max Weber und die literarische Moderne,* 257–98. Stuttgart: Metzler, 1994.

# 1995

Angermeier, John S. "Marienbad and Goethe as a Source of Motifs for Mann's *Der Tod in Venedig.*" *German Life and Letters* 48.1 (January 1995): 12–24.

———. "The Punica Granatum Motif in Mann's *Der Tod in Venedig.*" *Germanic Notes and Reviews* 26.1 (Spring 1995): 12–15.

Appiah, Anthony. *Another Death in Venice.* London: Constable, 1995.

Dieterle, Bernard. *Die versunkene Stadt: Sechs Kapitel zum literarischen Venedig-Mythos.* Frankfurt am Main: Lang, 1995.

Fieguth, Rolf. "Zur literarischen Bedeutung des Bedeutungslosen: Das Polnische in Thomas Manns Novelle 'Der Tod in Venedig.'" In *Studien zur Kulturgeschichte des deutschen Polenbildes 1848–1939,* edited by Hendrik Feindt, 130–47. Wiesbaden: Harassowitz, 1995.

Harpprecht, Klaus. *Thomas Mann: Eine Biographie.* [Reinbek bei Hamburg]: Rowohlt, 1995.

Hayman, Ronald. *Thomas Mann: A Biography.* New York: Scribner, 1995.

Herwig, Oliver. "Wolfgang Koeppens Absage an den Ästhetizismus: Die Strategie der literarischen Auseinandersetzung mit Thomas Mann im Roman 'Der Tod in Rom.'" *Zeitschrift für Germanistik,* n.s., 5.3 (1995): 544–53.

Hoffmann, Martina. *Thomas Manns "Der Tod in Venedig": Eine Entwicklungsgeschichte im Spiegel philosophischer Konzeptionen.* Frankfurt am Main: Lang, 1995.

Ohl, Hubert. *Ethos und Spiel: Thomas Manns Frühwerk und die Wiener Moderne.* Freiburg im Breisgau: Rombach, 1995.

Prater, Donald. *Thomas Mann: A Life.* Oxford: Oxford UP, 1995.

Schirnding, Albert von. "Dionysos und sein Widersacher: Zu Thomas Manns Rezeption der Antike." *Thomas Mann Jahrbuch* 8 (1995): 93–108.

Schneider, Ursula W. *Ars amandi: The Erotic of Extremes in Thomas Mann and Marguerite Duras.* New York: Lang, 1995.

Szendi, Zoltán. "Die doppelte Optik von Versteck- und Entlarvungsspiel: Zur Funktion der mythischen Parallelen in Thomas Manns Novelle *Der Tod in Venedig.*" *Jahrbuch der ungarischen Germanistik* (1995): 31–44.

Vice, Sue. "Addicted to Love." In *Romance Revisited,* edited by Lynne Pearce and Jackie Stacey, 117–27. London: Lawrence & Wishart, 1995.

Vischer, Ute Heidmann. "Récit mythologique et récit de rêve: Deux formes de représentation littéraire chez Marguerite Yourcenar, Thomas Mann et Christa Wolf." *Colloquium Helveticum* 21 (1995): 27–44.

# 1996

Alexander, Doris. "The Birth of *Death in Venice.*" In her *Creating Literature out of Life: The Making of Four Masterpieces,* 7–21. University Park: Pennsylvania State UP, 1996.

Clerc, Jeanne-Marie. "Littérature et cinéma: *Mort à Venise* et le mythe faustien." In *L'imaginaire des âges de la vie,* edited by Danièle Chauvin, 263–80. Grenoble: Ellug Université Stendhal, 1996.

Harrison, Andrew, and Richard Hibbitt. "D. H. Lawrence and Thomas Mann." *Notes and Queries* 241 [n.s., 43].4 (December 1996): 443.

Heilbut, Anthony. "Death in Venice." In his *Thomas Mann: Eros and Literature,* 247–67. New York: Knopf, 1996.

Kawalec, Urszula. "Fiktion und Realität — Die polnische Episode in der Aschenbach-Novelle: Zur Arbeitsweise Thomas Manns." In *Annäherungsversuche: Germanistische Beiträge,* edited by Norbert Honsza, 143–47. Wrocław: Wydawnictwo Uniwersytetu Wrocławskiego, 1996.

Meredith, Don. "Where the Tigers Were: In Search of the Hotel des Bains." *Poets & Writers Magazine* 24.5 (September/October 1996): 44–51.

Mudford, Peter. "Thomas Mann: *Death in Venice.*" In his *Memory and Desire: Representations of Passion in the Novella,* 142–54. London: Duckworth, 1996.

O'Neill, Patrick. "*Death in Venice:* Narrative Situations in Thomas Mann's *Der Tod in Venedig.*" In his *Acts of Narrative: Textual Strategies in Modern German Fiction,* 16–38. Toronto: U of Toronto P, 1996.

Reed, Terence James. "Der falsche Text des *Tod in Venedig,* oder: wie ist ein Meistersatz zu retten?" *Thomas Mann Jahrbuch* 9 (1996): 293–302.

———. "The Frustrated Poet: Homosexuality and Taboo in *Der Tod in Venedig.*" In *Taboos in German Literature,* edited by David Jackson, 119–34. Providence, RI: Berghahn Books, 1996.

Shalabi, Andrée. *Die Olympische Verschwörung: Ein Beitrag zur Interpretation von Thomas Manns Erzählung "Der Tod in Venedig."* Hamburg: Kovač, 1996.

Tateno, Hideo. "Aschenbachs Tod als Flucht vor der Moderne." In *Literatur und Kulturhermeneutik,* herausgegeben von der Japanischen Gesellschaft für Germanistik, 189–95. Munich: Iudicium, 1996.

Treitel, Ilona. "Two Beasts in the Jungle: *The Beast in the Jungle, Death in Venice.*" In her *The Dangers of Interpretation: Art and Artists in Henry James and Thomas Mann,* 115–48. New York: Garland, 1996.

Wysling, Hans. "Thomas Manns Goethe-Nachfolge" (1978) and "Schopenhauer-Leser Thomas Mann" (1983) in his *Ausgewählte Aufsätze 1963–1995*, edited by Thomas Sprecher and Cornelia Bernini, 17–64, 65–88. Thomas-Mann-Studien 13. Frankfurt am Main: Klostermann, 1996.

# 1997

Bergenholtz, Rita A. "Mann's *Death in Venice*." *Explicator* 55.3 (Spring 1997): 145–47.

Bertellini, Giorgio. "A Battle *d'Arrière-Garde:* Notes on Decadence in Luchino Visconti's *Death in Venice*." *Film Quarterly* 50.4 (Summer 1997): 11–19.

Binion, Rudolph. "Death Beckoning: Thomas Mann's *Death in Venice*." In his *Sounding the Classics: From Sophocles to Thomas Mann*, 135–44. Westport, CT: Greenwood, 1997.

Brunel, Pierre. "Sous le regard d'Hermès: Aschenbach et ses doubles." In his *Transparences du roman: Le romancier et ses doubles au XXe siècle*, 65–109. Paris: Corti, 1997.

Dierks, Manfred. "'Der Tod in Venedig.'" In his *Der Wahn und die Träume: Eine fast wahre Erzählung aus dem Leben Thomas Manns*, 264–67. Düsseldorf: Artemis & Winkler, 1997.

Elsaghe, Yahya A. "Zur Sexualisierung des Fremden im *Tod in Venedig*." *Archiv* 234 (1997): 19–32.

Fischlin, Daniel. "'Eros Is in the Word': Music, Homoerotic Desire, and the Psychopathologies of Fascism, or The 'Strangely Fruitful Intercourse' of Thomas Mann and Benjamin Britten." In *The Work of Opera: Genre, Nationhood, and Sexual Difference*, edited by Richard Dellamora and Daniel Fischlin, 209–33. New York: Columbia UP, 1997.

Fleissner, R. F. "Death in [The Merchant of] Venice." *Germanic Notes and Reviews* 28.1 (Spring 1997): 11–15.

Hickel, Werner. "*Der Tod in Venedig*— Aschenbach zwischen Rausch und Erlösung." In his *"Freund Hain," die erotische Süßigkeit und die Stille des Nirwanas: Thomas Manns Rezeption der Erlösungsthematik zwischen Schopenhauer, Nietzsche und Wagner*, 82–105. Hamburg: Kovač, 1997.

Kraske, Bernd M. "Von der *Wollust des Untergangs:* Die Künstler-Novelle *Der Tod in Venedig*." In his *Nachdenken über Thomas Mann: Sechs Vorträge*, 77–102. Glinde: Böckel, 1997.

Martin, Robert K. "Gustav von Aschenbach Goes to the Movies: Thomas Mann and the Joy Rio Stories of Tennessee Williams." *International Fiction Review* 24.1–2 (1997): 57–64.

Meiners, Nicole. *Heimat in orphischen Tiefen: Mystische Dispositionen in Thomas Manns frühen Novellen*. Frankfurt am Main: Lang, 1997.

Sackey, Edward. "Kwame Anthony Appiah: The Philosopher as Novelist." In *Contemporary African Fiction*, edited by Derek Wright, 245–53. Bayreuth: Breitinger, 1997.

Schaller, Angelika. "Auge und Blick im Tod in Venedig." In her *Und seine Begierde ward sehend": Auge, Blick und visuelle Wahrnehmung in der Prosa Thomas Manns,* 201–36. Würzburg: Ergon, 1997.

Schmidgall, Gary. "Death in Venice, Life in Zurich: Mann's 'Late Something for the Heart.'" *Southwest Review* 82.3 (Summer 1997): 293–324.

Schmidt-Dengler, Wendelin. "Brüderlich durch Hermes vereint: Zur Rezeption antiker Mythologie bei Thomas Mann und Max Frisch." In *Mythos und Utopie,* 24–36. Linz: Adalbert-Stifter Institut, 1997.

Todd, Natalya. "Jenseits der Schrift: Viscontis *Death in Venice*." In *Text und Ton im Film,* edited by Paul Goetsch and Dietrich Scheunemann, 107–16. Tübingen: Narr, 1997.

Van Watson, William. "The Subject as Abject: Luchino Visconti's *Death in Venice* and the 'Art' of Pederasty." *Romance Languages Annual* 8 (1997): 335–41.

Zlotnick-Woldenberg, Carrie. "An Object-Relational Interpretation of Thomas Mann's 'Death in Venice.'" *American Journal of Psychotherapy* 51.4 (Fall 1997): 542–51.

# 1998

Berman, Russell A. "History and Community in *Death in Venice*." In Ritter, 1998, 263–80.

Brink, André. "The Tiger's Revenge: Thomas Mann: *Death in Venice*." In his *The Novel: Language and Narrative from Cervantes to Calvino,* 173–88. New York: New York UP, 1998.

Foster, John Burt, Jr. "Why is Tadzio Polish? *Kultur* and Cultural Multiplicity in *Death in Venice*." In Ritter, 1998, 192–210.

Furst, Lilian R. "The Potential Deceptiveness of Reading in *Death in Venice*." In Ritter, 1998, 158–70.

Luft, Klaus Peter. "*Der Tod in Venedig*." In his *Erscheinungsformen des Androgynen bei Thomas Mann,* 71–86. New York: Lang, 1998.

Reed, Terence James. "Ein Nebenweg." In *Begleittexte zum Reprint von Thomas Mann[:] Der Tod in Venedig,* 7–18. Frankfurt am Main: Fischer, 1998.

Ritter, Naomi. "A Critical History of *Death in Venice*." In Ritter, 1998, 91–109.

———, ed. *Thomas Mann: Death in Venice*. Boston: Bedford, 1998.

Sarkowski, Heinz. "Hans von Weber, 'Die Drucke für die Hundert' und der S. Fischer Verlag." In *Begleittexte zum Reprint von Thomas Mann[:] Der Tod in Venedig,* 19–29. Frankfurt am Main: Fischer, 1998.

Solway, Diane. *Nureyev: His Life*. New York: Morrow, 1998.

Symington, Rodney. "The Eruption of the Other: Psychoanalytic Approaches to *Death in Venice*." In Ritter, 1998, 127–41.

Tobin, Robert. "The Life and Work of Thomas Mann: A Gay Perspective." In Ritter, 1998, 225–44.

Troubetzkoy, Vladimir. "Comparatiste et Pédéraste: Humbert Humbert Réconcilié." In *Littérature et Interdits,* edited by Jacques Dugast and François Mouret, 157–66. Rennes: Presses Universitaires, 1998.

Wilson, Michael. "Art is Ambiguous: The Zoom in *Death in Venice.*" *Literature/Film Quarterly* 26.2 (1998): 153–56.

Woods, Gregory. *A History of Gay Literature.* New Haven: Yale UP, 1998.

# 1999

Brinkley, Edward S. "Fear of Form: Thomas Mann's *Der Tod in Venedig.*" *Monatshefte* 91.1 (1999): 2–27.

Catlin, Alan. "Death in Venice." *Literary Review* 42.3 (Spring 1999): 390–91.

Ghose, Indira. "Venice Confidential." In Pfister and Schaff, 1999, 213–24.

Halliwell, Martin. "Books and Ruins: Abject Decadence in Gide and Mann." In *Romancing Decay: Ideas of Decadence in European Culture,* edited by Michael St. John, 154–70. Aldershot: Ashgate, 1999.

Hoffmann, Martina. *Von Venedig nach Weimar: Eine Entwicklungsgeschichte paradigmatischen Künstlertums.* Frankfurt: Lang, 1999.

Kempton, Daniel. "The Games of Apollo in Benjamin Britten's *Death in Venice:* 'Strength, Agility and Skill — The Body's Praise.'" *Aethlon* 16.2 (Spring 1999): 55–61.

Kurzke, Hermann. "Der Tod in Venedig." In his *Thomas Mann: Das Leben als Kunstwerk,* 193–96. Munich: Beck, 1999.

Mahler, Andreas. "Writing Venice: Paradoxical Signification as Connotational Feature." In Pfister and Schaff, 1999, 29–44.

Otis, Laura. "Thomas Mann: The Tigers of Wrath and the Origin of Cholera." In her *Membranes: Metaphors of Invasion in Nineteenth-Century Literature, Science, and Politics,* 148–67. Baltimore: Johns Hopkins UP, 1999.

Pausch, Holger A. and Diana Spokiene. "Walter Benjamin, Roland Barthes und die Dialektik der Modesprache im Werk Thomas Manns." *Wirkendes Wort* 49.1 (April 1999): 86–104.

Perosa, Sergio. "Literary Deaths in Venice." In Pfister and Schaff, 1999, 115–28.

Pfister, Manfred, and Barbara Schaff. *Venetian Views, Venetian Blinds: English Fantasies of Venice.* Amsterdam: Rodopi, 1999.

Said, Edward W. "Not all the way to the tigers: Britten's *Death in Venice.*" *Critical Quarterly* 41.2 (Summer 1999): 46–54.

Schwarz, Olaf. "' . . . eine Art schweifender Unruhe': Zur Funktionalisierung des 'Reisens' in deutschsprachigen Erzähltexten um und nach 1900." *Kodikas/Code: Ars Semeiotica* 22.1–2 (1999): 25–42.

Seaboyer, Judith. "Robert Coover's *Pinocchio in Venice:* An Anatomy of a Talking Book." In Pfister and Schaff, 1999, 237–55.

Von der Lippe, George B. "Death in Venice in Literature and Film: Six 20th-Century Versions." *Mosaic* 32.1 (March 1999): 35–54.

Weathers, Winston. "Der Tod in Venedig." *Literary Review* 42.3 (Spring 1999): 451–53.

Widmaier-Haag, Susanne. *Es war das Lächeln des Narziß: Die Theorien der Psychoanalyse im Spiegel der literaturpsychologischen Interpretationen des "Tod in Venedig."* Würzburg: Königshausen & Neumann, 1999.

Zorzi, Rosella Mamoli. "Intertextual Venice: Blood and Crime and Death Renewed in Two Contemporary Novels." In Pfister and Schaff, 1999, 225–36.

# 2000

Elsaghe, Yahya. "Der Tod in Venedig." In his *Die imaginäre Nation: Thomas Mann und das "Deutsche,"* 27–60. Munich: Fink, 2000.

Goll, Thomas. *Die Deutschen und Thomas Mann: Die Rezeption des Dichters in Abhängigkeit von der Politischen Kultur Deutschlands 1898–1955.* Baden-Baden: Nomos, 2000.

Izenberg, Gerald N. "Thomas Mann and the Feminine Passion for Transcendence." In his *Modernism and Masculinity: Mann, Wedekind, Kandinsky through World War I,* 97–159. Chicago: U of Chicago P, 2000.

Otis, Laura. "The Tigers of Wrath: Mann's *Death in Venice* as Myth and Medicine." In *Teaching Literature and Medicine,* edited by Anne Hunsaker Hawkins and Marilyn Chandler McEntyre, 243–51. New York: Modern Language Association, 2000.

Strobel, Jochen. *Entzauberung der Nation: Die Repräsentation Deutschlands im Werk Thomas Manns.* Dresden: Thelem, 2000.

# 2001

Meuthen, Erich. "Anmut ohne Würde: Thomas Manns Schiller-Widerruf: 'Der Tod in Venedig.'" In his *Eins und doppelt oder Vom Anderssein des Selbst: Struktur und Tradition des deutschen Künstlerromans,* 195–214. Tübingen: Niemeyer, 2001.

Prechtl-Fröhlich, Ulrike: *Die Dinge sehen, wie sie sind: Melancholie im Werk Thomas Manns.* Frankfurt am Main: Lang, 2001.

# 2002

Minden, Michael. "Mann's Literary Techniques." In Robertson, 2002, 43–63.

Reed, T. J. "Mann and History." In Robertson, 2002, 1–21.

Robertson, Ritchie, ed. *The Cambridge Companion to Thomas Mann.* Cambridge: Cambridge UP, 2002.

————. "Classicism and Its Pitfalls: *Death in Venice.*" In Robertson, 2002, 95–106.

Webber, Andrew J. "Mann's Man's World: Gender and Sexuality." In Robertson, 2002, 64–83.

# Index